Study Guide

Charles M. Seiger

Essentials of
Anatomy & Physiology

MARTINI / BARTHOLOMEW

Fourth Edition

PEARSON

Benjamin
Cummings

San Francisco   Boston   New York
Cape Town   Hong Kong   London   Madrid   Mexico City
Montreal   Munich   Paris   Singapore   Sydney   Tokyo   Toronto

Executive Editor: Leslie Berriman
Project Editor: Nicole George-O'Brien
Assistant Editor: Blythe Robbins
Editorial Assistant: Jon Duke
Managing Editor, Production: Deborah Cogan
Production Supervisor: Mary O'Connell
Manufacturing Buyer: Stacey Weinberger
Production Service/Compositor: The Left Coast Group
Executive Marketing Manager: Lauren Harp

Cover Photograph: Greg Epperson/Index Stock Imagery

ISBN 0-8053-7520-1

4 5 6 7 8—CRS—10 09 08
www.aw-bc.com

Contents

Preface

This Study Guide has been written to accompany Martini and Bartholomew's *Essentials of Anatomy & Physiology,* 4th Edition and serve as a resource to help students master the material in the one-semester Anatomy and Physiology course.

In the fourth edition of this Study Guide, the questions and exercises have been reviewed, refined, and, when needed, rewritten in an effort to help students more easily organize information and focus on facts and concepts. These changes have resulted in many significant improvements.

The inclusion of concept maps in each chapter has been highly praised by both instructors and students as an engaging means of aiding the learning process. All of the concept maps in this edition have been completely redesigned for greater clarity and organization and, in some cases, entirely rewritten to improve the content. The substantial revisions have resulted in an exceptional learning tool that encourages, develops, and supports students' ability to learn, apply information, and think critically.

In addition, the following revisions have been made:

- Many objective-based questions have been completely rewritten to correspond closely with concepts in the new edition of the text.
- Much of the artwork has been updated to correspond with the revisions in the text and the layout of the labeling exercises has been modified for clarification and ease of labeling.
- Most of the Matching exercises have been thoroughly revised and rewritten.

While many features have been improved, the basic sequence and organization of exercises remain largely unchanged from the previous edition. The objective-based questions correspond directly to the chapter objectives, and the comprehensive exercises tie together the major concepts in each chapter.

The objective-based questions include:

- Multiple choice
- Fill-in-the-blank
- Labeling exercises

The chapter comprehensive exercises include:

- Word elimination
- Matching
- Concept maps
- Crossword puzzles
- Short-answer questions

I have worked hard to provide an exceptional study tool and have made every effort to ensure quality and accuracy in this Study Guide. In each new edition, I seek to improve upon the last, and an integral part of this improvement is feedback from both instructors and the students. I value your input and encourage you to provide comments and make suggestions for the fifth edition. Please feel free to e-mail me at the address below.

Charles M. Seiger

Cseiger38@davtv.com

1

An Introduction to Anatomy and Physiology

Overview

For centuries, the study of the human body has aroused the curiosity of the human mind, just as it does today. A few years ago our knowledge of the human body was limited to what our senses could perceive; however, modern technology has changed the way we view and understand the physical and chemical makeup of living organisms. Even today, for many of you the study of anatomy and physiology may be an "adventure into the unknown." Are you curious to know the what, why, and how of your body? Knowledge of the body structures described by anatomists, and an understanding of the physical and chemical processes developed by physiologists, may provide the framework and foundation for your future career, your own personal health, or perhaps some necessary clinical applications.

Chapter 1 is an introduction to anatomy and physiology, citing the basic functions of living things, defining the various specialties of anatomy and physiology, and examining the major levels of organization in living organisms. The organ systems and their components are identified and the significance of homeostasis is explained. The chapter concludes with the use of anatomical terms to describe body sections, body regions, and major body cavities.

Review of Chapter Objectives

1. Describe the basic functions of living organisms.
2. Define anatomy and physiology and describe the various specialties within each discipline.
3. Identify the major levels of organization in living organisms.
4. Identify the organ systems of the human body, and the major components of each system.
5. Explain the significance of homeostasis.
6. Describe how negative feedback and positive feedback are involved in homeostatic regulation.
7. Use anatomical terms to describe body sections, body regions, and relative positions.
8. Identify the major body cavities and their subdivisions.

Part I: Objective-Based Questions

OBJECTIVE 1   Describe the basic functions of living organisms.

B   1. When organisms respond to changes and make adjustments in their environment, the properties involved are

   a. growth and development.
   b. irritability and adaptability.
   c. reproduction and movement.
   d. metabolism and respiration.

C   2. *Metabolism* is best defined as

   a. the creation of subsequent generations of similar organisms.
   b. the accumulation of changes that occur for an organism's survival.
   c. all the chemical operations that occur in the body.
   d. an organism's capability of producing internal and external movements.

A   3. Differentiation of cells during development is directly related to the function of

   a. growth.
   b. metabolism.
   c. reproduction.
   d. adaptability.

D   4. The term used to refer to the absorption, transport, and use of oxygen by cells is

   a. excretion.
   b. breathing.
   c. metabolism.
   d. respiration.

OBJECTIVE 2   Define anatomy and physiology and describe the various specialties within each discipline.

C   1. The word *structure* relates to the study of _____, whereas the word *function* relates to the science of _____.

   a. physiology; anatomy
   b. cytology; histology
   c. anatomy; physiology
   d. biology; chemistry

B   2. The study of *cytology* involves

   a. all aspects of specific organ systems.
   b. the microscopic anatomy concerning the internal structure of cells.
   c. the examination of groups of specialized cells and cell products.
   d. features visible with the unaided eye.

A   3. The specialized science that involves the study and examination of tissues is

   a. histology.
   b. cytology.
   c. cell biology.
   d. systemic anatomy.

Part II: Chapter Comprehensive Exercises

A. Word Elimination

Circle the term that does not belong in each of the following groupings.

1. responsiveness   growth   reproduction   biology   movement
2. anatomy   physiology   cytology   histology   organism
3. cell   digestion   tissue   organ   organism
4. organism   endocrine   skeletal   nervous   reproductive
5. receptor   effector   temperature   stimulus
6. cephalic   supine   cervical   axillary   brachial
7. transverse   frontal   sagittal   coronal   prone
8. anterior   posterior   coronal   cephalic   proximal
9. caudal   pelvic   pericardial   thoracic   abdominal
10. pericardium   mediastinum   pleura   peritoneum   mesentery

B. Matching

Match the terms in Column "B" with the terms in Column "A." Use letters for answers in the spaces provided.

COLUMN A	COLUMN B
___ 1. integumentary system	a. failure of homeostatic regulation
___ 2. thermoregulation	b. double sheets of peritoneum
___ 3. disease	c. pericardial and pleural cavities
___ 4. cephalic	d. serous membrane
___ 5. thoracic cavity	e. forms outer wall of body cavity
___ 6. mesenteries	f. viscera
___ 7. positive feedback	g. control of body temperature
___ 8. parietal	h. refers to head region
___ 9. peritoneum	i. labor contractions
___10. internal organs in thoracic and abdominopelvic cavities	j. controlled by negative feedback

C. Concept Map

The concept map summarizes and organizes the basic information on body cavities in Chapter 1. Using the following terms, fill in the circled numbered, blank spaces to complete the concept map. Follow the numbers that comply with the organization of the map.

Pelvic cavity

Heart

Spinal cord

Abdominopelvic cavity

Cranial cavity

Two pleural cavities

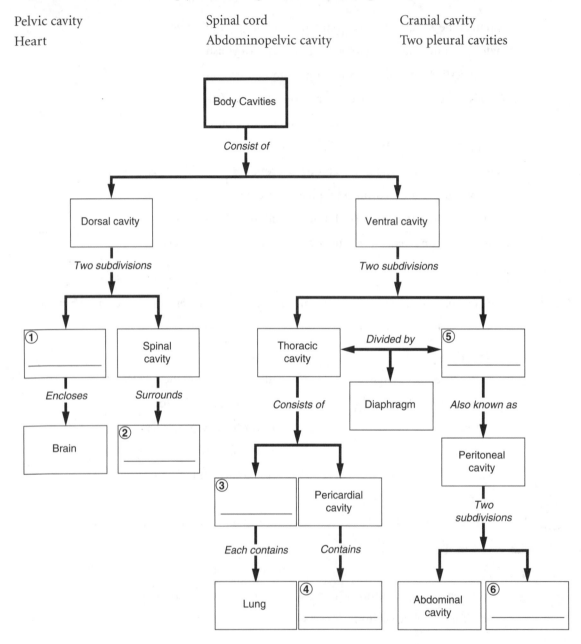

D. Crossword Puzzle

The following crossword puzzle reviews the material in Chapter 1. To complete the puzzle you must know the answers to the clues given, and you must be able to spell the terms correctly.

ACROSS

4. When the body is healthy, it is said to be in _____.
7. A lot of the scientific words we use are derived from the _____ language.
8. The body region typically referred to as the elbow is anatomically called the _____ region.
9. The visceral _____ membrane surrounds the lung.
10. The muscle that separates the thoracic cavity from the abdominal cavity is the _____.
11. The wrist bones are collectively called _____ (singular).

DOWN

1. The abdominal region located superior to the umbilicus is the _____.
2. The study of how the body works.
3. The homeostatic mechanism that is constantly fluctuating is called _____ feedback.
5. A group of organized cells working together.
6. The depression located posterior to the knee is known as the _____ region.

E. Short-Answer Questions

Briefly answer the questions in the spaces provided.

1. Despite obvious differences, all living things perform the same basic functions. List five functions that are active processes in living organisms.

2. List the levels of organization in living things in correct sequence, from the least complex to the most complex level.

3. What are the major differences between negative feedback and positive feedback?

4. Describe the position of the body when it is in anatomical position.

5. References are made by anatomists to the front, back, head, and tail of the body. What anatomical direction reference terms are used to describe each of these directions? (Your answer should be in the order listed above).

6. What is the difference between a sagittal section and a transverse section?

7. What are the two essential functions of body cavities in the human body?

2

The Chemical Level of Organization

Overview

Most students of anatomy and physiology are surprised to learn that the human body is made up of atoms and that the interactions of these atoms control the physiological processes within the body. To fully comprehend the functioning of the body as a whole, the basic concepts of inorganic and organic chemistry are studied, and mastery of chemical principles is necessary. Atomic structure and formation of molecules provide the basic framework for understanding how simple components interact to form more complex ordering and structuring found in all living things, whether plant or animal.

Even though over 100 chemical elements are known, only four (carbon, hydrogen, oxygen, and nitrogen) make up over 96% of all living matter. These four elements comprise the structure of the most abundant complex biological molecules such as proteins, fats, carbohydrates, and nucleic acids, which provide the building blocks and functional processes in the human body.

The exercises in this chapter focus on many of the important organic and inorganic chemical principles. The tests and activities are set up to reinforce students' understanding of basic chemical concepts and to increase their ability to apply these principles to the functioning of the body as a whole.

Review of Chapter Objectives

1. Describe an atom and an element.
2. Compare the ways in which atoms combine to form molecules and compounds.
3. Use chemical notation to symbolize chemical reactions.
4. Distinguish among the major types of chemical reactions that are important for studying physiology.
5. Describe the important role of enzymes in metabolism.
6. Distinguish between organic and inorganic compounds.
7. Explain how the chemical properties of water make life possible.
8. Describe the pH scale and the role of buffers in body fluids.
9. Describe the physiological roles of inorganic compounds.
10. Discuss the structure and functions of carbohydrates, lipids, proteins, nucleic acids, and high-energy compounds.

Part I: Objective-Based Questions

OBJECTIVE 1 Describe an atom and an element.

_D_ 1. The smallest units of matter whose identities cannot be altered by a chemical change are
   a. electrons.
   b. mesons.
   c. protons.
   d. atoms.

_B_ 2. The three subatomic particles that are stable constituents of atomic structures are
   a. carbon, hydrogen, and oxygen.
   b. protons, neutrons, and electrons.
   c. atoms, molecules, and compounds.
   d. cells, tissues, and organs.

_C_ 3. The subatomic particles found in the nucleus of an atom include
   a. protons and electrons.
   b. neutrons and electrons.
   c. protons and neutrons.
   d. protons, neutrons, and electrons.

_A_ 4. Isotopes of an element differ in the number of
   a. neutrons in the nucleus.
   b. protons in the nucleus.
   c. electrons in the nucleus.
   d. orbital electrons.

_B_ 5. The atomic number represents the number of
   a. protons and neutrons.
   b. protons in an atom.
   c. protons in an ion.
   d. neutrons in an atom.

_A_ 6. The protons and neutrons of an atom determine the
   a. mass number of an atom.
   b. atomic number of an atom.
   c. chemical behavior of an atom.
   d. stability of an atom.

_C_ 7. The number and arrangement of electrons determine the
   a. number of neutrons in the nucleus.
   b. electrical nature of the atom.
   c. chemical behavior of an atom.
   d. mass number of an atom.

8. A chemical _____ is a substance that consists entirely of atoms with the same atomic number.

9. The center of an atom is called the _____.

10. The areas surrounding the center of an atom represent _____ levels.

11. Draw an atom of *carbon* showing the number of protons, neutrons, and electrons it contains.

12. The atomic number of carbon is _____.

13. The atomic weight of carbon is _____.

14. How many electrons are needed to fill its outer shell?_____

15. Is this element inert or chemically active?_____

16. The symbol for the carbon atom is _____.

OBJECTIVE 2   Compare the ways in which atoms combine to form molecules and compounds.

_C_   1. When a chemical reaction occurs, the chemical structures that contain more than one atom are called

  a. ions.
  b. isotopes.
  c. molecules.
  d. buffers.

_A_   2. Ions with a positive charge are called

  a. cations.
  b. anions.
  c. radicals.
  d. isotopes.

_D_   3. Unequal sharing of a pair of electrons between two atoms forms a(n)

  a. double covalent bond.
  b. ionic bond.
  c. hydrogen bond.
  d. polar covalent bond.

_C_   4. Chemical structures that contain more than one atom bonded together by shared electrons are

  a. compounds.
  b. ionic bonds.
  c. molecules.
  d. electrolytes.

5. Any chemical substance made up of atoms of two or more elements, regardless of how the atoms achieve stability, is a(n)

        a. compound.
        b. molecule.
        c. ion.
        d. isotope.

 6. Which one of the following molecules is drawn correctly to show the proper covalent bonding?

        a. O–O
        b. N ≡ N
        c. H ≡ H
        d. O–C–O

 7. The formation of cations and anions illustrates the attraction between

        a. polar covalent bonds.
        b. ionic bonds.
        c. nonpolar covalent bonds.
        d. double covalent bonds.

8. Atoms that complete their outer shells by sharing electrons with other atoms result in molecules held together by _____.

9. When one atom loses an electron and another accepts that electron, the result is the formation of a(n) _____.

Labeling Exercise

In figures A and B below, identify which one is the covalent bond and which one is the ionic bond. Show the direction of electron transfer with an arrow.

FIGURE 2-1 Chemical Bonding

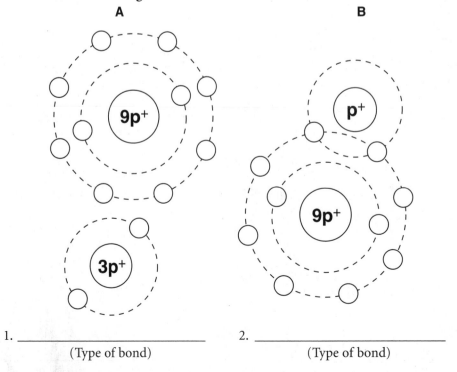

1. _____
(Type of bond)

2. _____
(Type of bond)

OBJECTIVE 3 Use chemical notation to symbolize chemical reactions.

D 1. Which one of the following statements about the reaction $H_2 + Cl_2 \rightarrow 2HCl$ is *not* correct?

    a. H_2 and Cl_2 are the reactants.
    b. HCl is the product.
    c. One molecule of hydrogen contains two atoms.
    d. All of the above are correct.

C 2. The symbol 2H means

    a. one molecule of hydrogen.
    b. two molecules of hydrogen.
    c. two atoms of hydrogen.
    d. a, b, and c are correct.

B 3. The symbol Na^+ refers to

    a. one sodium ion (has gained an electron).
    b. one sodium ion (has lost an electron).
    c. one sodium ion (has gained a proton).
    d. none of the above.

D 4. The balanced equation $2H_2 + O_2 \rightarrow 2H_2O$ means that

    a. one molecule of hydrogen and one molecule of oxygen have combined chemically to form one molecule of water.
    b. two molecules of hydrogen and two molecules of oxygen have combined chemically to form two molecules of water.
    c. two atoms of hydrogen and two atoms of oxygen have combined chemically to form four molecules of water.
    d. two molecules of hydrogen and one molecule of oxygen have combined chemically to form two molecules of water.

B 5. The chemical notation that would indicate "one molecule of hydrogen composed of two hydrogen atoms" would be

    a. $2H_2$.
    b. H_2.
    c. 2H.
    d. a, b, and c are correct.

OBJECTIVE 4 Distinguish among the major types of chemical reactions that are important for studying physiology.

A 1. A decomposition reaction is one in which

    a. a molecule is broken down into smaller fragments.
    b. larger molecules are assembled from smaller components.
    c. complex molecules are formed by removal of water.
    d. the components of the reaction are present in different combinations.

D 2. Which of the following is a synthesis reaction?

    a. AB → A + B
    b. A + B ↔ AB
    c. AB + CD → AD + CB
    d. A+B → AB

B 3. The reaction AB + CD → AD + CB is an example of

    a. a reversible reaction.
    b. an exchange reaction.
    c. a decomposition reaction.
    d. a catabolic reaction.

4. The decomposition reaction of complex molecules within cells is called _____.

5. When the rate of a synthesis reaction balances the rate of a decomposition reaction, the result is _____.

OBJECTIVE 5   Describe the important role of enzymes in metabolism.

A 1. Special molecules called enzymes found in cells

    a. speed up the reactions that support life.
    b. produce energy to start a chemical reaction.
    c. release activation energy for a reaction to proceed.
    d. All of the above are correct.

C 2. Enzymes belong to a class of substances called _____, which accelerate chemical reactions without themselves being permanently changed.

    a. metabolites
    b. buffers
    c. catalysts
    d. isotopes

B 3. When an enzyme promotes a chemical reaction by lowering the activation energy, it only affects the

    a. direction of the reaction.
    b. rate of the reaction.
    c. products that are formed.
    d. All of the above are correct.

D 4. *Exergonic* reactions, which are common in the body, are responsible for

    a. absorption of energy to activate a reaction.
    b. lowering activating energy requirements.
    c. a net gain of energy for the reaction to occur.
    d. generating the heat that maintains your body temperature.

B 5. The activation energy requirement of a reaction is much lower in the presence of

    a. a strong acid solution.
    b. an appropriate enzyme.
    c. extreme temperatures.
    d. cellular malfunctions.

C. Concept Map

This concept map summarizes and organizes some basic concepts covered in Chapter 2. Using the following terms, fill in the circled numbered, blank spaces to complete the concept map. Follow the numbers that comply with the organization of the map.

Dissacharides   DNA   Amino acids

Fatty acids   Nucleic acids   Lipids

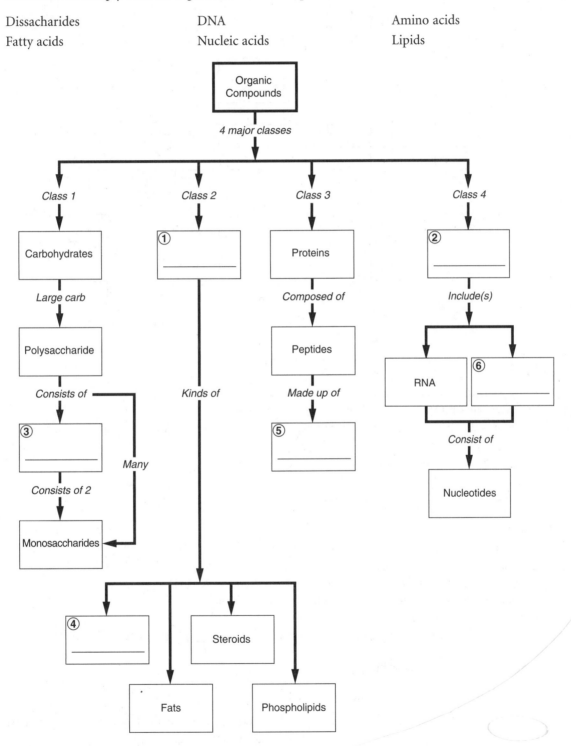

D. Crossword Puzzle

The following crossword puzzle reviews the material in Chapter 2. To complete the puzzle, you have to know the answers to the clues given, and you have to be able to spell the terms correctly.

ACROSS

1. The greater the concentration of _____ ions in solution, the lower the pH.
4. Neutrons and protons are located in the _____ of an atom.
5. Two atoms that have the same number of protons but a different number of neutrons are called _____.
8. A _____ consists of a chain of molecules called amino acids.
10. Fats and steroids are examples of _____.
11. The mass number of an atom changes if its number of _____ changes.

DOWN

2. The disaccharide sucrose consists of fructose bonded to _____.
3. A substance that helps stabilize pH is called a(n) _____.
5. An atom or molecule that has a positive or a negative charge is a(n) _____.
6. When an atom loses an electron, it exhibits a _____ charge.
7. When phosphorus becomes an ion, it exhibits a _____ 3 charge.
9. The high-energy compound produced by the body is _____ triphosphate.

E. Short-Answer Questions

Briefly answer the questions in the spaces provided.

1. Suppose an atom has 8 protons, 8 neutrons, and 8 electrons. Construct a diagram of the atom and identify the subatomic particles by placing them in their proper locations.

2. Why are the elements helium, argon, and neon called inert gases?

3. In a water molecule (H_2O), the unequal sharing of electrons creates a polar covalent bond. Why?

4. List four important characteristics of water that make life possible.

5. List the four major classes of organic compounds found in the human body and give an example of each one.

6. What is the difference between a saturated and an unsaturated fatty acid?

7. Using the four kinds of nucleotides that make up a DNA molecule, construct a model that will show the correct arrangement of the components that make up each nucleotide. Name each nucleotide.

8. What three components make up one nucleotide of ATP?

3

Cell Structure and Function

Overview

The basic unit of structure and function of all living things is the cell. In the living world a single cell can be a complete living thing or it can be one of billions of units that make up a complex living organism. In complex organisms such as humans, cells become specialized to form tissues and organs that perform specific functions. Cells differ in shape, size, and the roles they play in the human body. Cell structures called organelles perform the work of metabolism and are responsible for growth and reproduction, movement, responsiveness to internal and external stimuli, and maintenance of homeostasis.

The student activities and test questions in this chapter are designed to help you conceptualize, synthesize, and apply the principles of cell biology that provide the foundation for understanding how the body's organ systems work.

Review of Chapter Objectives

1. List the main points of the cell theory.
2. Describe the functions of the cell membrane and the structures that enable it to perform those functions.
3. Describe the various mechanisms that cells use to transport substances across the cell membrane.
4. Describe the organelles of a typical cell and indicate their specific functions.
5. Explain the functions of the cell nucleus.
6. Summarize the process of protein synthesis.
7. Describe the process of mitosis and explain its significance.
8. Define differentiation and explain its importance.

Part I: Objective-Based Questions

OBJECTIVE 1 List the main points of the cell theory.

_____ 1. The basic structural units of all plants and animals are

a. atoms.
b. cells.
c. molecules.
d. protons, neutrons, and electrons.

_____ 2. The smallest functioning units of life are

a. tissues.
b. organs.
c. atoms.
d. cells.

_____ 3. Cells are produced only by the division of

a. pre-existing cells.
b. tissues.
c. molecules.
d. organelles.

4. The primary function of each cell in the body is to maintain _____.

OBJECTIVE 2 Describe the functions of the cell membrane and the structures that enable it to perform those functions.

_____ 1. The major components of the cell membrane are

a. carbohydrates, lipids, ions, and vitamins.
b. carbohydrates, fats, proteins, and water.
c. phospholipids, proteins, glycolipids, and cholesterol.
d. amino acids, fatty acids, carbohydrates, and cholesterol.

_____ 2. Membrane proteins may function as

a. receptors and channels.
b. carriers and enzymes.
c. anchors or identifiers.
d. all of the above.

_____ 3. Physical isolation, sensitivity, structural support, and regulation of exchange with the environment are the primary functions of the

a. nuclear and mitochondrial membranes.
b. ribosomal and lysosomal membranes.
c. microtubules and microfilaments.
d. cell membrane or plasma membrane.

_____ 4. The characteristic that enables the cell membrane to act as a selective physical barrier is that

        a. hydrophobic lipid tails will not associate with water molecules.
        b. the cell membrane is extremely thin and delicate.
        c. movement across the membrane is both active and passive.
        d. all of the above are correct.

5. The molecular structure of the cell membrane consists of a(n) _____.

6. The outer boundary of the intracellular material is called the _____.

Labeling Exercise

Locate and identify the following cell structures. Place your answers in the spaces below the drawing.

carbohydrate chain	phospholipid bilayer	protein with channels
proteins	cholesterol	cell membrane
heads	tails	cytoskeleton

FIGURE 3-1 The Cell Membrane

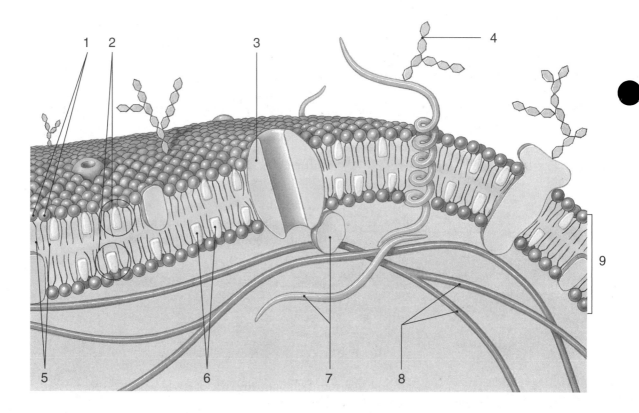

1. _____   6. _____

2. _____   7. _____

3. _____   8. _____

4. _____   9. _____

5. _____

OBJECTIVE 3   Describe the various mechanisms that cells use to transport substances across the cell membrane.

_____ 1. All transport through the cell membrane may be classified as

    a. active or passive.
    b. diffusion or osmosis.
    c. pinocytosis or phagocytosis.
    d. permeable or impermeable.

_____ 2. The cell membrane property called _selective permeability_ refers to

    a. allowing any substance to cross the membrane without difficulty.
    b. preventing any materials from crossing the cell membrane.
    c. allowing the free passage of some materials across the cell membrane and the restricted passage of others.
    d. All of the above are correct.

_____ 3. Ions and other small water-soluble materials cross the cell membrane only by passing through

    a. ligands.
    b. channels.
    c. receptor proteins.
    d. membrane anchors.

_____ 4. Whether or not a substance can cross the cell membrane is based on the substance's

    a. size and electrical charge.
    b. molecular shape.
    c. lipid solubility.
    d. All of the above are correct.

_____ 5. If a high-energy bond of ATP provides the energy needed to move ions or molecules across the cell membrane, the process is called

    a. facilitated diffusion.
    b. active transport.
    c. vesicular transport.
    d. receptor-mediated endocytosis.

_____ 6. Diffusion is described as the

    a. binding of specific ions or organic substrates by membrane proteins.
    b. binding of transported molecules to receptor sites on the carrier protein.
    c. movement of ions or molecules across the membrane by ATP energy.
    d. net movement of molecules from an area of high concentration to an area of low concentration.

_____ 7. During osmosis, water will always flow across a membrane toward the solution that has the

    a. highest concentration of solvents.
    b. highest concentration of solutes.
    c. equal concentration of solute.
    d. equal concentration of solvents.

_____ 8. Facilitated diffusion differs from ordinary diffusion in that

        a. ATP is expended during facilitated diffusion.

        b. molecules move against a concentration gradient.

        c. receptor sites on carrier proteins are involved.

        d. it is an active process utilizing carriers.

9. When hydrostatic pressure forces water across a membrane passively, the process is called

_____.

10. A white blood cell engulfing a bacterium illustrates the process of _____.

11. If a solution has the same solute concentration as the cytoplasm and will not cause a net

movement of fluid in or out of the cells, the solution is said to be _____.

Labeling Exercise

Using the diagrams and criteria below and applying the principle of osmosis, identify the diagrams
that represent a cell in a hypertonic solution, a hypotonic solution, and an isotonic solution. Draw
arrows to show the direction in which the net movement of water will occur.

FIGURE 3-2 Principles of Tonicity

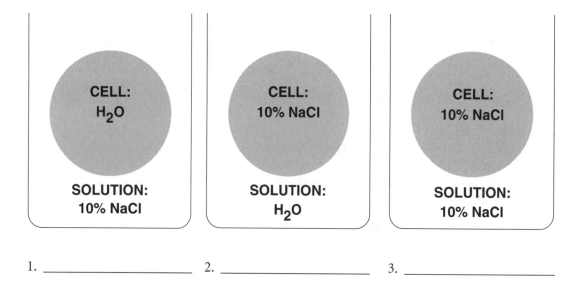

1. _____   2. _____   3. _____

OBJECTIVE 4   Describe the organelles of a typical cell and indicate their specific functions.

A 1. The mitochondria are small organelles in cells that

   a. provide energy for the cell.
   b. perform essential recycling functions inside the cell.
   c. absorb and break down fatty acids and other organic compounds.
   d. All of the above are correct.

C 2. The organelle that synthesizes ribosomal RNA and assembles the ribosomal subunits into functional ribosomes is the

   a. nucleus.
   b. proteasome.
   c. nucleolus.
   d. Golgi apparatus.

B 3. The four major functions of the endoplasmic reticulum are

   a. hydrolysis, diffusion, osmosis, and storage.
   b. synthesis, transport, storage, and detoxification.
   c. detoxification, packaging, modification, and storage.
   d. pinocytosis, phagocytosis, storage, and diffusion.

D 4. The functions of the Golgi apparatus include

   a. neutralization, absorption, assimilation, and secretion.
   b. strength, movement, control, and secretion.
   c. isolation, protection, sensitivity, and organization.
   d. synthesis, storage, alteration, and packaging.

B 5. The organelles that manufacture proteins, using information provided by the DNA of the nucleus, are the

   a. centrioles.
   b. ribosomes.
   c. proteasomes.
   d. lysosomes.

C 6. Vesicles filled with digestive enzymes that perform cleanup and recycling functions within the cells are the

   a. ribosomes.
   b. microvilli.
   c. lysosomes.
   d. proteasomes.

7. The intracellular fluid that contains dissolved nutrients, ions, soluble and insoluble proteins, and waste products is the ___cytosol___.

8. The primary components of the cytoskeleton that give the cell strength and rigidity, and anchor the positions of major organelles, are the ___microtobules___.

Labeling Exercise

Using the terms below, identify the cell organelles in Figure 3-3. Place your answers in the spaces provided below the drawing.

centrioles	Golgi apparatus	free ribosomes	cell membrane
nuclear envelope	nucleolus	mitochondrion	lysosome
smooth E.R.	rough E.R.	chromatin	fixed ribosomes
cytosol	secretory vesicles	nuclear pores	cytoskeleton
microvilli	cilia		

FIGURE 3-3 A Representative Cell

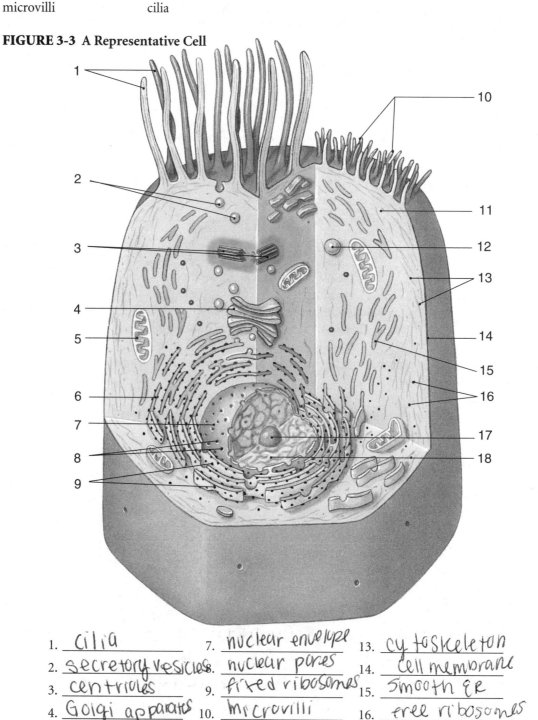

1. _cilia_
2. _secretory vesicles_
3. _centrioles_
4. _Golgi apparatus_
5. _mitochondrion_
6. _rough ER_
7. _nuclear envelope_
8. _nuclear pores_
9. _fixed ribosomes_
10. _microvilli_
11. _cytosol_
12. _lysosome_
13. _cytoskeleton_
14. _cell membrane_
15. _smooth ER_
16. _free ribosomes_
17. _nucleolus_
18. _chromatin_

OBJECTIVE 5   Explain the functions of the cell nucleus.

_____ 1. The major factor that allows the nucleus to control cellular operations is its

a. location within the cell.
b. regulation of protein synthesis.
c. ability to communicate chemically through nuclear pores.
d. "brain-like" sensory devices that monitor cell activity.

_____ 2. Ions, enzymes, RNA and DNA nucleotides, proteins, and small amounts of DNA and RNA are contained in the

a. nucleoli.
b. nucleoplasm.
c. cytosol.
d. ribosomes.

_____ 3. There are _____ chromosomes in the nucleus of a human cell, and these chromosomes consist of _____ made of _____.

a. 23; DNA; RNA
b. 46; DNA; genes
c. 23; genes; proteins
d. 46; genes; DNA

_____ 4. DNA in the nucleus stores instructions for protein synthesis, and the DNA is contained in

a. nucleoli.
b. the cytosol.
c. chromosomes.
d. the nuclear envelope.

_____ 5. The nuclear pores provide an exit for _____ into the cytosol so it can travel to the ribosomes.

a. RNA
b. DNA
c. ATP
d. chromosomes

OBJECTIVE 6   Summarize the process of protein synthesis.

_____ 1. Which of the following sequences of events correctly describes protein synthesis?

a. DNA transcribes the coded message to RNA; RNA (messenger RNA) exits the nuclear pores; RNA translates the coded message to ribosomes; ribosomes make protein.
b. DNA transcribes the coded message to RNA; RNA (transfer RNA) exits the nuclear pores; RNA carries the coded message to the ribosomes, where translation occurs; ribosomes make protein.
c. DNA translates the coded message to RNA; RNA exits the nuclear pores; RNA carries the coded message to the ribosomes, where transcription occurs; ribosomes make protein.
d. DNA transcribes the coded message to RNA; RNA (messenger RNA) exits the nuclear pores and translates the coded message to transfer RNA; tRNA carries the coded message to the ribosomes; ribosomes make protein.

_____ 2. The process of transcription involves the

    a. sequencing of codons forming amino acid chains.
    b. delivery of amino acids used by the ribosomes to assemble a protein.
    c. formation of messenger RNA (mRNA) from DNA.
    d. "start" codon of the mRNA strand.

_____ 3. The RNA that exits the nuclear pores to the cytosol on its way to the ribosomes is called

    a. messenger RNA.
    b. ribosomal RNA.
    c. transcription RNA.
    d. transfer RNA.

_____ 4. The process of translation results in

    a. complementary RNA molecules forming hydrogen bonds with DNA strands.
    b. RNA polymerase bonding the arriving nucleotides together into mRNA strands.
    c. reattachment of the two DNA strands.
    d. synthesis of a protein using the information provided by the sequence of codons along the mRNA strand.

_____ 5. The functional units of DNA that contain the instructions for making one or more proteins are the

    a. genes.
    b. multiple enzymes.
    c. three types of RNA.
    d. chromosomes.

_____ 6. If the DNA triplet is TAG, the corresponding codon on the messenger RNA would be

    a. ACT.
    b. AGC.
    c. ATC.
    d. AUC.

_____ 7. If the messenger RNA has the codons CCC CGG UUA, the corresponding transfer RNA anticodons would be

    a. GGG GCC AAU.
    b. CCC CGG TTA.
    c. GGG GCC AAT.
    d. CCC CGG TTU.

8. A protein consists of a sequence of _____ bonded together.

Labeling Exercise

Identify the numbers in Figure 3-4 that represent the following: DNA, mRNA, tRNA, ribosomes; nuclear pore, the process of transcription, and the process of translation. Place your answers in the spaces below the drawing.

FIGURE 3-4 Protein Synthesis

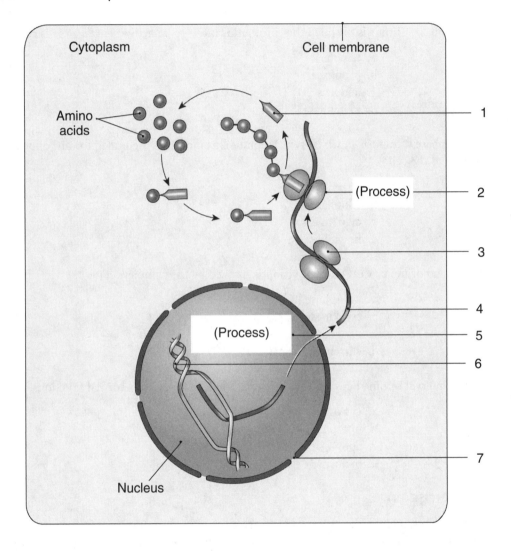

1. _____   5. _____

2. _____   6. _____

3. _____   7. _____

4. _____

OBJECTIVE 7 Describe the process of mitosis and explain its significance.

_____ 1. The four stages of mitosis in correct sequence are

    a. prophase, anaphase, metaphase, telophase.
    b. prophase, metaphase, telophase, anaphase.
    c. prophase, metaphase, anaphase, telophase.
    d. prophase, anaphase, telophase, metaphase.

_____ 2. The phase of mitosis in which the chromatids move to a narrow central zone is called

    a. telophase.
    b. prophase.
    c. anaphase.
    d. metaphase.

_____ 3. The phase of mitosis in which two daughter chromosomes are pulled toward opposite ends of the cell is

    a. anaphase.
    b. telophase.
    c. cytokinesis.
    d. metaphase.

_____ 4. The end of the process of cell division is marked by the completion of

    a. interphase.
    b. cytokinesis.
    c. telophase.
    d. chromatid formation.

_____ 5. The interval of time between cell divisions, when cells perform normal functions, is

    a. cytokinesis.
    b. interphase.
    c. apoptosis.
    d. meiosis.

Labeling Exercise

Using the terms below, identify the phases of mitosis and the structures involved in the process, seen in Figure 3-5 on the following page. Place your answers in the spaces provided beneath the figure.

anaphase	early prophase	nucleolus
centrioles	telophase	sister chromatids
spindle fibers	cytokinesis	interphase
nucleus	daughter chromosomes	daughter cell
metaphase	chromatin	metaphase plate
centromere	late prophase	

FIGURE 3-5 Mitosis

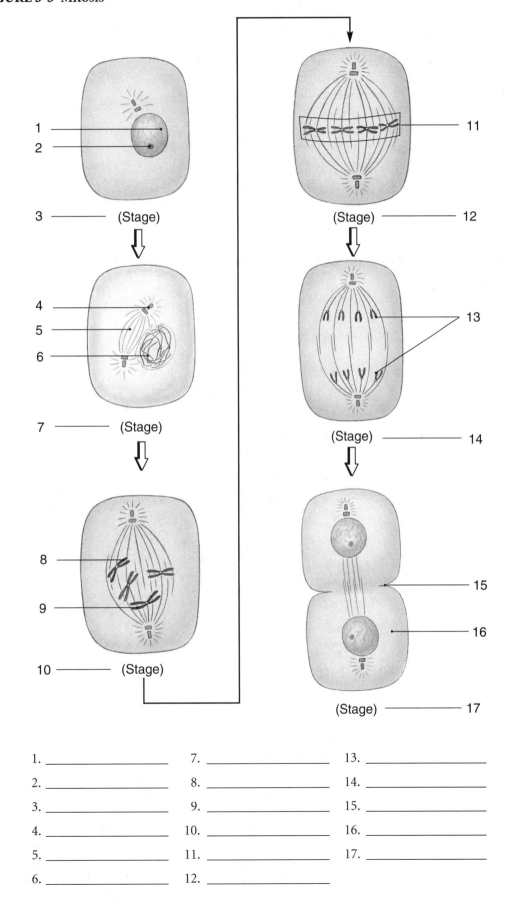

1. _____
2. _____
3. _____
4. _____
5. _____
6. _____

7. _____
8. _____
9. _____
10. _____
11. _____
12. _____

13. _____
14. _____
15. _____
16. _____
17. _____

OBJECTIVE 8 Define differentiation and explain its importance.

_____ 1. The specialization process that produces cells to perform specific functions is called

      a. selection.
      b. metastasis.
      c. differentiation.
      d. replication.

_____ 2. The process of differentiation, which causes cells to have different characteristics, involves

      a. gene activation and deactivation.
      b. the process of fertilization.
      c. embryonic development.
      d. protein denaturation.

_____ 3. The process that restricts a cell to performing specific functions is known as

      a. maturation.
      b. specialization.
      c. speciation.
      d. replication.

_____ 4. A single cell with all of its genetic potential intact is produced by

      a. mitosis.
      b. differentiation.
      c. replication.
      d. fertilization.

Part II: Chapter Comprehensive Exercises

A. Word Elimination

Circle the term that does not belong in each of the following groupings.

1. extracellular   interstitial   organelle   cytosol   intracellular

2. microvilli   lysosomes   cilia   cytoskeleton   centrosome

3. anchoring   recognition   receptor   carrier   glycocalyx

4. distance   diffusion   filtration   vesicular   carrier-mediated

5. isotonic   hypertonic   hyperosmotic   saturation   hypotonic

6. diffusion   endocytosis   phagocytosis   pinocytosis   exocytosis

7. enzymes   ribosomes   suicide packets   lysosome   autolysis

8. nucleoli   DNA   chromatin   nucleoplasm   mitochondria

9. codon   mRNA   DNA   anticodon   tRNA

10. prophase   interphase   metaphase   telophase   anaphase

B. Matching

Match the terms in Column "B" with the terms in Column "A". Use letters for answers in the spaces provided.

COLUMN A	COLUMN B
___ 1. passive processes	a. sodium–potassium exchange pump
___ 2. active processes	b. no energy expenditure required
___ 3. carrier-mediated transport	c. facilitated diffusion and active transport
___ 4. homeostasis	d. "cell eating"
___ 5. vesicular transport	e. "cell drinking"
___ 6. pinocytosis	f. move a cell through surrounding fluid
___ 7. phagocytosis	g. move fluids across cell membrane
___ 8. cilia	h. death of cells
___ 9. flagella	i. cellular energy expenditure required
___10. apoptosis	j. endocytosis and exocytosis

C. Concept Map

This concept map summarizes and organizes some basic concepts in Chapter 3. Using the following terms, fill in the circled numbered, blank spaces to complete the concept map. Follow the numbers that comply with the organization of the map.

Centrioles   Membranous
Proteins   Nucleus
Cytosol

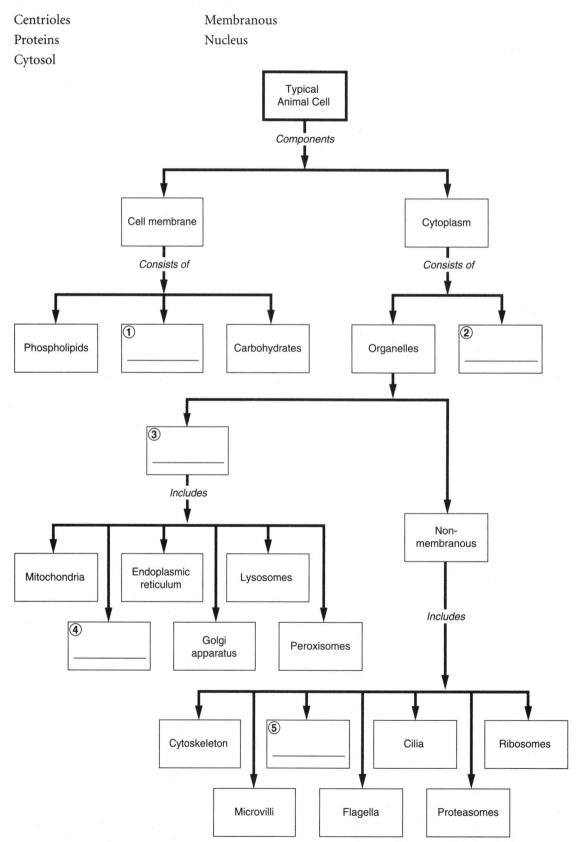

D. Crossword Puzzle

The following crossword puzzle reviews the material in Chapter 3. To complete the puzzle, you have to know the answers to the clues given, and you have to be able to spell the terms correctly.

ACROSS

   5. A solution that has a lower concentration of solutes than that within the cell.
   7. The second phase of mitosis.
   9. Molecules that bond together to produce a protein.
   10. A type of RNA that delivers information to the ribosomes.
   11. A cell structure that contains DNA.

DOWN

   1. A cell organelle that digests incoming material.
   2. The organelle responsible for making ATP.
   3. Cell organelles that produce protein.
   4. A genetic change in the DNA.
   5. A solution that has a greater concentration of solutes than that within the cell.
   6. The process by which a cell engulfs particles.
   8. The movement of water from an area of high concentration to an area of low concentration.

E. Short-Answer Questions

Briefly answer the following questions in the spaces provided.

1. Confirm your understanding of cell specialization by citing five systems in the human body and naming a specialized cell found in each system.

2. List four general functions of the cell membrane.

3. List three ways in which the cytosol differs chemically from the extracellular fluid.

4. What organelles would be necessary to construct a functional "typical" cell? Assume the presence of cytosol and a cell membrane.

5. What are the functional differences among centrioles, cilia, and flagella?

6. What three major factors determine whether a substance can diffuse across a cell membrane?

Labeling Exercise

Identify the type of membrane that is located within each of the body regions identified by the arrows in Figure 4-3. Write your answers in the spaces provided below.

serous   mucous   cutaneous   synovial

FIGURE 4-3 Body Membranes

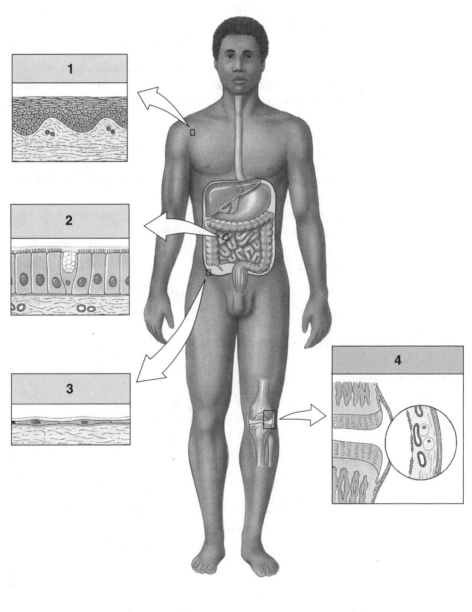

1. _____   3. _____

2. _____   4. _____

OBJECTIVE 6   Describe the three types of muscle tissue and the special structural features of each.

_____ 1. The three types of muscle tissue found in the body are

        a. elastic, hyaline, and fibrous.
        b. striated, nonstriated, and fibrous.
        c. voluntary, involuntary, and nonstriated.
        d. skeletal, cardiac, and smooth.

_____ 2. Skeletal muscle fibers are very unusual because they may be

        a. a foot or more in length, and each cell contains hundreds of nuclei.
        b. subject to pacemaker cells, which establish contraction rates.
        c. devoid of striations, and spindle shaped with a single nucleus.
        d. capable of division, unlike smooth muscle cells.

_____ 3. _Smooth muscle tissue_ is most likely found in the

        a. entrances and exits to the digestive and respiratory systems.
        b. walls of hollow internal organs.
        c. areas of the body where contractions are associated with strength.
        d. areas where joints articulate with bones.

_____ 4. Cardiac muscle is different than skeletal muscle in that

        a. cardiac muscle is under involuntary control.
        b. cardiac muscle has striations.
        c. cardiac muscle has intercalated discs.
        d. a and c are correct.

_____ 5. Smooth muscle is like cardiac muscle in that

        a. smooth muscle cells have a single nucleus.
        b. smooth muscle cells are under involuntary control.
        c. smooth muscle cells have intercalated discs.
        d. Only a and b are correct.

6. A unique feature of muscle tissue is that it is capable of _____.

7. Striated, voluntary, and multinucleated describes the structural and functional characteristics of _____ muscle.

Labeling Exercise

Identify the muscle tissue types and structures in the following drawings. Place your answers in the spaces below the drawings. Note: A few terms may be used more than once.

cardiac muscle tissue   smooth muscle tissue   nucleus   muscle fiber (cell)
intercalated disc   striations   skeletal muscle tissue   smooth muscle cell

FIGURE 4-4 Muscle Tissue

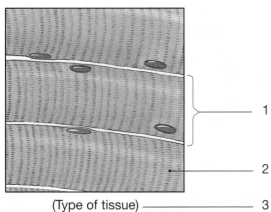

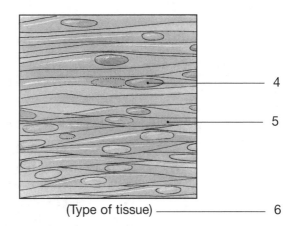

(Type of tissue) ———————— 3

1

2

(Type of tissue) ———————— 6

4

5

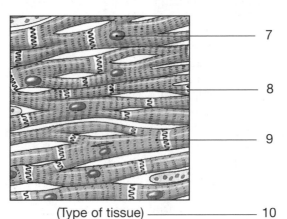

(Type of tissue) ———————— 10

7

8

9

1. _____   6. _____
2. _____   7. _____
3. _____   8. _____
4. _____   9. _____
5. _____   10. _____

OBJECTIVE 7 Discuss the basic structure and role of neural tissue.

_____ 1. Neural tissue is specialized to

        a. contract and produce movement.
        b. conduct electrical impulses throughout the body.
        c. provide structural support and fill internal spaces.
        d. line internal passageways and body cavities.

_____ 2. The major function of neurons in neural tissue is to

        a. provide a supporting framework for neural tissue.
        b. regulate the composition of the interstitial fluid.
        c. act as phagocytes that defend neural tissue.
        d. transmit signals that take the form of changes in the transmembrane potential.

_____ 3. Structurally, neurons are unique because they are the only cells in the body that have

        a. lacunae and canaliculi.
        b. axons and dendrites.
        c. satellite cells and neuroglia.
        d. soma and stroma.

_____ 4. Cells of the nervous system that function to protect, provide nourishment to, and support the neural tissue are

        a. neuroglia.
        b. neurons.
        c. nephrons.
        d. All of the above are correct.

_____ 5. The unidirectional pathway for an impulse to travel through a neuron is

        a. dendrite → axon → soma.
        b. dendrite → soma → axon.
        c. axon → soma → dendrite.
        d. soma → dendrite → axon.

Labeling Exercise

Identify the structures in the following figure. Place the answers in the spaces next to the numbers.

FIGURE 4-5 A Typical Neuron

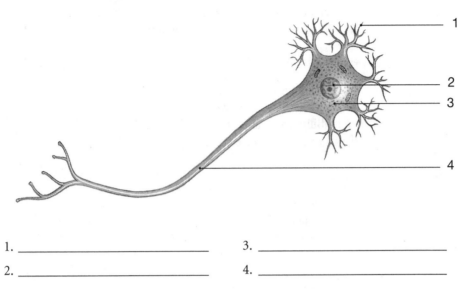

1. _____   3. _____

2. _____   4. _____

OBJECTIVE 8   Explain how tissues respond in a coordinated manner to maintain homeostasis.

_____ 1. The restoration of homeostasis after an injury involves two related processes, which are

        a. necrosis and fibrosis.
        b. infection and immunization.
        c. inflammation and regeneration.
        d. isolation and reconstruction.

_____ 2. Redness, warmth, and swelling are responses due to

        a. the release of histamine by mast cells at an injury site.
        b. fibroblasts producing a dense network of collagen fibers.
        c. the process of fibrosis, which occurs in response to injury.
        d. reconstruction and repair before cleanup operations.

_____ 3. Inflammation is the first evidence of

        a. connective tissue fragility.
        b. thinner and less resilient tissue due to injury.
        c. deterioration in membrane function.
        d. the tissue repair process.

_____ 4. In the second phase of repair following injury, damaged tissues are replaced to restore normal function through the process of

        a. cloning.
        b. regeneration.
        c. reconstruction.
        d. fibrosis.

> **OBJECTIVE 9** Describe how aging affects the tissues of the body.

_____ 1. The two primary requirements for maintaining tissue homeostasis over time are

a. exercise and supplements.
b. hormonal therapy and adequate nutrition.
c. metabolic turnover and adequate nutrition.
d. supplements and hormonal therapy.

_____ 2. Tissue changes with age include

a. thinner epithelial tissue.
b. more brittle connective tissue.
c. inability to repair cardiac and nerve cells.
d. All of the above are correct.

_____ 3. Tissue changes with age can be the result of

a. hormonal changes.
b. improper nutrition.
c. an inadequate amount of activity.
d. All of the above are correct.

Part II: Chapter Comprehensive Exercises

A. Word Elimination

Circle the term that does not belong in each of the following groupings.

1. epithelial   connective   adipose   muscle   neural

2. protection   permeability   sensation   storage   secretion

3. microvilli   gap junction   tight junction   desmosomes   intercellular cement

4. microvilli   stereocilia   cilia   flagella   villus

5. squamous   cuboidal   columnar   connective   transitional

6. support   covering   transporting   storing   defending

7. fibroblasts   macrophages   matrix   adipocytes   mast cells

8. lymph   canaliculi   lacunae   osteocytes   matrix

9. mucous   serous   visceral   cutaneous   synovial

10. soma   neuroglia   dendrites   nucleus   axon

B. Matching

Match the terms in column "B" with the terms in column "A." Use letters for answers in the spaces provided.

COLUMN A

___ 1. exocrine secretions

___ 2. endocrine secretions

___ 3. CAMs (cell adhesion molecules)

___ 4. desmosome

___ 5. stem cells

___ 6. mucin

___ 7. sebaceous glands

___ 8. pericardium

___ 9. pleura

___ 10. fibrosis

___ 11. tendons

___ 12. ligament

COLUMN B

a. cell junctions

b. unspecialized germinative cells

c. holocrine secretion

d. merocrine secretion

e. connects bone to bone

f. hormones

g. connect muscle to bone

h. replacement of normal tissue

i. enzymes, milk, perspiration

j. epithelial cell interconnection

k. covers the lungs

l. covers the heart

C. Concept Map

This concept map organizes and summarizes the concepts presented in Chapter 4. Using the following terms, fill in the circled numbered, blank spaces to complete the concept map. Follow the numbers that comply with the organization of the map.

Adipose   Loose   Connective   Cartilage   Skeletal

Columnar   Blood   Neuron   Ligament

D. Crossword Puzzle

The following crossword puzzle reviews the material in Chapter 4. To complete the puzzle, you must know the answers to the clues given, and must be able to spell the terms correctly.

ACROSS
5. Describes discs found in cardiac cells.
10. Tissue that has the ability to contract.
11. Type of tissue that conducts impulses.
12. An elongated cell that can conduct impulses.
13. Cells that appear to be flat and that line some organs.

DOWN
1. Describes cells that connect skin to muscle.
2. Cells that have a liquid matrix.
3. The portion of a neuron that contains the organelles.
4. Tissues that connect muscle to bone.
6. The tissue that makes up the lining of many organs.
7. The tissue that has a matrix associated with the cells.
8. Tissues that connect bone to bone.
9. Cells that form concentric rings around blood vessels.

E. Short-Answer Questions

Briefly answer the following questions in the spaces provided.

1. What are the four primary tissue types in the body?

2. Summarize the four essential functions of epithelial tissue.

3. What is the functional difference between microvilli and cilia on the exposed surfaces of epithelial cells?

4. How do the processes of merocrine, apocrine, and holocrine secretion differ?

5. List the types of exocrine glands in the body and identify their secretions.

6. What three basic components are found in all connective tissues?

7. What three classifications are recognized to classify connective tissues?

8. What three basic types of fibers are found in connective tissue?

9. What four kinds of membranes—consisting of epithelial and connective tissues that cover and protect other structures and tissues—are found in the body?

10. What are the three types of muscle tissue?

11. What two types of cell populations make up neural tissue, and what is the primary function of each type?

The Integumentary System

Overview

Do you know what the largest organ in the human body is? If you answered "skin" you are correct. The skin, which makes up the greatest part of the integumentary system, is considered to be the largest structurally integrated organ in the body. In addition to the skin, the integumentary system consists of associated structures, including hair, nails, and a variety of glands. Of all the body systems, the integument is the only one that is seen every day. Millions of dollars are spent each year for skin, hair, and nail care to enhance their appearance and prevent disorders that may alter desirable structural features on or below the surface of the skin. All of the four tissue types studied in Chapter 4 are found in the structural makeup of the skin, each contributing to the many functions performed by the skin and its associated structures. These functions include protection, excretion, secretion, absorption, synthesis, storage, sensitivity, and temperature regulation.

Completion and mastery of the exercises in Chapter 5 will increase your awareness of the structural and functional features of the integument and the important roles the skin, hair, and nails play in our lives.

Review of Chapter Objectives

1. Describe the general functions of the integumentary system.
2. Describe the main structural features of the epidermis, and explain their functional significance.
3. Explain what accounts for individual differences in skin, such as skin color.
4. Describe how the integumentary system helps to regulate body temperature.
5. Discuss the effects of ultraviolet radiation on the skin and the role played by melanocytes.
6. Discuss the functions of the skin's accessory structures.
7. Explain the mechanisms that produce hair and determine hair texture and color.
8. Explain how the skin responds to injury and repairs itself.
9. Summarize the effects of the aging process on the skin.

Part I: Objective-Based Questions

OBJECTIVE 1   Describe the general functions of the integumentary system.

_____ 1. The two functional components of the integument include

        a. dermis and epidermis.
        b. hair and skin.
        c. cutaneous membrane and accessory structures.
        d. elastin and keratin.

_____ 2. Regulating heat exchange with the environment is the mechanism that the skin uses to

        a. maintain normal body temperature.
        b. prevent excessive loss of body fluids.
        c. maintain large reserves of lipids.
        d. transmit information to the nervous system.

_____ 3. The structure(s) of the integumentary system involved in protection is(are)

        a. hair.
        b. skin.
        c. nails.
        d. all of the above.

_____ 4. All of the following are functions of the integumentary system except

        a. protection of underlying tissue.
        b. synthesis of vitamin A.
        c. maintenance of body temperature.
        d. excretion.

_____ 5. Receptors in the skin represent the

        a. method by which body temperature is maintained.
        b. release of chemicals from metabolism.
        c. areas of synthesis and storage of nutrients.
        d. link between the integument and the nervous system.

OBJECTIVE 2   Describe the main structural features of the epidermis, and explain their functional significance.

_____ 1. The layers of the epidermis, beginning with the deepest layer and *proceeding outwardly,* include the strata

        a. corneum, granulosum, spinosum, germinativum.
        b. granulosum, spinosum, germinativum, corneum.
        c. spinosum, germinativum, corneum, granulosum.
        d. germinativum, spinosum, granulosum, corneum.

_____ 2. Stem cells and melanocytes dominate the stratum germinativum, making it the layer where

        a. new cells are generated and skin colors are synthesized.
        b. the protein keratin produces cornified cells.
        c. dead epithelial cells accumulate in large amounts.
        d. the cells are flattened, densely packed, and filled with keratin.

_____ 3. Epidermal cells in the stratum spinosum and stratum germinativum function as chemical factories in that they can convert

        a. steroid precursors to vitamin D when exposed to sunlight.
        b. eleidin to keratin.
        c. keratohyalin to eleidin.
        d. a and c only

_____ 4. The two pigments contained in the epidermis in variable amounts are

        a. melanin and keratin.
        b. carotene and keratin.
        c. vitamin D and melanin.
        d. carotene and melanin.

5. Keratin, a fibrous protein, would be found primarily in the _____.

6. The layer where the skin is thick, such as the palms of the hands and the soles of the feet, is called the _____.

Labeling Exercise

Identify the various components of the integumentary system in Figure 5-1. Place your answers in the spaces provided on the following page.

FIGURE 5-1 Components of the Integumentary System

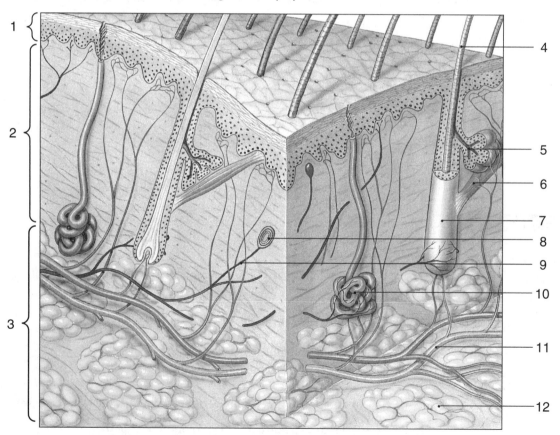

1. _____   7. _____

2. _____   8. _____

3. _____   9. _____

4. _____   10. _____

5. _____   11. _____

6. _____   12. _____

OBJECTIVE 3 Explain what accounts for individual differences in skin, such as skin color.

_____ 1. Differences in skin color among individuals reflect

  a. numbers of melanocytes.
  b. melanocyte distribution patterns.
  c. levels of melanin synthesis.
  d. UV responses and nuclear activity.

_____ 2. Dermal blood supply and epidermal pigmentation are the two basic factors interacting to

  a. produce melanocytes and provide skin coloration.
  b. provide oxygen and carbon dioxide for skin respiration.
  c. produce skin pigments and avoid albinism.
  d. produce skin color.

_____ 3. Even though melanocytes are of normal abundance and distribution, in the inherited condition of albinism

  a. melanin is not produced by the melanocytes.
  b. sunlight inhibits production of melanin.
  c. there is a decrease in blood supply to the skin.
  d. melanocytes are destroyed before they mature.

_____ 4. Some people only "burn" when exposed to the sun. The reason they don't tan is that

  a. they do not have a gene for tanning.
  b. their melanocytes are inactive.
  c. they don't have a sufficient number of melanocytes.
  d. all of the above are true.

_____ 5. Albinos have

  a. no melanocytes.
  b. fewer melanocytes than non-albinos.
  c. the same number of melanocytes as non-albinos.
  d. overactive melanocytes.

6. Small amounts of ultraviolet (UV) radiation are beneficial because it stimulates the

synthesis of _____.

7. The pigment that absorbs ultraviolet radiation before it can damage mitochondrial DNA is

_____.

OBJECTIVE 4 Describe how the integumentary system helps to regulate body temperature.

_____ 1. Cooling the surface of the skin and producing perspiration is the primary function of

      a. ceruminous gland activity.
      b. sebaceous gland activity.
      c. apocrine gland activity.
      d. merocrine gland activity.

_____ 2. If body temperature drops below normal, heat is conserved by _____ in the diameter of dermal blood vessels.

      a. an increase
      b. no change
      c. a decrease
      d. None of the above are correct.

_____ 3. When body temperature becomes abnormally high, thermoregulatory homeostasis is maintained by

      a. an increase in sweat gland activity and blood flow to the skin.
      b. a decrease in blood flow to the skin and sweat gland activity.
      c. an increase in blood flow to the skin and a decrease in sweat gland activity.
      d. an increase in sweat gland activity and a decrease in blood flow to the skin.

_____ 4. Excessive perspiration to maintain normal body temperature may cause

      a. excessive secretion of sebum by sebaceous glands.
      b. dangerous fluid and electrolyte losses.
      c. the apocrine glands to discharge a sticky, cloudy, odorous secretion.
      d. All of the above are correct.

_____ 5. Perspiration (or sweat) produced by eccrine sweat glands consists of

      a. 50 percent water, 1 percent sebum, 40 percent wastes, and 9 percent nutrients.
      b. 90 percent water, 5 percent electrolytes, and 5 percent wastes and nutrients.
      c. 1 percent sebum, 9 percent wastes and nutrients, and 90 percent water.
      d. 99 percent water, and 1 percent electrolytes, organic nutrients, and wastes.

OBJECTIVE 5 Discuss the effects of ultraviolet radiation on the skin and the role played by melanocytes.

_____ 1. Melanin prevents skin damage due to UV light by

      a. covering and protecting the epidermal layers.
      b. absorbing UV light.
      c. protecting the nuclei of epidermal cells.
      d. b and c are correct.

_____ 2. Excessive exposure to UV light may damage

        a. cellular DNA, resulting in mutations.

        b. connective tissue and cause wrinkling.

        c. chromosomes and cause cancer.

        d. all of the above.

_____ 3. Excessive exposure to UV light may cause

        a. a decrease in the number of melanocytes.

        b. an increase in the number of melanocytes.

        c. a decrease in vitamin D production.

        d. damage to the DNA in cells in the stratum germinativum.

4. Melanocytes prevent skin damage due to UV light by protecting the _____ within the nuclei of epidermal cells.

5. Melanocytes begin producing melanin when they are exposed to _____.

OBJECTIVE 6   Discuss the functions of the skin's accessory structures.

_____ 1. Accessory structures of the skin include

        a. the dermis, epidermis, hypodermis, subcutaneous layer, and hair follicles.

        b. a cutaneous and subcutaneous layer, dermis, epidermis, and hair.

        c. hair, hair follicles, sebaceous glands, sweat glands, and nails.

        d. blood vessels, macrophages, neurons, hair papillae, and the cuticle.

_____ 2. Hairs are best described as

        a. living structures that are produced in the dermis and extend into the epidermis.

        b. nonliving epithelial cells that undergo keratinization and die.

        c. living structures containing a cortex and medulla.

        d. nonliving structures produced in organs called hair follicles.

_____ 3. The sensitivity mechanism in hair follicles that provides an early warning system that may help prevent injury is the presence of a

        a. cortex and medulla making up the core of the hair.

        b. cuticular surface layer of cells.

        c. sensory nerve fiber associated with the base of each hair follicle.

        d. Hairs are nonliving; there is no sensitivity mechanism.

_____ 4. Natural body odor is produced by the _____ glands.

        a. apocrine

        b. eccrine

        c. sebaceous

        d. sweat

_____ 5. During adolescence, the sebaceous glands are especially prone to

        a. producing excessive perspiration while sweating.

        b. developing acne.

        c. causing redness of the skin due to blood vessel dilation.

        d. all the above are correct.

_____   6. Other types of modified sweat glands with specialized secretions are

a. holocrine glands and sudoriferous glands.
b. mammary glands and ceruminous glands.
c. merocrine glands and eccrine glands.
d. endocrine and exocrine glands.

7. Protection for the tips of the fingers and toes is provided by the _____.

8. Hair develops from a group of epidermal cells at the base of a tube-like depression called

a(n) _____.

9. The accessory structures that prevent the entry of foreign particles into the eye are the

_____.

10. The arrector pili are muscles of the integument involved in creating _____.

Labeling Exercise

Identify the structures in Figure 5-2 (a) and (b). Place your answers in the spaces provided below the drawings.

FIGURE 5-2 Nail Structure: (a) Nail Surface (b) Sectional View

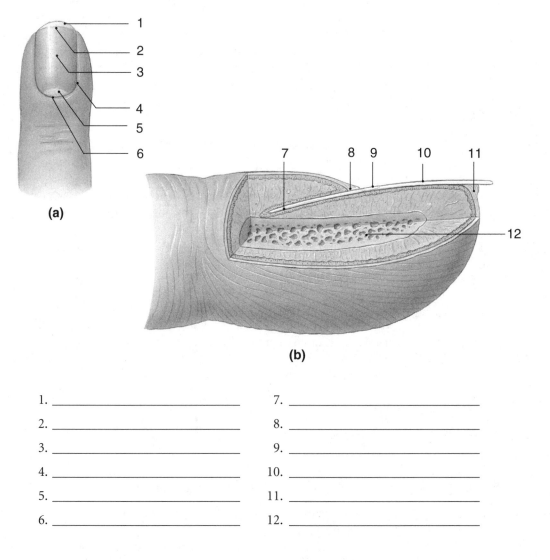

(a)

(b)

1. _____	7. _____
2. _____	8. _____
3. _____	9. _____
4. _____	10. _____
5. _____	11. _____
6. _____	12. _____

OBJECTIVE 7   Explain the mechanisms that produce hair and determine hair texture and color.

_____ 1. Hair production begins at the

         a. reticular layer of the dermis.
         b. papillary layer of the dermis.
         c. hypodermis.
         d. base of a hair follicle.

_____ 2. Except for red hair, the natural factor responsible for various shades of hair color is

         a. the number of melanocytes.
         b. the amount of carotene production.
         c. the type of pigment present.
         d. all of the above.

_____ 3. The development of gray hair is due to the

         a. death of hair follicles.
         b. production of air bubbles in the hair.
         c. production of gray pigments.
         d. reduction of melanocyte activity.

_____ 4. The various types of hair are due to the

         a. arrector pili.
         b. follicles.
         c. hair papilla.
         d. melanocytes.

_____ 5. The shaft of the hair is stiff due to the presence of a protein substance called

         a. elastin.
         b. collagen.
         c. keratin.
         d. vellus.

_____ 6. The fine "peach fuzz" hairs formed over much of the body surface are called

         a. vellus.
         b. lunula.
         c. arrector pili.
         d. eccrines.

OBJECTIVE 8   Explain how the skin responds to injury and repairs itself.

_____ 1. The immediate response by the skin to an injury is that

         a. bleeding occurs, and mast cells trigger an inflammation response.
         b. the epidermal cells are immediately replaced.
         c. fibroblasts in the dermis create scar tissue.
         d. a scab is formed.

_____ 2. The practical limit to the healing process in the skin is the formation of inflexible, fibrous, noncellular

   a. scabs.
   b. skin grafts.
   c. ground substance.
   d. scar tissue.

_____ 3. The appearance of blisters and very painful sensations is indicative of

   a. a first-degree burn.
   b. a second-degree burn.
   c. a third-degree burn.
   d. none of the above.

_____ 4. The granulation tissue that appears during the healing process is a combination of

   a. a scab, fibrin, and macrophages.
   b. a keloid, a blood clot, and newly arriving phagocytes.
   c. a blood clot, fibroblasts, and an extensive capillary network.
   d. macrophages, fibroblasts, pathogens, and phagocytes.

_____ 5. An essential part of the healing process during which the edges of a wound are pulled closer together is called

   a. cyanosing.
   b. regressing.
   c. regeneration.
   d. contraction.

OBJECTIVE 9   Summarize the effects of the aging process on the skin.

_____ 1. Dangerously high body temperatures occur sometimes in the elderly due to

   a. reduction in the number of Langerhans cells.
   b. decreased blood supply to the dermis.
   c. decreased sweat gland activity.
   d. b and c only.

_____ 2. A factor that causes increased skin damage and infection in the elderly is

   a. decreased sensitivity of the immune system.
   b. decreased vitamin D production.
   c. a decline in melanocyte activity.
   d. a decline in glandular activity.

_____ 3. Hair turns gray or white due to

   a. a decline in glandular activity.
   b. a decrease in the number of Langerhans cells.
   c. decreased melanocyte activity.
   d. decreased blood supply to the dermis.

_____ 4. Sagging and wrinkling of the integument results from

        a. a decline of germinativum cell activity in the epidermis.
        b. a decrease in the elastic fiber network of the dermis.
        c. a decrease in vitamin D production.
        d. deactivation of sweat glands.

5. In older Caucasians, the skin becomes very pale because of a decline in _____ activity.

6. In older adults, dry and scaly skin is usually a result of a decrease in _____ activity.

Part II: Chapter Comprehensive Exercises

A. Word Elimination

Circle the term that does not belong in each of the following groupings.

1. protection   fat storage   excretion   secretion   cutaneous

2. dermis   germinativum   spinosum   granulosum   lucidum

3. touch   pain   secretion   pressure   temperature

4. hair follicles   melanocytes   sebaceous glands   sweat glands   nails

5. protect   cushion   stabilize   insulate   guard

6. sebaceous   holocrine   acne   sebum   apocrine

7. apocrine   merocrine   sebaceous   eccrine   sweat

8. cuticle   arrector pili   lunula   nail root   eponychium

9. increased immunity   dry skin   gray hair   wrinkling   weak muscles

10. papillary   reticular   collagen   dermis   epidermis

B. Matching

Match the terms in Column "B" with the terms in Column "A." Write letters for answers in the spaces provided.

COLUMN A	COLUMN B
____ 1. subcutaneous layer	a. decreased oxygen to skin
____ 2. epidermis	b. life-threatening skin cancer
____ 3. stratum granulosum	c. contains desmosomes
____ 4. stratum corneum	d. thickened area of scar tissue
____ 5. cyanosis	e. hypodermis
____ 6. melanoma	f. activated arrector pili
____ 7. papillary layer (dermis)	g. produces keratin
____ 8. "goose bumps"	h. no blood vessels
____ 9. eponychium	i. cuticle
____10. keloid	j. contains capillaries and nerves

C. Concept Map

This concept map summarizes and organizes some of the ideas in Chapter 5. Using the following terms, fill in the circled numbered, blank spaces to complete the concept map. Follow the numbers that comply with the organization of the map.

Hair   Loose connective tissue   Sweat glands
Dermis   Elastic and collagen fibers   Deep reticular layer

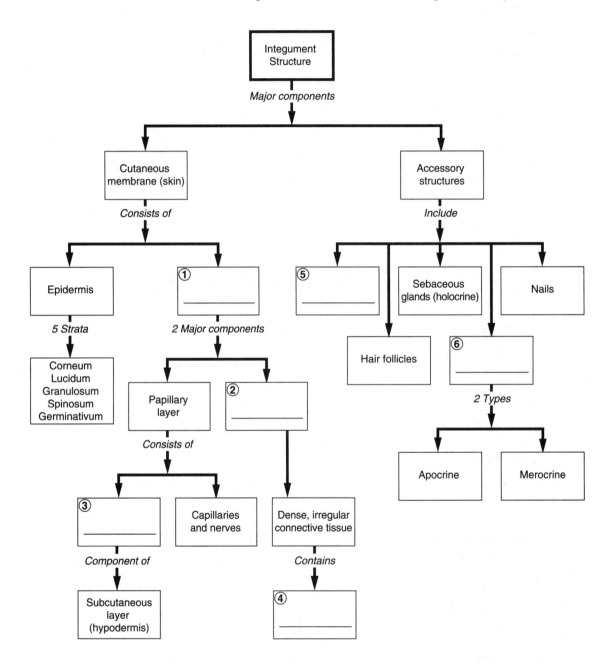

D. Crossword Puzzle

This crossword puzzle reviews the material in Chapter 5. To complete the puzzle, you must know the answers to the clues given, and you must be able to spell the terms correctly.

ACROSS
1. The stratum _____ is the outermost layer of the epidermis.
4. The stratum _____ is the layer of epidermis where the cells are actively growing.
7. Melanin protects a cell's nuclear ____.
8. This layer of skin contains most of the accessory structures.
9. The ____ pili muscles are responsible for goose bumps.
11. Freckles are spot concentrations of ____.
13. The stratum corneum layer is a part of this layer of skin.
14. A blocked sebaceous gland can result in this skin condition.
15. The integumentary system includes the skin, hair, nails, and ____.

DOWN
2. Skin is the largest ____ of the body.
3. Albinos have the same number of ____ as non-albinos.
5. A term that refers to skin and its accessory structures.
6. The skin becomes pale if ____ is(are) underactive.
10. This gland helps maintain proper body temperature.
12. This gland produces "natural body odor."

E. Short-Answer Questions

Briefly answer the following questions in the spaces provided.

1. A friend says to you, "Don't worry about what you say to her; she is thick skinned." Anatomically speaking, what areas of the body would your friend be referring to? Why are these areas thicker?

2. Two women are discussing their dates. One of them says, "I liked everything about him except he had body odor." What is the cause of body odor?

3. A hypodermic needle is used to introduce drugs into the loose connective tissue of the hypodermis. Beginning on the surface of the skin in the region of the thigh, list, in order, the layers of tissue the needle would penetrate to reach the hypodermis.

4. The general public associates a tan with good health. What is wrong with this assessment?

5. Many shampoo advertisements suggest that some ingredients, such as honey, kelp extracts, beer, vitamins, and other nutrients, are beneficial to the hair. Why could this be considered false advertising?

6. Two teenagers are discussing their problems with acne. One says to the other, "Sure wish I could get rid of these whiteheads." The other replies, "At least you don't have blackheads like I do." What is the difference between a "whitehead" and a "blackhead"?

The Skeletal System

Overview

Can you imagine what the human body would be like if it were devoid of bones or some other form of supporting framework? Picture a "blob" utilizing amoeboid movement. Ugh! The skeletal system consists of bones and related connective tissues, which include cartilage, tendons, and ligaments. Bone is a living tissue and is functionally dynamic. It provides a supportive framework for vital body organs, serves as areas for muscle attachment, articulates at joints for stability and movement, and assists in respiratory movements. In addition, it provides areas of storage for substances such as calcium and lipids, and blood cell formation occurs within the cavities containing bone marrow.

The skeletal system consists of 206 bones, 80 of which are found in the axial division, and 126 of which make up the appendicular division. Many of the bones of the body, especially those of the appendicular skeleton, provide a system of levers used in movement, and are utilized in numerous ways to control the environment that surrounds you every second of your life. Few people relate the importance of movement as one of the factors necessary for maintaining life, but the body doesn't survive very long without the ability to produce movements.

The study and review for this chapter includes microscopic and macroscopic features of bone, bone development and growth, location and identification of bones, joint classification, and the structure of representative articulations.

Review of Chapter Objectives

1. Describe the functions of the skeletal system.
2. Compare the structures and functions of compact and spongy bones.
3. Discuss bone growth and development, and account for variations in the internal structure of specific bones.
4. Describe the remodeling and repair of the skeleton, and discuss homeostatic mechanisms responsible for regulating mineral deposition and turnover.
5. Name the components and functions of the axial and appendicular skeletons.
6. Identify the bones of the skull.
7. Discuss the differences in the structure and function of the various vertebrae.

8. Relate the structural differences between the pectoral and pelvic girdles to their various functional roles.

9. Distinguish among different types of joints, and link structural features to joint functions.

10. Describe the dynamic movements of the skeleton and the structure of representative articulations.

11. Explain the relationship between joint structure and mobility, using specific examples.

12. Discuss the functional relationship between the skeletal system and other body systems.

Part I: Objective-Based Questions

OBJECTIVE 1 Describe the functions of the skeletal system.

_____ 1. The function(s) of the skeletal system is(are)

        a. structural support and storage for calcium and lipids.
        b. blood cell production.
        c. protection and leverage.
        d. all of the above.

_____ 2. Storage of lipids that represent an important energy reserve in bone occurs in areas of

        a. red marrow.
        b. yellow marrow.
        c. bone matrix.
        d. ground substance.

_____ 3. Of the five major functions of the skeleton, the two that depend on the dynamic nature of bone are

        a. support and storage of minerals.
        b. blood cell formation and lipid storage.
        c. storage of lipids and calcium.
        d. support and blood cell formation.

_____ 4. The support tissues in the body consist of

        a. bone and muscle.
        b. collagen and elastin.
        c. bone and cartilage.
        d. all of the above.

OBJECTIVE 2   Compare the structures and functions of compact and spongy bones.

_____ 1. One of the basic histological differences between compact and spongy bone is that in compact bone,

   a. the basic functional unit is the osteon/Haversian system.
   b. there is a lamella arrangement.
   c. there are plates or struts called trabeculae.
   d. osteons are not present.

_____ 2. Compact bone is usually found where

   a. bones are not heavily stressed.
   b. stresses arrive from many directions.
   c. trabeculae are aligned with extensive cross-bracing.
   d. stresses arrive from a limited range of directions.

_____ 3. Spongy and cancellous bone, unlike compact bone, resembles a network of bony struts separated by spaces that are normally filled with

   a. osteocytes.
   b. lacunae.
   c. bone marrow.
   d. lamellae.

_____ 4. Spongy bone is found primarily at the

   a. bone surfaces of long bones, except inside joint capsules.
   b. expanded ends of long bones, where they articulate with other skeletal elements.
   c. epiphyses of long bones.
   d. exterior region of the bone shaft of long bones, to withstand forces applied at either end.

5. The basic functional unit of compact bones is the _____.

6. The expanded region of a long bone consisting of spongy bone is called the

_____.

Labeling Exercises

Identify the following structures in a long bone. Place your answers in the spaces provided below the drawing.

compact bone   distal epiphysis   marrow cavity
blood vessels   spongy bone   proximal epiphysis
articular cartilage   endosteum   diaphysis
periosteum

FIGURE 6-1 Structure of a Long Bone

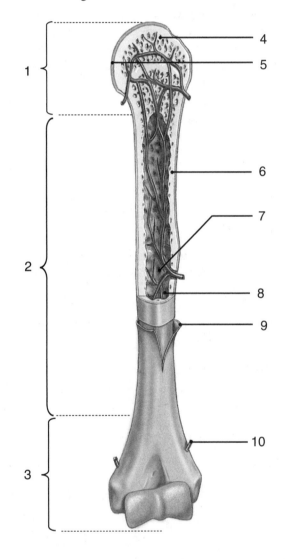

1. _____   6. _____
2. _____   7. _____
3. _____   8. _____
4. _____   9. _____
5. _____   10. _____

Identify the following structures in a typical bone. Place your answers in the spaces provided below the drawing.

osteons	vein	trabeculae	perforating canal
artery	compact bone	central canal	endosteum
periosteum	lamellae		

FIGURE 6-2 Structure of a Typical Bone

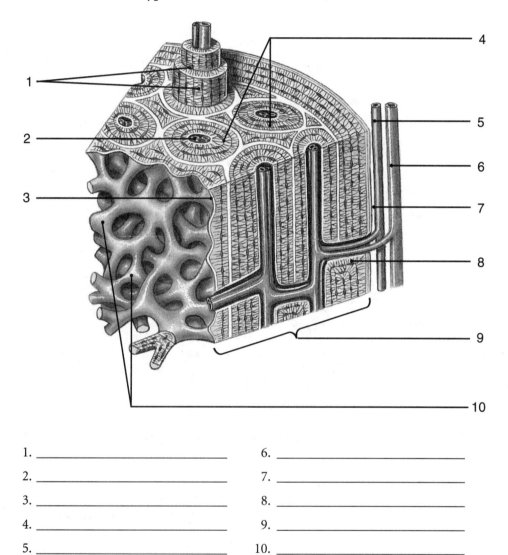

1. _____   6. _____

2. _____   7. _____

3. _____   8. _____

4. _____   9. _____

5. _____   10. _____

OBJECTIVE 3   Discuss bone growth and development, and account for variations in the internal structure of specific bones.

_____   1. The ossification process first occurs in the

       a. diaphysis.

       b. distal end of the bone.

       c. epiphysis.

       d. proximal end of the bone.

_____ 2. From the following steps, identify the correct sequence in the process of endochondral ossification.

(1) Inner layer of perichondrium differentiates into osteoblasts.
(2) Blood vessels invade epiphyses; osteoblasts form secondary centers of ossification.
(3) Chondrocytes enlarge and calcify, and then die.
(4) Bone enlarges; osteoclasts break down spongy bone, creating a narrow cavity.
(5) Osteoblasts form spongy bone at a primary center of ossification.

        a. 1, 5, 3, 4, 2
        b. 3, 1, 5, 4, 2
        c. 1, 3, 5, 4, 2
        d. 2, 3, 1, 5, 4

_____ 3. Secondary ossification centers occur

        a. in the medullary cavity of the diaphysis.
        b. at the outer surface of the diaphysis.
        c. in the center of the epiphysis.
        d. at the surface of the epiphysis.

_____ 4. When sexual hormone production increases, bone growth

        a. slows down.
        b. increases, but only in thickness.
        c. accelerates rapidly.
        d. is not affected.

_____ 5. Endochondral ossification begins with the formation of a

        a. cartilage model.
        b. calcified model.
        c. membranous mode.
        d. fibrous connective tissue model.

_____ 6. Variations in body size and proportions relative to bone growth between men and women are due to

        a. differences in sex hormones.
        b. vitamin B supplementation.
        c. the degree to which breast milk is available to an infant.
        d. all of the above.

_____ 7. The vitamins that play an important role in normal bone growth and maintenance are

        a. Ca, P, K, Fe
        b. A, C, D$_3$
        c. Ca, B, P, K
        d. A, Ca, B, P

Labeling Exercise

Identify the following structures in Figure 6-3. Place your answers in the spaces provided below the drawings.

disintegrating chondrocytes   enlarging chondrocytes

blood vessels   epiphyseal plate

marrow cavity   epiphysis

diaphysis

FIGURE 6-3 Endochondral Ossification

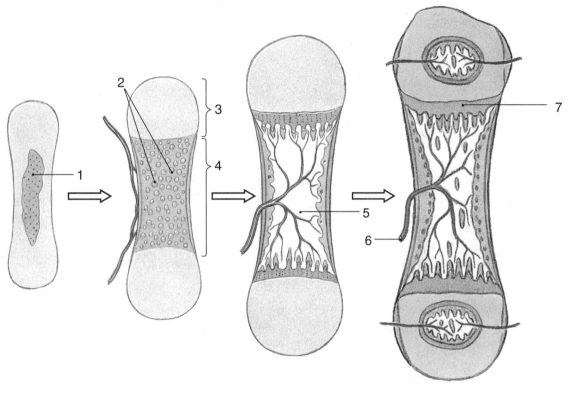

1. _____   5. _____

2. _____   6. _____

3. _____   7. _____

4. _____

OBJECTIVE 4 Describe the remodeling and repair of the skeleton, and discuss homeostatic mechanisms responsible for regulating mineral deposition and turnover.

_____ 1. The process of *remodeling* in bone involves the

      a. inactivation of osteoclasts, and increased activation of osteoblasts.
      b. activation of osteoclasts, and the inactivation of osteoblasts.
      c. removal and replacement of the protein and mineral components of bone.
      d. formation of osteons by osteoclasts and destruction by osteoblasts.

_____ 2. During bone renewal, as one osteon forms through the activity of osteoblasts, another is destroyed by

      a. osteocytes.
      b. osteoclasts.
      c. chondrocytes.
      d. calcification.

_____ 3. An important and essential way to maintain bone strength and bone mass is to

      a. avoid stressing the bones during exercise.
      b. avoid exercises that involve lifting weights.
      c. decrease the weight of an exercise and increase the repetitions.
      d. apply stress to bones during exercise.

_____ 4. Bones will usually heal after they have been severely damaged so long as the cellular components of the endosteum and periosteum survive and there is a(n)

      a. blood supply.
      b. ossification center.
      c. increase in osteoclast activity.
      d. decrease in osteoblast activity and an increase in osteoclast activity.

_____ 5. Two hormones—parathyroid hormone and calcitriol—work together to

      a. elevate calcium levels in body fluids.
      b. decrease calcium levels in body fluids.
      c. absorb and transport calcium in the blood.
      d. regulate vitamin and mineral deposition in bones.

_____ 6. Of the following selections, the one that describes a homeostatic mechanism of the skeleton is

      a. as one osteon forms through the activity of osteoblasts, another is destroyed by osteoclasts.
      b. mineral absorption from the mother's bloodstream during prenatal development.
      c. vitamin D stimulating the absorption and transport of calcium and phosphate ions.
      d. a, b, and c are correct.

_____ 7. Of the following nutrients, the one that is essential for absorption of calcium and phosphate ions in the digestive tract is

      a. vitamin A.
      b. vitamin C.
      c. vitamin K.
      d. vitamin D.

_____ 8. The most abundant _mineral_ in the human body, 99 percent of which is deposited in the skeleton, is

      a. phosphorus.
      b. iron.
      c. calcium.
      d. potassium.

_____ 9. Bones not subjected to ordinary stresses become

      a. thicker.
      b. thin and brittle.
      c. longer.
      d. all of the above.

_____ 10. The hormone calcitonin functions to

      a. decrease the rate of calcium excretion.
      b. increase the rate of calcium absorption.
      c. stimulate osteoclast activity.
      d. depress the level of calcium in body fluids.

OBJECTIVE 5   Name the components and functions of the axial and appendicular skeletons.

_____ 1. The axial skeleton provides an extensive surface area for the attachment of muscles that

      a. stabilize or position elements of the appendicular skeleton.
      b. perform respiratory movements.
      c. adjust the positions of the head, neck, and trunk.
      d. do all of the above.

_____ 2. Of the following selections, the one that includes bones found exclusively in the axial skeleton is

      a. ear ossicles, scapula, clavicle, sternum, hyoid.
      b. vertebral, ischium, ilium, skull, ribs.
      c. skull, vertebrae, ribs, sternum, hyoid.
      d. sacrum, ear ossicles, skull, scapula, ilium.

_____ 3. The axial skeleton creates a framework that supports and protects organ systems in the

      a. dorsal and ventral body cavities.
      b. pleural cavity.
      c. abdominal cavity.
      d. pericardial cavity.

_____ 4. The bones that make up the appendicular division of the skeleton consist of the

        a. bones that form the longitudinal axis of the body.
        b. rib cage and vertebral column.
        c. skull and the arms and legs.
        d. pectoral and pelvic girdles, and the upper and lower limbs.

_____ 5. One of the major functional differences between the appendicular and axial divisions is that the appendicular division

        a. serves to adjust the position of the head, neck, and trunk.
        b. protects organ systems in the dorsal and ventral body cavities.
        c. makes you an active, mobile individual.
        d. assists directly in respiratory movements.

_____ 6. A composite structure that includes portions of both the appendicular and axial skeleton is the

        a. pelvis.
        b. pectoral girdle.
        c. pelvic girdle.
        d. a, b, and c are correct.

_____ 7. The unique compromise of the articulations in the appendicular skeleton is

        a. the stronger the joint, the less restricted the range of motion.
        b. the weaker the joint, the more restricted the range of motion.
        c. the stronger the joint, the more restricted the range of motion.
        d. the strength of the joint and range of motion are unrelated.

8. The bones of the skeleton provide an extensive surface area for the attachment of

_____.

9. The appendicular skeleton includes the bones of the pectoral and pelvic girdles and the upper and lower _____.

10. The only direct connection between the pectoral girdle and the axial skeleton is the

_____.

Labeling Exercise

Identify all the bones of the skeleton designated by leader lines. Place your answers in the spaces provided below the drawing.

FIGURE 6-4 The Skeleton—Axial and Appendicular Divisions

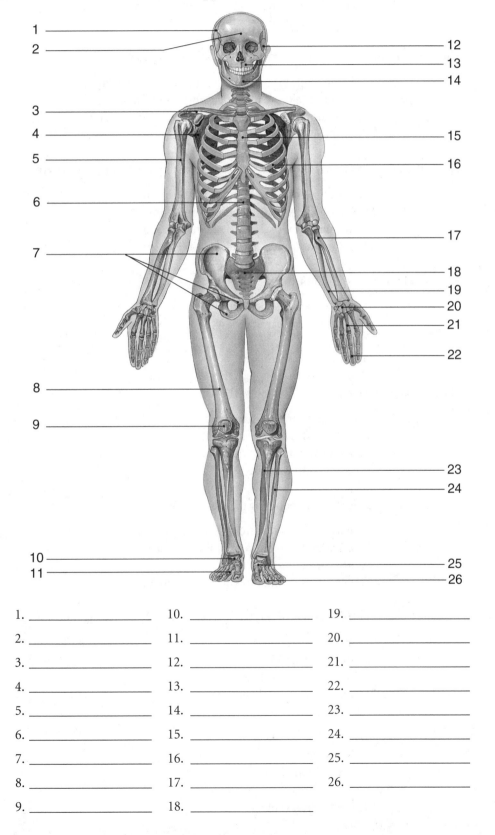

1. _____	10. _____	19. _____
2. _____	11. _____	20. _____
3. _____	12. _____	21. _____
4. _____	13. _____	22. _____
5. _____	14. _____	23. _____
6. _____	15. _____	24. _____
7. _____	16. _____	25. _____
8. _____	17. _____	26. _____
9. _____	18. _____	

OBJECTIVE 6   Identify the bones of the skull.

_____ 1. At birth, the bones of the skull can be distorted without damage because of the

a. cranial foramina.
b. fontanels.
c. alveolar process.
d. cranial ligaments.

_____ 2. The most significant growth in the skull occurs before age 5 when the

a. brain stops growing and cranial sutures develop.
b. brain development is incomplete until maturity.
c. cranium of a child is larger than that of an adult.
d. ossification and articulation process is completed.

_____ 3. The bones of the cranium that exclusively represent single, unpaired bones are

a. occipital, parietal, frontal, and temporal.
b. occipital, frontal, sphenoid, and ethmoid.
c. frontal, temporal, parietal, and sphenoid.
d. ethmoid, frontal, parietal, and temporal.

_____ 4. The paired bones of the cranium are the

a. ethmoid and sphenoid.
b. frontal and occipital.
c. occipital and parietal.
d. parietal and temporal.

_____ 5. The associated bones of the skull include the

a. mandible and maxilla.
b. nasal and lacrimal.
c. hyoid and auditory ossicles.
d. vomer and palatine.

_____ 6. The sutures that articulate the bones of the skull are the

a. parietal, occipital, frontal, and temporal.
b. calvaria, foramen, condyloid, and lacerum.
c. posterior, anterior, laternal, and dorsal.
d. lambdoid, sagittal, coronal, and squamous.

_____ 7. Foramina, located on the bones of the skull, serve primarily as passageways for

a. air and secretions.
b. sight and sound.
c. nerves and blood vessels.
d. muscle fibers and nerve tissue.

_____ 8. Areas of the head that are involved in the formation of the skull are called

a. fontanels.
b. craniocephalic.
c. craniulums.
d. ossification centers.

_____ 9. The sinuses or internal chambers in the skull are found in the

        a. sphenoid, ethmoid, vomer, and lacrimal bones.

        b. sphenoid, frontal, ethmoid, and maxillary bones.

        c. ethmoid, frontal, lacrimal, and maxillary bones.

        d. lacrimal, vomer, ethmoid, and frontal bones.

Labeling Exercises

Identify the following structures in Figure 6-5. Place your answers in the spaces provided below the drawing.

frontal bone	parietal bone	mandible
mastoid process	sphenoid bone	ethmoid bone
temporal bone	zygomatic bone	maxilla
occipital bone	styloid process	nasal bone
lacrimal bone	zygomatic arch	

FIGURE 6-5 Lateral View of the Skull

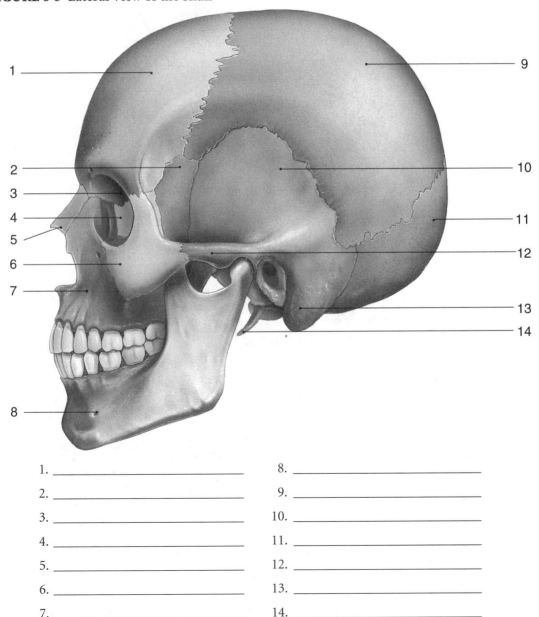

1. _____   8. _____

2. _____   9. _____

3. _____   10. _____

4. _____   11. _____

5. _____   12. _____

6. _____   13. _____

7. _____   14. _____

Labeling Exercises, continued

Identify the following structures in Figure 6-6. Place your answers in the spaces provided below the drawing.

frontal bone	temporal bone	zygomatic bone
vomer	parietal bone	ethmoid bone
maxilla	nasal bone	sphenoid bone
lacrimal bone	mandible	nasal concha

FIGURE 6-6 Anterior View of the Skull

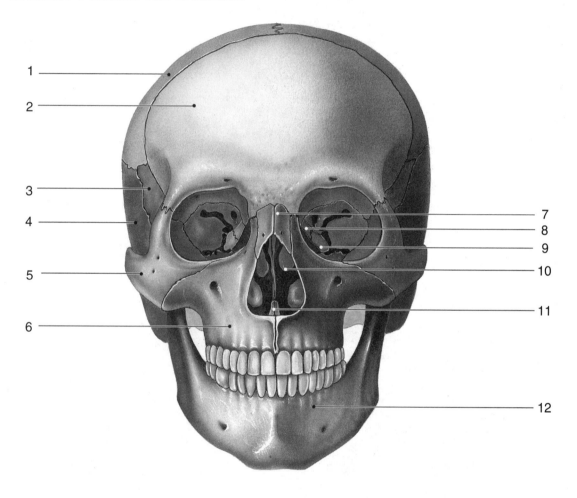

1. _____   7. _____

2. _____   8. _____

3. _____   9. _____

4. _____   10. _____

5. _____   11. _____

6. _____   12. _____

Identify the following structures in Figure 6-7. Place your answers in the spaces provided below the drawing.

zygomatic bone   vomer   sphenoid bone
foramen magnum   maxillary bone   palatine bone
temporal bone   styloid process   occipital bone
mastoid process   occipital condyle zygomatic arch

FIGURE 6-7 Inferior View of the Skull

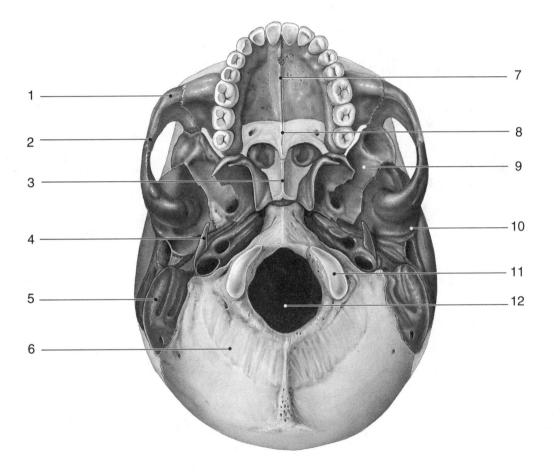

1. _____   7. _____

2. _____   8. _____

3. _____   9. _____

4. _____   10. _____

5. _____   11. _____

6. _____   12. _____

Labeling Exercises, continued

Identify the following structures in Figure 6-8. Place your answers in the spaces provided below the drawings. <u>One term is used twice.</u>

coronal suture

frontal bone

mastoid fontanel

occipital fontanel

mandible

sphenoidal fontanel

squamosal suture

occipital bone

parietal bone

sagittal suture

lambdoidal suture

frontal fontanel

maxillary bone

FIGURE 6-8 Infant Skull

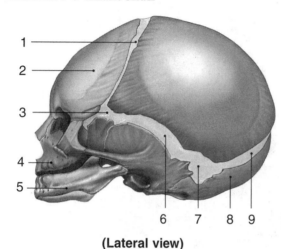

(Lateral view)   (Superior view)

1. _____

2. _____

3. _____

4. _____

5. _____

6. _____

7. _____

8. _____

9. _____

10. _____

11. _____

12. _____

13. _____

14. _____

OBJECTIVE 7   Discuss the differences in the structure and function of the various vertebrae.

_____ 1. The vertebrae that indirectly effect changes in the volume of the rib cage are the

        a. cervical vertebrae.

        b. thoracic vertebrae.

        c. lumbar vertebrae.

        d. sacral vertebrae.

_____ 2. The lumbar vertebrae are the

        a. vertebrae that effect changes in the volume of the rib cage.

        b. most mobile and least massive of the vertebrae.

        c. most massive and least mobile of the vertebrae.

        d. result of the fusion of five embryonic vertebrae.

_____ 3. Of the following selections, the one that correctly identifies the sequence of the vertebrae from superior to inferior is

    a. thoracic, cervical, lumbar, coccyx, sacrum.
    b. cervical, lumbar, thoracic, sacrum, coccyx.
    c. cervical, thoracic, lumbar, sacrum, coccyx.
    d. cervical, thoracic, sacrum, lumbar, coccyx.

_____ 4. The _atlas_ and _axis_ are vertebrae identified as

    a. T_1 and T_2.
    b. C_1 and C_2.
    c. L_1 and L_2.
    d. S_1 and S_2.

_____ 5. Gaps that permit the passage of nerves running to or from the enclosed spinal cord are called

    a. lamina propria.
    b. vertebral pedicles.
    c. intervertebral foramina.
    d. intervertebral discs.

_____ 6. The vertebral column contains _____ cervical vertebrae, _____ thoracic vertebrae, and _____ lumbar vertebrae.

    a. 7; 12; 5
    b. 5; 12; 7
    c. 7; 5; 12
    d. 12; 7; 5

_____ 7. Cervical vertebrae can usually be distinguished from other vertebrae by the presence of

    a. transverse processes.
    b. transverse foramina.
    c. large spinous processes.
    d. facets for articulations of the ribs.

_____ 8. The odontoid process is found in the

    a. sacrum.
    b. coccyx.
    c. axis.
    d. atlas.

_____ 9. Costal processes are located on the _____ vertebrae.

    a. thoracic
    b. cervical
    c. lumbar
    d. sacral

_____ 10. Thoracic vertebrae can be distinguished from other vertebrae by the presence of

    a. transverse processes.
    b. transverse foramina.
    c. facets for the articulation of ribs.
    d. costal cartilages.

11. An attachment site for a muscle that closes the anal opening is the primary purpose of the

    _____.

12. The vertebra that holds up the head and articulates with the occipital condyles of the skull

    is the _____.

13. The vertebrae that stabilize relative positions of the brain and spinal cord are the

    _____ vertebrae.

Labeling Exercises

Identify the following structures in Figure 6-9. Place your answers in the spaces provided on the following page.

cervical   sacral   lumbar

thoracic   coccygeal

FIGURE 6-9 The Vertebral Column

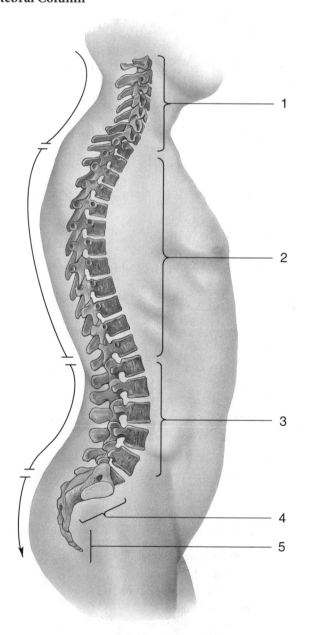

1. _____   4. _____

2. _____   5. _____

3. _____

Identify the following structures in Figure 6-10. Place your answers in the spaces provided below the drawing.

vertebral body   spinous process   vertebral foramen
transverse process   pedicle   lamina

FIGURE 6-10 A Typical Vertebra

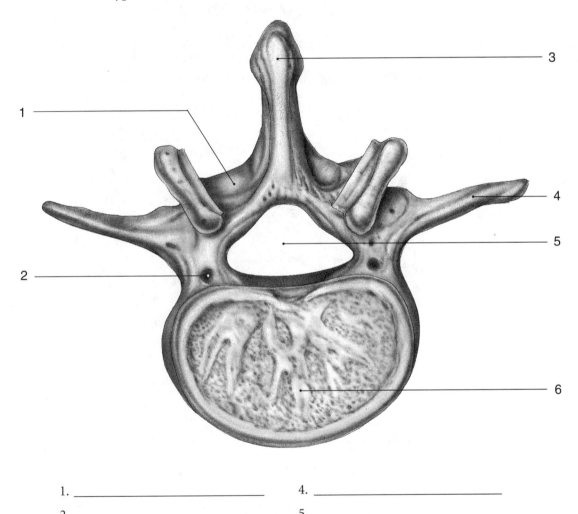

1. _____   4. _____

2. _____   5. _____

3. _____   6. _____

Labeling Exercises, continued

Identify the following structures in Figure 6-11. Place your answers in the spaces provided below the drawing.

true ribs	manubrium	false ribs
xiphoid process	sternum	body of sternum
costal cartilage	floating ribs	

FIGURE 6-11 The Ribs and Sternum

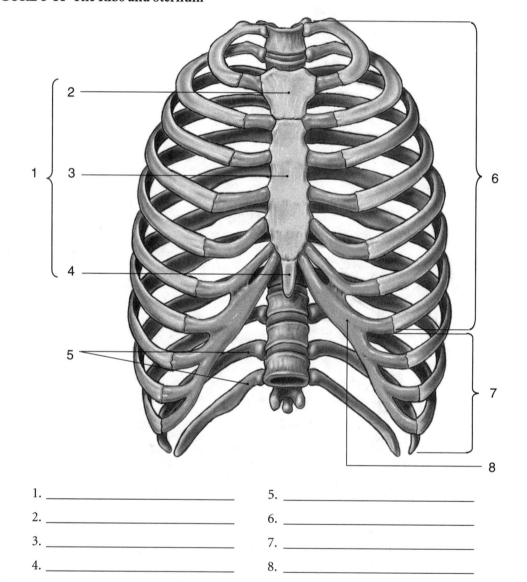

1. _____   5. _____

2. _____   6. _____

3. _____   7. _____

4. _____   8. _____

OBJECTIVE 8   Relate the structural differences between the pectoral and pelvic girdles to their various functional roles.

_____ 1. The bones of the pectoral girdle include the

        a. clavicles and scapulae.
        b. ilium and ischium.
        c. humerus and femur.
        d. ulna and radius.

_____ 2. The primary function of the pectoral girdle is to

        a. protect the organs of the thorax.
        b. provide areas for articulation with the vertebral column.
        c. position the shoulder joint and provide a base for arm movement.
        d. support and maintain the position of the skull.

_____ 3. The bones of the pelvic girdle include the

        a. tibia and fibula.
        b. ilium, pubis, and ischium.
        c. ilium, ischium, and acetabulum.
        d. coxa, patella, and acetabulum.

_____ 4. The heavy bones and the strong, stable joints of the pelvic girdle

        a. bear the weight of the body.
        b. allow a high degree of flexibility at the hip joint.
        c. allow for a wide range of motion.
        d. do all of the above.

_____ 5. The primary type of tissue responsible for stabilizing, positioning, and bracing the pectoral girdle is

        a. tendons.
        b. ligaments.
        c. cartilage.
        d. muscles.

_____ 6. The large posterior process on the scapula that articulates with the distal end of the clavicle is the

        a. coracoid process.
        b. acromion process.
        c. olecranon process.
        d. styloid process.

_____ 7. At the glenoid cavity, the scapula articulates with the proximal end of the humerus to form the

        a. subscapular fossa.
        b. deltoid tuberosity.
        c. elbow joint.
        d. shoulder joint.

_____ 8. The parallel bones that support the forearm are the

        a. ulna and radius.
        b. humerus and femur.
        c. tibia and fibula.
        d. scapula and clavicle.

_____ 9. The pubic symphysis is the articulation that

        a. limits movement of the femur in the acetabulum.
        b. allows rotation of the hips.
        c. limits movement between the two pubic bones.
        d. allows slight movement of the sciatic notch.

_____ 10. The bone that articulates with the coxa at the acetabulum is the

      a. humerus.
      b. femur.
      c. sacrum.
      d. tibia.

_____ 11. The longest and heaviest bone in the body is the

      a. tibia.
      b. fibula.
      c. femur.
      d. humerus.

_____ 12. Compared to the pelvis of males, the pelvis of females is

      a. heart shaped.
      b. robust, heavy, and rough.
      c. relatively deep.
      d. broad, light, and smooth.

_____ 13. The eight carpal bones represent the bones of the

      a. wrist.
      b. foot.
      c. hand.
      d. fingers.

_____ 14. The bones of the foot are called the

      a. metacarpals.
      b. carpals.
      c. tarsals.
      d. metatarsals.

_____ 15. The anatomical name for the heel bone is the

      a. navicular.
      b. calcaneus.
      c. talus.
      d. cuboid.

_____ 16. The bones of the fingers and toes are collectively referred to as

      a. tarsals and metatarsals.
      b. carpals and tarsals.
      c. phalanges.
      d. carpals and metacarpals.

17. The only direct connection between the pectoral girdle and the axial skeleton is the

_____.

18. The pelvic girdle consists of six bones collectively referred to as the _____.

19. The ulna and radius both have long shafts that contain like processes called

_____ processes.

20. The process that the tibia and fibula have in common that acts as a shield for the ankle is

    the _____.

21. At the hip joint on either side, the head of the femur articulates with the

    _____.

22. The popliteal ligaments are responsible for reinforcing the back of the _____.

23. An enlarged pelvic outlet in the female is an adaptation for _____.

24. The bone that cannot resist strong forces but provides the only fixed support for the pec-

    toral girdle is the _____.

25. The thin lateral bone of the lower leg is the _____.

Labeling Exercises

Identify the following structures in Figure 6-12. Place your answers in the spaces provided below the drawing.

medial border	lateral border	superior border
coracoid process	glenoid cavity	acromion process
spine	body	

FIGURE 6-12 The Scapula

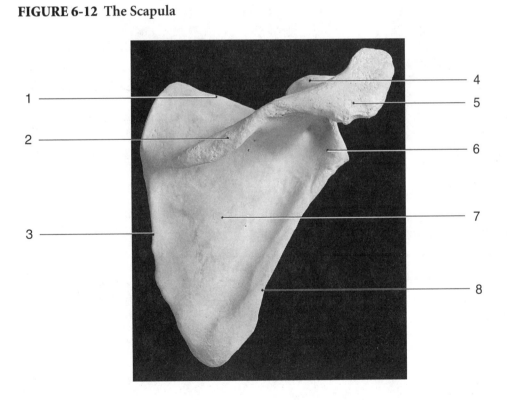

1. _____   5. _____

2. _____   6. _____

3. _____   7. _____

4. _____   8. _____

Labeling Exercises, continued

Identify the following components of the pelvis. Place your answers in the spaces provided below the drawing.

ilium	sacrum	iliac crest
ischium	coccyx	obturator foramen
pubis	symphysis pubis	acetabulum

FIGURE 6-13 The Pelvis—Anterior View

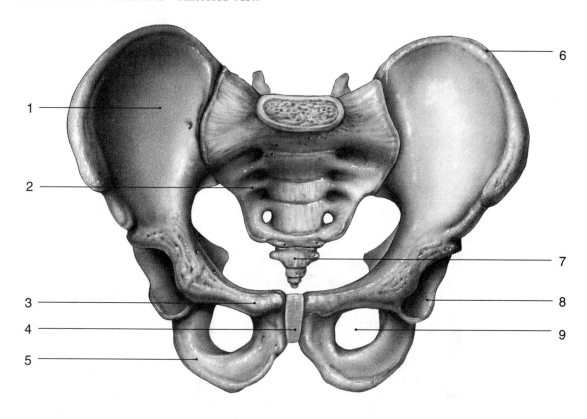

1. _____   6. _____
2. _____   7. _____
3. _____   8. _____
4. _____   9. _____
5. _____

Identify the following bones in the wrist and hand. Place your answers in the spaces provided below the drawing.

ulna   radius   carpals
metacarpals   phalanges

FIGURE 6-14 Bones of the Wrist and Hand

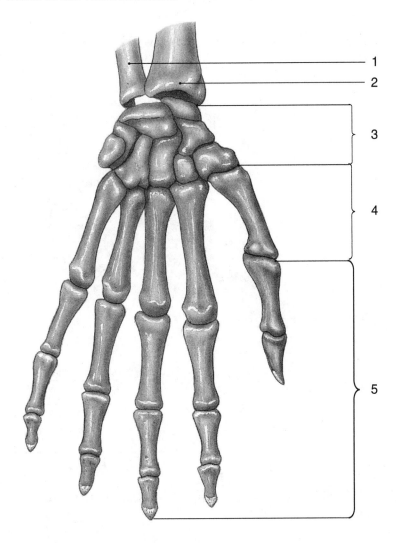

1. _____   4. _____

2. _____   5. _____

3. _____

Labeling Exercises, continued

Identify the following bones in the ankle and foot. Place your answers in the spaces provided below the drawing.

calcaneous   navicular bone   talus

metatarsals   tarsals   phalanges

tibia   cuneiform bone

FIGURE 6-15 Bones of the Ankle and Foot (Medial View — Right Foot)

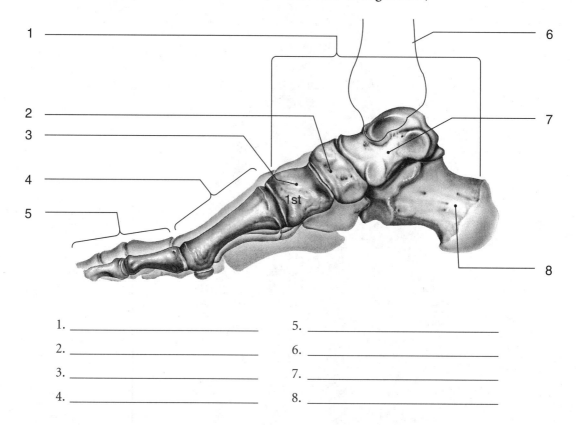

1. _____   5. _____
2. _____   6. _____
3. _____   7. _____
4. _____   8. _____

OBJECTIVE 9   Distinguish among different types of joints, and link structural features to joint functions.

_____ 1. The two types of joints that reflect the type of connective tissue binding them together are

        a. fibrous and synovial joints.
        b. synovial and cartilaginous joints.
        c. fibrous and cartilaginous joints.
        d. synovial and diarthrosis joints.

_____ 2. Sutures, gomphoses, synchondroses, and synarthroses are terms used to identify

        a. movable joints.
        b. immovable joints.
        c. slightly movable joints.
        d. joints with a wide range of motion.

_____ 3. The freely movable joints typically found at the ends of long bones are called

      a. synarthroses or synchondroses.

      b. amphiarthroses or syndesmoses.

      c. gomphoses or symphyses.

      d. diarthroses or synovial joints.

_____ 4. The joint that permits the greatest range of motion of any joint in the body is the

      a. hip joint.

      b. shoulder joint.

      c. elbow joint.

      d. knee joint.

_____ 5. The joint that is correctly matched with the type of joint indicated is

      a. symphysis pubis – fibrous.

      b. knee – synovial.

      c. sagittal suture – cartilaginous.

      d. intervertebral disc – synovial.

_____ 6. The synovial fluid that fills a joint cavity

      a. nourishes the chondrocytes.

      b. provides lubrication.

      c. acts as a shock absorber.

      d. does all of the above.

_____ 7. The primary function(s) of menisci in synovial joints is(are) to

      a. subdivide a synovial cavity.

      b. channel flow of synovial fluid.

      c. allow for variations in the shapes of articular surfaces.

      d. do all of the above.

8. A synarthrotic joint found only between the bones of the skull is a _____.

9. A totally rigid immovable joint resulting from fusion of bones is a _____.

10. The amphiarthrotic joint where bones are separated by a wedge or pad of fibrocartilage is a _____.

11. Diarthrotic joints that permit a wide range of motion are called _____ joints.

12. The extremely stable joint that is almost completely enclosed in a bony socket is the _____ joint.

13. The joint that resembles three separate joints with no single unified capsule or common synovial cavity is the _____ joint.

14. The radial collateral, annular, and ulnar collateral ligaments provide stability for the _____ joint.

Labeling Exercise

Identify the following structures in the knee joint. Place your answers in the spaces provided below the drawing.

femur   tibia   extensor muscle

tendon   fat pad   intracapsular ligament

bursa   meniscus   patellar ligament

patella   joint cavity   joint capsule

FIGURE 6-16 **A Sectional View of the Knee (Synovial) Joint**

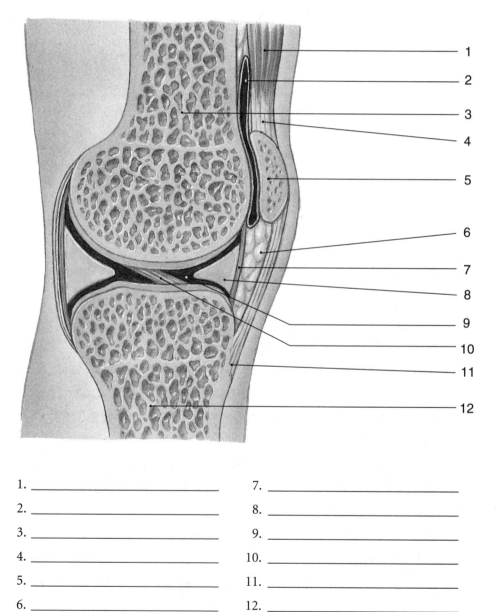

1. _____   7. _____

2. _____   8. _____

3. _____   9. _____

4. _____   10. _____

5. _____   11. _____

6. _____   12. _____

OBJECTIVE 10   Describe the dynamic movements of the skeleton and the structure of representative articulations.

_____ 1. *Flexion* is movement in the anterior–posterior plane that

    a. reduces the angle between the articulating elements.
    b. increases the angle between the articulating elements.
    c. moves away from the longitudinal axis of the body.
    d. abducts in the frontal plane of the body.

_____ 2. The movement that allows you to gaze at the ceiling is

    a. rotation.
    b. circumduction.
    c. hyperextension.
    d. elevation.

_____ 3. Movements of the vertebral column are limited to

    a. flexion and extension.
    b. lateral flexion.
    c. rotation.
    d. all of the above.

_____ 4. The opposing movement of pronation, in which the palm is turned forward, is called

    a. supination.
    b. opposition.
    c. circumduction.
    d. protraction.

_____ 5. A movement toward the midline of the body is called

    a. abduction.
    b. inversion.
    c. eversion.
    d. adduction.

_____ 6. The movement of the thumb that allows for grasping is

    a. inversion.
    b. opposition.
    c. supination.
    d. retraction.

_____ 7. Twiddling your thumbs during a lecture demonstrates the action that occurs at a

    a. hinge joint.
    b. ball and socket joint.
    c. saddle joint.
    d. gliding joint.

_____ 8. Contraction of the biceps brachii muscle produces

    a. pronation of the forearm and extension of the elbow.
    b. supination of the forearm and extension of the elbow.
    c. supination of the forearm and flexion of the elbow.
    d. pronation of the forearm and flexion of the elbow.

_____ 9. Movements such as dorsiflexion and plantar flexion involve moving the

    a. leg.
    b. hip.
    c. arm.
    d. foot.

_____ 10. To do a lateral split, the initial movement of the legs is

    a. abduction.
    b. adduction.
    c. extension.
    d. flexion.

Labeling Exercises

Identify the body movements in the following illustrations. Place your answers in the spaces provided below the drawings.

FIGURE 6-17 Body Movements

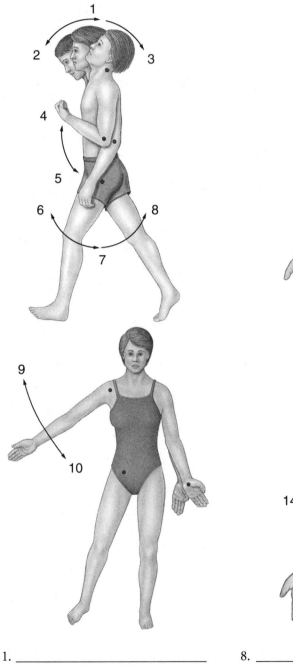

1. _____	8. _____
2. _____	9. _____
3. _____	10. _____
4. _____	11. _____
5. _____	12. _____
6. _____	13. _____
7. _____	14. _____

Labeling Exercises, continued

Identify the special movements in the following illustrations. Place your answers in the spaces provided below the drawings.

FIGURE 6-18 Special Movements

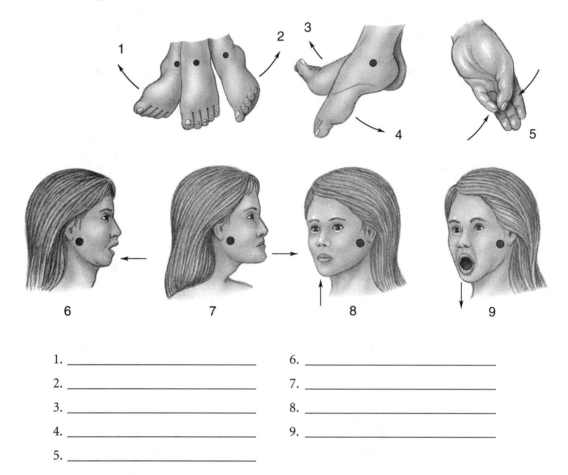

1. _____   6. _____

2. _____   7. _____

3. _____   8. _____

4. _____   9. _____

5. _____

OBJECTIVE 11   Explain the relationship between joint structure and mobility, using specific
examples.

_____   1. The elbow joint is quite stable because

     a. the bony surfaces of the humerus and the ulna lock.
     b. the articular capsule is very thick.
     c. the capsule is reinforced by stout ligaments.
     d. all of the above.

_____   2. In the hip joint, the arrangement that keeps the head of the femur from moving away from
the acetabulum is the

     a. formation of a complete bony socket.
     b. presence of fat pads covered by synovial membranes.
     c. articular capsule enclosing the femoral head and neck.
     d. tight fit of the acetabular bones and the femoral head.

_____   3. The knee joint functions as a _____ joint.

     a. hinge
     b. ball-and-socket
     c. saddle
     d. gliding

_____   4. The reason the points of contact in the knee joint are constantly changing is

     a. there is no single unified capsule or a common synovial cavity.
     b. the menisci conform to the shape of the surface of the femur.
     c. the rounded femoral condyles roll across the top of the tibia.
     d. all of the above.

_____   5. The special movement of the thumb that enables it to grasp and hold an object is

     a. supination.
     b. opposition.
     c. pronation.
     d. eversion.

_____   6. The function(s) of the intervertebral discs is(are) to

     a. act as shock absorbers.
     b. prevent bone-to-bone contact.
     c. allow for flexion and rotation of the vertebral column.
     d. a, b, and c are correct.

Labeling Exercise

Using the following selections, identify the types of synovial joints, seen in Figure 6-19. Place your answers in the spaces provided below each type of joint.

hinge joint   ball-and-socket joint   pivot joint
saddle joint   ellipsoidal joint   gliding joint

FIGURE 6-19 **Types of Synovial Joints**

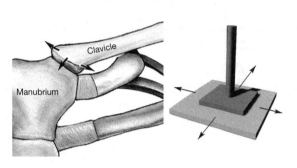

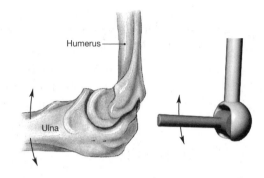

1. _____   2. _____

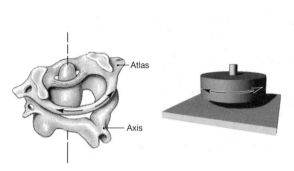

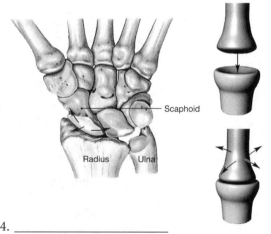

3. _____   4. _____

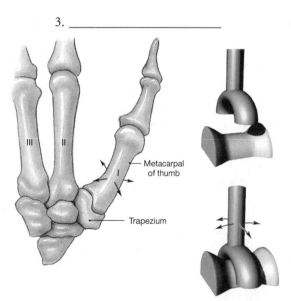

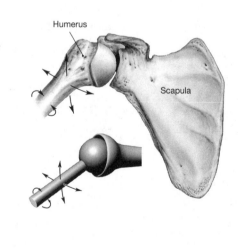

5. _____   6. _____

OBJECTIVE 12   Discuss the functional relationship between the skeletal system and other body systems.

_____ 1. The skeletal system is associated with all the other systems in the body in that it

a. provides mechanical support.
b. stores energy reserves.
c. stores calcium and phosphate reserves.
d. does all of the above.

_____ 2. The functional relationship of the skeletal system to the nervous system is that the skeletal system

a. stores calcium for neural functions.
b. has receptors at joints that provide information about body positions.
c. protects the brain and spinal cord.
d. a, b, and c are correct.

_____ 3. The respiratory system is functionally associated with the skeletal system because the respiratory system provides

a. nutrients, including calcium and phosphate ions.
b. oxygen and eliminates carbon dioxide.
c. skeletal growth regulated by hormones.
d. protection for the lungs and associated structures.

_____ 4. The urinary system supports the skeletal system by

a. disposing of waste products.
b. conserving calcium and phosphate ions.
c. protecting the kidneys and ureters.
d. Both a and b are correct.

Part II: Chapter Comprehensive Exercises

A. Word Elimination

Circle the term that does not belong in each of the following groupings.

1. support   protection   secretion   storage   leverage

2. vitamin D_3 growth hormone   calcitriol   PTH   sex hormones

3. colles   ostopenia   greenstick   Pott's   comminuted

4. skull   vertebral column   pelvis   sternum   rib cage

5. pelvic   pectoral   upper limbs   lower limbs   hyoid bone

6. mandible   maxilla   occipital   zygomatic   lacrimal

7. occipital   sphenoid   frontal   maxilla   mastoid

8. cervical   scoliosis   thoracic   lumbar   sacral

9. olecranon   scaphoid   lunate   trapezium   capitate

10. gliding   hinge   pronation   ellipsoidal   saddle

B. Matching

Match the terms in Column "B" with the terms in Column "A." Write letters for answers in the spaces provided.

COLUMN A	COLUMN B
___ 1. menisci	a. osteogenesis
___ 2. appositional growth	b. movement toward the midline
___ 3. osteoblasts	c. exaggerated thoracic curvature
___ 4. osteocytes	d. articular discs
___ 5. kyphosis	e. odontoid process
___ 6. scoliosis	f. kneecap
___ 7. "dens"	g. enlargement process
___ 8. adduction	h. abnormal lateral curvature
___ 9. patella	i. mature bone cells
___ 10. abduction	j. slightly movable joint
___ 11. ligaments	k. bone-to-bone attachment
___ 12. amphiarthrosis	l. movement away from midline

C. Concept Map I - Skeletal System

This concept map is a review of Chapter 6. Using the following terms, fill in the circled numbered, blank spaces to complete the concept map. Follow the numbers that comply with the organization of the map.

Ribs   Pectoral girdle   Coxal bone   Cranium (8 bones)

Vertebral column   Upper limb   Lower limb

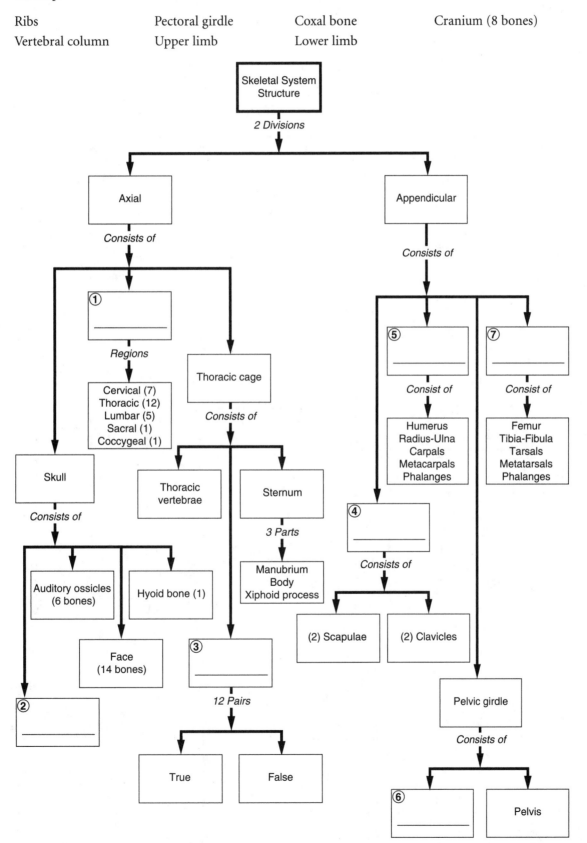

Concept Map II - Joints

Using the following terms, fill in the circled numbered, blank spaces to complete the concept map. Follow the numbers that comply with the organization of the map.

Amphiarthrosis   No movement   Cartilaginous   Synovial   Fibrous
Symphysis   Sutures   Wrist   Monoaxial

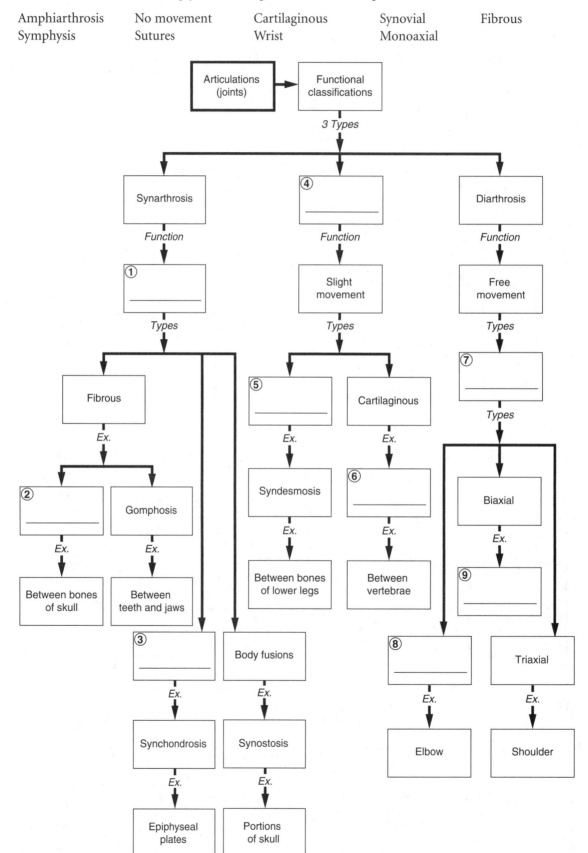

D. Crossword Puzzle

The following puzzle reviews the material in Chapter 6. To complete the puzzle, you must know the answers to the clues given, and you must be able to spell the terms correctly.

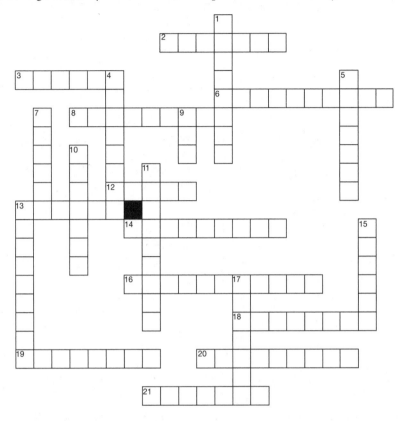

ACROSS

2. The most inferior portion of the sternum.
3. The lateral bone of the antebrachium.
6. The cavity that serves as the "socket" into which the femur fits.
8. The anatomical name for the cheekbone.
12. The division of the skeletal system that includes the skull.
13. The capitate is a _____ bone.
14. This term refers to the ends of the bone.
16. The bone-forming cells.
18. The anatomical name for the collarbone.
19. The fluid that is associated with many joints.
20. A baby's "soft spots."
21. Because osteoclasts remodel bone, they are probably responsible for creating _____.

DOWN

1. The vertebrae to which the ribs attach.
4. The suture that connects the two parietal bones.
5. The cavity that serves as the "socket" of the scapula.
7. The lateral bone of the lower leg.
9. The number of coxae bones that make up the hip.
10. The type of bone that is made of osteons.
11. This term refers to the shaft of the bone.
13. The anatomical name for the heel bone.
15. The fluid-filled sacs that reduce friction at some joint areas.
17. The depressions in the osteons in which the osteocytes set in.

E. Short-Answer Questions

Briefly answer the following questions in the spaces provided.

1. What five major functions is the skeletal system responsible for in the human body?

2. What are the primary histological differences between compact bone and spongy bone?

3. How does the process of *calcification* differ from *ossification*?

4. Compare and contrast the primary curves and secondary curves of the spinal column.

5. Distinguish among the abnormal spinal curvature distortions of kyphosis, lordosis, and scoliosis.

6. Differentiate between the beginning stages of intramembranous ossification and endochondral ossification.

7. What bones comprise the pectoral girdle? The pelvic girdle?

8. What is the functional difference between a ligament and a tendon?

9. What are the structural and functional differences between (a) a bursa and (b) a meniscus?

10. What are the functional roles of synovial fluid in a diarthrotic joint?

11. Functionally, what type of joint are the elbow and knee joints?

12. Functionally, what is the commonality between the shoulder joint and the hip joint?

13. What regions of the vertebral column do not contain intervertebral discs? Why are they unnecessary in these regions?

14. Identify the unusual types of movements that apply to each of the following examples:

   (a) twisting motion of the foot that turns the sole inward

   (b) grasping and holding an object with the thumb

   (c) standing on tiptoes

   (d) crossing the arms

   (e) opening the mouth

   (f) shrugging the shoulders

7

The Muscular System

Overview

This chapter focuses on the three types of muscle tissue, with emphasis on the organization of skeletal muscle tissue and the functional organization of the muscular system. Muscles are specialized tissues that support and facilitate body movement and the movement of materials within the body. Movement is an important function of life for adjusting to changing conditions, both in the external environment in which we live, and in the internal environment within the body.

Most of the muscle or "red meat" of the body is skeletal or voluntary muscle. It is called skeletal muscle because it is attached to the bony skeleton by ligaments. If you weigh 150 pounds, approximately 60 pounds or 40% of your body weight consists of skeletal muscle. Cardiac and smooth muscles form the walls of the heart and hollow organs and are involved in transporting materials within the body.

After reviewing and successfully completing the exercises in Chapter 7, you should be able to understand the microscopic and gross structure of muscle, the basic principles of muscle physiology, the locations of major skeletal muscles, and muscle performance (including body movements).

Review of Chapter Objectives

1. Describe the functions of skeletal muscle tissue.
2. Describe the organization of muscle at the tissue level.
3. Identify the structural components of a sarcomere.
4. Explain the key steps involved in the contraction of a skeletal muscle fiber.
5. Compare the different types of muscle contractions.
6. Describe the mechanisms by which muscles obtain and use energy to power contractions.
7. Relate the types of muscle fibers to muscular performance. Distinguish between aerobic and anaerobic endurance, and explain their implications for muscular performance.
8. Contrast skeletal, cardiac, and smooth muscles in terms of structure and function.
9. Identify the main axial muscles of the body, along with their actions. Identify the main appendicular muscles of the body, along with their actions.
10. Describe the effects of aging on muscle tissue.
11. Discuss the functional relationships between the muscular system and other organ systems.

Part I: Objective-Based Questions

OBJECTIVE 1 Describe the functions of skeletal muscle tissue.

_____ 1. Highly coordinated activities such as swimming, skiing, or typing are examples of the skeletal muscle function of

a. supporting soft tissues.
b. producing movement.
c. maintaining body temperature.
d. guarding entrances and exits.

_____ 2. Voluntary control over swallowing, defecation, and urination are controlled by skeletal muscles that

a. maintain body temperature.
b. produce movements.
c. support soft tissues.
d. guard entrances and exits.

_____ 3. The function of layers of skeletal muscles that comprise the abdominal wall and floor of the pelvic cavity is to

a. produce movements.
b. guard entrances and exits.
c. support soft tissues.
d. maintain posture and body position.

_____ 4. The ability of skeletal muscles to produce continuous contractions results in the ability of the body to

a. maintain posture and body position.
b. support soft tissue.
c. release energy to pull on ligaments and move bones.
d. do all of the above.

OBJECTIVE 2   Describe the organization of muscle at the tissue level.

_____ 1. The three layers of connective tissues comprising each muscle are

      a. cardiac, smooth, and skeletal.
      b. epimysium, perimysium, and endomysium.
      c. sarcolemma, sarcomeres, and T tubules.
      d. A band, I band, and Z lines.

_____ 2. The dense layer of collagen fibers that surrounds an entire skeletal muscle is the

      a. epimysium.
      b. tendon.
      c. perimysium.
      d. fascicle.

_____ 3. Bundles of muscle fibers called fascicles make up the connective tissue fibers of the

      a. epimysium.
      b. endomysium.
      c. myofibrils.
      d. perimysium.

_____ 4. _Tendons_ are bundles of collagen fibers at the end of a skeletal muscle that

      a. attach muscle to muscle.
      b. connect different skeletal muscles.
      c. allow blood vessels and nerves to innervate muscle tissue.
      d. attach muscle to bone.

_____ 5. The layer of connective tissue that contains blood vessels and nerves is the

      a. epimysium.
      b. endomysium.
      c. perimysium.
      d. fascicle.

_____ 6. The endomysium is the layer of connective tissue that

      a. surrounds each skeletal muscle fiber and ties adjacent muscle fibers together.
      b. surrounds the entire muscle and separates the muscle from other tissues.
      c. divides the skeletal muscle into a series of compartments.
      d. contains blood vessels and nerves that supply the fascicles.

Labeling Exercise

Identify the following structures in Figure 7-1. Place your answers in the spaces provided below the drawing.

epimysium   perimysium   endomysium
blood vessels and nerves   skeletal muscle   muscle fascicle
muscle fiber   tendon

FIGURE 7-1 Organization of Skeletal Muscle

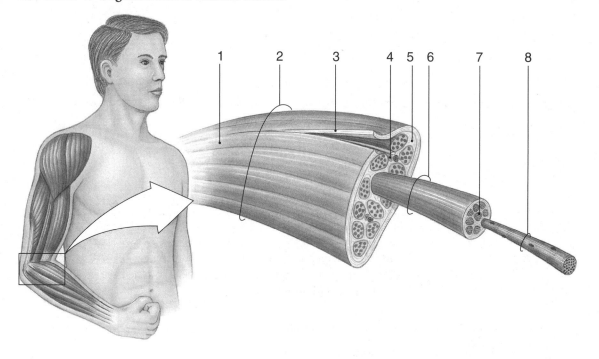

1. _____   5. _____

2. _____   6. _____

3. _____   7. _____

4. _____   8. _____

OBJECTIVE 3   Identify the structural components of a sarcomere.

_____ 1. The thin filaments of a sarcomere consist of

        a. actin.
        b. myosin.
        c. troponin.
        d. tropomyosin.

_____ 2. The thick filaments of a sarcomere consist of

        a. actin.
        b. myosin.
        c. troponin.
        d. muscle fibers.

_____ 3. Thin filaments at either end of the sarcomere are attached to interconnecting filaments that make up the

        a. T tubules.
        b. A band.
        c. I band.
        d. Z lines.

_____ 4. The command to contract is distributed throughout a muscle fiber by the

        a. T tubules.
        b. sarcolemma.
        c. myofibrils.
        d. sarcomere.

_____ 5. The smallest functional unit of the muscle fiber is the

        a. myofilament.
        b. sarcomere.
        c. T tubule.
        d. cisterna.

Labeling Exercise

Identify the following parts of a sarcomere. Place your answers in the spaces provided.

actin	myosin	A band
I band	M line	Z line

FIGURE 7-2 Sarcomere Structure

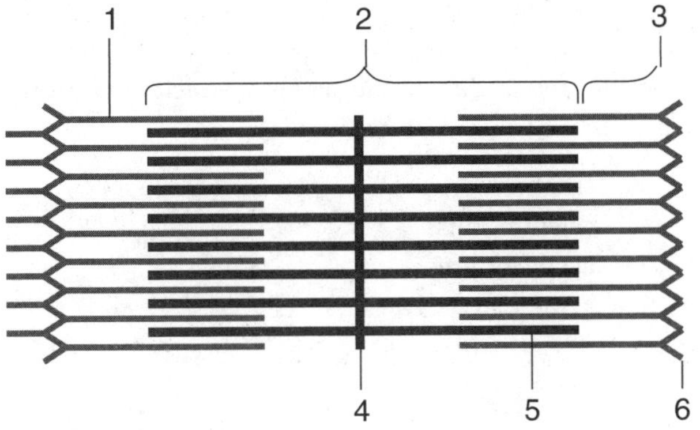

1. _____   4. _____

2. _____   5. _____

3. _____   6. _____

OBJECTIVE 4 Explain the key steps involved in the contraction of a skeletal muscle fiber.

_____ 1. Skeletal muscle fiber contraction begins when

      a. the muscle cell relaxes and lengthens.
      b. depolarization occurs and an action potential is generated.
      c. the calcium ion concentration at the myofilament increases.
      d. acetylcholine is released into the neuromuscular junction and binds to receptors on the sarcolemma.

_____ 2. The final step involved in skeletal muscle contraction is

      a. the muscle cell relaxes and returns passively to its resting length.
      b. the sarcoplasmic reticulum absorbs calcium ions.
      c. action potential generation ceases as ACh is removed.
      d. repeated cycles of cross-bridge binding occur.

_____ 3. Active sites on the actin become available for binding when

      a. actin binds to troponin.
      b. myosin binds to troponin.
      c. calcium binds to troponin.
      d. troponin binds to tropomysosin.

_____ 4. In response to action potentials arriving from the transverse tubules, calcium ions are released from the

      a. synaptic cleft.
      b. sarcoplasmic reticulum.
      c. neuromuscular junction.
      d. motor plate.

_____ 5. The neurotransmitter released from the synaptic vesicles that initiates an action potential in the sarcolemma is

      a. troponin.
      b. calcium ions.
      c. acetylcholine.
      d. actin.

Labeling Exercise

Identify the steps in the contraction process (1–6). Place your answers in the spaces provided below each drawing.

FIGURE 7-3 Summary of Contraction Process

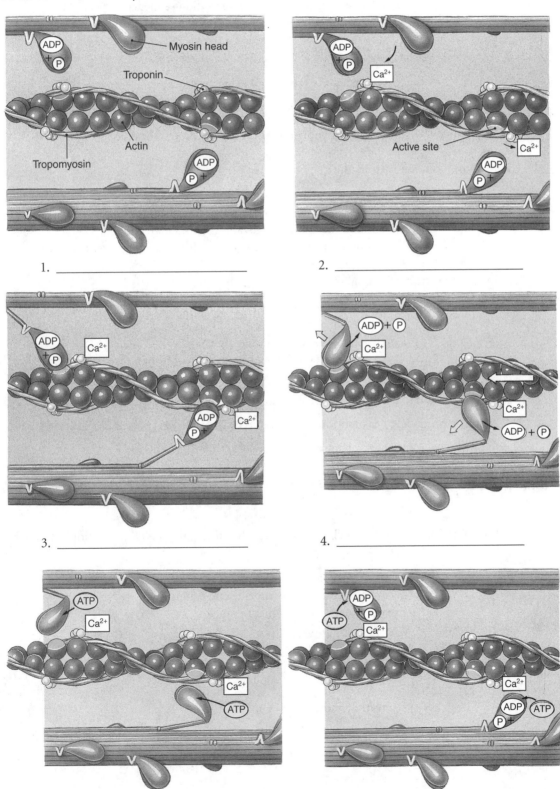

1. _____

2. _____

3. _____

4. _____

5. _____

6. _____

OBJECTIVE 5 Compare the different types of muscle contractions.

_____ 1. A twitch is the type of contraction represented by a

      a. successive arrival of stimuli before the relaxation phase is completed.
      b. frequency of stimulation that eliminates the relaxation phase.
      c. single stimulus-contraction-relaxation sequence.
      d. summation of more powerful contractions.

_____ 2. The process of recruitment is the smooth but steady increase in muscle tension produced by

      a. increasing the number of active motor units.
      b. increasing the number of neurons innervating a single muscle fiber.
      c. increasing the size of the motor units.
      d. generating enough tension to overcome resistance.

_____ 3. In an isotonic contraction, the

      a. tension in the muscle varies as it shortens.
      b. muscle length doesn't change due to resistance.
      c. tension rises and the skeletal muscle's length changes.
      d. tension in the muscle decreases as the resistance increases.

_____ 4. In an isometric contraction, the

      a. tension produced never exceeds the resistance and the length of the muscle remains constant.
      b. tension rises and the muscle shortens.
      c. tension produced by the muscle is greater than the resistance.
      d. tension of the muscle increases as the resistance decreases.

5. Resting tension in a skeletal muscle is called _____.

6. A muscle producing peak tension during rapid cycles of contraction and relaxation is said to be in _____ tetany.

OBJECTIVE 6 Describe the mechanisms by which muscles obtain and use energy to power contractions.

_____ 1. Mitochondrial activities are relatively efficient, but their rate of ATP generation is limited by the

      a. presence of enzymes.
      b. availability of carbon dioxide and water.
      c. energy demands of other organelles.
      d. availability of oxygen.

_____ 2. When muscles are actively contracting, the process requires large amounts of energy in the form of

      a. creatine phosphate (CP).
      b. oxygen.
      c. ATP.
      d. ADP.

_____ 3. The primary energy reserve in muscle tissue is

    a. creatine phosphate (CP).
    b. adenosine triphosphate (ATP).
    c. adenosine diphosphate (ADP).
    d. adenosine monophosphate (AMP).

_____ 4. During anaerobic glycolysis,

    a. a large amount of ATP energy is produced.
    b. NAD is oxidized via electron transport.
    c. pyruvic acid is produced.
    d. all of the above.

_____ 5. When energy reserves in a muscle are exhausted or lactic acid levels increase,

    a. fatigue occurs.
    b. the muscle contracts.
    c. tetany is occurring.
    d. recruitment resumes.

_____ 6. A resting muscle generates most of its ATP by

    a. anaerobic respiration.
    b. aerobic respiration.
    c. glycolysis.
    d. electron transport.

OBJECTIVE 7   Relate the types of muscle fibers to muscular performance. Distinguish between aerobic and anaerobic endurance, and explain their implications for muscular performance.

_____ 1. Fast fibers are the type of muscle fibers that

    a. are best adapted for endurance.
    b. produce powerful contractions but fatigue rapidly.
    c. contain the red pigment myoglobin.
    d. contain a relatively large number of mitochondria.

_____ 2. Slow fibers are the type of muscle fibers that contain

    a. an extensive network of capillaries.
    b. the red pigment myoglobin.
    c. a relatively large number of mitochondria.
    d. all of the above.

_____ 3. In humans, slow fibers are not found in the muscles of the

    a. arms and legs.
    b. eyes and hands.
    c. calf and the back.
    d. thorax and pelvis.

_____ 4. The length of time a muscle can continue to contract while supported by mitochondrial activities is referred to as

      a. anaerobic endurance.
      b. aerobic endurance.
      c. hypertrophy.
      d. recruitment.

_____ 5. _____ exercise requires oxygen and is of _____ duration than _____ exercise.

      a. Anaerobic; longer; aerobic
      b. Aerobic; longer; anaerobic
      c. Anaerobic; shorter; aerobic
      d. Aerobic; shorter; anaerobic

_____ 6. The amount of oxygen used in the recovery period to restore normal pre-exertion conditions is referred to as the

      a. endurance rate.
      b. citric acid cycle.
      c. electron transport system.
      d. oxygen debt.

_____ 7. An example of an activity that requires anaerobic endurance is

      a. a 50-yard dash.
      b. a 3-mile run.
      c. a 10-mile bicycle ride.
      d. running a marathon.

_____ 8. Athletes training to develop anaerobic endurance perform

      a. a few, long, relaxing workouts.
      b. a combination of weight training and running marathons.
      c. frequent, brief, intensive workouts.
      d. stretching, flexibility, and relaxation exercises.

OBJECTIVE 8 Contrast skeletal, cardiac, and smooth muscles in terms of structure and function.

_____ 1. The presence of intercalated discs is a characteristic unique to

      a. smooth muscle cells.
      b. skeletal muscle cells.
      c. cardiac muscle cells.
      d. all of the above.

_____ 2. The type of muscle tissue that lacks myofibrils, sarcomeres, and striations is

      a. cardiac muscle tissue.
      b. skeletal muscle tissue.
      c. voluntary muscle tissue.
      d. smooth muscle tissue.

_____ 3. The type of muscle cells that contract either automatically or in response to environmental or hormonal stimulation are

   a. skeletal muscle cells.
   b. those muscle cells innervated by neurons.
   c. cardiac muscle cells.
   d. smooth muscle cells.

OBJECTIVE 9   Identify the main axial muscles of the body, along with their actions. Identify the main appendicular muscles of the body, along with their actions.

_____ 1. The axial musculature consists of

   a. muscles of the head and neck.
   b. muscles of the spine and pelvic floor.
   c. muscles of the trunk.
   d. all of the above.

_____ 2. From the following selections, choose the one that includes only muscles of facial expression.

   a. lateral rectus, medial rectus, hypoglossus, stylohyoid
   b. splenius, masseter, scalenus, platymsa
   c. procerus, capitis, cervicis, zygomaticus
   d. buccinator, orbicularis oris, risorius, frontalis

_____ 3. The names of the muscles of the tongue are readily identified because their descriptive names end in

   a. genio.
   b. glossus.
   c. pollicus.
   d. hallucis.

_____ 4. The superficial muscles of the spine are identified by subdivisions that include

   a. cervicis, thoracis, and lumborum.
   b. iliocostalis, longissimus, and spinalis.
   c. longissimus, transversus, and longus.
   d. capitis, splenius, and spinalis.

_____ 5. The muscular floor of the pelvic cavity is formed by muscles that make up the

   a. urogenital and anal triangle.
   b. sacrum and coccyx.
   c. ischium and the pubis.
   d. ilium and the ischium.

_____ 6. During a specific action, the insertion is the

   a. more stationary end of the muscle.
   b. stabilized point of the origin.
   c. more movable end of a muscle.
   d. fixator that stabilizes the synergistic effect of a prime mover.

_____ 7. A muscle that inserts on the body of the mandible is probably involved in

       a. hissing.

       b. blowing.

       c. frowning.

       d. chewing.

_____ 8. Muscles that insert on the olecranon process of the ulna act to

       a. extend the forearm.

       b. flex the forearm.

       c. abduct the forearm.

       d. adduct the forearm.

_____ 9. The origin of the frontalis muscle is the

       a. frontal bone.

       b. galea aponeurotica.

       c. temporal bone.

       d. sphenoid bone.

_____ 10. The iliac crest is the origin of the

       a. longissimus.

       b. iliocostalis.

       c. quadratus lumborum.

       d. supraspinatus.

_____ 11. Of the following selections, the one that includes muscles that move the shoulder girdle is the

       a. teres major, deltoid, pectoralis major, and triceps.

       b. procerus, capitis, pterygoid, and brachialis.

       c. trapezius, levator scapulae, pectoralis minor, and subclavius.

       d. internal oblique, thoracis, deltoid, and pectoralis minor.

_____ 12. From the following selections, choose the one that includes the muscles that move the upper arm.

       a. deltoid, teres major, latissimus dorsi, pectoralis major

       b. trapezius, pectoralis minor, subclavius, triceps

       c. rhomboideus, serratus anterior, subclavius, trapezius

       d. brachialis, brachioradialis, pronator, supinator

_____ 13. Two of the muscles comprising the rotator cuff are the

       a. deltoid and teres major.

       b. extensor digitorum and palmaris longus.

       c. deltoid and trapezius.

       d. infraspinatus and teres major.

_____ 14. When the gluteus maximus contracts it

      a. extends the thigh anteriorly.
      b. extends the thigh backward.
      c. moves the thigh laterally.
      d. adducts the thigh.

_____ 15. The quadriceps are a group of anterior thigh muscles that include the _____ muscles.

      a. semitendinosus, biceps femoris, semimembranosus, and sartorius
      b. gastrocnemius, soleus, tibialis anterior, and gracilis
      c. rectus femoris, vastus medialis, vastus lateralis, and vastus intermedius
      d. sartorius, gracilis, peroneus, and popliteus

_____ 16. The hamstrings are a group of posterior thigh muscles that include the _____ muscles.

      a. rectus femoris, vastus medialis, and vastus lateralis
      b. semimembranosus, rectus femoris, and semitendinosus
      c. semitendinosus, biceps femoris, and semimembranosus
      d. rectus femoris, biceps femoris, and semitendinosus

_____ 17. The muscles that arise on the humerus and the forearm and rotate the radius without producing flexion or extension of the elbow are the

      a. pronator teres and supinator.
      b. brachialis and brachioradialis.
      c. triceps and biceps brachii.
      d. carpi ulnaris and radialis.

_____ 18. The muscle that inserts on the acromion process and scapular spine is the

      a. pectoralis major.
      b. trapezius.
      c. sternocleidomastoid.
      d. latissimus dorsi.

_____ 19. The muscle that inserts on the iliotibial tract and gluteal tuberosity of the femur is the

      a. gracilis.
      b. rectus femoris.
      c. sartorius.
      d. gluteus maximus.

_____ 20. The muscle that originates along the entire length of the linea aspera of the femur is the

      a. biceps femoris.
      b. vastus medialis.
      c. vastus lateralis.
      d. rectus femoris.

Labeling Exercises

Identify the following muscles on the axial and appendicular skeleton, seen in Figure 7–4.

temporalis	rectus abdominis	orbicularis oris	tensor fascia lata
vastus medialis	tibialis anterior	external oblique	deltoid
gracilis	peroneus longus	transversus abdominis	vastus lateralis
rectus femoris	sartorius	zygomaticus	pectoralis major
masseter	biceps brachii	orbicularis oculi	
sternocleidomastoid	adductor muscles	frontalis	

FIGURE 7-4 Principal Skeletal Muscles—Anterior View

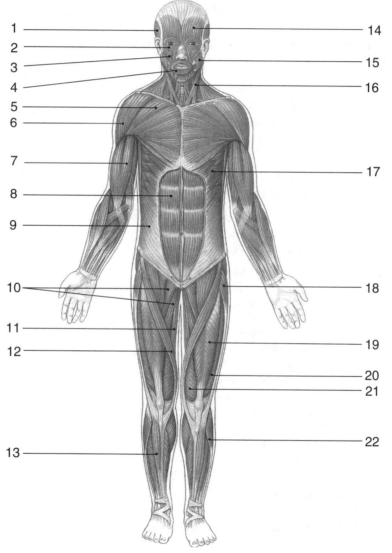

1. _____
2. _____
3. _____
4. _____
5. _____
6. _____
7. _____
8. _____

9. _____
10. _____
11. _____
12. _____
13. _____
14. _____
15. _____
16. _____

17. _____
18. _____
19. _____
20. _____
21. _____
22. _____

Identify the following muscles on the axial and appendicular skeleton.

soleus   gluteus maximus   semimembranosus

deltoid   external oblique   gastrocnemius

occipitalis   biceps femoris   semitendinosus

trapezius   triceps brachii   latissimus dorsi

gluteus medius

FIGURE 7-5 Principal Skeletal Muscles—Posterior View

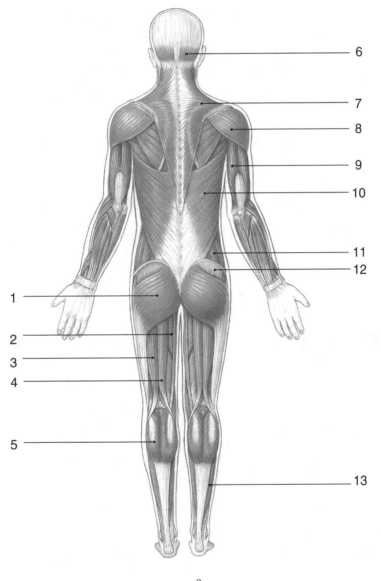

1. _____   8. _____

2. _____   9. _____

3. _____   10. _____

4. _____   11. _____

5. _____   12. _____

6. _____   13. _____

7. _____

OBJECTIVE 10   Describe the effects of aging on muscle tissue.

_____ 1. There is clear evidence that the benefits of regular exercise throughout life include

   a. control of body weight.
   b. increase in bone strength.
   c. improving the quality of life.
   d. all of the above.

_____ 2. In the aging process, skeletal muscle fibers decrease in diameter, causing

   a. decreased muscular strength and endurance, and rapid fatigue.
   b. excessive formation of scar tissue.
   c. decreased thermoregulatory ability.
   d. decreased recovery from muscular injuries.

_____ 3. The development of fibrosis in the elderly causes

   a. reduced muscle fiber diameter and decreased endurance.
   b. rapid fatigue and limited repair capabilities following injury.
   c. skeletal muscles to become less elastic, restricting movement and circulation.
   d. a reduction in thermoregulatory ability.

_____ 4. The typical result of repairing aging skeletal muscle tissue is

   a. rapid muscular fatigue.
   b. a decrease in the amount of fibrous connective tissue.
   c. formation of scar tissue.
   d. overheating of muscle tissue.

OBJECTIVE 11   Discuss the functional relationships between the muscular system and other organ systems.

1. The system that provides for muscle attachment in the body is the _____ system.

2. The system that accelerates oxygen delivery and carbon dioxide removal in muscles is the _____ system.

3. The system that defends skeletal muscles against infection and assists in tissue repairs after injury is the _____ system.

4. The system that releases hormones that adjust muscle metabolism and growth is the _____ system.

5. The system that controls skeletal muscle contractions is the _____ system.

Part II: Chapter Comprehensive Exercises

A. Word Elimination

Circle the term that does not belong in each of the following groupings.

1. excitability   contractility   support   extensibility   elasticity

2. actin   thick filament   myosin   thin filament   sarcomere

3. exposure   attachment   contraction   pivoting   detachment

4. twitch   tetany   myogram   isometric   isotonic

5. ADP   CP   ATP   glucose   DNA

6. myoglobin   fast fibers   white muscles   slow fibers   red muscles

7. 50-yard dash   jogging   pole vault   weight-lifting   50-yard swim

8. automaticity   pacemaker cells   uninucleate   intercalated discs   anaerobic

9. occipitalis   parietal   temporal   sartorius   frontalis

10. cardiovascular   respiratory   heart   integumentary   nervous

B. Matching

Match the terms in Column "B" with the terms in Column "A." Write letters for answers in the spaces provided.

COLUMN A	COLUMN B
___ 1. aponeurosis	a. protein cover of active sites
___ 2. cisternae	b. attach, pivot, detach, return
___ 3. tropomyosin	c. sliding filament theory
___ 4. sarcomere contraction	d. a neurotransmitter
___ 5. "cross-bridging"	e. broad sheet of collagen fibers
___ 6. acetylcholine	f. addition of one twitch to another
___ 7. summation	g. expanded chambers of SR
___ 8. complete tetanus	h. no tension produced
___ 9. latent period	i. enlargement
___10. hypertrophy	j. produces maximum tension

C. Concept Map I - Muscle Tissue

Using the following terms, fill in the circled numbered, blank spaces to complete the concept map. Follow the numbers that comply with the organization of the map.

Smooth   Involuntary   Striated   Heart
Multinucleated   Bones   Nonstriated

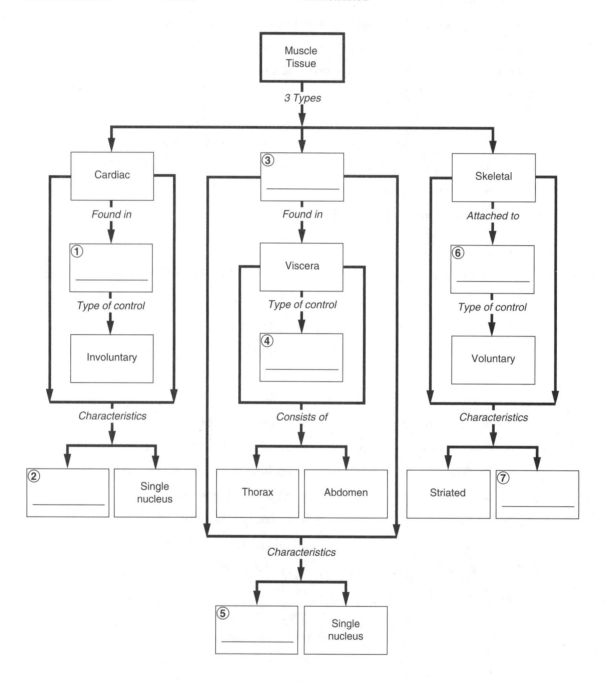

Concept Map II - Muscle Structure

Using the following terms, fill in the circled numbered, blank spaces to complete the concept map. Follow the numbers that comply with the organization of the map.

Z lines
Actin
H zone
Muscle bundles (fascicles)
Thick filaments
Myofibrils
Sarcomeres

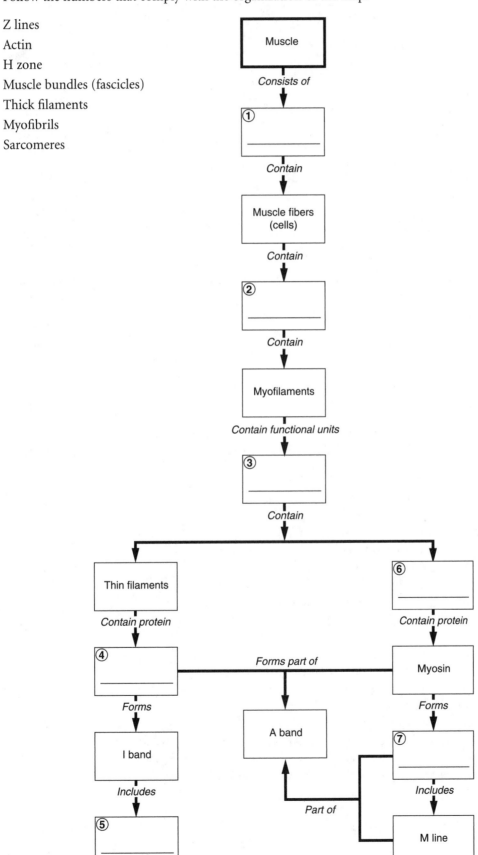

D. Crossword Puzzle

This crossword puzzle reviews the material in Chapter 7. To complete the puzzle, you must know the answers to the clues given, and you must be able to spell the terms correctly.

ACROSS

1. The gracilis will _____ the leg.
3. One of the quadriceps muscles (two words).
4. The biceps brachii will _____ the antebrachium.
5. The filament that slides.
7. The involuntary type of muscle.
10. A unit of muscle that is made of actin and myosin.
12. The muscle associated with the cheeks.
14. The rectus femoris will _____ the lower leg.
15. A major lower back muscle (two words).
16. This type of metabolism requires the use of oxygen.
17. This type of metabolism does not require the use of oxygen.
18. The deltoid will _____ the arm.

DOWN

2. A major upper back muscle.
5. A sheath that connects the frontalis to the occipitalis.
6. The thick filament that has cross-bridges.
7. The voluntary type of muscle.
8. These connect muscle to bone.
9. A neuromuscular junction is the connection between a motor neuron and a muscle _____.
11. The biceps brachii and the triceps brachii are examples of _____ muscles.
13. Cardiac muscle has _____ discs. No other muscle has them.
16. A muscle that is not used may undergo _____.

E. Short-Answer Questions

Briefly answer the following questions in the spaces provided.

1. What are the five functions performed by skeletal muscles?

2. What are the three layers of connective tissue that are part of each muscle?

3. What is the relationship among fatigue, anaerobic glycolysis, and oxygen debt?

4. What are the differences between an isometric contraction and an isotonic contraction?

5. List the three muscles that are included in the hamstrings.

6. List the four muscles that are included in the quadriceps.

7. Why do fast fibers fatigue more rapidly than slow fibers?

8. What is the primary functional difference between an origin and an insertion?

9. What are the four groups of muscles that comprise the axial musculature?

10. What two major groups of muscles comprise the appendicular musculature?

The Nervous System

Overview

The nervous system includes all the neural tissues in the body, and along with the endocrine system, the nervous system coordinates organ system activities in response to changes in environmental conditions. Due to the complexity and versatility of the nervous system, the structures are described in terms of two major anatomical divisions: the central nervous system (CNS) and the peripheral nervous system (PNS). The CNS consists of the brain and spinal cord and is responsible for integrating and coordinating sensory data and motor commands. The CNS is also the seat of higher functions, such as intelligence, memory, and emotion. The PNS, consisting of cranial nerves and spinal nerves and ganglia, provides the communication pathways between the CNS and the muscles, glands, and sensory receptors.

The peripheral nervous system (PNS) consists of all the neuron cell bodies and processes located outside the brain and spinal cord. All sensory information and motor commands are carried by axons of the PNS, which facilitate communication processes via pathways, nerve tracts, and nuclei that relay sensory and motor information from the spinal cord to the higher centers in the brain. The peripheral nerves of the PNS connected to the brain are called cranial nerves, and those attached to the spinal cord are called spinal nerves.

An understanding of the integration and interrelation of the nervous system with all other body systems is an integral part of comprehending how the body functions as a whole and how the nervous system's control mechanisms provide the necessary adjustments to meet changing internal and external environmental conditions.

Review of Chapter Objectives

1. Describe the two anatomical divisions of the nervous system and their general functions.
2. Distinguish between neurons and neuroglia on the basis of their structures and functions.
3. Discuss the events that generate action potentials in the membranes of nerve cells.
4. Explain the mechanisms of nerve impulse transmission at the synapse.
5. Describe the three meningeal layers that surround the central nervous system.
6. Discuss the structure and functions of the spinal cord.
7. Name the major regions of the brain and describe their functions.
8. Locate the motor, sensory, and association areas of the cerebral cortex, and discuss their functions.

9. Identify the cranial nerves, and relate each pair of cranial nerves to its principal functions.

10. Relate the distribution pattern of spinal nerves to the regions they innervate.

11. Describe the components of a reflex arc.

12. Identify the principal sensory and motor pathways.

13. Compare and contrast the functions and structures of the sympathetic and parasympathetic divisions.

14. Summarize the effects of aging on the nervous system.

15. Discuss the interrelationships among the nervous system and other organ systems.

Part I: Objective-Based Questions

OBJECTIVE 1   Describe the two anatomical divisions of the nervous system and their general functions.

_____ 1. The two major anatomical divisions of the nervous system are the

     a. central nervous system (CNS) and the peripheral nervous system (PNS).
     b. somatic nervous system (SNS) and the autonomic nervous system (ANS).
     c. neurons and neuroglia.
     d. afferent division and the efferent division.

_____ 2. The central nervous system (CNS) consists of

     a. afferent and efferent divisions.
     b. somatic and visceral divisions.
     c. the brain and spinal cord.
     d. autonomic and somatic divisions.

_____ 3. The primary function(s) of the nervous system include(s)

     a. monitoring the internal and external environments.
     b. integrating sensory information.
     c. coordinating voluntary and involuntary responses of other organ systems.
     d. all of the above.

_____ 4. The peripheral nervous system consists of two divisions, the

     a. autonomic and somatic.
     b. cranial nerves and spinal nerves.
     c. efferent and afferent.
     d. sympathetic and parasympathetic.

_____ 5. _____ nerves carry impulses from the PNS to the CNS; _____ nerves carry impulses from the CNS to the PNS.

     a. Afferent; efferent
     b. Autonomic; somatic
     c. Somatic; autonomic
     d. Efferent; afferent

_____ 6. Voluntary control of skeletal muscles is provided by the

      a. somatic nervous system.
      b. autonomic nervous system.
      c. sympathetic nervous system.
      d. parasympathetic nervous system.

OBJECTIVE 2   Distinguish between neurons and neuroglia on the basis of their structures and functions.

_____ 1. The types of neuroglia (glial cells) in the central nervous system are

      a. unipolar, bipolar, and multipolar cells.
      b. astrocytes, oligodendrocytes, microglia, and ependymal cells.
      c. efferent, afferent, and association cells.
      d. motor, sensory, and interneuron cells.

_____ 2. The white matter of the CNS represents a region dominated by the presence of

      a. astrocytes.
      b. neuroglia.
      c. oligodendrocytes.
      d. unmyelinated neurons.

_____ 3. The control of functions in the nervous system—communication and information processing—are performed by the

      a. neuroglia.
      b. Schwann cells and satellite cells.
      c. sensory and motor pathways.
      d. neurons.

_____ 4. Neurons are classified on the basis of their structure as

      a. motor, sensory, association, and interneurons.
      b. unipolar, bipolar, and multipolar.
      c. astrocytes, oligodendrocytes, microglia, and ependymal.
      d. efferent, afferent, association, and interneurons.

_____ 5. Neurons are classified on the basis of their function as

      a. unipolar, bipolar, and multipolar.
      b. somatic, visceral, and autonomic.
      c. motor, sensory, and association.
      d. central, peripheral, and somatic.

_____ 6. Small phagocytic cells that are quite obvious in damaged tissue in the CNS are the

      a. microglia.
      b. Schwann cells.
      c. astrocytes.
      d. oligodendrocytes.

_____ 7. The *motor neurons* of the efferent division of the PNS carry

      a. instructions from the PNS to the brain and spinal cord.
      b. sensory information to the CNS from the PNS.
      c. motor commands from muscles and glands to the CNS.
      d. instructions from the CNS to muscles, glands, and adipose tissue.

_____ 8. A synaptic terminal is a part of the *synapse*, a site where

      a. neurons control the interstitial environment.
      b. intercellular communication between neurons occurs.
      c. neural processing occurs in the CNS and PNS.
      d. the neuroglia provide support for the CNS.

_____ 9. Interneurons or association neurons

      a. are found only within the brain and the spinal cord.
      b. carry only sensory impulses.
      c. carry only motor impulses.
      d. are found between neurons and their effectors.

_____ 10. The two types of neuroglia found in the PNS are

      a. astrocytes and microglia.
      b. oligodendrocytes and ependymal cells.
      c. Schwann cells and satellite cells.
      d. interneurons and neurons.

Labeling Exercises

Identify and label the structures in a typical neuron. Place your answers in the spaces provided on the following page.

axon	soma	neurilemma
dendrite	nucleus	axon terminals/synaptic knobs
axon hillock		

FIGURE 8-1 Neuron Structure

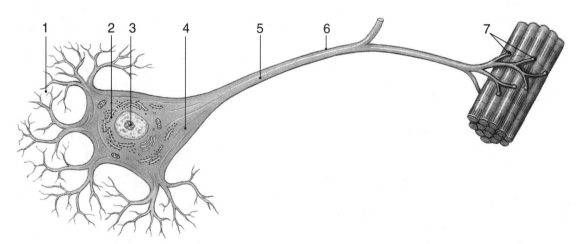

1. _____   5. _____

2. _____   6. _____

3. _____   7. _____

4. _____

8. On the basis of structure, the neuron illustrated in Figure 8-1 is _____.

Identify and label the following structures in Figure 8-2. Place your answers in the spaces provided below the drawings.

myelinated axon   microglial cell   oligodendrocyte
neuron   astrocyte   capillary

FIGURE 8-2 Neurons and Neuroglia

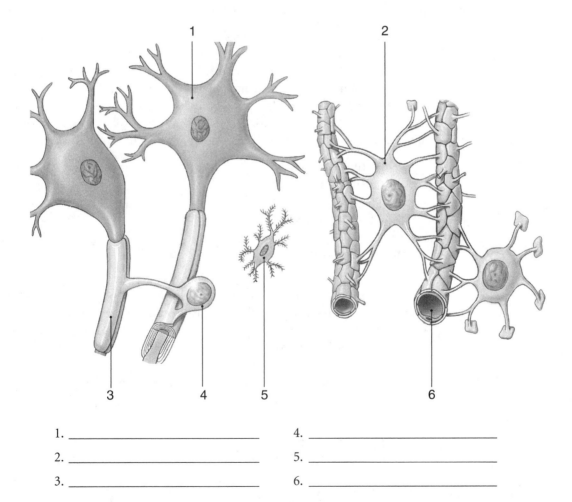

1. _____   4. _____

2. _____   5. _____

3. _____   6. _____

OBJECTIVE 3 Discuss the events that generate action potentials in the membranes of nerve cells.

_____ 1. At the site of an action potential, the membrane contains an

      a. excess of negative ions inside and an excess of negative ions outside.
      b. excess of positive ions inside and an excess of negative ions outside.
      c. equal amount of positive and negative ions on either side of the membrane.
      d. equal amount of positive ions on either side of the membrane.

_____ 2. If the resting membrane potential is -70 mV, a hyperpolarized membrane is

      a. 0 mV.
      b. $+30$ mV.
      c. -80 mV.
      d. -65 mV.

_____ 3. In the first step in the generation of an action potential,

      a. a graded depolarization brings an area of excitable membrane to threshold.
      b. sodium channel activation occurs.
      c. potassium channels open and potassium moves out.
      d. a temporary hyperpolarization occurs.

_____ 4. Opening of sodium channels in the membrane of a neuron results in

      a. hyperpolarization.
      b. depolarization.
      c. repolarization.
      d. none of the above.

_____ 5. The sodium–potassium exchange pump

      a. transports sodium ions into the cell during depolarization.
      b. transports potassium ions out of the cell during repolarization.
      c. moves sodium and potassium in the direction of their chemical gradients.
      d. requires ATP energy to function.

_____ 6. A propagated change in the membrane potential of the entire cell membrane is

      a. a graded potential.
      b. transmembrane potential.
      c. its resting potential.
      d. an action potential.

_____ 7. The all-or-none principle states that

      a. all stimuli will produce identical action potentials.
      b. stimuli that are strong enough to bring the membrane to threshold will produce identical action potentials.
      c. the greater the magnitude of the stimuli, the greater the intensity of the action potential.
      d. only motor stimuli can activate action potentials.

OBJECTIVE 4   Explain the mechanism of nerve impulse transmission at the synapse.

_____ 1. The most common type of synapse found in the nervous system is

      a. chemical.
      b. electrical.
      c. mechanical.
      d. time released.

_____ 2. At cholinergic synapses, calcium ions entering the synaptic knobs trigger the exocytosis of the synaptic vesicles and cause the release of

      a. noradrenaline.
      b. nitric oxide and carbon monoxide.
      c. acetylcholine.
      d. dopamine and serotonin.

_____ 3. The neurotransmitters that function primarily in the CNS are

      a. noradrenaline and norepinephrine.
      b. dopamine and serotonin.
      c. nitric oxide and carbon monoxide.
      d. acetylcholine and norepinephrine.

_____ 4. Adrenergic synapses release the neurotransmitter

      a. norepinepherine.
      b. adrenalin.
      c. dopamine.
      d. acetylcholine.

_____ 5. The processing of the same information at the same time by several neuronal pools is called

      a. serial processing.
      b. parallel processing.
      c. convergent processing.
      d. divergent processing.

_____ 6. In the last event to occur at a typical cholinergic synapse,

      a. calcium ions enter the cytoplasm of the synaptic cleft.
      b. ACh release ceases because Ca^{2+} are removed from the cytoplasm.
      c. ACh is broken down into acetate and choline by AChE.
      d. the synaptic knob reabsorbs choline from the synaptic cleft and uses it to resynthesize ACh.

OBJECTIVE 5   Describe the three meningeal layers that surround the central nervous system.

_____ 1. Absorption of shock and giving physical stability to the brain and spinal cord is provided by the

      a. dural sinus and subdural space.
      b. arachnoid and subarachnoid space.
      c. three layers of specialized meninges.
      d. cranium and intervertebral discs.

_____ 2. Blood vessels servicing the spinal cord are found in the

      a. pia mater.
      b. dura mater.
      c. epidural space.
      d. subarachnoid space.

_____ 3. The pia mater is the meninx that is

      a. firmly bound to neural tissue and deep to the other meninges.
      b. the outermost covering of the central nervous system.
      c. filled with a quantity of lymphatic fluid that reduces friction between the opposing surfaces.
      d. a layer of squamous cells forming a delicate web of collagen and elastic fibers.

_____ 4. Progressing from the outward layer to the inward layer, the correct sequence of meningeal layers of the spinal cord is

      a. dura mater, pia mater, epidural space, arachnoid, subarachnoid space.
      b. arachnoid, subarachnoid space, epidural space, dura mater, pia mater.
      c. epidural space, dura mater, arachnoid, subarachnoid space, pia mater.
      d. pia mater, subarachnoid space, arachnoid, dura mater, epidural space.

_____ 5. When cerebrospinal fluid is drawn during a spinal tap, a needle is inserted into the

      a. subdural space.
      b. subarachnoid space.
      c. epidural space.
      d. dura mater.

_____ 6. The epidural space between the dura mater of the spinal cord and the walls of the vertebral canal contains

      a. a small quantity of lymphatic fluid, which reduces friction between surfaces.
      b. loose connective tissue, blood vessels, and adipose tissue.
      c. large collecting veins and dural folds.
      d. large vessels that branch over the surfaces of the brain.

OBJECTIVE 6   Discuss the structure and functions of the spinal cord.

_____ 1. The spinal cord serves as the major passageway for

      a. motor impulses to the brain and sensory impulses from the brain.
      b. automatic sensory responses involved with complex reflex patterns.
      c. conscious thoughts, sensations, and intellectual functions.
      d. sensory impulses to the brain and motor impulses from the brain.

_____ 2. In the spinal cord, cerebrospinal fluid is found within the

    a. central canal and epidural space.
    b. subarachnoid and epidural space.
    c. central canal and subarachnoid space.
    d. subdural and epidural space.

_____ 3. The white matter of the spinal cord contains

    a. cell bodies of neurons and glial cells.
    b. somatic and visceral sensory nuclei.
    c. large numbers of myelinated and unmyelinated axons.
    d. sensory and motor nuclei.

_____ 4. The area of the spinal cord that surrounds the central canal and is dominated by the cell bodies of neurons and glial cells is the

    a. white matter.
    b. gray matter.
    c. ascending tracts.
    d. descending tracts.

_____ 5. The posterior gray horns of the spinal cord contain

    a. somatic and visceral sensory nuclei.
    b. somatic and visceral motor nuclei.
    c. ascending and descending tracts.
    d. anterior and posterior columns.

_____ 6. The axons in the white matter of the spinal cord that carry sensory information up toward the brain are organized into

    a. anterior white columns.
    b. descending rami.
    c. descending tracts.
    d. ascending tracts.

Labeling Exercise

Identify and label the following structures of the spinal cord. Place your answers in the spaces provided below the drawing.

white matter   anterior median fissure   posterior median sulcus
gray commissure   subarachnoid space   central canal
dura mater   anterior horn   dorsal root
ventral root   spinal nerve   posterior horn
pia mater

FIGURE 8-3 Organization of the Spinal Cord

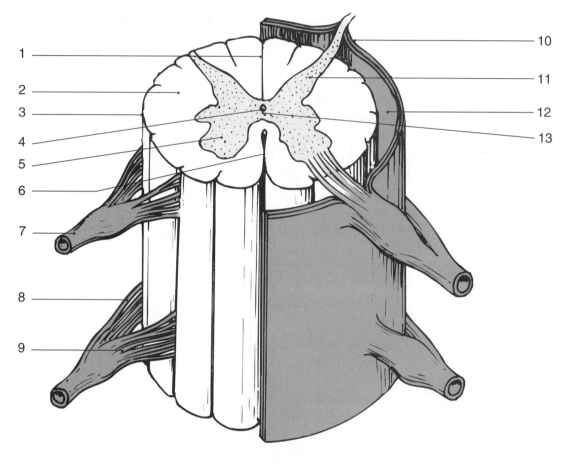

Anterior

1. _____   8. _____

2. _____   9. _____

3. _____   10. _____

4. _____   11. _____

5. _____   12. _____

6. _____   13. _____

7. _____

OBJECTIVE 7 Name the major regions of the brain and describe their functions.

_____ 1. The major region of the brain responsible for conscious thought processes, sensations, intellectual functions, memory, and complex motor patterns is the

  a. cerebellum.
  b. medulla.
  c. pons.
  d. cerebrum.

_____ 2. The region of the brain that adjusts voluntary and involuntary motor activities on the basis of sensory information and stored memories of previous movements is the

  a. cerebrum.
  b. cerebellum.
  c. medulla.
  d. diencephalon.

_____ 3. The brain stem consists of the

  a. midbrain, pons, and medulla oblongata.
  b. cerebellum, medulla, and pons.
  c. thalamus, hypothalamus, and medulla.
  d. spinal cord, cerebellum, and medulla.

_____ 4. The largest portion of the diencephalon—the thalamus—contains

  a. centers for involuntary somatic motor responses.
  b. relay and processing centers for sensory information.
  c. nuclei involved with visceral motor control.
  d. centers involved with emotions and hormone production.

_____ 5. The hypothalamus contains centers involved with

  a. voluntary somatic motor responses.
  b. somatic and visceral motor control.
  c. maintenance of consciousness.
  d. emotions, autonomic function, and hormone production.

_____ 6. The primary link between the nervous system and the endocrine system is the

  a. pineal gland.
  b. pituitary gland.
  c. medulla oblongata.
  d. mesencephalon.

_____ 7. Major centers concerned with autonomic control of breathing, blood pressure, heart rate, and digestive activities are located in the

  a. medulla oblongata.
  b. pons.
  c. midbrain.
  d. diencephalon.

_____ 8. The cerebellum is an automatic processing center that

      a. adjusts the postural muscles of the body to maintain balance.
      b. compares motor commands with proprioceptive information.
      c. programs and fine-tunes movements consciously and subconsciously.
      d. does all of the above.

_____ 9. The lateral ventricles communicate with the third ventricle in the diencephalon via the

      a. mesencephalic aqueduct.
      b. choroid plexus.
      c. interventricular foramen.
      d. pons.

_____ 10. Cerebrospinal fluid that circulates between the different ventricles is produced at the

      a. mesencephalic aqueduct.
      b. choroid plexus.
      c. central canal.
      d. corpus callosum.

Labeling Exercises

Identify and label the structures in Figure 8-4. Place your answers in the spaces provided on the following page.

frontal lobe	parietal lobe	temporal lobe
occipital lobe	central sulcus	lateral fissure
precentral gyrus	medulla oblongata	parieto-occipital fissure
cerebellum	postcentral gyrus	pons

FIGURE 8-4 Lateral View of the Human Brain

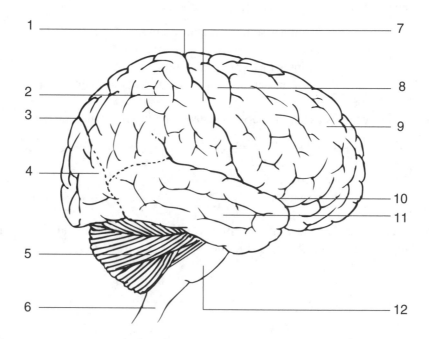

1. _____   7. _____

2. _____   8. _____

3. _____   9. _____

4. _____   10. _____

5. _____   11. _____

6. _____   12. _____

Identify and label the structures in Figure 8-5. Place your answers in the spaces provided below the drawing.

cerebral hemispheres   corpus callosum   pineal gland
cerebellum   thalamus   fornix
third ventricle   pituitary gland   pons
medulla oblongata   mammilary gland   choroid plexus
cerebral peduncle   cerebral aqueduct   fourth ventricle
corpora quadrigemina   optic chiasma

FIGURE 8-5 Sagittal View of the Human Brain

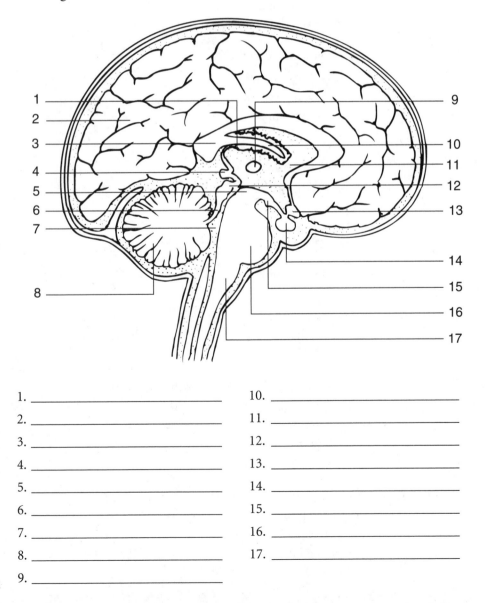

1. _____   10. _____

2. _____   11. _____

3. _____   12. _____

4. _____   13. _____

5. _____   14. _____

6. _____   15. _____

7. _____   16. _____

8. _____   17. _____

9. _____

OBJECTIVE 8   Locate the motor, sensory, and association areas of the cerebral cortex, and discuss their functions.

_____ 1. The neurons in the primary sensory cortex receive somatic information from

a. commisural fibers.
b. touch, pressure, pain, taste, and temperature receptors.
c. visual and auditory receptors in the eyes and ears.
d. receptors in muscle spindles and Golgi tendon organs.

_____ 2. The neurons of the primary motor cortex are responsible for directing

a. visual and auditory responses.
b. responses to taste and temperature.
c. voluntary movements.
d. involuntary movements.

_____ 3. The somatic nervous system issues somatic motor commands that

a. control smooth and cardiac muscles.
b. direct the contractions of skeletal muscles.
c. control involuntary movements.
d. control the ability to hear, see, and smell.

_____ 4. The primary motor areas are located in the

a. precentral gyrus area.
b. postcentral gyrus area.
c. corpus callosum.
d. limbic system.

_____ 5. The primary sensory areas are located in the

a. choroid plexus.
b. amygdaloid bodies.
c. postcentral gyrus area.
d. cerebral peduncles.

_____ 6. The interpretive association area for vision is in the

a. occipital lobe.
b. parietal lobe.
c. frontal lobe.
d. temporal lobe.

_____ 7. The inability to interpret what is read or heard indicates that there is damage to the

a. left hemisphere.
b. right hemisphere.
c. cerebellum.
d. medulla oblongata.

_____ 8. The auditory cortex is located in the

a. occipital lobe.
b. parietal lobe.
c. temporal lobe.
d. frontal lobe.

_____ 9. Interconnecting neurons and communication between cerebral hemispheres occurs through the

      a. hypothalamus.

      b. medulla oblongata.

      c. pons.

      d. corpus callosum.

_____ 10. The series of elevated ridges that increase the surface area of the cerebral hemispheres and the number of neurons in the cortical areas are called

      a. sulci.

      b. gyri.

      c. fissures.

      d. all of the above.

Labeling Exercise

Identify and label the primary association areas in Figure 8-6. Place the answers in the spaces provided below the drawing.

occipital lobe	parietal lobe	central sulcus
premotor cortex	frontal lobe	temporal lobe
precentral gyrus	postcentral gyrus	

FIGURE 8-6 Left Cerebral Hemisphere—Association Areas

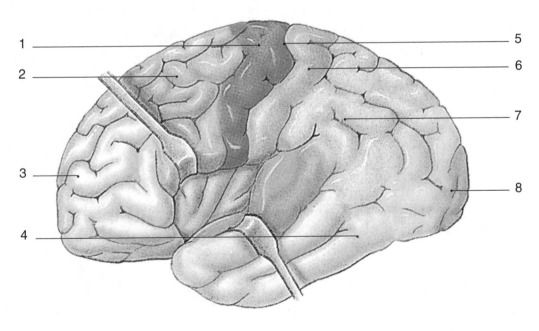

1. _____   5. _____

2. _____   6. _____

3. _____   7. _____

4. _____   8. _____

OBJECTIVE 9 Identify the cranial nerves, and relate each pair of cranial nerves to its principal functions.

_____ 1. The special sensory cranial nerves include the

      a. oculomotor, trochlear, and abducens.
      b. spinal accessory, hypoglossal, and glossopharyngeal.
      c. olfactory, optic, and vestibulocochlear.
      d. vagus, trigeminal, and facial.

_____ 2. Cranial nerves III, IV, VI, and XI, which provide motor control, are the

      a. trigeminal, facial, glossopharyngeal, and vagus nerves.
      b. oculomotor, trochlear, abducens, and spinal accessory nerves.
      c. olfactory, optic, vestibulocochlear, and hypoglossal nerves.
      d. oculomotor, hypoglossal, optic, and olfactory nerves.

_____ 3. The cranial nerves that carry sensory information and involuntary motor commands are

      a. I, II, III, and IV.
      b. II, IV, VI, and VIII.
      c. V, VI, VIII, and XII.
      d. V, VII, IX, and X.

4. The cranial nerve responsible for the sense of smell is the _____.

5. The cranial nerve responsible for vision is the _____.

6. The pair of cranial nerves that controls the pupil of the eye is the _____.

7. The cranial nerve involved when a person feels a sinus headache is the _____.

8. The number of the pair of cranial nerves involved in taste is _____.

9. The cranial nerve that controls the diaphragm is the _____.

10. The hypoglossal cranial nerves control movement of the _____.

Labeling Exercise

Identify and label the cranial nerves and their number in Figure 8-7 (e.g., olfactory N I). Place your answers in the spaces provided below the drawing.

FIGURE 8-7 The 12 Pairs of Cranial Nerves

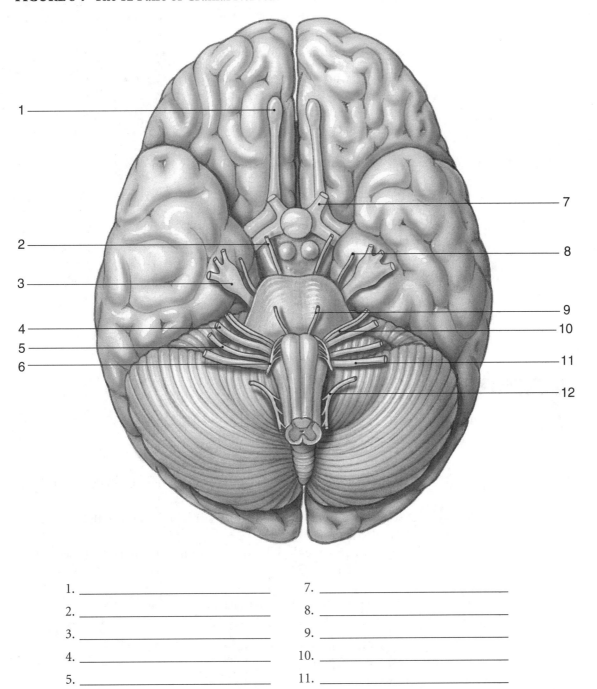

1. _____   7. _____

2. _____   8. _____

3. _____   9. _____

4. _____   10. _____

5. _____   11. _____

6. _____   12. _____

OBJECTIVE 10 Relate the distribution pattern of spinal nerves to the regions they innervate.

_____ 1. The 31 pairs of spinal nerves include

        a. 12 pr. cervical; 8 pr. thoracic; 5 pr. lumbar; 5 pr. sacral; 1 pr. coccygeal.
        b. 8 pr. cervical; 12 pr. thoracic; 5 pr. lumbar; 5 pr. sacral; 1 pr. coccygeal.
        c. 5 pr. cervical; 12 pr. thoracic; 8 pr. lumbar; 5 pr. sacral; 1 pr. coccygeal.
        d. 8 pr. cervical; 10 pr. thoracic; 7 pr. lumbar; 5 pr. sacral; 1 pr. coccygeal.

_____ 2. The cervical plexus innervates the muscles of the

        a. neck and extends into the thoracic cavity to control the diaphragm.
        b. shoulder girdle and upper limb.
        c. pelvic girdle and lower limb.
        d. upper and lower limbs.

_____ 3. Spinal nerves innervate and supply the pelvic girdle and lower limb via the

        a. cervical plexus.
        b. brachial plexus.
        c. brachiocervical plexus.
        d. lumbar plexus and sacral plexus.

_____ 4. The spinal nerve supply to the shoulder girdle and upper limb is provided by the

        a. cervical plexus.
        b. lumbar plexus.
        c. brachial plexus.
        d. sacral plexus.

OBJECTIVE 11 Describe the components of a reflex arc.

_____ 1. In a reflex arc, a stimulus initiates a nerve impulse that travels along a

        a. sensory neuron to the CNS, which sends an impulse via a motor neuron to the effector.
        b. motor neuron to the CNS, which sends an impulse to the effector via a sensory neuron.
        c. sensory neuron to the PNS, which sends an impulse to the effector via a motor neuron.
        d. sensory neuron to the effector, which stimulates the CNS to send an impulse to the PNS.

_____ 2. The sensory neuron associated with a reflex arc transmits the impulse

        a. away from the interneuron.
        b. away from the spinal cord.
        c. toward the effector.
        d. toward the CNS.

_____ 3. The motor neuron associated with a reflex arc transmits the impulse

        a. toward the effector.
        b. away from the CNS.
        c. toward the CNS.
        d. a and b are correct.

_____ 4. In a typical reflex arc, the correct pathway of an action potential beginning with the receptor is

        a. interneuron → motor neuron in CNS → sensory neuron → effector.
        b. sensory neuron → interneuron in CNS → motor neuron → effector.
        c. motor neuron → interneuron in PNS → sensory neuron → effector.
        d. sensory neuron → motor neuron in CNS → interneuron → effector.

_____ 5. In a reflex arc, neurotransmitter activity occurs at

        a. the site of stimulation.
        b. the effector.
        c. synapses.
        d. the receptor.

Labeling Exercise

In the drawing below, identify and label the parts of a reflex arc. Place your answers in the spaces provided below the drawings.

effector	interneuron	gray matter
receptor	synapse	stimulus
sensory neuron	motor neuron	white matter

FIGURE 8-8 The Reflex Arc

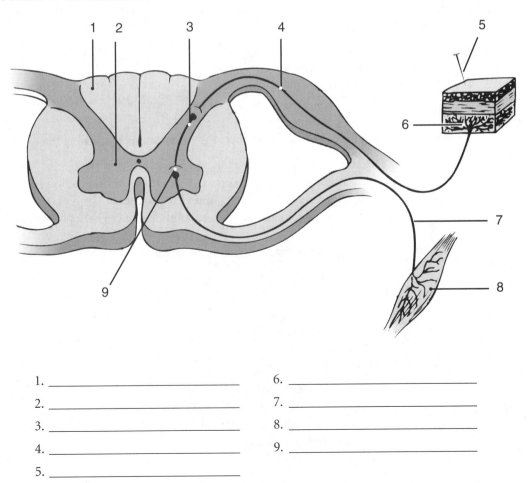

1. _____   6. _____

2. _____   7. _____

3. _____   8. _____

4. _____   9. _____

5. _____

OBJECTIVE 12 Identify the principal sensory and motor pathways.

_____ 1. The three major somatic sensory pathways include

      a. first-order, second-order, and third-order pathways.
      b. the nuclear, cerebellar, and thalamic pathways.
      c. the posterior column, spinothalamic, and spinocerebellar pathways.
      d. the anterior, posterior, and lateral pathways.

_____ 2. The motor (descending) pathways include the

      a. spinothalamic and cerebellar pathways.
      b. corticospinal, medial, and lateral pathways.
      c. posterior and anterior column pathways.
      d. cerebral and cerebellar systems.

_____ 3. If the name of a tract begins with the prefix _spino,_ the tract

      a. starts in the brain and ends in the spinal cord.
      b. starts in the spinal cord and ends in the brain.
      c. has axons that start in the higher centers and end in the medulla oblongata.
      d. has afferent fibers that arrive at the cerebral cortex from the spinal cord.

_____ 4. Poorly localized sensations of touch, pressure, pain, and temperature to the primary sensory cortex are the functions of the

      a. spinothalamic pathway.
      b. posterior column pathway.
      c. medial and lateral pathways.
      d. corticospinal pathway.

_____ 5. The spinocerebellar pathway delivers proprioceptive information concerning the

      a. positions of skeletal muscles, bones, and joints to the cerebral cortex.
      b. sensations of touch, pressure, and vibrations to the cerebral cortex.
      c. conscious control of skeletal muscles throughout the body.
      d. positions of muscles, bones, and joints to the cerebellar cortex.

_____ 6. Conscious, voluntary control of skeletal muscles is provided by the

      a. spinothalamic pathway.
      b. corticospinal pathway.
      c. spinocerebellar pathway.
      d. posterior column pathway.

_____ 7. The pyramidal system consists of

      a. rubrospinal and reticulospinal tracts.
      b. vestibulospinal and tectospinal tracts.
      c. corticobulbar and corticospinal tracts.
      d. sensory and motor neurons.

_____ 8. The crossing over of corticospinal axons causes the

          a. left side of the body to be controlled by the left cerebral hemisphere.

          b. right side of the body to be controlled by the right cerebral hemisphere.

          c. right and left sides of the body to be controlled by the medulla oblongata.

          d. left side of the body to be controlled by the right cerebral hemisphere.

_____ 9. The medial and lateral pathways provide reflexive skeletal muscle responses to

          a. equilibrium sensations and strong visual and auditory stimuli.

          b. conscious control of skeletal muscles throughout the body.

          c. localized sensations of touch, pressure, and temperature.

          d. positions of bones, muscles, and joints.

Labeling Exercise

Identify and label the following pathways in Figure 8-9. Place your answers in the spaces below the drawing.

posterior spinocerebellar	anterior corticospinal	lateral spinothalamic
anterior spinothalamic	anterior spinocerebellar	lateral corticospinal

FIGURE 8-9 Sensory and Motor Pathways of the Spinal Cord

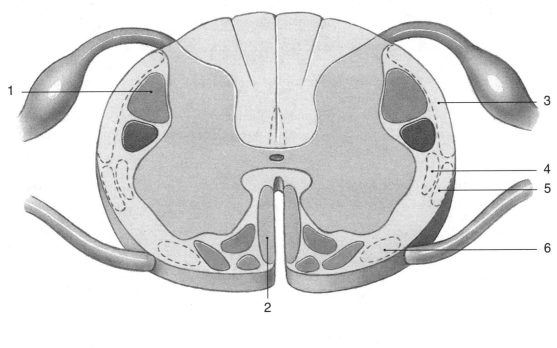

1. _____   4. _____

2. _____   5. _____

3. _____   6. _____

OBJECTIVE 13   Compare and contrast the functions and structures of the sympathetic and parasympathetic divisions.

_____ 1. Sympathetic (preganglionic) neurons originate between

a. T_1 and T_2 of the spinal cord.
b. T_1 and L_2 of the spinal cord.
c. L_1 and L_4 of the spinal cord.
d. S_2 and S_4 of the spinal cord.

_____ 2. Among the important functions of the postganglionic fibers that enter the thoracic cavity in autonomic nerves is

a. accelerating the heart rate.
b. increasing the force of cardiac contractions.
c. dilating the respiratory passageways.
d. a, b, and c are correct.

_____ 3. Preganglionic neurons in the parasympathetic division of the ANS originate in the

a. peripheral ganglia adjacent to the target organ.
b. thoracolumbar area of the spinal cord.
c. walls of the target organ.
d. brain stem and sacral segments of the spinal cord.

_____ 4. Because second-order neurons in the parasympathetic division are all located in the same ganglion, the effects of parasympathetic stimulation are

a. more diversified and less localized than those of the sympathetic division.
b. less diversified but less localized than those of the sympathetic division.
c. more specific and localized than those of the sympathetic division.
d. more diversified and more localized than those of the sympathetic division.

_____ 5. The parasympathetic division of the ANS includes visceral motor nuclei associated with cranial nerves

a. I, II, III, and IV.
b. III, VII, IX, and X.
c. IV, V, VI, and VIII.
d. V, VI, VII, and XII.

_____ 6. At their synaptic terminals, all cholinergic preganglionic autonomic fibers release

a. norepinephrine.
b. serotonin.
c. acetylcholine.
d. noradrenalin.

_____ 7. At neuroeffector junctions, typical sympathetic postganglionic fibers release

     a. epinephrine.
     b. norepinephrine.
     c. acetylcholine.
     d. dopamine.

_____ 8. At synapse and neuroeffector junctions, all preganglionic and postganglionic fibers in the parasympathetic division release

     a. epinephrine.
     b. norepinephrine.
     c. acetylcholine.
     d. a, b, and c are correct.

_____ 9. The functions of the parasympathetic division center on

     a. accelerating the heart rate and the force of contraction.
     b. dilation of the respiratory passageways.
     c. relaxation, food processing, and energy absorption.
     d. a, b, and c are correct.

_____ 10. During a crisis, the event necessary for an individual to cope with stressful and potentially dangerous situations is called

     a. the effector response.
     b. sympathetic activation.
     c. parasympathetic activation.
     d. a, b, and c are correct.

_____ 11. Parasympathetic preganglionic fibers of the vagus nerve entering the thoracic cavity join the

     a. cardiac plexus.
     b. pulmonary plexus.
     c. hypogastric plexus.
     d. a and b are correct.

_____ 12. The major structural difference between sympathetic pre- and postganglionic fibers is that

     a. preganglionic fibers are short and postganglionic fibers are long.
     b. preganglionic fibers are long and postganglionic fibers are short.
     c. preganglionic fibers are close to target organs, and postganglionic fibers are close to the spinal cord.
     d. preganglionic fibers innervate target organs while postganglionic fibers originate from cranial nerves.

_____ 13. The effects of parasympathetic stimulation are usually

     a. brief in duration and restricted to specific organs and sites.
     b. long in duration and diverse in distribution.
     c. brief in duration and diverse in distribution.
     d. long in duration and restricted to specific organs and sites.

14. Because the sympathetic division of the PNS stimulates tissue metabolism and increases alertness, it is called the _____ or _____ division.

15. Because the parasympathetic division of the ANS conserves energy and promotes sedentary activity, it is known as the _____ and _____ division.

OBJECTIVE 14 Summarize the effects of aging on the nervous system.

_____ 1. Differences in the brains of elderly and younger individuals include

      a. narrower gyri, wider sulci, and large subarachnoid space in the young.
      b. narrower gyri, wider sulci, and large subarachnoid space in the elderly.
      c. decreased numbers of cortical neurons in the young.
      d. increased blood flow to the brain in the elderly.

_____ 2. Changes that occur in the CNS during the aging process include

      a. increased numbers of synaptic connections.
      b. increased numbers of cortical neurons.
      c. reduction in brain size and weight.
      d. reduction of abnormal intracellular deposits in neurons.

_____ 3. Alzheimer's disease is characterized by

      a. decreased blood flow to the brain.
      b. reduced neuronal loss due to dementia.
      c. an increased rate of neurotransmitter production.
      d. a gradual deterioration of mental organization.

OBJECTIVE 15 Discuss the interrelationships among the nervous system and other organ systems.

1. Sexual hormones that affect CNS development and sexual behaviors result from the activity of the _____ system.

2. Storage of calcium for neural function and protection of the brain and spinal cord results from the activity of the _____ system.

3. Hormonal effect on CNS neural metabolism and CNS development results from the activity of the _____ system.

4. The system that provides nutrients for energy production and neurotransmitter synthesis for the nervous system is the _____ system.

5. The system that provides endothelial cells to maintain the blood–brain barrier is the _____ system.

Part II: Chapter Comprehensive Exercises

A. Word Elimination

Circle the term that does not belong in each of the following groupings.

1. afferent   efferent   somatic   autonomic   CNS

2. sensory   excitatory   motor   muscle   inhibitory

3. soma   dendrites   neuroglia   axon   synaptic knob

4. astrocyte   neuron   oligodendrocyte   microglia   ependymal cells

5. resting   threshold   conduction   depolarization repolarization

6. norepinephrine   dopamine   serotonin   GABA   adrenergic

7. trigeminal   opthalmic   N IV   maxillary   mandibular

8. axons   peripheral nerves   cell bodies   ganglia   CNS

9. frontal   parietal   occipital   gyrus   temporal

10. cerebrum   meninges   diencephalon   cerebellum   medulla oblongata

B. Matching

Match the terms in Column "B" with the terms in Column "A." Write letters for answers in the spaces provided.

COLUMN A	COLUMN B
___ 1. graded potential	a. smell sensations
___ 2. hyperpolarization	b. voluntary control of skeletal muscle
___ 3. somatic nervous system	c. pineal gland
___ 4. autonomic nervous system	d. speech center
___ 5. epithalamus	e. taste sensations
___ 6. gustatory cortex	f. affects limited portion of cell membrane
___ 7. olfactory cortex	g. involuntary control of smooth and cardiac muscle
___ 8. neurotransmitters	h. change in membrane potential from -70 mV to -80 mV
___ 9. Broca's area	i. general interpretive area
___10. Wernicke's area	j. nitric oxide and carbon monoxide

C. Concept Map I - Nervous System Overview

Using the following terms, fill in the circled numbered, blank spaces to complete the concept map. Follow the numbers that comply with the organization of the map.

Motor neurons   Gray matter   Ascending and descending tracts
Arachnoid mater   Columns   Central nervous system (CNS)
Cell bodies   Afferent division

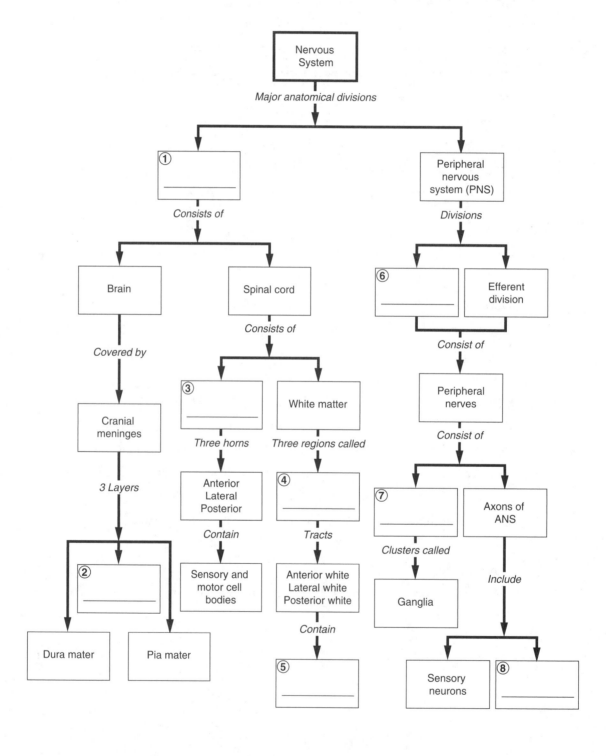

Concept Map II - Major Regions of the Brain

Using the following terms, fill in the circled numbered, blank spaces to complete the concept map. Follow the numbers that comply with the organization of the map.

2 Cerebellar hemispheres   Pons

Hypothalamus   Corpora quadrigemina

Diencephalon   Medulla oblongata

```
                              ┌─────────────┐
                              │  Six Major  │
                              │   Regions   │
                              │ of the Brain│
                              └──────┬──────┘
```

Region 1   Region 2   Region 3   Region 4   Region 5   Region 6

| Cerebrum | ① _____ | Mesencephalon | Cerebellum | ⑤ _____ | ⑥ _____ |

Consists of   Consists of   Consists of   Consists of   Contains   Contains

2 cerebral hemispheres

④ _____

Cerebral peduncles   ③ _____   Nuclei   Ascending and descending tracts

Walls called the   Floor called the   Roof called the

Thalamus   ② _____   Epithalamus

Nuclei   Reflex centers

Ascending and descending tracts

Concept Map III - Autonomic Nervous System

Using the following terms, fill in the circled numbered, blank spaces to complete the concept map. Follow the numbers that comply with the organization of the map.

Ganglia outside CNS   Motor neurons   Sympathetic

Smooth muscle   Postganglionic   First-order neurons

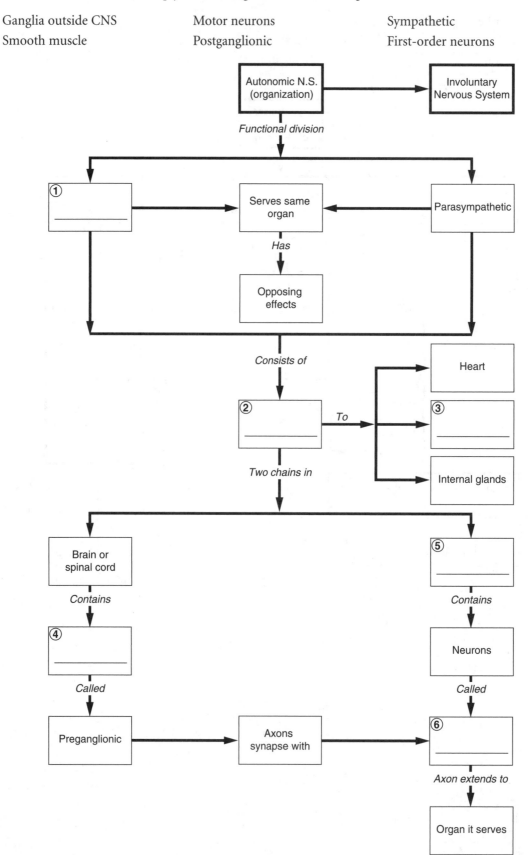

Concept Map IV - Sympathetic Division of ANS

Using the following terms, fill in the circled numbered, blank spaces to complete the concept map. Follow the numbers that comply with the organization of the map.

Adrenal medulla (paired)

Second-order neurons (postganglionic)

Thoracolumbar

Sympathetic chain of ganglia (paired)

Spinal segments T_1–L_2

Visceral effectors

General circulation

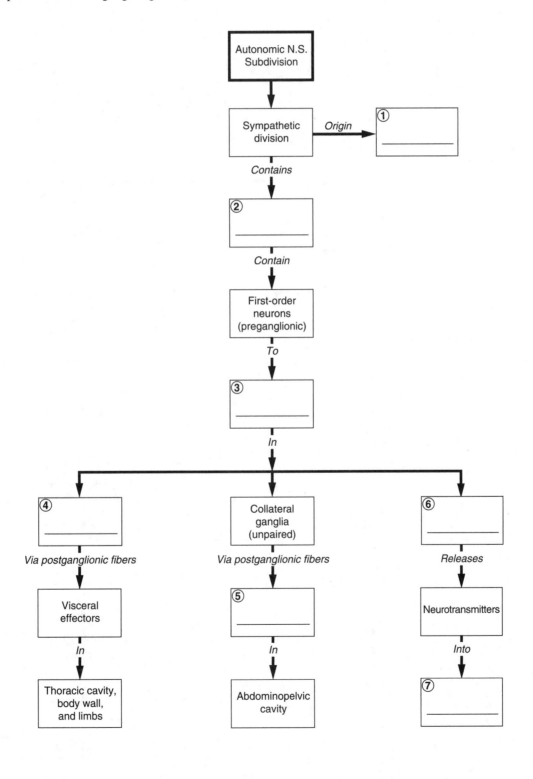

Concept Map V - Parasympathetic Division of ANS

Using the following terms, fill in the circled numbered, blank spaces to complete the concept map. Follow the numbers that comply with the organization of the map.

Lower abdominopelvic cavity

Nasal, tear, salivary glands

Craniosacral

Segments S_2–S_4

Otic ganglia

Intramural ganglia

Ciliary ganglion

N X

N VII

Brain stem

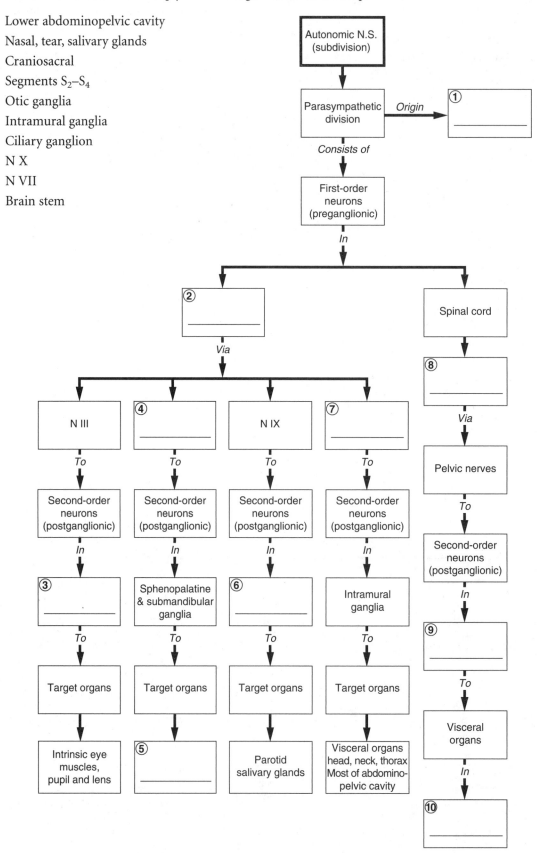

D. Crossword Puzzle I

The following crossword puzzles review the material in Chapter 8. To complete the puzzle, you must know the answers to the clues given, and you must be able to spell the terms correctly.

ACROSS

1. One of the many types of neurotransmitters.
5. Nerves antagonistic to the parasympathetic nervous system.
6. An integral part of the autonomic nervous system.
7. The same as a sensory nerve.
9. The abbreviation for acetylcholine.
10. There are seven cervical vertebrae but _____ pairs of cervical nerves.
11. A nerve emerging from the cervical plexus involved in breathing.
12. The descending tracts in the spinal cord are _____ nerves.

DOWN

2. One of the two components of the CNS.
3. A major nerve of the lumbosacral plexus.
4. The portion of the neuron that contains organelles.
8. The same as a motor nerve.

Crossword Puzzle II

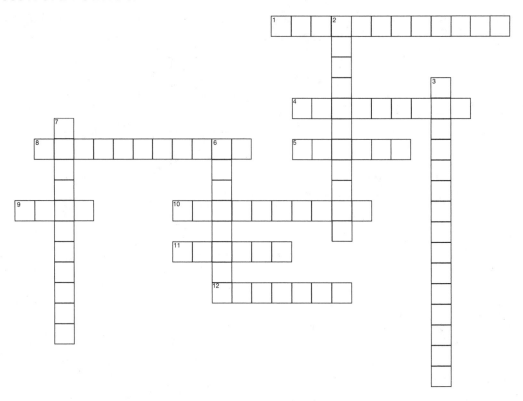

ACROSS

1. Fanning of the toes in infants (two words).
4. The system that provides voluntary control over skeletal muscles.
5. A type of withdrawal reflex.
8. CN responsible for tongue movements.
9. Type of innervation in which instructions come from both ANS divisions.
10. N III is the _____ nerve.
11. A network of a nerve trunk.
12. An example of a monosynaptic reflex.

DOWN

2. Found between a sensory neuron and a motor neuron.
3. Rest and repose division of the ANS.
6. N VI is the _____ nerve.
7. Fight or flight division of the ANS.

E. Short-Answer Questions

Briefly answer the following questions in the spaces provided.

1. What are the three major functions of the nervous system?

2. What are the major components of the central nervous system and the peripheral nervous system?

3. What four types of glial cells are found in the central nervous system?

4. Functionally, what is the major difference between neurons and neuroglia?

5. List the six major regions in the adult brain.

6. What are the two primary functions of the cerebellum?

7. What are the three major components of the sympathetic division?

8. What are the two major components of the parasympathetic division of the ANS?

9. Why is the sympathetic division of the ANS called the "fight or flight" system?

10. Why is the parasympathetic division of the ANS known as the "rest and repose" system?

11. List four of the anatomical changes in the nervous system that are commonly associated with the aging process.

The General and Special Senses

Overview

Seeing, hearing, smelling, tasting, and balance: These special senses that allow us to be aware of the world within and around us by reacting to stimuli are usually taken for granted. In fact, it is not unusual to ignore their importance until we don't have them. Our chances for survival would be severely limited if the general senses of temperature, pain, touch, pressure, vibration, and proprioception would cease to allow us to respond in positive or negative ways so that we are consciously aware of the sensory information we receive. All these specialized parts of the nervous system allow the body to assess and make adjustments to changing conditions and maintain homeostasis. Sensory receptors in the specialized sensory structures receive stimuli, initiating production of action potentials that are transmitted on neurons to the CNS. There the sensations are processed, resulting in motor responses that preserve the integrity of the body's steady state and ability to survive.

The activities and exercises in Chapter 9 are designed to reinforce your understanding of the structure and function of general sensory receptors and specialized receptor cells, which are structurally more complex than those of the general senses. The concept maps will be a valuable resource tool to help you synthesize, organize, and master the material regarding the general and special senses.

Review of Chapter Objectives

1. Distinguish between the general senses and the special senses.
2. Identify the receptors for the general senses, and describe how they function.
3. Describe the receptors and processes involved in the sense of smell.
4. Discuss the receptors and processes involved in the sense of taste.
5. Identify the parts of the eye and their functions.
6. Explain how we are able to see objects and distinguish colors.
7. Discuss how the central nervous system processes information related to vision.
8. Discuss the receptors and processes involved in the sense of equilibrium.
9. Describe the parts of the ear and their roles in the process of hearing.
10. Describe the effects of aging on smell, taste, vision, and hearing.

Part I: Objective-Based Questions

OBJECTIVE 1 Distinguish between the general senses and the special senses.

_____ 1. The term general senses refers to sensations of

      a. smell, taste, balance, hearing, and vision.
      b. pain, smell, pressure, balance, and vision.
      c. temperature, pain, touch, pressure, vibration, and proprioception.
      d. touch, taste, balance, vibration, and hearing.

_____ 2. The special senses refer to

      a. balance, taste, smell, hearing, and vision.
      b. temperature, pain, taste, touch, and hearing.
      c. touch, pressure, vibration, and proprioception.
      d. proprioception, smell, touch, and taste.

_____ 3. Receptors for special senses are located

      a. in specific sense organs.
      b. throughout the body.
      c. in the cerebral area.
      d. in the integument.

_____ 4. The general senses

      a. are localized in specific areas of the body.
      b. involve receptors that are relatively simple.
      c. are located in the sense organs.
      d. do not require action potentials for effector responses.

OBJECTIVE 2 Identify the receptors for the general senses, and describe how they function.

_____ 1. The receptors for the general senses are the

      a. axons of the sensory neurons.
      b. cell bodies of sensory neurons.
      c. dendrites of sensory neurons.
      d. All of the above are correct.

_____ 2. The three classes of mechanoreceptors are

      a. Meissner's corpuscles, Pacinian corpuscles, and Merkel's discs.
      b. fine touch, crude touch, and pressure receptors.
      c. tactile receptors, baroreceptors, and proprioceptors.
      d. slow-adapting, fast-adapting, and central-adapting receptors.

_____ 3. The free nerve endings that function as pain receptors are called

      a. nociceptors.
      b. mechanoreceptors.
      c. baroreceptors.
      d. proprioceptors.

_____ 4. Sensory receptors that monitor the position of joints are called

      a. nociceptors.
      b. baroreceptors.
      c. chemoreceptors.
      d. proprioceptors.

_____ 5. Sensory receptors that monitor blood pressure in the walls of major blood vessels are called

      a. nociceptors.
      b. baroreceptors.
      c. chemoreceptors.
      d. proprioceptors.

_____ 6. Tactile receptors respond to all of the following except

      a. vibration.
      b. touch.
      c. pain.
      d. pressure.

_____ 7. Receptors that monitor the pH and the carbon dioxide and oxygen concentrations of arterial blood are

      a. baroreceptors.
      b. nociceptors.
      c. proprioceptors.
      d. chemoreceptors.

OBJECTIVE 3 Describe the receptors and processes involved in the sense of smell.

_____ 1. Olfactory reception occurs as dissolved chemicals interact with receptors called

      a. odorant binding proteins.
      b. columnar cells.
      c. basal cells.
      d. olfactory glands.

_____ 2. The CNS interprets smell on the basis of the particular pattern of

      a. cortical arrangement.
      b. neuronal replacement.
      c. receptor activity.
      d. sensory impressions.

_____ 3. The only type of sensory information that reaches the cerebral cortex without synapsing in the thalamus is _____ stimuli.

      a. visual
      b. olfactory
      c. gustation
      d. All of the above are correct.

_____ 4. The olfactory epithelium of each olfactory organ contains

        a. olfactory receptor cells.
        b. supporting cells.
        c. regenerative basal cells.
        d. all of the above.

_____ 5. The cerebral interpretation of smell occurs in the

        a. olfactory cortex.
        b. hypothalamus.
        c. portions of the limbic system.
        d. All of the above are correct.

Labeling Exercise

In the following structures, identify and label the parts. Place the labels in the spaces provided below the drawing.

olfactory tract	cilia	afferent nerve fiber
cribriform plate	mucus layer	basal cell
olfactory bulb	olfactory gland	bipolar neuron

FIGURE 9-1 (a) Structure of Olfactory Organ (b) Olfactory Receptor

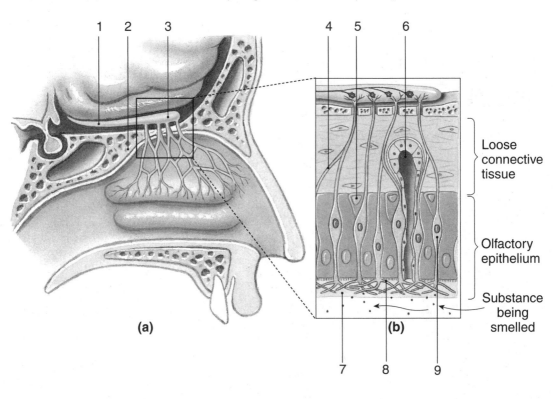

1. _____   6. _____

2. _____   7. _____

3. _____   8. _____

4. _____   9. _____

5. _____

OBJECTIVE 4 Discuss the receptors and processes involved in the sense of taste.

_____ 1. Most of the taste buds on the surface of the tongue are associated with

       a. large gustatory cilia.

       b. umami and water receptors.

       c. small cupula and macular papillae.

       d. large circumvallate papillae.

_____ 2. Taste buds are monitored by cranial nerves

       a. VII, IX, and X.

       b. IV, V, and VI.

       c. I, II, and III.

       d. VIII, XI, and XII.

_____ 3. After synapsing in the thalamus, gustatory information is transmitted to the appropriate portion of

       a. the medulla.

       b. the medial lemniscus.

       c. the primary sensory cortex.

       d. cranial nerves VII, IX, and X.

_____ 4. The sensation of taste is due to receptors called

       a. papillae.

       b. gustatory cells.

       c. taste buds.

       d. taste pores.

Labeling Exercise

Identify and label the following structures in Figure 9-2. Place the answers in the spaces provided below the drawings.

sweet taste

bitter taste

stratified squamous epithelium

salty taste

taste buds

cranial nerve fibers

gustatory cell

sour taste

taste hairs

transitional cell

FIGURE 9-2 Gustatory Reception

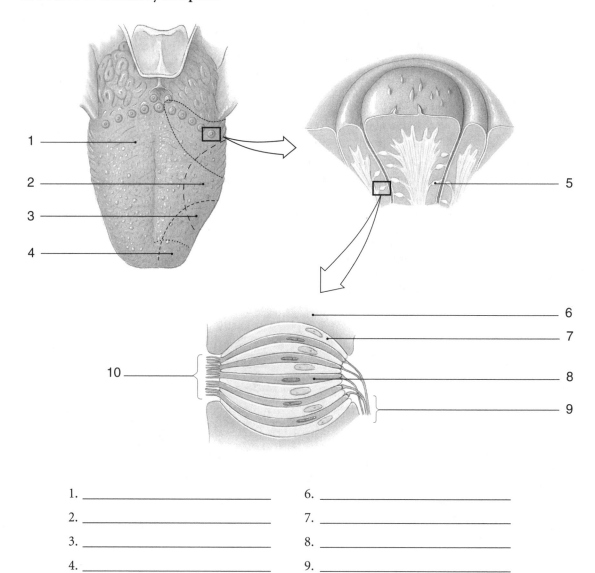

1. _____

2. _____

3. _____

4. _____

5. _____

6. _____

7. _____

8. _____

9. _____

10. _____

OBJECTIVE 5   Identify the parts of the eye and their functions.

_____ 1. The large posterior cavity of the hollow eyeball contains the

      a. aqueous humor.
      b. lacrimal fluid.
      c. vitreous body.
      d. orbital fat.

_____ 2. The fibrous tunic, the outermost layer covering the eye, consists of the

      a. iris and choroid.
      b. pupil and ciliary body.
      c. sclera and cornea.
      d. lacrimal sac and orbital fat.

_____ 3. The vascular tunic consists of three distinct structures that include the

      a. iris, ciliary body, and choroid.
      b. sclera, cornea, and iris.
      c. choroid, pupil, and lacrimal sac.
      d. retina, cornea, and iris.

_____ 4. The function of the vitreous body in the eye is to

      a. provide a fluid cushion that protects the eye.
      b. serve as a route for nutrient and waste transport.
      c. maintain the shape of the eye and give physical support to the retina.
      d. serve as a medium for cleansing the inner eye.

_____ 5. The primary function of the lens of the eye is to

      a. absorb light as it passes through the retina.
      b. biochemically interact with the photoreceptors of the retina.
      c. focus the visual image on the photoreceptors.
      d. integrate visual information for the retina.

_____ 6. When looking directly at an object, its image falls upon the portion of the retina called the ,

      a. fovea centralis.
      b. choroid layer.
      c. sclera.
      d. focal point.

_____ 7. The center of color vision and the site of sharpest vision is the

      a. macula lutea.
      b. rods.
      c. bipolar cells.
      d. fovea centralis.

_____ 8. The most detailed information about a visual image is provided by the

      a. cones.
      b. rods.
      c. optic disc.
      d. rods and cones.

9. Most of the ocular surface of the eye is covered by the _____.

10. The opening surrounded by the iris is called the _____.

11. The photoreceptors that enable us to see in dimly lit rooms, at twilight, or in pale moonlight are the _____.

12. The photoreceptors that account for the perception of color are the _____.

13. Visual information is integrated in the cortical area of the _____ lobe.

Labeling Exercises

Identify and label the following structures in Figure 9-3. Place the answers in the spaces below the drawing.

vitreous humor	suspensory ligament	retina	iris
fovea centralis	aqueous humor	optic nerve	ciliary body
lens	cornea	choroid coat	sclera
optic disc			

FIGURE 9-3 Anatomy of the Eye

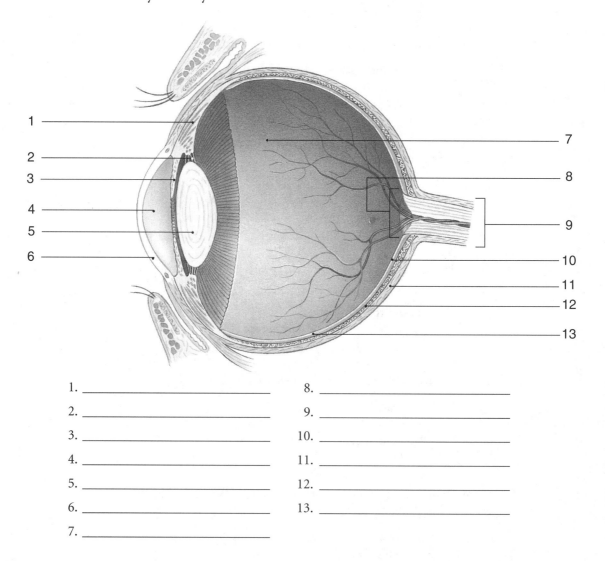

1. _____   8. _____

2. _____   9. _____

3. _____   10. _____

4. _____   11. _____

5. _____   12. _____

6. _____   13. _____

7. _____

Identify and label the following structures in Figure 9-4. Place the answers in the spaces below the drawing.

superior oblique   inferior oblique   superior rectus

lateral rectus   inferior rectus

FIGURE 9-4 Extrinsic Eye Muscles

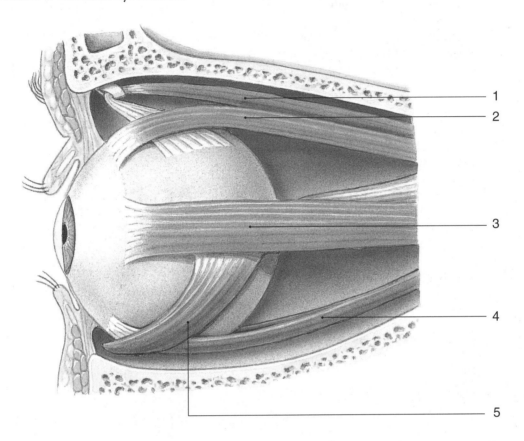

1. _____   4. _____

2. _____   5. _____

3. _____

OBJECTIVE 6 Explain how we are able to see objects and distinguish colors.

_____ 1. When the cones in the retina are stimulated, the result is

        a. the ability to see in dim light.
        b. the ability to distinguish patterned images.
        c. perception of colors.
        d. accommodation.

_____ 2. The area of the retina that contains a high concentration of cones and is the site of sharpest vision is the

        a. iris.
        b. fovea centralis.
        c. optic disc.
        d. neural tunic.

_____ 3. The rods are the photoreceptors that enable us to see

        a. in dimly lit rooms or pale moonlight.
        b. in color.
        c. sharp, clear images.
        d. in bright light.

_____ 4. The "blind spot" in the retina occurs where

        a. ganglion cells synapse with bipolar cells.
        b. rod cells cluster to form the macula.
        c. the optic nerve attaches to the retina.
        d. there is an accumulation of amacrine cells.

_____ 5. Light absorption requires the presence of

        a. neurotransmitters.
        b. visual pigments.
        c. rods and cones.
        d. vitamin A.

_____ 6. The _____ changes in diameter in response to the intensity of light entering the eye. Light is necessary to activate the cells of the _____.

        a. lens; retina
        b. pupil; optic disc
        c. retina; pupil
        d. pupil; retina

7. The muscles of the eye responsible for changing the diameter of the pupil are contained in the _____.

8. Nearsightedness, or being able to see "up close," is called _____.

9. The absence of rods in the retina is apparent in a region called the _____.

10. The process of focusing an image on the retina by changing the shape of the lens is called _____.

Labeling Exercise

Identify and label the following structures in Figure 9-5. Place the answers in the spaces provided below the drawing.

amacrine cell   cone   pigment layer of retina

ganglion cells   horizontal cell   rod

bipolar cells

FIGURE 9-5 Cellular Organization of the Retina

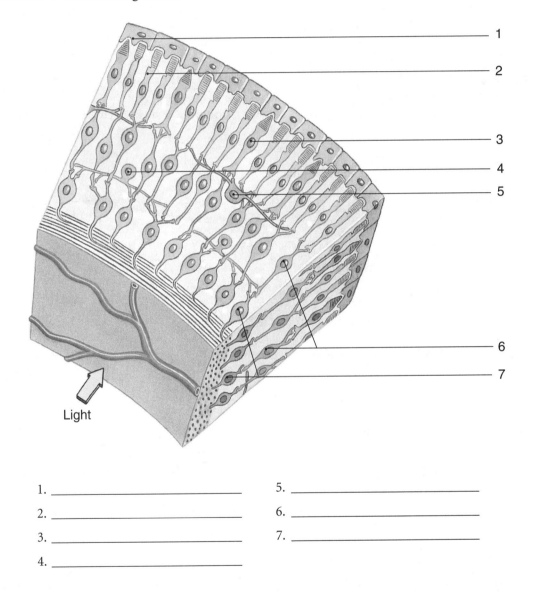

Light

1. _____   5. _____

2. _____   6. _____

3. _____   7. _____

4. _____

OBJECTIVE 7   Discuss how the central nervous system processes information related to vision.

_____ 1. Axons converge on the optic disk, penetrate the wall of the eye, and proceed toward the

        a. retina at the posterior part of the eye.

        b. diencephalon at the optic nerve (N II).

        c. retinal processing areas below the choroid coat.

        d. cerebral cortex area of the parietal lobes.

_____ 2. The sensation of vision arises from the integration of information arriving at the

        a. lateral geniculate of the left side.
        b. lateral geniculate of the right side.
        c. visual cortex of the cerebrum.
        d. reflex centers in the brain.

_____ 3. Visual input from the hypothalamus and pineal gland establish a daily pattern of activity called _____, which is tied to the day-night cycle.

        a. the biological time clock
        b. visual photoreception
        c. crossover charisma
        d. circadian rhythm

OBJECTIVE 8   Discuss the receptors and processes involved in the sense of equilibrium.

_____ 1. The branch of cranial nerves responsible for monitoring changes in equilibrium is the _____ branch.

        a. cochlear
        b. vestibular
        c. auditory
        d. trigeminal

_____ 2. The sense of equilibrium and hearing are provided by receptors in the

        a. external ear.
        b. middle ear.
        c. inner ear.
        d. All of the above are correct.

_____ 3. All equilibrium sensations are provided by hair cells of the

        a. cochlea.
        b. vestibular complex.
        c. organ of Corti.
        d. auditory ossicles.

_____ 4. The parts of the vestibular complex that provide information about your position with respect to gravity are the

        a. malleus and stapes.
        b. vestibular and tympanic ducts.
        c. oval and round windows.
        d. saccule and utricle.

_____ 5. Equilibrium is achieved when the fluid in the

        a. ear moves, and a signal is sent to the brain via the cochlear branch of CN VIII.
        b. cochlea moves, and a signal is sent to the brain via CN VIII.
        c. cochlea moves, and a signal is sent to the brain via the vestibular portion of CN VIII.
        d. semicircular canals move, and a signal is sent via CN VIII.

_____ 6. The structures that monitor dynamic equilibrium, which aids in maintaining balance when the head and body are moved suddenly, are the

    a. saccules and utricles.
    b. cochlear ducts.
    c. semicircular ducts.
    d. auditory ossicles.

OBJECTIVE 9   Describe the parts of the ear and their roles in the process of hearing.

_____ 1. The structure that provides the surface for sound collection is the

    a. tympanic membrane.
    b. oval window.
    c. basilar membrane.
    d. vestibular duct.

_____ 2. In the middle ear, sound waves vibrate the _____, which converts sound energy into mechanical movements of the ossicles, which consist sequentially of the _____.

    a. oval window; malleus, incus, and stapes
    b. round window; malleus, incus, and stapes
    c. tympanum; stapes, incus, and malleus
    d. tympanum; malleus, incus, and stapes

_____ 3. The receptors that provide the sensation of hearing are located in the

    a. vestibular complex.
    b. cochlea.
    c. ampulla.
    d. tympanic membrane.

_____ 4. The number of hair cells responding in a given region of the organ of Corti provides information on the

    a. sense of position and movement.
    b. frequency of the perceived sound.
    c. intensity of the sound.
    d. pitch of the sound.

_____ 5. The dividing line between the external ear and middle ear is the

    a. pharyngotympanic tube.
    b. tympanic membrane.
    c. round window.
    d. oval window.

_____ 6. The structure in the cochlea of the inner ear that provides information to the CNS is the

    a. scala tympani.
    b. tectorial membrane.
    c. organ of Corti.
    d. basilar membrane.

_____ 7. The fluid in the vestibular and tympanic ducts that is affected by sound vibrations is

   a. endolymph.
   b. ceruminal fluid.
   c. perilymph.
   d. lymphoid fluid.

Labeling Exercise

Identify and label the following structures of the ear. Place the answers in the spaces provided below the drawing.

middle ear	outer ear	inner ear
malleus	pinna	incus
vestibular complex	stapes	temporal bone
vestibulocochlear nerve	cochlea	bony labyrinth
auditory tube	tympanum	external auditory canal

FIGURE 9-6 Anatomy of the Ear

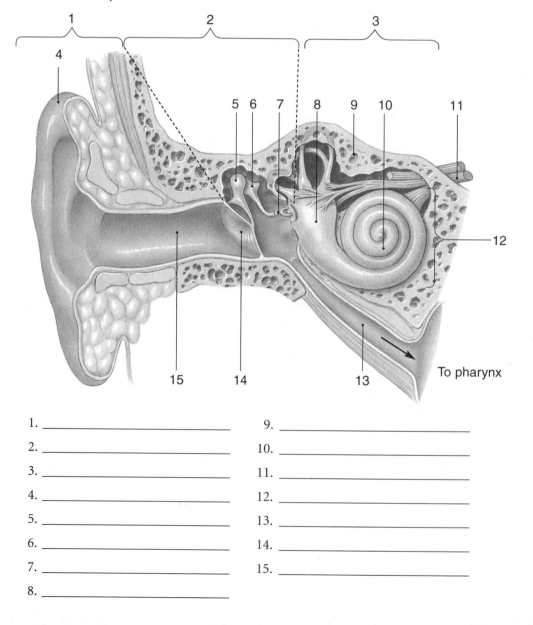

1. _____   9. _____

2. _____   10. _____

3. _____   11. _____

4. _____   12. _____

5. _____   13. _____

6. _____   14. _____

7. _____   15. _____

8. _____

OBJECTIVE 10   Describe the effects of aging on smell, taste, vision, and hearing.

_____ 1. Elderly individuals have difficulty detecting odors in low concentrations because

      a. the muscous membranes become thin.
      b. the membranes of the nose lose their elasticity.
      c. the number of olfactory cells declines with age.
      d. the population of olfactory cells increases with age.

_____ 2. If elderly induviduals are to be able to smell their own perfume or aftershave, they must

      a. buy strong, expensive scents.
      b. apply excessive amounts to their skin.
      c. increase the conduction of motor action potentials
      d. increase the abundance of stereocilia from the nasal hair cells.

_____ 3. Tasting abilities change with age due to the

      a. purchase of bland food by the elderly.
      b. lack of nutritional information by the elderly.
      c. increase of mucosal tissue covering the taste buds.
      d. thinning of mucous membranes and reduction in the number and sensitivity of taste buds.

_____ 4. The most common visual disorders associated with normal aging involve the

      a. lens and the neural part of the retina.
      b. vitreous and aqueous humor.
      c. accessory structures of the eye.
      d. bipolar and ganglion cells.

_____ 5. The most common cause of senile cataracts is

      a. the gradual loss of rods and cones.
      b. macular degeneration.
      c. advancing age.
      d. excessive vascular growth.

_____ 6. The leading cause of blindness in individuals over 50 is

      a. macular degeneration.
      b. senile cataracts.
      c. deterioration of the rods and cones.
      d. extreme changes in lens transparency.

_____ 7. The inability of the elderly to see objects up close due to the inelasticity and stiffening of the lens results in a condition called

      a. nearsightedness.
      b. presbyopia.
      c. myopia.
      d. presbycusis.

_____ 8. The progressive loss of hearing that occurs with aging is called

      a. presbyopia.

      b. tympanisopia.

      c. nystagonus.

      d. presbycusis.

Part II: Chapter Comprehensive Exercises

A. Word Elimination

Circle the term that does not belong in each of the following groupings.

1. smell   taste   touch   hearing   vision

2. temperature   pain   pressure   balance   vibration

3. nociceptors   stereoreceptors   thermoreceptors   chemoreceptors   mechanoreceptors

4. cornea   eyelids   conjunctiva   lacrimal gland   extrinsic eye muscles

5. rods   cones   bipolar cells   choroid   ganglion cells

6. emmetropia   propriopia   myopia   hyperopia   presbyopia

7. tympanum   malleus   incus   stapes

8. tectorial membrane   basilar membrane   hair cells   nerve fibers   otolith

9. optic nerve   auditory tube   optic tract   projection fibers   occipital lobes

10. rhodopsin   retinal   opsin   cerumen   vitamin A

B. Matching

Match the terms in Column "B" with the terms in Column "A." Write letters for answers in the spaces provided.

COLUMN A	COLUMN B
___ 1. tactile discs	a. deep pressure receptors
___ 2. Meissner's corpuscles	b. pleasant taste response
___ 3. Pacinian corpuscles	c. sclera
___ 4. Ruffini corpuscles	d. earwax
___ 5. "white of the eye"	e. tears
___ 6. umami	f. Merkel's cells
___ 7. eyelids	g. elevated eye pressure
___ 8. lacrimal gland	h. fine touch and pressure
___ 9. cerumen	i. palpebrae
___10. glaucoma	j. skin distortion sensitivity

C. Concept Map I - Special Senses

Using the following terms, fill in the circled numbered, blank spaces to complete the concept map.
Follow the numbers that comply with the organization of the map.

Retina

Olfaction

Ears

Hearing

Balance and hearing

Taste buds

Rods and cones

Smell

Tongue

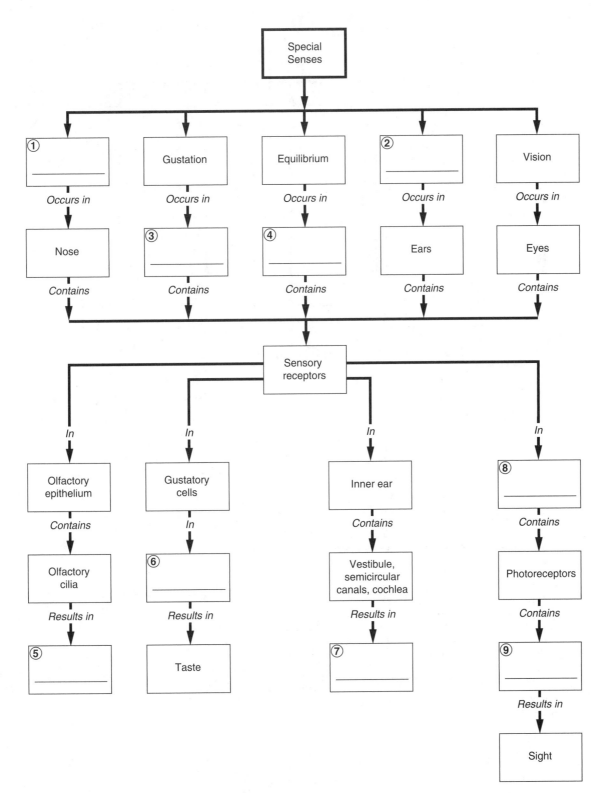

Concept Map II - General Senses

Using the following terms, fill in the circled numbered, blank spaces to complete the concept map. Follow the numbers that comply with the organization of the map.

Pacinian corpuscles   Aortic sinus   Muscle spindles   Pressure

Proprioception   Merkel's discs   Pain   Dendritic processes

Thermoreceptors   Tactile   Baroreceptors

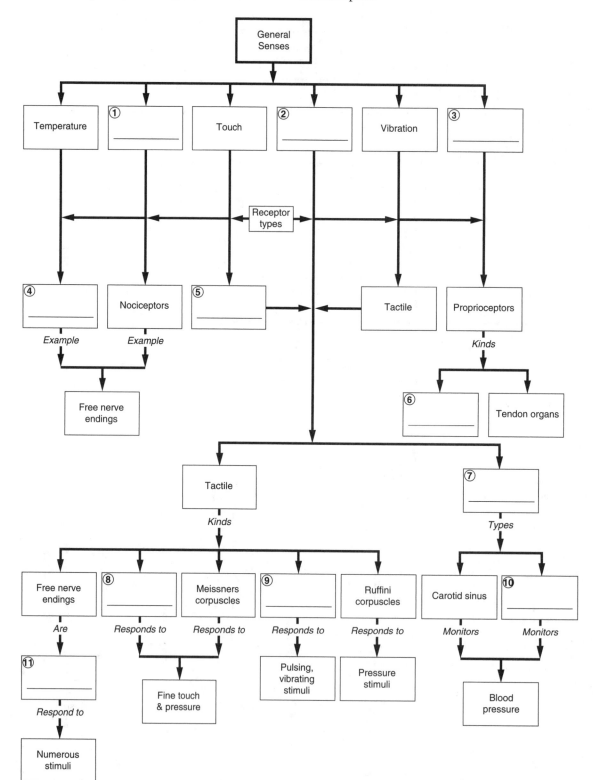

D. Crossword Puzzle

The following crossword puzzle reviews the material in Chapter 9. To complete the puzzle, you must know the answers to the clues given, and you must be able to spell the terms correctly.

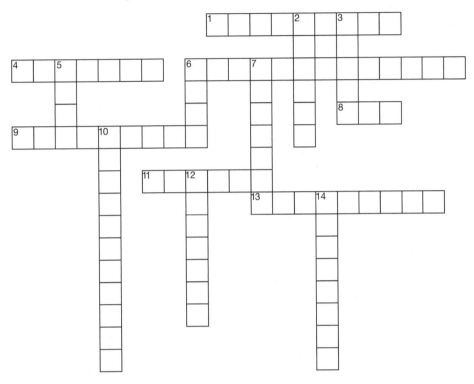

ACROSS

1. The portion of the retina where the optic nerve exits the eye (two words).
4. The name of earwax.
6. Rods and cones are a type of sensory receptor called a _____.
8. An infection of the lacrimal gland.
9. The process of tasting food.
11. A cranial nerve involved in taste.
13. The fluid in the semicircular canals.

DOWN

2. The transparent portion of the sclera.
3. The second ossicle involved in the sequence of transmitting sound waves.
5. The cells of the retina that cannot detect color.
6. _____ receptors are sensory nerve cells called free nerve endings.
7. Sensory receptors involved with touch.
10. Irregularities in the shape of the lens.
12. The location of the organ of Corti.
14. The three smallest bones of the body, which are located in the middle ear.

E. Short-Answer Questions

Briefly answer the following questions in the spaces provided.

1. What sensations are included as general senses?

2. What sensations are included as special senses?

3. What four kinds of "general sense" receptors are found throughout the body, and to what kind(s) of stimuli do they respond?

4. What is the functional difference between a baroreceptor and a proprioceptor?

5. Trace an olfactory sensation from the time it leaves the olfactory bulb until it reaches its final destinations in the higher centers of the brain.

6. What are the four primary taste sensations?

7. What sensations are provided by the saccule and utricle in the vestibule of the inner ear?

8. What are the three primary functions of the fibrous tunic, which consists of the sclera and the cornea?

9. What are the three primary functions of the vascular tunic, which consists of the iris, the ciliary body, and the choroid?

10. What are the primary functions of the neural tunic, which consists of an outer pigment layer and an inner retina that contains the visual receptors and associated neurons?

11. When referring to the eye, what is the purpose of accommodation, and how does it work?

10

The Endocrine System

Overview

Along with the nervous system, the endocrine system plays an important role in maintaining homeostasis by monitoring and regulating the activity of cells throughout the body. Chemical messengers, called hormones, orchestrate ongoing and long-term cellular changes in target tissues throughout the body. The influence of these chemical messengers results in facilitating processes that include growth and development, sexual maturation and reproduction, and the maintenance of homeostasis of many body systems.

To simplify the study of the endocrine system, ask and answer the following questions:
- Where is the endocrine gland located in the body?
- What hormone(s) does the gland secrete?
- What is the hormone's target organ in the body?
- What effect does the hormone have on the body?
- What are the consequences of the hormone's hyper- or hyposecretion?

Chapter 10 tests your knowledge of the endocrine organs and their functions, and it presents opportunities for you to affirm your understanding of the effects of endocrine activity within the body.

Review of Chapter Objectives

1. Compare the similarities between the endocrine and nervous systems.
2. Compare the major chemical classes of hormones.
3. Explain the general mechanisms of hormonal action.
4. Describe how endocrine organs are controlled.
5. Discuss the location, hormones, and functions of the following endocrine glands and tissues: pituitary gland, thyroid gland, parathyroid glands, adrenal glands, pineal gland, pancreas, kidneys, heart, thymus gland, testes, ovaries, and adipose tissue.
6. Explain how hormones interact to produce coordinated physiological responses.
7. Identify the hormones that are especially important to normal growth, and discuss their roles.
8. Explain how the endocrine system responds to stress.
9. Discuss the results of abnormal hormone production.
10. Discuss the functional relationships between the endocrine system and other body systems.

Part I: Objective-Based Questions

OBJECTIVE 1   Compare the similarities between the endocrine and nervous systems.

_____ 1. Coordination by the nervous and endocrine systems results in

   a. cellular communication over greater distances.
   b. regulation by negative feedback control mechanisms.
   c. release of chemicals that bind to specific receptors on target cells.
   d. all of the above.

_____ 2. An example of a functional similarity between the nervous system and the endocrine system is

   a. both systems secrete hormones into the bloodstream.
   b. the cells of the endocrine system and nervous system are functionally the same.
   c. compounds used as hormones by the endocrine system may also function as neurotransmitters inside the CNS.
   d. both produce very specific responses to environmental stimuli.

_____ 3. The coordinating centers that regulate the activities of the nervous and endocrine systems are in the

   a. pituitary gland.
   b. hypothalamus.
   c. medulla oblongata.
   d. cerebrum.

_____ 4. The chemical messengers in the endocrine system are called _____; those in the nervous system are called _____.

   a. neurotransmitters; hormones
   b. steroids; eicosanoids
   c. hormones; neurotransmitters
   d. neurotransmitters; eicosanoids

OBJECTIVE 2   Compare the major chemical classes of hormones.

_____ 1. Peptide hormones consist of chains of

   a. glucose molecules.
   b. fatty acids.
   c. polysaccharides.
   d. amino acids.

_____ 2. Steroid hormones are derived from

   a. prostaglandins.
   b. cholesterol.
   c. arachidonic acid.
   d. muscle tissue.

_____ 3. Epinephrine, norepinephrine, melatonin, and the thyroid hormones are small

      a. peptide hormones.
      b. steroids and eicosanoids.
      c. amino acid derivatives.
      d. lipid derivatives.

_____ 4. Steroid hormones are released by the

      a. adrenal glands and reproductive organs.
      b. pituitary gland and thymus.
      c. thyroid and parathyroid glands.
      d. All of the above are correct.

OBJECTIVE 3   Explain the general mechanisms of hormonal action.

_____ 1. A cell's hormonal sensitivities are determined by the

      a. chemical nature of the hormone.
      b. quantity of circulating hormone.
      c. shape of the hormone molecule.
      d. presence or absence of specific receptors.

_____ 2. Hormones alter cellular operations by changing the

      a. cell membrane permeability properties.
      b. identities, activities, quantities, or properties of important enzymes.
      c. arrangement of the molecular complex of the cell membrane.
      d. rate at which hormones affect target cells.

_____ 3. The net result of the function of a second messenger in hormonal action is

      a. to produce a G-protein enzyme complex.
      b. to activate specific genes in the nucleus.
      c. an increase in the mitochondrial rates of ATP production.
      d. a change in the cell's metabolic activities.

_____ 4. Steroid hormones affect target organ cells by

      a. targeting receptors in peripheral tissues.
      b. releasing second messengers at cell membrane receptors.
      c. binding to receptors in the cell membrane.
      d. binding to target receptors in the cytoplasm or nucleus.

_____ 5. When adenyl cyclase is activated,

      a. cyclic AMP is formed.
      b. cyclic AMP is broken down.
      c. steroids are produced.
      d. protein kinases are metabolized.

_____ 6. The target organ of a hormone is the

    a. origin of the hormone.
    b. stimulus that has caused the release of the hormone.
    c. site of the hormone's destination.
    d. production site of the hormone.

OBJECTIVE 4   Describe how endocrine organs are controlled.

_____ 1. The basis of control for endocrine activity is provided by

    a. increased metabolic activity.
    b. negative feedback mechanisms.
    c. the nervous system.
    d. all of the above.

_____ 2. The hypothalamus secretes regulatory hormones that control the activity of endocrine cells in the

    a. anterior pituitary gland.
    b. adrenal glands.
    c. pancreas.
    d. thyroid gland.

_____ 3. The two hormones synthesized by the hypothalamus that are released into the circulation at the posterior pituitary gland are

    a. testosterone and estrogen.
    b. TSH and ACTH.
    c. ADH and oxytocin.
    d. FSH and prolactin.

_____ 4. Hormones modify cellular activities by

    a. altering membrane permeability.
    b. activating or inactivating key enzymes.
    c. changing genetic activity.
    d. doing all of the above.

_____ 5. The gland that is activated when blood calcium ion levels are too high is the

    a. hypothalamus.
    b. thyroid.
    c. pituitary.
    d. parathyroid.

_____ 6. If blood calcium ion levels become too low, the hormone that will appear in higher concentrations in the blood is

    a. calcitonin.
    b. thyroxin.
    c. antidiuretic hormone.
    d. parathyroid hormone.

OBJECTIVE 5 Discuss the location, hormones, and functions of the following endocrine glands and tissues: pituitary gland, thyroid gland, parathyroid glands, adrenal glands, pineal gland, pancreas, kidneys, heart, thymus gland, testes, ovaries, and adipose tissue.

1. ADH and oxytocin are secreted by the _____ gland.

2. The hormone that initiates uterine contractions is _____.

3. The pituitary hormone that controls the release of glucocorticoids from the adrenal cortex is _____.

4. The pituitary hormone that promotes egg development in ovaries, and sperm development in testes, is _____.

5. The pituitary hormone that stimulates melanocytes to produce melanin is

    _____.

6. The C cells of the thyroid gland produce _____.

7. Thyroid hormone contains the mineral _____.

8. The glands responsible for producing a hormone that increases the level of calcium ions in the blood are the _____ glands.

9. The gland responsible for the calorigenic effect is the _____.

10. The adrenal medulla produces _____.

11. Cells of the adrenal cortex produce _____.

12. Calcitrol, erythropoietin, and renin are hormones released by the _____.

13. The hormone ANP, which lowers blood volume, is released by the _____.

14. When blood glucose levels rise, insulin is secreted and released by the _____.

15. The alpha cells of the pancreas produce the hormone _____.

16. Testosterone and inhibin are hormones produced by cells in the _____.

17. When stimulated by FSH, follicle cells in the ovary produce large quantities of

    _____.

18. The gland that is believed to be involved with the establishment and maintenance of circadian rhythms is the _____ gland.

Labeling Exercises

Identify and label the endocrine organs and tissues in Figure 10-1. Place your answers in the spaces provided below the drawing.

testis   thyroid   thymus

adrenals   hypothalamus   parathyroids

pancreas   ovary   atria (heart)

pituitary   pineal

FIGURE 10-1 The Endocrine System

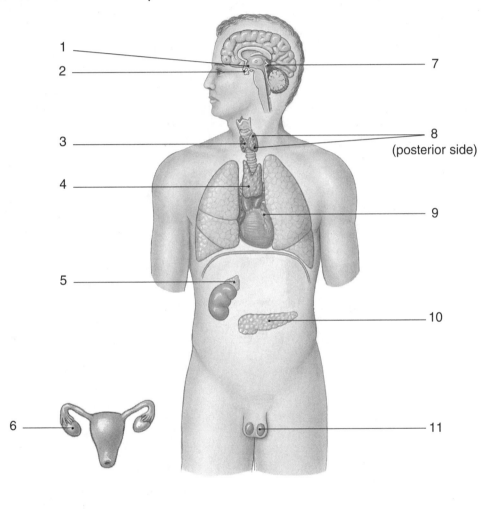

1. _____   7. _____

2. _____   8. _____

3. _____   9. _____

4. _____   10. _____

5. _____   11. _____

6. _____

Labeling Exercises, continued

In Figure 10-2, identify the pituitary secretions in column A, and identify the actions of those pituitary secretions in column B.

FIGURE 10-2 Pituitary Secretions, Hormones, Their Targets, and Actions

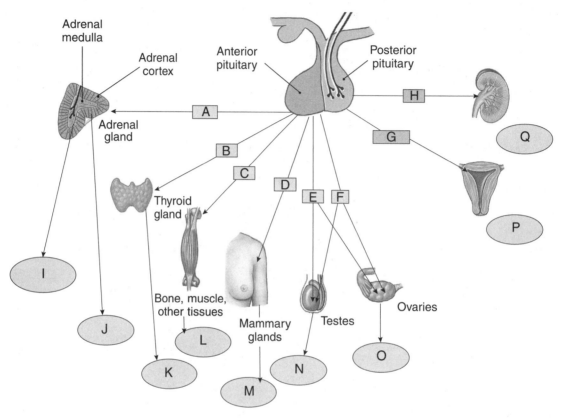

A

Hormones released from the pituitary gland (letters A through H)

____ 1. adrenocorticotropic hormone

____ 2. antidiuretic hormone

____ 3. follicle-stimulating hormone

____ 4. growth hormone

____ 5. luteinizing hormone

____ 6. oxytocin

____ 7. prolactin

____ 8. thyroid-stimulating hormone

B

Actions due to the pituitary secretions (letters I through Q)

____ 9. causes bone growth

____ 10. causes milk production

____ 11. causes the release of thyroid hormones

____ 12. causes the release of epinephrine

____ 13. causes the release of glucocorticoids

____ 14. causes the release of testosterone

____ 15. causes the retention of water

____ 16. causes the release of progesterone

____ 17. causes uterine contractions

OBJECTIVE 6   Explain how hormones interact to produce coordinated physiological responses.

_____ 1. When a cell receives instructions from two different hormones at the same time, the results may be

      a. antagonistic or synergistic.
      b. permissive.
      c. integrative.
      d. all of the above.

_____ 2. If one hormone has a permissive effect on another, the

      a. first hormone is needed for the second to produce its effect.
      b. hormones produce different but complementary results in specific tissues.
      c. two hormones have opposing effects.
      d. two hormones have additive effects.

_____ 3. The hormone that is the antagonist of insulin is

      a. calcitonin.
      b. glucagon.
      c. adrenalin.
      d. aldosterone.

_____ 4. Stimulation of mammary gland development by prolactin, estrogens, and GH is an example of the _____ effect.

      a. antagonistic
      b. synergistic
      c. permissive
      d. integrative

OBJECTIVE 7   Identify the hormones that are especially important to normal growth, and discuss their roles.

_____ 1. The important hormones for normal growth include

      a. growth hormone, LH, ADH, and parathormone.
      b. insulin, prolactin, ADH, and MSH.
      c. thyroid hormones, TSH, ACTH, insulin, and LH.
      d. growth hormone, thyroid hormones, insulin, parathyroid, and reproductive hormones.

_____ 2. The reason insulin is important to normal growth is that it promotes

      a. changes in skeletal proportions and calcium deposition in the body.
      b. the passage of glucose and amino acids across cell membranes.
      c. muscular development via protein synthesis.
      d. all of the above.

_____ 3. Undersecretion of growth hormone can lead to

         a. gigantism.

         b. pituitary dwarfism.

         c. cretinism.

         d. all of the above.

OBJECTIVE 8   Explain how the endocrine system responds to stress.

_____ 1. Physical or emotional conditions that threaten homeostasis are forms of

         a. stress.

         b. hormonal adjustments.

         c. physiological responses.

         d. resistance patterns.

_____ 2. The alarm phase of the general adaptation syndrome (GAS) is under the direction of the

         a. somatic nervous system (SNS).

         b. parasympathetic division of the ANS.

         c. sympathetic division of the ANS.

         d. Both b and c are correct.

_____ 3. The dominant hormone during the alarm phase is

         a. epinephrine.

         b. aldosterone.

         c. insulin.

         d. growth hormone.

_____ 4. The dominant hormones of the resistance phase of the GAS are

         a. mineralocorticoids.

         b. glucocorticoids.

         c. gonadal hormones.

         d. pancreatic hormones.

_____ 5. The exhaustive phase of the GAS begins when

         a. energy reserves are mobilized.

         b. the body prepares to escape from the source of stress.

         c. homeostatic regulation breaks down.

         d. increases in heart and respiratory rates occur.

OBJECTIVE 9   Discuss the results of abnormal hormone production.

_____ 1. Excessive secretion of growth hormone prior to puberty will cause

         a. dwarfism.

         b. gigantism.

         c. acromegaly.

         d. diabetes.

_____ 2. The inability of the pancreas to produce insulin results in

      a. acromegaly.
      b. cretinism.
      c. diabetes mellitus.
      d. diabetes insipidus.

_____ 3. Hyposecretion of glucocorticoids results in

      a. Addison's disease.
      b. Cushing's disease.
      c. diabetes insipidus.
      d. goiter.

_____ 4. Increased aggressive behavior is associated with increased secretion of

      a. progesterone.
      b. growth hormone.
      c. mineralocorticoids.
      d. testosterone.

OBJECTIVE 10   Discuss the functional relationships between the endocrine system and other body systems.

1. The system that controls the adrenal medulla and secretes ADH and oxytocin is the

    _____system.

2. The system that distributes hormones throughout the body is the _____

    system.

3. The system that includes the endocrine cells of the pancreas, which secrete insulin and

    glucagon, is the _____ system.

4. The system that releases renin and erythropoietin and produces calcitrol is the

    _____ system.

5. The system primarily affected by endocrine hormones that affect energy production and

    growth is the _____ system.

Part II: Chapter Comprehensive Exercises

A. Word Elimination

Circle the term that does not belong in each of the following groupings.

1. hypothalamus   prostate   pituitary   thyroid   pineal

2. adrenalin   norepinephrine   thyroxine   keratin   melatonin

3. ACTH   GH   PTH   FSH   LH

4. estrogen   testosterone   progesterone   inhibin   elastin

5. aldosterone   cortisol   hydrocortisone   corticosterone   cortisone

6. calcitrol   erythropoietin   renin   hemoglobin   angiotensin II

7. alpha cells   glucagon   beta cells   insulin   calcitonin

8. testes   follicles   estrogen   corpus luteum   progesterone

9. growth hormone   melatonin   insulin   thyroid hormone   gonadal hormones

10. exhaustion   alarm   GAS   resistance   permissive

B. Matching

Match the terms in Column "B" with the terms in Column "A." Write letters for answers in the spaces provided.

COLUMN A	COLUMN B
____ 1. prostaglandin	a. cyclic AMP
____ 2. thymus	b. produces leptin and resistin
____ 3. second messenger	c. milk letdown
____ 4. pituitary gland	d. red blood cell production
____ 5. adipose tissue	e. eicosanoid
____ 6. prolactin	f. produce calcitonin
____ 7. oxytocin	g. milk production
____ 8. C cells	h. development of immunity
____ 9. erythropoietin	i. melatonin
____10. pineal gland	j. hypophysis

C. Concept Map I - Endocrine Glands

Using the following terms, fill in the circled numbered, blank spaces to complete the concept map. Follow the numbers that comply with the organization of the map.

Male/female gonads

Pineal

Testosterone

Peptide hormones

Pituitary

Hormones

Heart

Epinephrine

Bloodstream

Parathyroids

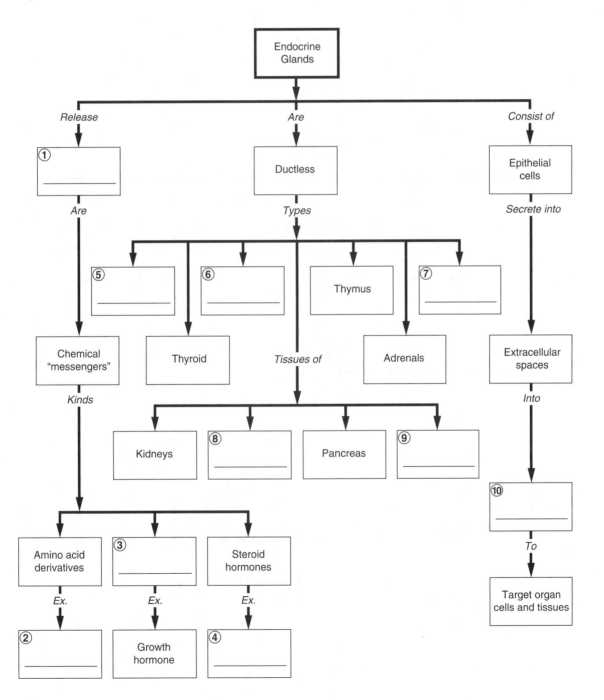

Concept Map II - Endocrine System Functions

Using the following terms, fill in the circled numbered, blank spaces to complete the concept map. Follow the numbers that comply with the organization of the map.

Homeostasis

Target cells

Ion channel opening

Hormones

Contraction

Cellular communication

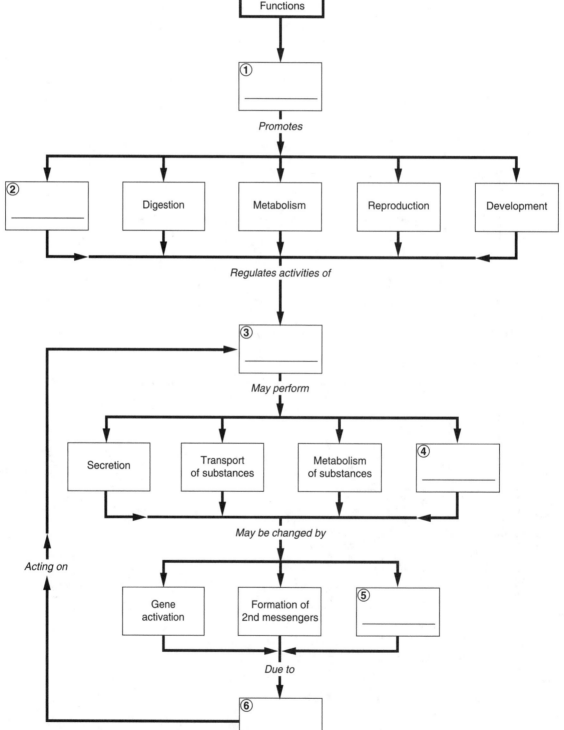

D. Crossword Puzzle

The following crossword puzzle reviews the material in Chapter 10. To complete the puzzle, you must know the answers to the clues given, and must be able to spell the terms correctly.

ACROSS

4. A hormone that prevents the loss of sodium ions.
5. A hormone produced by adipose cells.
7. A hormone that prepares the body for pregnancy.
8. A hormone involved in secondary sex characteristics in males.
10. A hormone involved in secondary sex characteristics in females.
13. A dietary ingredient necessary to make thyroxine.

DOWN

1. A steroid hormone that reduces inflammation.
2. After a hormone leaves a gland, it travels to a(n) _____ organ.
3. The _____ is both an endocrine organ and an exocrine organ.
4. A hormone that causes the loss of sodium ions.
6. A type of gland that secretes hormones into the blood.
9. The hormone that lowers blood glucose levels.
11. The hormone that raises blood glucose levels.
12. A gland involved with the immune system.

E. Short-Answer Questions

Briefly answer the following questions in the spaces provided.

1. What three mechanisms does the hypothalamus use to regulate the activities of the nervous and endocrine systems?

2. What hypothalamic control mechanisms are used to effect endocrine activity in the anterior pituitary?

3. How does the calorigenic effect of thyroid hormones help us adapt to cold temperatures?

4. How does the kidney hormone erythropoietin cause an increase in blood pressure?

5. How do you explain the relationship between the pineal gland and circadian rhythms?

6. What are the possible results when a cell receives instructions from two different hormones at the same time?

The Cardiovascular System: Blood

Overview

Blood is a specialized fluid connective tissue consisting of two basic components: (1) the formed elements (including blood cells and cell fragments) and (2) the fluid plasma, in which the formed elements are carried. The blood is a greater part of a transportation system that supplies every cell in the body with a continuous supply of vital nutrients and oxygen, and provides the means by which the body disposes of metabolic wastes. The life-sustaining blood makes up approximately 7 percent of the body's total weight and serves to maintain the integrity of cells by regulating the pH and electrolyte composition of interstitial cells throughout the body. It also defends against toxins and pathogens and helps stabilize body temperature.

The exercises in Chapter 11 provide opportunities for you to identify and study the components of blood, and to understand the functional roles of the blood in providing essential homeostatic services to the trillions of human body cells. The phases of the homeostatic process, along with clinical notes citing clotting abnormalities, are also considered.

Review of Chapter Objectives

1. Describe the important components and major functions of blood.
2. Discuss the composition and functions of plasma.
3. Describe the origin and production of the formed elements in blood.
4. Discuss the characteristics and functions of red blood cells.
5. Explain the factors that determine a person's blood type, and why blood types are important.
6. Categorize the various white blood cells on the basis of their structure and functions.
7. Describe the mechanisms that reduce blood loss after an injury.

Part I: Objective-Based Questions

OBJECTIVE 1   Describe the important components and major functions of blood.

_____ 1. The formed elements of the blood consist of

a. antibodies, metalloproteins, and lipoproteins.
b. red and white blood cells, and platelets.
c. albumins, globulins, and fibrinogen.
d. electrolytes, nutrients, and organic wastes.

_____ 2. Loose connective tissue and cartilage contain a network of insoluble fibers, whereas plasma, a fluid connective tissue, contains

a. dissolved proteins.
b. a network of collagen and elastic fibers.
c. elastic fibers only.
d. collagen fibers only.

_____ 3. Blood transports dissolved gases, bringing oxygen from the lungs to the tissues and carrying

a. carbon dioxide from the lungs to the tissues.
b. carbon dioxide from one peripheral cell to another.
c. carbon dioxide from the interstitial fluid to the cell.
d. carbon dioxide from the tissues to the lungs.

_____ 4. The "patrol agents" in the blood that defend the body against toxins and pathogens are

a. hormones and enzymes.
b. albumins and globulins.
c. white blood cells and antibodies.
d. red blood cells and platelets.

_____ 5. The unique composition of whole blood consists of

a. serum and intracellular fluid.
b. plasma and interstitial fluid.
c. serum and plasma.
d. plasma and formed elements.

OBJECTIVE 2   Discuss the composition and functions of plasma.

_____ 1. In addition to water and proteins, the plasma contains

a. erythrocytes, leukocytes, and platelets.
b. electrolytes, nutrients, and organic wastes.
c. albumins, globulins, and fibrinogen.
d. all of the above.

_____ 2. The three primary classes of plasma proteins are

a. antibodies, metalloproteins, and lipoproteins.
b. serum, fibrin, and fibrinogen.
c. albumins, globulins, and fibrinogen.
d. heme, porphyrin, and globin.

_____ 3. The primary function(s) of plasma is(are)

      a. absorbing and releasing heat as needed by the body.
      b. transporting ions.
      c. transporting red blood cells.
      d. all the above.

_____ 4. The plasma proteins that attack foreign proteins and pathogens are called

      a. fibrinogen.
      b. albumins.
      c. immunoglobulins.
      d. lipoproteins.

_____ 5. The fluid left after the clotting proteins are removed from plasma is known as

      a. serum.
      b. albumin.
      c. fibrin.
      d. interstitial fluid.

OBJECTIVE 3   Describe the origin and production of the formed elements in blood.

_____ 1. Formed elements in the blood are produced by the process of

      a. hemolysis.
      b. hemopoiesis.
      c. diapedesis.
      d. erythrocytosis.

_____ 2. The stem cells that produce all the blood cells are called

      a. erythroblasts.
      b. rouleaux.
      c. hemocytoblasts.
      d. plasma cells.

_____ 3. In adults, the only site of RBC and WBC production is the

      a. liver.
      b. red bone marrow.
      c. spleen.
      d. yellow bone marrow.

_____ 4. Megakaryocytes are large cells that continuously shed cytoplasm in small membrane-enclosed pockets called

      a. lymphocytes.
      b. leukocytes.
      c. erythrocytes.
      d. platelets.

5. The term used to describe the formation of red blood cells is _____.

6. The term used to describe the formation of white blood cells is _____.

7. The term used to describe the formation of platelets is _____.

OBJECTIVE 4 Discuss the characteristics and functions of red blood cells.

_____ 1. The primary function(s) of a mature red blood cell is(are)

        a. transport of respiratory gases.
        b. delivery of enzymes to target tissues.
        c. defense against toxins and pathogens.
        d. all the above.

_____ 2. Circulating mature red blood cells lack

        a. mitochondria.
        b. ribosomes.
        c. nuclei.
        d. all the above.

_____ 3. RBC production is regulated by the hormone

        a. thymosin.
        b. angiotensin.
        c. renin.
        d. erythropoietin.

_____ 4. The average lifespan of a red blood cell is

        a. 7 days.
        b. 1 month.
        c. 120 days.
        d. 6 months.

_____ 5. The function of hemoglobin is to

        a. carry oxygen.
        b. protect the body against infectious agents.
        c. aid in the process of blood clotting.
        d. All of the above are correct.

_____ 6. Aged and damaged erythrocytes are broken down by macrophages in the

        a. spleen.
        b. liver.
        c. bone marrow.
        d. All of the above are correct.

_____ 7. The important effect(s) on RBCs due to their unusual shape is(are)

        a. it enables RBCs to form stacks.
        b. it gives each RBC a large surface area-to-volume ratio.
        c. it enables RBCs to bend and flex when entering small capillaries.
        d. all of the above.

_____ 8. Red blood cells are called

        a. leukocytes.
        b. thrombocytes.
        c. erythrocytes.
        d. none of the above.

OBJECTIVE 5   Explain the factors that determine a person's blood type, and why blood types are important.

_____ 1. A person's blood type is determined by the

a. shape and size of the red blood cells.
b. presence or absence of specific antigens on the cell membrane.
c. number of specific antigens in the cell membrane.
d. chemical nature of hemoglobin.

_____ 2. A person with type A blood has

a. A agglutinins on their RBC.
b. A agglutinins in their plasma.
c. B agglutinogens on their RBC.
d. B agglutinins in their plasma.

_____ 3. Agglutinogens are contained (on, in) the _____, while the agglutinins are found (on, in) the _____.

a. plasma; cell membrane of RBCs
b. nucleus of the RBC; mitochondria
c. cell membrane of RBC; plasma
d. mitochondria; nucleus of RBCs

_____ 4. The blood of a person with type O blood

a. contains anti-A and anti-B agglutinins.
b. contains anti-O agglutinins.
c. contains anti-A and anti-B agglutinogens.
d. lacks agglutinins.

_____ 5. Rh-negative blood indicates the

a. presence of the Rh antigen.
b. presence of antigen A.
c. absence of the Rh antigen.
d. absence of antigen B.

_____ 6. A type O person can donate blood to a type A person because

a. a type O person does not have any antigens to be attacked by the type A blood.
b. a type O person does not have any antigens to attack the type A blood.
c. a type O person does not have any plasma antibodies to be attacked by the type A blood.
d. a type O person is a universal donor.

_____ 7. When blood types are incompatible, the blood will

a. clot.
b. clump.
c. agglutinate.
d. Both b and c are correct.

Labeling Exercises

A person with AB type blood has A antigens and B antigens. In Figure 11-1, identify which number represents the A antigen, and which number represents the B antigen of type AB blood. Place your answers in the numbered spaces below the illustrations.

FIGURE 11-1 Blood Types and Antigens

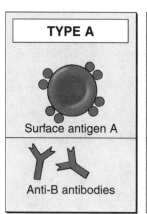

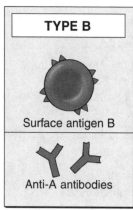

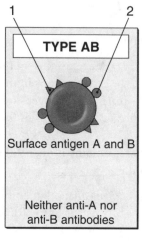

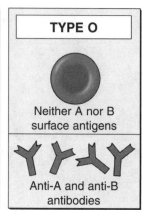

1. _____   2. _____

In Figure 11-2, identify which numbers represent a safe blood donation, and which numbers represent an unsafe blood donation. In the corresponding blanks, write the words "compatible" or "incompatible."

FIGURE 11-2 Cross-Reactions between Different Blood Types

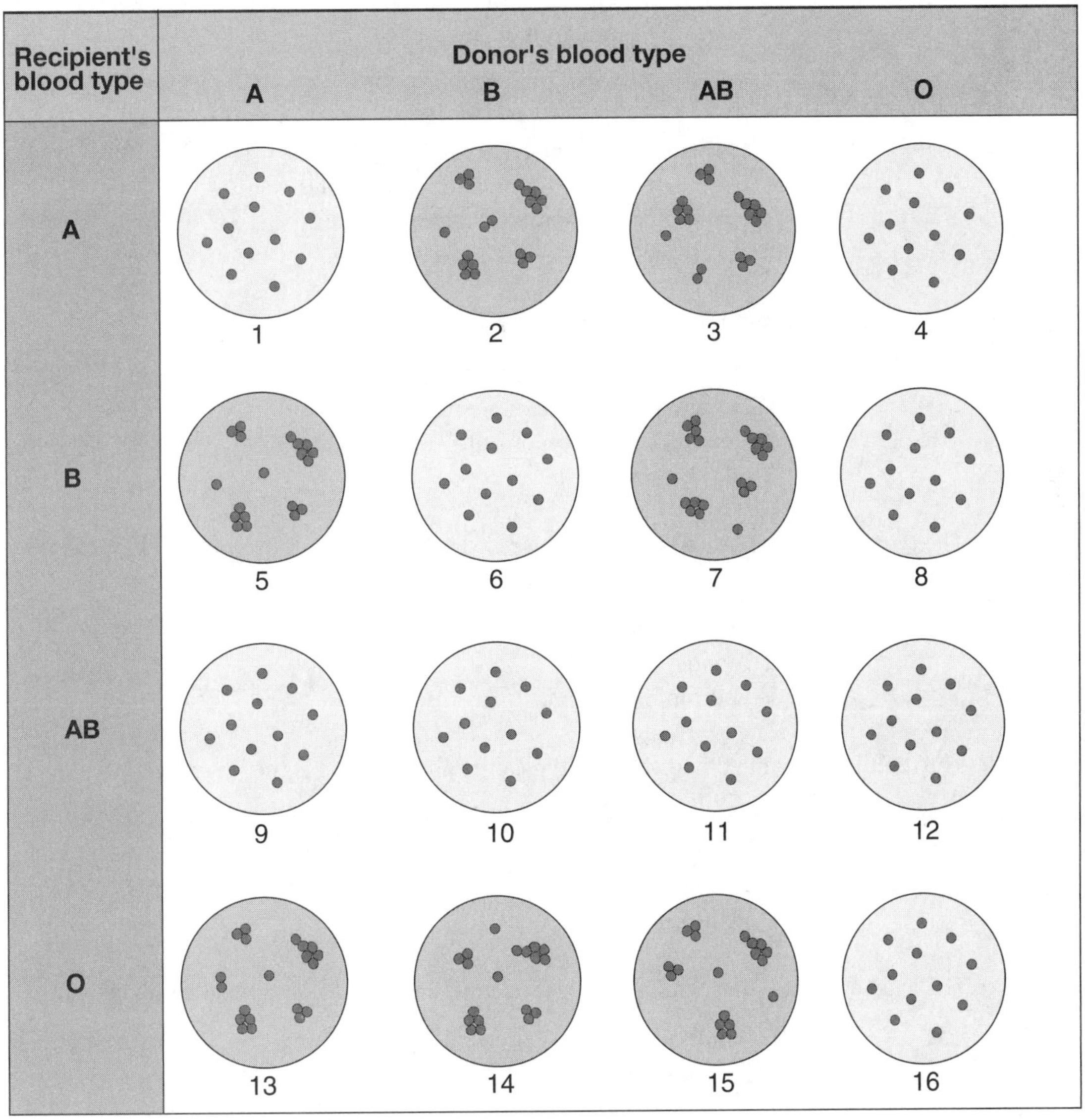

1. _____

2. _____

3. _____

4. _____

5. _____

6. _____

7. _____

8. _____

9. _____

10. _____

11. _____

12. _____

13. _____

14. _____

15. _____

16. _____

OBJECTIVE 6   Categorize the various white blood cells on the basis of their structure and functions.

_____ 1. The two types of agranular leukocytes found in the blood are

   a. neutrophils and eosinophils.
   b. leukocytes and lymphocytes.
   c. monocytes and lymphocytes.
   d. neutrophils and monocytes.

_____ 2. Based on their staining characteristics, the types of granular leukocytes found in the blood are

   a. lymphocytes, monocytes, and erythrocytes.
   b. neutrophils, monocytes, and lymphocytes.
   c. eosinophils, basophils, and lymphocytes.
   d. neutrophils, eosinophils, and basophils.

_____ 3. The number of eosinophils increases dramatically during

   a. an allergic reaction or a parasitic infection.
   b. an injury to a tissue or a bacterial infection.
   c. tissue degeneration or cellular deterioration.
   d. all the above.

_____ 4. The type of leukocyte responsible for the red swollen condition in inflamed tissue is the

   a. basophil.
   b. lymphocyte.
   c. monocyte.
   d. neutrophil.

_____ 5. The multilobed white blood cell that typically fights bacteria is the

   a. basophil.
   b. lymphocyte.
   c. monocyte.
   d. neutrophil.

_____ 6. The leukocyte that fuses with another of its kind to create a giant phagocytic cell is the

   a. lymphocyte.
   b. monocyte.
   c. neutrophil.
   d. basophil.

_____ 7. The most numerous WBCs in a normal WBC differential are the

   a. neutrophils.
   b. eosinophils.
   c. lymphocytes.
   d. basophils.

_____ 8. WBCs that release histamine at the site of an injury are

   a. neutrophils.
   b. eosinophils.
   c. basophils.
   d. lymphocytes.

_____   9. The WBCs that are important in producing antibodies are the

            a. eosinophils.
            b. lymphocytes.
            c. neutrophils.
            d. basophils.

_____   10. The normal number of WBCs in a healthy person is _____/mm^3.

            a. 6000–9000
            b. 100,000–150,000
            c. 1000–2000
            d. 25,000–50,000

Labeling Exercise

Identify the white blood cells in the following illustrations. Place your answers in the spaces provided below each example.

FIGURE 11-3 White Blood Cells

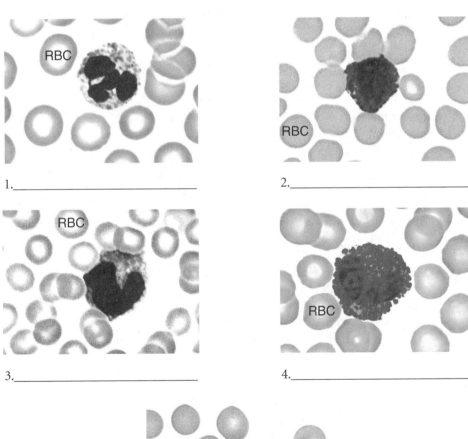

1._____   2._____

3._____   4._____

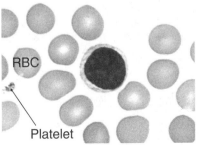

5._____

OBJECTIVE 7 Describe the mechanisms that reduce blood loss after an injury.

_____ 1. Basophils are specialized WBCs that

    a. contain microphages that engulf invading bacteria.

    b. contain histamine that exaggerates the inflammatory response at the injury site.

    c. are enthusiastic phagocytes, often attempting to engulf items as large or larger than themselves.

    d. produce and secrete antibodies that attack cells or proteins in distant portions of the body.

_____ 2. Hemostasis is a process consisting of three overlapping phases. The correct order of the phases is

    a. coagulation phase, platelet phase, vascular phase.

    b. platelet phase, coagulation phase, vascular phase.

    c. coagulation phase, vascular phase, platelet phase.

    d. vascular phase, platelet phase, coagulation phase.

_____ 3. The extrinsic pathway in blood clotting involves the release of

    a. platelet factors and platelet thromboplastin.

    b. Ca^{2+} and clotting factors VIII, IX, XI, and XIII.

    c. tissue factor by damaged endothelial cells.

    d. prothrombin and fibrinogen.

_____ 4. The "common pathway" in blood clotting involves the following events, in correct sequential order.

    a. tissue factors $\rightarrow Ca^{2+} \rightarrow$ plasminogen $\rightarrow$ plasmin

    b. prothrombin $\rightarrow$ thrombin $\rightarrow$ fibrinogen $\rightarrow$ fibrin

    c. platelet factors $\rightarrow Ca^{2+} \rightarrow$ fibrinogen $\rightarrow$ fibrin

    d. prothrombin and fibrinogen

_____ 5. During the clotting process, platelets function in

    a. transporting chemicals important for clotting.

    b. contraction after clot formation.

    c. initiating the clotting process.

    d. all of the above.

_____ 6. A blood clot attached to a blood vessel wall is called

    a. a thrombus.

    b. an embolus.

    c. a plaque.

    d. a platelet plug.

_____ 7. The process of fibrinolysis

    a. activates fibrinogen.

    b. forms emboli.

    c. dissolves clots.

    d. forms thrombi.

_____ 8. The vitamin needed for the formation of clotting factors is

         a. vitamin A.

         b. vitamin K.

         c. vitamin E.

         d. vitamin D.

_____ 9. A drifting blood clot is called

         a. a thrombus.

         b. a plaque.

         c. a platelet plug.

         d. an embolus.

_____ 10. A clotting protein found in the bloodstream and made by the liver is

         a. fibrin.

         b. fibrinogen.

         c. prothrombin.

         d. thrombin.

Part II: Chapter Comprehensive Exercises

A. Word Elimination

Circle the term that does not belong in each of the following groupings.

1. transportation   regulation   analysis   defense   stabilization

2. plasma   lymph   WBCs   RBCs   platelets

3. serum   albumins   globulins   antibodies   transport proteins

4. amino acids   iron   vitamin B_{12} folic acid   vitamin D

5. Hct   Hb   urinalysis   MCV   MCHC

6. Rh factor   Type A   Type B   Type AB   Type O

7. neutrophil   eosinophil   platelets   basophil   monocyte

8. T cells   B cells   NK cells   RBCs   plasma cells

9. hemocytoblast   stem cell   erythroblast   reticulocyte   platelet

10. prothrombin   thrombin   transferrin   fibrinogen   fibrin

B. Matching

Match the terms in Column "B" with the terms in Column "A." Write letters for answers in the spaces provided.

COLUMN A	COLUMN B
___ 1. hemopoiesis	a. dehydration
___ 2. hematocrit	b. neutrophils, eosinophils
___ 3. increased hematocrit	c. excessive WBCs
___ 4. decreased hematocrit	d. agglutinins
___ 5. leukocytosis	e. blood cell formation
___ 6. microphages	f. hemocytoblasts
___ 7. antibodies	g. agglutinogens
___ 8. stem cells	h. packed cell volume
___ 9. surface antigens	i. WBC migration
___10. diapedesis	j. internal bleeding

C. Concept Map I - Blood

Using the following terms, fill in the circled numbered, blank spaces to complete the concept map.
Follow the numbers that comply with the organization of the map.

Solutes   Leukocytes   Plasma   Albumins

Oxygen   Monocytes   Neutrophils

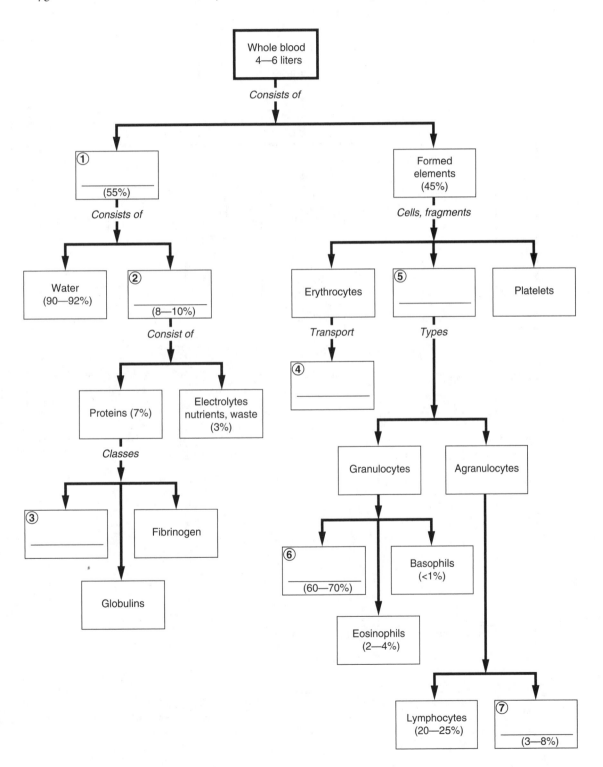

Concept Map II - Blood Clotting

Using the following terms, fill in the circled numbered, blank spaces to complete the concept map. Follow the numbers that comply with the organization of the map.

Clot dissolution   Platelet phase   Blood clot

Plasminogen   Plasmin   Vascular spasm

Plug   Clot retraction

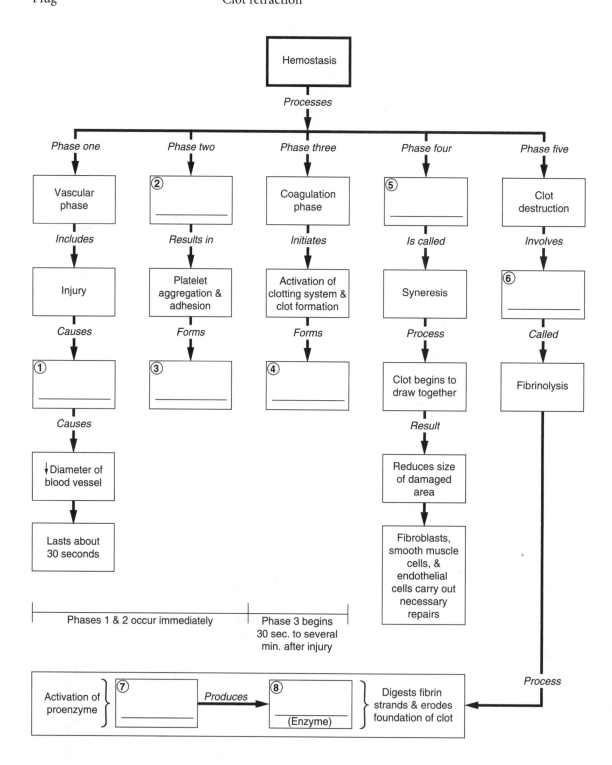

D. Crossword Puzzle

The following crossword reviews the material in Chapter 11. To complete the puzzle, you must know the answers to the clues given, and must be able to spell the terms correctly.

ACROSS
1. The rarest WBC in a healthy person.
3. A moving clot.
5. _____ cells contain only the antigens and not the antibodies.
6. Type B whole blood contains antigens and _____.
11. The process of blood clotting.
12. The fluid portion of blood.
15. If type A blood was given to a person with type B blood, the type B blood would begin to
    _____.
16. A blood clotting protein made in the liver.
17. Term for the formation of red blood cells.
18. Term for the formation of blood.

DOWN
2. Term for the formation of white blood cells.
4. The most common WBC in a healthy person.
7. After about 120 days, red blood cells begin to _____.
8. Type AB blood has A and B _____.
9. Type AB people are universal _____.
10. A normal count of white blood cells is 6000–9000 per cubic _____.
13. Some white blood cells produce these proteins that attack invading organisms.
14. Type O people are considered to be universal _____.

E. Short-Answer Questions

Briefly answer the following questions in the spaces provided.

1. List the five primary functions of the blood.

2. What are the three primary classes of plasma proteins?

3. List and describe the three kinds of granular leukocytes and the two kinds of agranular WBCs.

4. What are the three primary functions of platelets?

5. List the events in the clotting response, and summarize the results of each occurrence.

6. What is the difference between an embolus and a thrombus?

12

The Cardiovascular System: The Heart

Overview

The heart is an efficient and durable double pump. Every single day it beats 60–80 times per minute, supplying oxygen and other essential nutrients to every cell in the body and moving wastes for elimination from the lungs and the kidneys. The pumping action of this muscular organ pushes blood through a closed network of blood vessels consisting of a pulmonary circuit to the lungs and a systemic circuit serving the other regions of the body. The one-way direction of blood flow through the heart is maintained by a system of valves. Special coronary arteries that encircle the heart like a crown deliver nutrient and oxygen supplies to the tissues of the heart. The heart's electrical system includes a group of specialized pacemaker cells, which are located in a sinus node in the right atrium and are responsible for maintaining normal cardiac rhythm.

When you have successfully completed the exercises in Chapter 12, you should be able to describe the general features of the heart both internally and externally; identify the major blood vessels, chambers, and heart valves; understand the conducting system of the heart; and describe the cardiac cycle. The activities (which include heart dynamics) are designed to help you master the factors that control cardiac output and the effects of autonomic innervation in the heart.

Review of Chapter Objectives

1. Describe the location and general features of the heart.

2. Identify the layers of the heart wall.

3. Trace the flow of blood through the heart, identifying the major blood vessels, chambers, and heart valves.

4. Describe the differences in the action potential and twitch contractions of skeletal muscle fibers and cardiac muscle cells.

5. Describe the components and functions of the conducting system of the heart.

6. Explain the events of the cardiac cycle, and relate the heart sounds to specific events in this cycle.

7. Define stroke volume and cardiac output, and describe the factors that influence each.

Part I: Objective-Based Questions

OBJECTIVE 1   Describe the location and general features of the heart.

_____ 1. The "double pump" function of the heart includes the right side, which serves as the _____ circuit pump; the left side serves as the _____ pump.

    a. systemic; pulmonary
    b. pulmonary; hepatic portal
    c. hepatic portal; cardiac
    d. pulmonary; systemic

_____ 2. The major difference between the left and right ventricles relative to their role in heart function is that

    a. the L.V. pumps blood through the short, low-resistance pulmonary circuit.
    b. the R.V. pumps blood through the low-resistance systemic circulation.
    c. the L.V. pumps blood through the high-resistance systemic circulation.
    d. the R.V. pumps blood through the short, high-resistance pulmonary circuit.

_____ 3. The average maximum pressure developed in the right ventricle is about

    a. 15–28 mm Hg.
    b. 50–60 mm Hg.
    c. 67–78 mm Hg.
    d. 80–120 mm Hg.

_____ 4. The heart is surrounded by the

    a. pericardial cavity.
    b. coronary sulcus.
    c. intercostal space.
    d. mediastinum of the thorax.

_____ 5. The function of the chordae tendineae is to

    a. anchor the semilunar valve flaps and prevent backward flow of blood into the ventricles.
    b. anchor the AV valve flaps and prevent backflow of blood into the atria.
    c. anchor the bicuspid valve flaps and prevent backflow of blood into the ventricles.
    d. anchor the aortic valve flaps and prevent backflow into the ventricles.

_____ 6. The folds of fibrous tissue that ensure a one-way flow of blood from the atria into the ventricles are the

    a. aortic semilunar valves.
    b. pulmonary semilunar valves.
    c. interatrial valves.
    d. atrioventricular valves.

_____ 7. The portion of the pericardial membrane that lies on the surface of the heart is the

      a. visceral pericardium.
      b. visceral endocardium.
      c. parietal pericardium.
      d. parietal myocardium.

_____ 8. The visceral pericardium is the same as the

      a. mediastinum.
      b. epicardium.
      c. parietal pericardium.
      d. myocardium.

_____ 9. The functions of the pericardium include which of the following?

      a. returning blood to the atria
      b. pumping blood into circulation
      c. removing excess fluid from the heart chambers
      d. anchoring the heart to surrounding structures

10. The thin-walled chambers in the heart that are highly distensible are the

      _____.

11. The dense bands of tough, elastic connective tissue that form the internal network of the heart are called the _____.

12. Each cardiac muscle cell contacts several others at specialized sites known as

      _____.

Labeling Exercise

Identify and label the structures in Figure 12-1. Place your answers in the spaces provided below the drawing.

base   aortic arch   coronary vessels   pulmonary trunk
right side   apex   left side

FIGURE 12-1 External View of the Heart

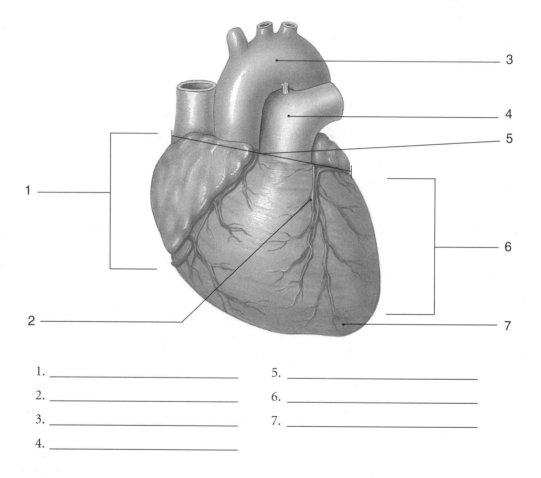

1. _____   5. _____
2. _____   6. _____
3. _____   7. _____
4. _____

OBJECTIVE 2   Identify the layers of the heart wall.

_____ 1. The outer surface of the heart is covered by the

        a. epicardium.
        b. endocardium.
        c. myocardium.
        d. papillary muscles.

_____ 2. The layer of the heart wall that contains cardiac muscle tissue, blood vessels, and nerves is the

        a. endocardium.
        b. epicardium.
        c. myocardium.
        d. chordae tendineae.

_____   3. The heart's inner surface, including the heart valves, is covered by the

        a. chordae tendineae.
        b. endocardium.
        c. papillary muscles.
        d. visceral pericardium.

_____   4. The principal kind of tissue making up the endocardium and epicardium is

        a. muscle tissue.
        b. serous membrane.
        c. epithelial tissue.
        d. nervous tissue.

Labeling Exercise

Using the selections below, identify and label the areas in Figure 12-2. Place your answers in the spaces provided below the drawing.

pericardial cavity	endocardium	individual muscle cells
myocardium	epicardium	parietal pericardium

FIGURE 12-2 Layers of the Heart Wall

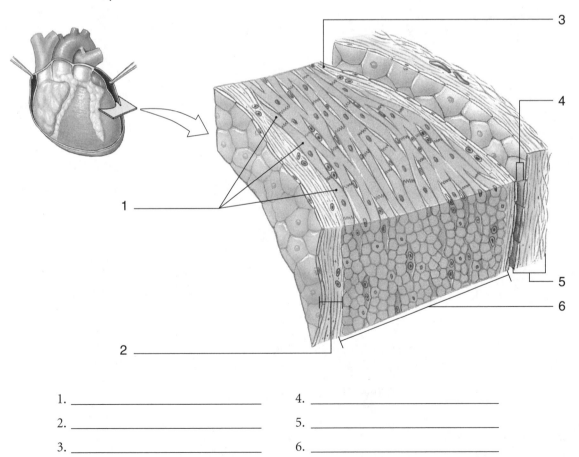

1. _____   4. _____

2. _____   5. _____

3. _____   6. _____

OBJECTIVE 3 Trace the flow of blood through the heart, identifying the major blood vessels, chambers, and heart valves.

_____ 1. Blood returning from the systemic circuit first enters the

        a. right atrium.
        b. right ventricle.
        c. left atrium.
        d. left ventricle.

_____ 2. Blood returning from the lungs enters the

        a. right atrium.
        b. right ventricle.
        c. left atrium.
        d. left ventricle.

_____ 3. The right ventricle pumps blood to the

        a. left ventricle.
        b. lungs.
        c. left atrium.
        d. systemic circuit.

_____ 4. The left ventricle pumps blood to the

        a. lungs.
        b. left atrium.
        c. right ventricle.
        d. systemic circuit.

_____ 5. The right atrium receives blood from the

        a. pulmonary veins.
        b. aorta.
        c. inferior vena cava.
        d. pulmonary trunk.

_____ 6. The atrioventricular valve located on the right side of the heart is the

        a. tricuspid valve.
        b. mitral valve.
        c. bicuspid valve.
        d. aortic semilunar valve.

_____ 7. Blood leaving the right ventricle enters the

        a. aorta.
        b. pulmonary artery.
        c. pulmonary veins.
        d. inferior vena cava.

_____ 8. The pulmonary semilunar valve guards the entrance to the

        a. aorta.
        b. pulmonary veins.
        c. pulmonary trunk.
        d. left ventricle.

_____ 9. The bicuspid or mitral valve is located

    a. in the opening of the aorta.
    b. in the opening of the pulmonary trunk.
    c. where the venae cavae join the right atrium.
    d. between the left atrium and left ventricle.

_____ 10. The entrance to the ascending aorta is guarded by

    a. an atrioventricular valve.
    b. the bicuspid valve.
    c. a semilunar valve.
    d. the tricuspid valve.

_____ 11. The function of an atrium is

    a. to collect blood.
    b. to pump blood to the lungs.
    c. to pump blood into the systemic circuit.
    d. to pump blood to the heart muscle.
    e. all of the above.

_____ 12. The following is a list of vessels and structures that are associated with the heart.

    1. right atrium
    2. left atrium
    3. right ventricle
    4. left ventricle
    5. venae cavae
    6. aorta
    7. pulmonary trunk
    8. pulmonary veins

What is the correct order for the flow of blood entering from the systemic circulation?

    a. 1, 2, 7, 8, 3, 4, 6, 5
    b. 5, 1, 3, 7, 8, 2, 4, 6
    c. 1, 7, 3, 8, 2, 4, 6, 5
    d. 5, 3, 1, 7, 8, 4, 2, 6

_____ 13. The left and right pulmonary arteries carry blood to the

    a. heart.
    b. intestines.
    c. lungs.
    d. brain.

_____ 14. The left and right pulmonary veins carry blood to the

    a. heart.
    b. intestines.
    c. lungs.
    d. liver.

Labeling Exercises

Using the following terms, identify the structures of the heart by labeling Figure 12-3. Place the answers in the spaces provided below the drawing.

interventricular septum

pulmonary trunk

aortic arch

aortic semilunar valve

left ventricle

papillary muscles

tricuspid valve

fossa ovalis

left pulmonary veins

right ventricle

right pulmonary arteries

superior vena cava

interatrial septum

chordae tendineae

left pulmonary arteries

pulmonary semilunar valve

bicuspid valve

inferior vena cava

right atrium

opening of coronary sinus

aorta

FIGURE 12-3 Anatomy of the Heart (Ventral View)

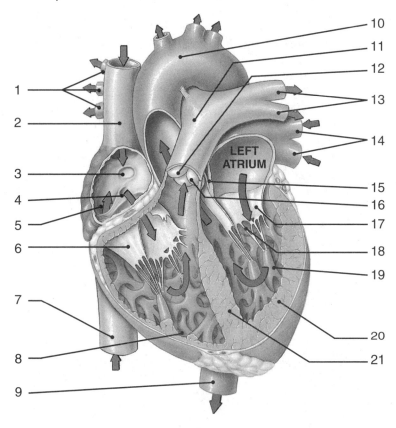

1. _____

2. _____

3. _____

4. _____

5. _____

6. _____

7. _____

8. _____

9. _____

10. _____

11. _____

12. _____

13. _____

14. _____

15. _____

16. _____

17. _____

18. _____

19. _____

20. _____

21. _____

In the drawing below, identify valves 1 through 8 and indicate whether each valve is open (O) or closed (C). Place your answers in the spaces provided below the drawing.

pulmonary semilunar valve (O)   bicuspid AV valve (O)

tricuspid (right AV) valve (C)   aortic semilunar valve (O)

tricuspid valve (O)   bicuspid valve (C)

pulmonary semilunar valve (C)   aortic semilunar valve (C)

FIGURE 12-4 Valves of the Heart

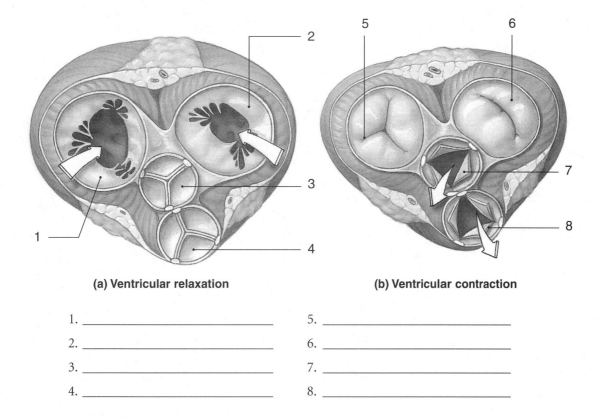

(a) Ventricular relaxation   **(b) Ventricular contraction**

1. _____ 5. _____

2. _____ 6. _____

3. _____ 7. _____

4. _____ 8. _____

OBJECTIVE 4 Describe the differences in the action potential and twitch contractions of skeletal muscle fibers and cardiac muscle cells.

_____ 1. The correct sequential path of a normal action potential in the heart is

   a. SA node → AV bundle → AV node → Purkinje fibers.
   b. AV node → SA node → AV bundle → bundle of His.
   c. SA node → AV node → bundle of His → bundle branches → Purkinje fibers.
   d. SA node → AV node → bundle branches → AV bundle → Purkinje fibers.

_____ 2. In a cardiac muscle cell, an action potential lasts approximately _____ times longer than the duration of an action potential in a skeletal muscle cell.

      a. 2–4
      b. 10–15
      c. 25–30
      d. 35–40

_____ 3. Specialized noncontractile muscle cells of the conducting system are necessary to

      a. initiate rapid depolarization at threshold.
      b. produce the repolarization that restores the resting potential.
      c. control and coordinate the activities of the contractile cells.
      d. produce tetany and summation.

_____ 4. In cardiac muscle,

      a. neither summation nor tetany can occur.
      b. both summation and tetany can occur.
      c. only summation can occur.
      d. only tetany can occur.

OBJECTIVE 5   Describe the components and functions of the conducting system of the heart.

_____ 1. The pacemaker cells of the heart are located in the

      a. bundle of His.
      b. SA node.
      c. AV node.
      d. wall of the left ventricle.

_____ 2. The following are the components of the conducting system of the heart:
(1) Purkinje cells (2) AV bundle (3) AV node (4) SA node (5) bundle branches.
The sequence in which an action potential would move through this system is

      a. 1, 4, 3, 2, 5.
      b. 4, 2, 3, 5, 1.
      c. 3, 2, 4, 5, 1.
      d. 4, 3, 2, 5, 1.

_____ 3. In contrast to skeletal muscle, cardiac muscle contracts on its own (in the absence of neural or hormonal stimulation) due to a property known as

      a. tachycardia.
      b. summation.
      c. autorhythmicity.
      d. tetany.

_____ 4. In the heart's conducting system, nodal cells and conducting cells do not

      a. contract.
      b. initiate and distribute electrical impulses.
      c. establish the rate of cardiac contraction.
      d. distribute the stimulus to the general myocardium.

_____   5. Ventricular contraction occurs when the impulse travels through the

           a. AV node.
           b. SA node.
           c. AV bundle.
           d. Purkinje fibers.

Labeling Exercise

Identify and label the following structures in Figure 12-5. Place the answers in the spaces provided below the drawing.

AV bundle	Purkinje fibers	SA node
bundle branches	AV node	

FIGURE 12-5 The Conducting System of the Heart

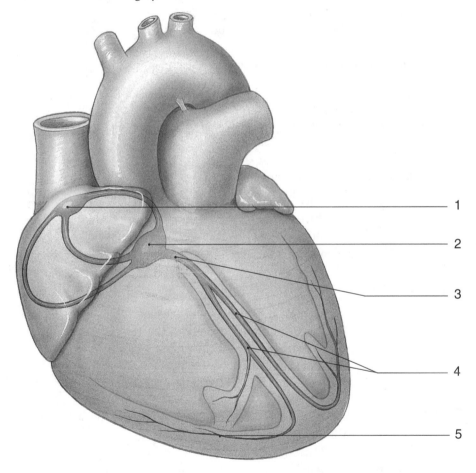

1. _____   4. _____

2. _____   5. _____

3. _____

OBJECTIVE 6   Explain the events of the cardiac cycle, and relate the heart sounds to specific events in this cycle.

_____ 1. The "lubb-dupp" sounds of the heart have practical clinical value because they provide information concerning the

a. strength of ventricular contraction.
b. strength of the pulse.
c. efficiency of the heart valves.
d. relative time the heart spends in systole and diastole.

_____ 2. When a chamber of the heart fills with blood and prepares for the start of the next cardiac cycle, the heart is in

a. systole.
b. ventricular ejection.
c. diastole.
d. isovolumetric contraction.

_____ 3. At the start of atrial systole, the ventricles are filled to approximately

a. 10 percent of capacity.
b. 30 percent of capacity.
c. 50 percent of capacity.
d. 70 percent of capacity.

_____ 4. The first heart sound is heard when the

a. AV valves open.
b. AV valves close.
c. semilunar valves close.
d. blood enters the aorta.

_____ 5. Systole and diastole refer to

a. contraction and relaxation of the heart.
b. relaxation and contraction of the heart.
c. atrial and ventricular contraction.
d. ventricular and atrial contraction.

OBJECTIVE 7   Define stroke volume and cardiac output, and describe the factors that influence each.

_____ 1. The amount of blood ejected by the left ventricle per minute is the

a. stroke volume.
b. cardiac output.
c. end-diastolic volume.
d. end-systolic volume.

_____ 2. The amount of blood pumped out of each ventricle during a single beat is the

   a. stroke volume.
   b. EDV.
   c. cardiac output.
   d. ESV.

_____ 3. Cardiac output is equal to the

   a. difference between the diastolic volume and the systolic volume.
   b. product of heart rate and stroke volume.
   c. difference between the stroke volume at rest and the stroke volume during exercise.
   d. stroke volume less the systolic volume.

_____ 4. Each of the following factors will increase cardiac output except one. Identify the exception.

   a. increased venous return
   b. increased parasympathetic stimulation
   c. increased sympathetic stimulation
   d. increased heart rate

_____ 5. According to Starling's law of the heart, cardiac output is directly related to the

   a. size of the ventricle.
   b. heart rate.
   c. venous return.
   d. thickness of the myocardium.

Part II: Chapter Comprehensive Exercises

A. Word Elimination

Circle the term that does not belong in each of the following groupings.

1. L. atrium   R. atrium   L. pulmonary artery   L. ventricle   R. ventricle

2. tricuspid   bicuspid   mitral   R. (AV) valve   semilunar

3. chordae tendineae   endocardium   myocardium   epicardium

4. SA node   AV bundle   AV node   anastomoses   Purkinje cells

5. EKG   systole   P wave   QRS complex   T wave

6. blood volume reflex   autonomic innervation   tachycardia   hormones   ECF ions

7. arteries   auricles   veins   capillaries   efferent vessels

8. pulmonary artery   pulmonary vein   superior vena cava   aortic arch   AV valve

9. single nucleus   central nucleus   syncytium   multinucleated   intercalated discs

10. R. coronary artery   aortic arch   L. coronary artery   anterior cardiac vein
    great cardiac vein

B. Matching

Match the terms in Column "B" with the terms in Column "A." Write letters for answers in the spaces provided.

COLUMN A	COLUMN B
____ 1. left AV valve	a. depolarization of ventricles
____ 2. right AV valve	b. lowers heart rate
____ 3. repolarization	c. depolarization of atria
____ 4. depolarization	d. slower than normal heart rate
____ 5. tachycardia	e. increases heart rate
____ 6. bradycardia	f. tricuspid
____ 7. P wave	g. K^+ out of cell
____ 8. QRS complex	h. faster than normal heart rate
____ 9. acetylcholine	i. mitral valve
____ 10. norepinephrine	j. Na^+ into cell

C. Concept Map I - The Heart

Using the following terms, fill in the circled numbered, blank spaces to complete the concept map.
Follow the numbers that comply with the organization of the map.

Epicardium

Aortic

Two semilunar

Oxygenated blood

Pacemaker cells

Tricuspid

Two atria

Endocardium

Blood from atria

Deoxygenated blood

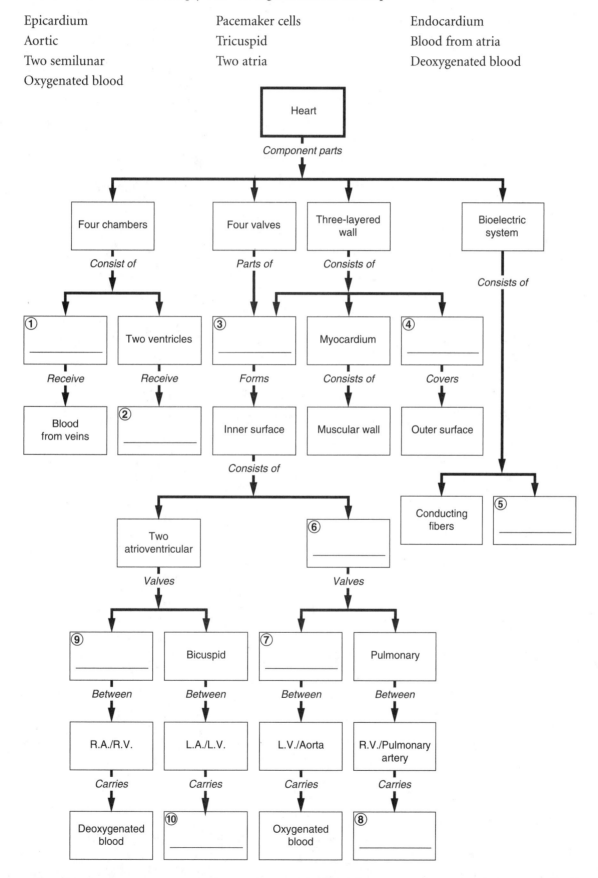

Concept Map II - Path of Blood Flow through the Heart

Use the heart map and the following list of terms to follow a drop of blood as it flows through the heart and peripheral blood vessels. Identify each numbered structure sequentially.

aortic semilunar valve	tricuspid valve	aorta
inferior vena cava	pulmonary semilunar valve	pulmonary arteries
pulmonary veins	systemic arteries	superior vena cava
left ventricle	systemic veins	right ventricle
right atrium	L. common carotid artery	bicuspid valve
left atrium		

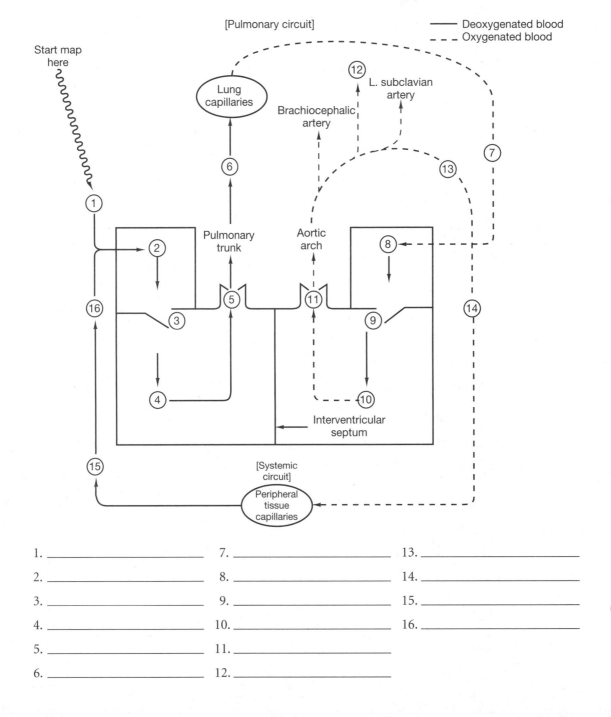

Ventral View of Heart Path of Circulation: "Heart Map"

1. _____   7. _____   13. _____

2. _____   8. _____   14. _____

3. _____   9. _____   15. _____

4. _____   10. _____   16. _____

5. _____   11. _____

6. _____   12. _____

D. Crossword Puzzle

The following crossword puzzle reviews the material in Chapter 12. To complete the puzzle, you must know the answers to the clues given, and must be able to spell the terms correctly.

ACROSS

1. The sinoatrial node is the heart's _____.
3. Is the aortic arch closer to the base or to the apex of the heart?
5. When these fibers are activated, the ventricles will contract.
8. Vessels that carry blood away from the heart.
11. The 80 in 120/80 represents the _____ value of blood pressure.
12. Arteries flow into _____ then into venules.
13. Blood entering the inferior vena cava could have come from the _____ vein.
16. The main muscular portion of the heart.
19. Blood leaving the placenta and going to the fetus travels in the umbilical _____.
20. Blood in the _____ artery enters the brachial artery.

DOWN

1. Blood leaving the femoral artery enters the _____ artery.
2. A heart _____ is a condition in which the AV valves do not close properly.
4. The name of the blood pressure apparatus.
6. The jugular vein and the subclavian vein join to form the _____ vein.
7. Another name for the bicuspid valve.
9. The valve located between the right atrium and the right ventricle.
10. Contraction of the heart.
14. The aortic arch arches to the _____ as it emerges from the heart.
15. Blood in the popliteal vein enters the _____ vein.
17. An opening between the two atria of a fetal heart is called the foramen _____.
18. The hormone that helps lower blood pressure.

E. Short-Answer Questions

Briefly answer the following questions in the spaces provided.

1. If the heart rate (HR) is 80 beats per minute and the stroke volume (SV) is 75 ml, what is the cardiac output (CO) (l/min)?

2. What are anastomoses, and how do they benefit the blood supply to the heart?

3. If the heart rate increases to 250 beats/min, what conditions would occur relative to the following factors? (Use vertical arrows to indicate an increase or decrease.)

   _____ CO, _____SV, _____ length of diastole, _____ ventricular filling

4. If the cardiac output (CO) is 5 l/min and the heart rate (HR) is 100 beats/min (bpm), what is the stroke volume (SV)?

5. What is the difference between the visceral pericardium and the parietal pericardium?

6. What three distinct layers comprise the tissues of the heart wall?

7. Because of specialized sites known as intercalated discs, cardiac muscle is a functional syncytium. What does this statement mean?

8. Beginning with the SA node, trace the pathway of an action potential through the conducting network of the heart. (Use arrows to indicate direction.)

9. What two common clinical problems result from abnormal pacemaker function? Explain what each term means.

10. What three important factors have a direct effect on heart rate and force of contraction?

13

The Cardiovascular System: Blood Vessels and Circulation

Overview

Blood is transported through a system of vessels that includes arteries, veins, and capillaries. The arteries are the high-pressure conduits, the veins are the low-pressure vessels, and the capillaries allow exchange of gases, nutrients, and wastes between the blood and cells throughout the body. The general plan of the circulatory system includes a pulmonary circuit and a systemic circuit. The pulmonary circuit carries deoxygenated blood from the right side of the heart through pulmonary arteries to the lung capillaries where the blood is oxygenated. The oxygenated blood is transported through pulmonary veins to the left side of the heart. After circulating through the left side of the heart, the oxygenated blood enters the aorta and is transported throughout the systemic circulation to all parts of the body, where it becomes deoxygenated. The deoxygenated blood returns to the right side of the heart to continue the cycle of circulation.

Blood vessels in the muscles, the skin, the cerebral circulation, and the hepatic portal circulation are specifically adapted to serve the functions of organs and tissues in these specialized areas of cardiovascular activity.

The major topics of the student activities in this chapter include the anatomy of blood vessels, cardiovascular physiology, and patterns of response in the regulation of blood flow. You will be expected to be able to identify the major blood vessels and know the structural and functional interactions among the cardiovascular system and other body systems.

Review of Chapter Objectives

1. Distinguish among the types of blood vessels on the basis of their structure and function.

2. Explain the mechanisms that regulate blood flow through arteries, capillaries, and veins.

3. Discuss the mechanisms and various pressures involved in the movement of fluids between capillaries and interstitial spaces.

4. Describe the factors that influence blood pressure and the mechanisms that regulate blood pressure.

5. Describe how central and local control mechanisms interact to regulate blood flow and pressure in tissues.

6. Explain how the activities of the cardiac, vasomotor, and respiratory centers are coordinated to control blood flow through the tissues.

7. Explain how the circulatory system responds to the demands of exercise and hemorrhage.

8. Identify the major arteries and veins and the areas they serve.

9. Describe the age-related changes that occur in the cardiovascular system.

10. Discuss the structural and functional interactions among the cardiovascular system and other organ systems.

Part I: Objective-Based Questions

OBJECTIVE 1   Distinguish among the types of blood vessels on the basis of their structure and function.

_____ 1. The layer of vascular tissue that consists of an endothelial lining and an underlying layer of connective tissue dominated by elastic fibers is the

    a. tunica interna.
    b. tunica media.
    c. tunica externa.
    d. tunica adventitia.

_____ 2. Smooth muscle fibers in arteries and veins are found in the

    a. endothelial lining.
    b. tunica externa.
    c. tunica interna.
    d. tunica media.

_____ 3. One of the major characteristics of arteries supplying peripheral tissues is that they are

    a. elastic.
    b. muscular.
    c. rigid.
    d. all of the above.

_____ 4. The blood vessels that play the most important role in the regulation of blood flow and blood pressure are the

    a. arteries.
    b. veins.
    c. arterioles.
    d. capillaries.

_____ 5. The blood vessels that have valves are the

    a. arteries.
    b. arterioles.
    c. capillaries.
    d. veins.

_____ 6. The vessels that carry blood to the heart are the

    a. veins.
    b. arteries.
    c. capillaries.
    d. arterioles.

Labeling Exercise

In Figure 13-1 identify the following blood vessels on the basis of their structural features. Place your answers in the spaces provided below the drawings.

artery   vein   capillaries
arteriole   venule

FIGURE 13-1 Types of Blood Vessels

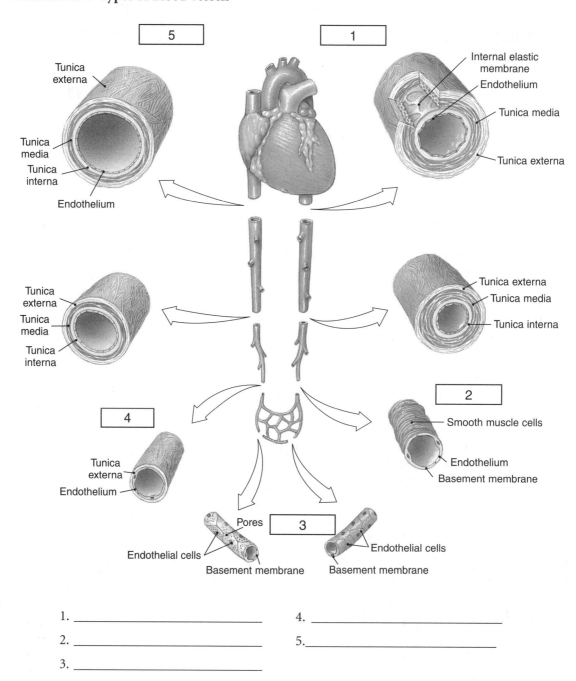

1. _____   4. _____

2. _____   5. _____

3. _____

OBJECTIVE 2   Explain the mechanisms that regulate blood flow through arteries, capillaries, and veins.

_____ 1. Blood flow through a capillary is regulated by the

a. endothelium.
b. action of the heart.
c. precapillary sphincter.
d. smooth muscle tissue.

_____ 2. Blood returns to the heart through veins

a. because the pressure in the veins is lower than in the arteries.
b. with the aid of contractions of skeletal muscles.
c. with the aid of thoracic cavity pressure changes.
d. All of the above are correct.

_____ 3. Blood flow through the circulatory system is affected by

a. pressure differences.
b. the viscosity of the blood.
c. the length and diameter of the blood vessels.
d. all of the above.

_____ 4. Of the following blood vessels, the greatest resistance to blood flow occurs in the

a. veins.
b. capillaries.
c. arterioles.
d. venules.

_____ 5. The most important determinant of vascular resistance is

a. a combination of neural and hormonal mechanisms.
b. differences in the length of the blood vessels.
c. friction between the blood and the vessel walls.
d. the diameter of the arterioles.

OBJECTIVE 3   Discuss the mechanisms and various pressures involved in the movement of fluids between capillaries and interstitial spaces.

_____ 1. Blood osmotic pressure is most affected by changes in the plasma concentration of

a. sodium ions.
b. proteins.
c. metabolic wastes.
d. glucose.

_____ 2. Capillary hydrostatic pressure (CHP) tends to push water

a. out of the capillary.
b. into the capillary.
c. out of the interstitial space.
d. into the blood.

_____ 3. In filtration, hydrostatic pressure pushes water molecules from an area of

    a. low pressure to an area of higher pressure.

    b. high pressure to an area of lower pressure.

    c. equal pressures on each side of the membrane.

    d. pressure differences in the nucleus and interstitial space.

_____ 4. Blood osmotic pressure (BOP) tends to

    a. reabsorb water back into the blood.

    b. draw water out of the blood.

    c. suppress the movement of water.

    d. cause dehydration and ultimately the death of cells.

5. The force that pushes water molecules out of solution is _____.

6. A force that pulls water into a solution is _____.

OBJECTIVE 4   Describe the factors that influence blood pressure and the mechanisms that regulate blood pressure.

_____ 1. The two factors that help overcome gravity and propel venous blood toward the heart are

    a. capillary hydrostatic pressure and blood osmotic pressure.

    b. filtration and diffusion.

    c. stroke volume and cardiac output.

    d. muscular compression and the respiratory pump.

_____ 2. From the following selections, choose the one that correctly identifies all the factors that would increase blood pressure. (Note: CO=Cardiac Output; SV=Stroke Volume; VR=Venous Return; PR=Peripheral Resistance; BV=Blood Volume)

    a. increased CO; increased SV; decreased VR; decreased PR; increased BV

    b. increased CO; increased SV; increased VR; increased PR; increased BV

    c. increased CO; increased SV; decreased VR; increased PR; decreased BV

    d. increased CO; decreased SV; increased VR; decreased PR; increased BV

_____ 3. As blood travels from the aorta toward the capillaries, the

    a. pressure increases.

    b. resistance increases.

    c. viscosity increases.

    d. All of the above are correct.

_____ 4. Blood pressure is determined by measuring the

    a. rate of the pulse.

    b. pressure in the left ventricle.

    c. degree of turbulence in a closed blood vessel.

    d. force exerted by blood in a vessel against air in a closed cuff.

_____ 5. Blood pressure increases with increased

    a. cardiac output.

    b. peripheral resistance.

    c. blood volume.

    d. All of the above are correct.

_____ 6. The difference between the systolic pressure and the diastolic pressure is called the

    a. mean arterial pressure.

    b. pulse pressure.

    c. blood pressure.

    d. circulatory pressure.

OBJECTIVE 5   Describe how central and local control mechanisms interact to regulate blood flow and pressure in tissues.

_____ 1. The mechanisms involved in the regulation of cardiovascular function include

        a. the skeletal muscle pump and respiratory movements.

        b. autoregulation and neural and endocrine mechanisms.

        c. viscosity, pressure, and resistance.

        d. turbulence, volume, and cardiac output.

_____ 2. According to the equation $F = P/R$,

        a. increased F results from increased P and decreased R.

        b. increased F results from decreased P and increased R.

        c. decreased F results from increased P and increased R.

        d. increased F results from decreased P and decreased R.

_____ 3. Atrial natriuretic peptide (ANP) reduces blood volume and blood pressure by

        a. blocking release of ADH.

        b. stimulating peripheral vasodilation.

        c. increasing water loss by the kidneys.

        d. all of the above.

_____ 4. Which of the following does not cause an increase in blood pressure?

        a. increased levels of aldosterone

        b. increased levels of angiotensin II

        c. increased blood volume

        d. increased levels of ANP

_____ 5. Which of the following will not result in increased blood flow to tissues?

        a. increased blood volume

        b. increased vessel diameter

        c. increased blood pressure

        d. decreased peripheral resistance

OBJECTIVE 6   Explain how the activities of the cardiac, vasomotor, and respiratory centers are coordinated to control blood flow through the tissues.

_____ 1. The central regulation of cardiac output primarily involves the activities of the

        a. somatic nervous system.

        b. autonomic nervous system.

        c. central nervous system.

        d. All of the above are correct.

_____ 2. An increase in cardiac output normally occurs during

        a. widespread sympathetic stimulation.

        b. widespread parasympathetic stimulation.

        c. the process of vasomotion.

        d. stimulation of the vasomotor center.

_____ 3. Stimulation of the vasomotor center in the medulla causes _____, and inhibition of the vasomotor center causes _____.

        a. vasodilation; vasoconstriction

        b. increased diameter of arterioles; decreased diameter of arterioles

        c. hyperemia; ischemia

        d. vasoconstriction; vasodilation

_____ 4. Hormonal regulation by epinephrine, angiotensin II, and norepinephrine results in

      a. increased peripheral vasodilation.

      b. decreased peripheral vasoconstriction.

      c. increased peripheral vasoconstriction.

      d. all of the above.

_____ 5. Chemoreceptor reflexes respond to

      a. dilation of arterioles throughout the body.

      b. increased cardiac output and increased peripheral resistance.

      c. the inhibition of vasomotor centers.

      d. changes in carbon dioxide, oxygen, or pH in the blood.

_____ 6. Baroreceptors that function in cardiovascular regulation are located in the

      a. aortic sinuses.

      b. walls of the carotid sinuses.

      c. walls of the right atrium.

      d. All of the above are correct.

OBJECTIVE 7   Explain how the circulatory system responds to the demands of exercise and hemorrhage.

_____ 1. The three primary interrelated changes that occur as exercise begins are

      a. decreased vasodilation, increased venous return, and increased cardiac output.

      b. increased vasodilation, decreased venous return, and increased cardiac output.

      c. increased vasodilation, increased venous return, and increased cardiac output.

      d. decreased vasodilation, decreased venous return, and decreased cardiac output.

_____ 2. The only area of the body where the blood supply is unaffected by exercising at maximum levels is the

      a. hepatic portal circulation.

      b. pulmonary circulation.

      c. brain.

      d. peripheral circulation.

_____ 3. In response to hemorrhage,

      a. decreased vasomotor tone occurs.

      b. increased parasympathetic stimulation of the heart occurs.

      c. mobilization of the venous reserve occurs.

      d. all of the above occur.

_____ 4. Symptoms of shock include

      a. decreased urine formation.

      b. rapid, weak pulse.

      c. acidosis.

      d. all of the above.

_____ 5. Homeostatic mechanisms can compensate for circulatory shock during the
   a. ischemic stage.
   b. progressive stage.
   c. compensated stage.
   d. reversible stage.

OBJECTIVE 8   Identify the major arteries and veins and the areas they serve.

1. The ring-shaped anastomosis that forms the cerebral arterial circle is known as the _____.

2. The four large blood vessels, two from each lung, that empty into the left atrium, completing the pulmonary circuit are the _____.

3. The blood vessels that provide blood to capillary networks that surround the alveoli in the lungs are the _____.

4. Blood from the brain returns to the heart by way of the _____.

5. After passing the first rib, the subclavian artery becomes the _____ artery.

6. In the upper arm, the axillary artery becomes the _____ artery.

7. The brachial artery branches to form the _____ and _____ arteries.

8. The two vertebral arteries fuse to form the large _____ artery.

9. The _____ divides the aorta into a superior thoracic aorta and an inferior abdominal aorta.

10. The inferior abdominal aorta branches to form the _____ arteries.

11. The external iliac artery branches to form the _____ and _____ arteries.

12. The blood vessel that receives blood from the head, neck, chest, shoulders, and arms is the _____.

13. The dural sinuses collect blood from the _____.

14. The radial and ulnar veins fuse to form the _____ vein.

15. The vein that is formed from the fusion of the subclavian with the internal and external jugulars is the _____ vein.

16. The fusion of the brachiocephalic veins forms the _____.

17. When the popliteal vein reaches the femur, it becomes the _____ vein before penetrating the abdominal wall.

18. The two common iliac veins form the _____.

19. Nutrients from the digestive tract enter the _____ vein.

20. The large blood vessel that collects most of the venous blood from organs below the diaphragm is the _____.

Labeling Exercises

In Figure 13-2, identify and label the major *arteries*. Put your answers in the spaces on the following page.

FIGURE 13-2 Overview of the Arterial System

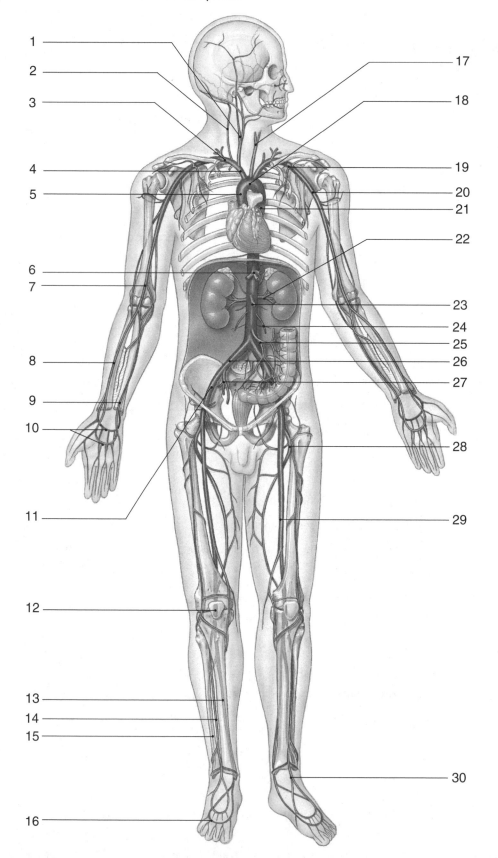

1. _____

2. _____

3. _____

4. _____

5. _____

6. _____

7. _____

8. _____

9. _____

10. _____

11. _____

12. _____

13. _____

14. _____

15. _____

16. _____

17. _____

18. _____

19. _____

20. _____

21. _____

22. _____

23. _____

24. _____

25. _____

26. _____

27. _____

28. _____

29. _____

30. _____

Labeling Exercises, continued

In Figure 13-3, identify and label the major *veins*. Put your answers in the spaces on the following page.

FIGURE 13-3 Overview of the Venous System

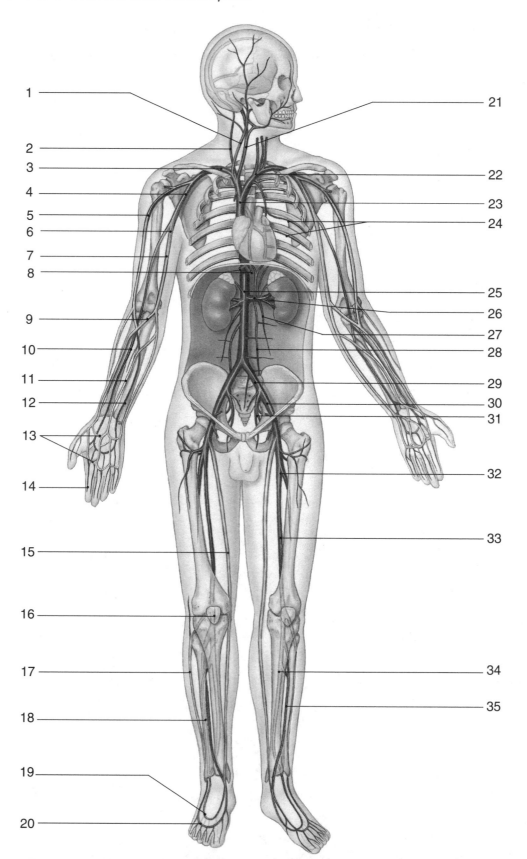

1. _____

2. _____

3. _____

4. _____

5. _____

6. _____

7. _____

8. _____

9. _____

10. _____

11. _____

12. _____

13. _____

14. _____

15. _____

16. _____

17. _____

18. _____

19. _____

20. _____

21. _____

22. _____

23. _____

24. _____

25. _____

26. _____

27. _____

28. _____

29. _____

30. _____

31. _____

32. _____

33. _____

34. _____

35. _____

Labeling Exercises, continued

In Figure 13-4, identify and label the *arteries* that supply blood to the brain. Place your answers in the spaces provided below the figure. Make your selections from the following choices.

anterior communicating   anterior cerebral

internal carotid   posterior communicating

posterior cerebral   middle cerebral

basilar   vertebral

circle of Willis   anterior cerebral

FIGURE 13-4 Arterial Supply to the Brain

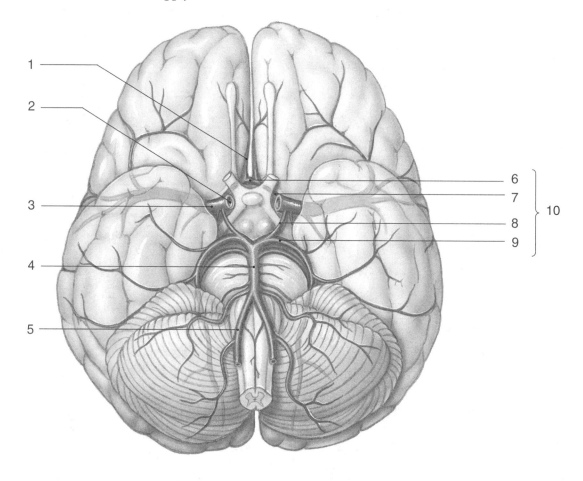

1. _____   6. _____

2. _____   7. _____

3. _____   8. _____

4. _____   9. _____

5. _____   10. _____

In Figure 13-5, identify and label the blood vessels and structures of the hepatic portal system. Make your selections from the following list of blood vessels and structures of the digestive system. Place your answers in the spaces below the figure.

aorta
pancreas
colic veins
hepatic portal vein
splenic vein
superior mesenteric vein
inferior mesenteric vein
superior rectal vein

liver
stomach
inferior vena cava
ascending colon
hepatic veins
left gastric vein
sigmoid branches

spleen
esophagus
left colic vein
descending colon
cystic vein
gastroepiploic veins
small intestine

FIGURE 13-5 The Hepatic Portal System

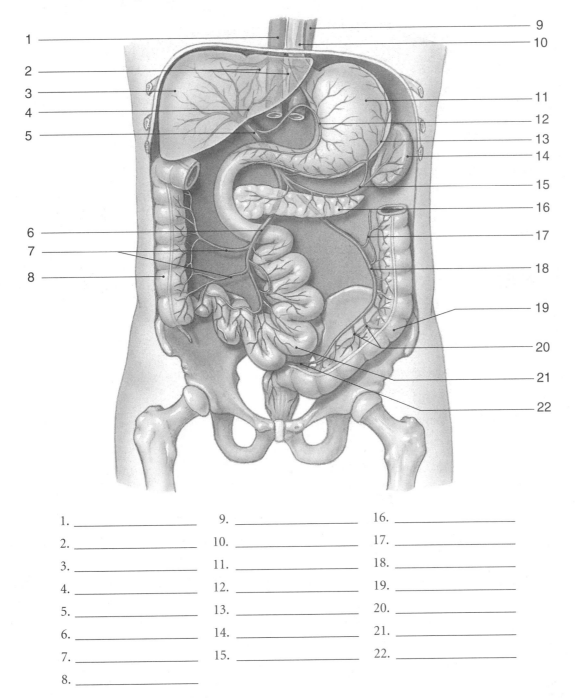

1. _____   9. _____   16. _____

2. _____   10. _____   17. _____

3. _____   11. _____   18. _____

4. _____   12. _____   19. _____

5. _____   13. _____   20. _____

6. _____   14. _____   21. _____

7. _____   15. _____   22. _____

8. _____

OBJECTIVE 9   Describe the age-related changes that occur in the cardiovascular system.

_____ 1. Elderly individuals usually have

      a. elevated hematocrits.
      b. stiff, inelastic arteries.
      c. decreased blood pressure.
      d. all of the above.

_____ 2. Elderly individuals are more prone to suffer from _____ than younger individuals.

      a. hypertension
      b. venous thrombosis
      c. arteriosclerosis
      d. All of the above are correct.

_____ 3. The primary cause of varicose veins is

      a. improper diet.
      b. aging.
      c. swelling due to edema in the veins.
      d. inefficient venous valves.

_____ 4. The primary effect of a decrease in the hematocrit of elderly individuals is

      a. thrombus formation in the blood vessels.
      b. a lowering of the oxygen-carrying capacity of the blood.
      c. a reduction in the maximum cardiac output.
      d. damage to ventricular cardiac muscle fibers.

OBJECTIVE 10   Discuss the structural and functional interactions among the cardiovascular system and other organ systems.

1. Of all the body systems, the most extensive communication occurs between the cardiovascular and _____ systems.

2. The system that modifies heart rate and regulates blood pressure is the _____ system.

3. The system that releases renin to elevate blood pressure and erythropoietin to accelerate RBC production is the _____ system.

4. The system that may slow development of arteriosclerosis with age is the _____ system.

5. The system that stores calcium needed for normal cardiac muscle contraction is the _____ system.

Part II: Chapter Comprehensive Exercises

A. Word Elimination

Circle the term that does not belong in each of the following groupings.

1. arteries   valves   arterioles   venules   veins

2. tunica interna   tunica media   tunica externa   tunica adventitia   tunica lumen

3. autoregulation   ANS   compression   endocrine factors   hormones

4. baroreceptors   increased acidity   rise in CO_2 decreased plasma O_2 decreased pH

5. NE   ACh   ADH   EPO   ANP

6. hypotension   acidosis   "clammy" skin   increased pH   disorientation

7. aortic arch   pulmonary vein   L. common carotid   brachiocephalic   L. subclavian

8. carotid A.   axillary A.   brachial A.   radial A.   ulnar A.

9. median cubital   cephalic   radial   phrenic   median antebrachial

10. decreased CO_2 increased hematocrit   decreased elasticity   increased scar tissue   atherosclerosis

B. Matching

Match the terms in Column "B" with the terms in Column "A." Place letters for answers in the spaces provided.

COLUMN A	COLUMN B
____ 1. sphygmomanometer	a. connected blood vessels
____ 2. autoregulation	b. immediate, localized, homeostatic adjustments
____ 3. systole	c. vasomotor center
____ 4. diastole	d. weakened vascular wall
____ 5. anastomosis	e. vasodilation
____ 6. peripheral resistance	f. brain circulation
____ 7. atrial natriuretic peptide	g. peak blood pressure
____ 8. circle of Willis	h. used to measure blood pressure
____ 9. medulla	i. viscosity and turbulence
____ 10. aneurysm	j. minimum blood pressure

C. Concept Map I - The Cardiovascular System

Using the following terms, fill in the circled numbered, blank spaces to complete the concept map. Follow the numbers that comply with the organization of the map.

Systemic circuit   Veins and venules   Pulmonary arteries

Pulmonary veins   Arteries and arterioles

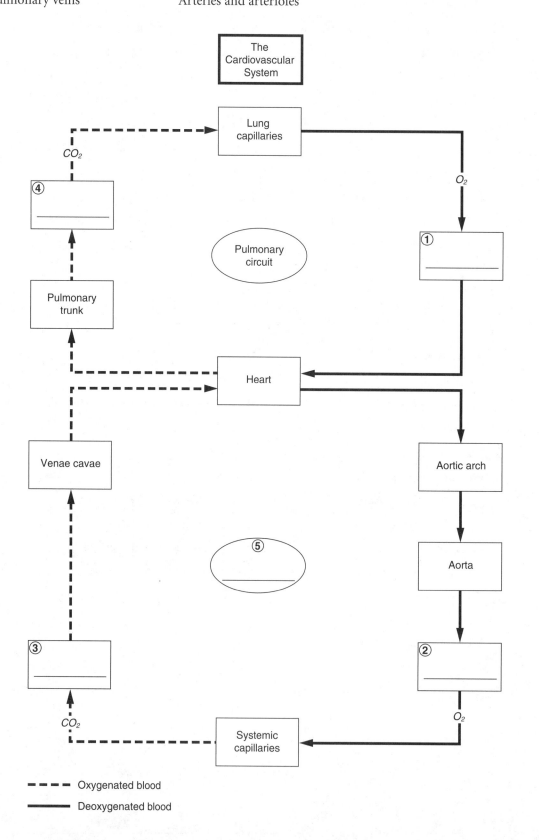

Concept Map II - Major Branches of the Aorta

Using the following terms, fill in the circled numbered, blank spaces to complete the concept map. Follow the numbers that comply with the organization of the map.

L. subclavian artery
Ascending aorta
Superior mesenteric artery
R. gonadal artery
L. common iliac artery
Celiac trunk
Thoracic aorta
Brachiocephalic artery

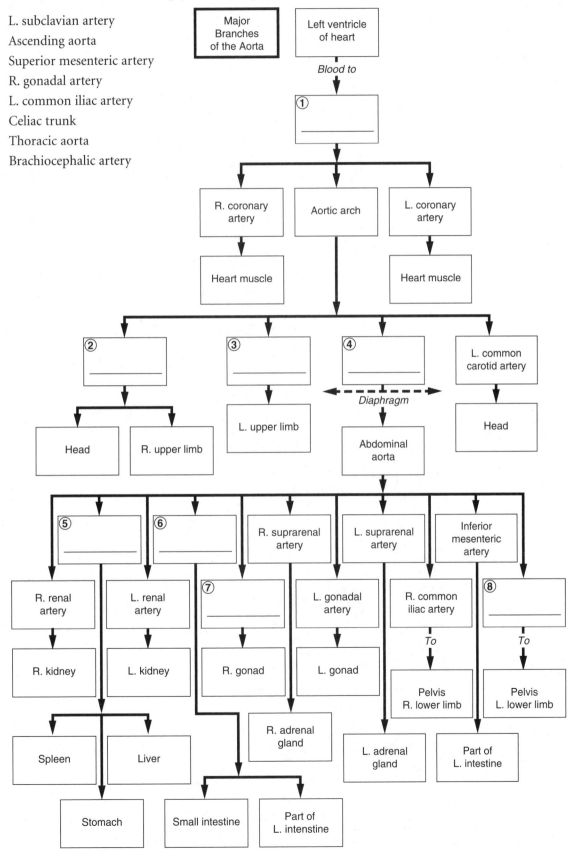

Concept Map III - Major Veins

Using the following terms, fill in the circled numbered, blank spaces to complete the concept map. Follow the numbers that comply with the organization of the map. (Note the direction of arrows on this map.)

Azygous vein
Superior vena cava
L. hepatic veins
L. renal vein
L. common iliac vein
R. suprarenal vein

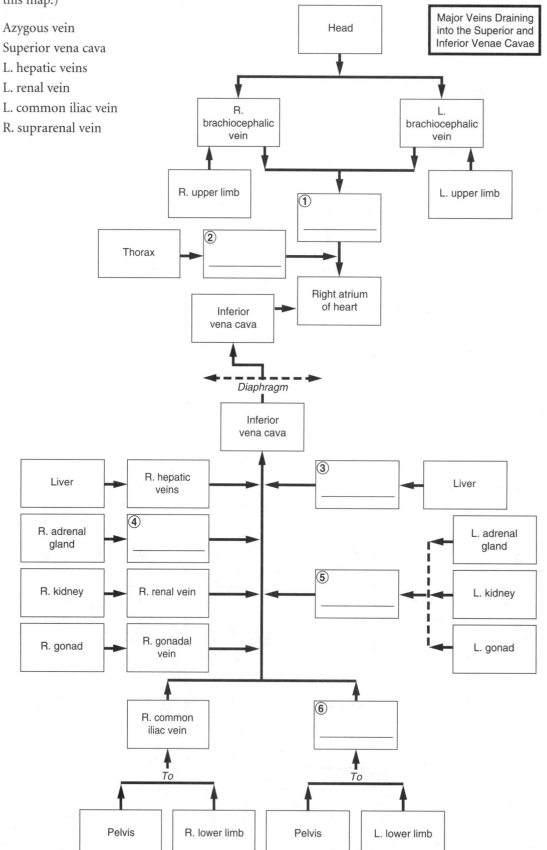

D. Crossword Puzzle

This crossword puzzle reviews the material in Chapter 13. To complete the puzzle you must know the answers to the clues given, and you must be able to spell the terms correctly.

ACROSS

2. Small air pockets surrounded by capillary networks.
4. Stimulates water reabsorption from urine.
6. Carry blood away from heart.
7. Alternating contraction and relaxation.
8. Minimum blood pressure.
9. Peak blood pressure.
10. Reflexes that respond to O_2 levels in the blood.
12. Movement of water across a semipermeable membrane.
13. Hormone produced by specialized cardiac cells.

DOWN

1. Aortic and carotid sinuses.
3. Permit exchanges between blood and interstitial fluid.
5. Only blood vessels that contain valves.
6. Stimulates water conservation at kidneys (abbreviation).
7. Carry blood to the heart.
11. Stimulates red blood cell production.

E. Short-Answer Questions

Briefly answer the following questions in the spaces provided.

1. Beginning with the heart, list (in order) the structures through which a drop of blood would pass during a single passage through the systemic circulation. Use arrows to indicate the direction of flow.

2. Relative to gaseous exchange, what is the primary difference between the pulmonary circuit and the systemic circuit?

3. (a) What are the three primary sources of peripheral resistance?

   (b) Which one can be adjusted by the nervous or endocrine system to regulate blood flow?

4. Write an equation that summarizes the relationships among blood pressure (BP), peripheral resistance (PR), and blood flow (F). State what the equation means.

5. Explain what is meant by $BP = \dfrac{120 \text{ mm Hg}}{80 \text{ mm Hg}}$.

6. What are the three primary factors that influence blood pressure and blood flow?

7. What three major baroreceptor populations enable the cardiovascular system to respond to alterations in blood pressure?

8. What hormones are responsible for the long-term and short-term regulation of cardiovascular performance?

9. How does arteriosclerosis affect blood vessels?

14

The Lymphatic System and Immunity

Overview

All the organ systems in the human body interact structurally and functionally to keep us alive and healthy. In this battle for survival, the lymphatic system plays a major role. The major enemies of the body's system of defense include an assortment of viruses, bacteria, fungi, and parasites. These potential disease-causing agents are responsible for many human diseases. The lymphatic system protects against disease-causing organisms primarily through the activities of lymphocytes. It is also responsible for the return of fluid and solutes from peripheral tissues to the blood, and for the distribution of hormones, nutrients, and waste products from their tissues of origin to the venous circulation.

Structurally, the lymphatic system consists of (1) a fluid called lymph; (2) a network of lymphatic vessels; (3) specialized cells called lymphocytes; and (4) lymphoid organs and tissues distributed throughout the body. Chapter 14 provides exercises that focus on topics that include the organization of the lymphatic system, the body's defense mechanisms, patterns of immune response, and the interactions between the lymphatic system and the other systems of the body.

Review of Chapter Objectives

1. Identify the major components of the lymphatic system and explain their functions.
2. Discuss the importance of lymphocytes and describe where they are found in the body.
3. List the body's nonspecific defenses and explain how each functions.
4. Define specific resistance and identify the forms and properties of immunity.
5. Distinguish between cell-mediated immunity and antibody-mediated (humoral) immunity.
6. Discuss the different types of T cells and the role played by each in the immune response.
7. Describe the structure of antibody molecules and explain how they function.
8. Describe the primary and secondary responses to antigen exposure.
9. Relate allergic reactions and autoimmune disorders to immune mechanisms.
10. Describe the changes in the immune system that occur with aging.
11. Discuss the structural and functional interactions among the lymphatic system and other body systems.

Part I: Objective-Based Questions

OBJECTIVE 1   Identify the major components of the lymphatic system and explain their functions.

_____ 1. The major components of the lymphatic system include

      a. lymph nodes, lymph, lymphocytes, and the thymus.
      b. the spleen, the thymus, tonsils, and fluid.
      c. the thoracic duct, R. lymphatic duct, lymph nodes, and lymphocytes.
      d. lymphatic vessels, lymph, lymphoid organs, and lymphocytes.

_____ 2. Lymphatic organs found in the lymphatic system include

      a. the thoracic duct, R. lymphatic duct, and lymph nodes.
      b. lymphatic vessels, tonsils, and lymph nodes.
      c. the spleen, the thymus, and lymph nodes.
      d. all of the above.

_____ 3. The body's ability to resist infection and disease through the action of specific defenses is called

      a. lymphocytosis.
      b. phagocytosis.
      c. pyrogenesis.
      d. immunity.

_____ 4. The lymphatic system

      a. helps maintain normal blood volume.
      b. fights infection.
      c. eliminates variations in the composition of interstitial fluid.
      d. All of the above are correct.

_____ 5. Anatomically, lymph vessels resemble

      a. arterioles.
      b. veins.
      c. elastic arteries.
      d. the vena cava.

6. Most of the lymph returns to the venous circulation by way of the _____.

7. The structures in the lymphatic system that act as a "way station" for cancer cells are the

_____.

Labeling Exercise

Identify and label the following structures of the lymphatic system. Place your answers in the spaces provided below the drawing.

inguinal lymph nodes   R. lymphatic duct   axillary lymph nodes

lumbar lymph nodes   thymus   spleen

thoracic duct   L. lymphatic duct

FIGURE 14-1 The Lymphatic System

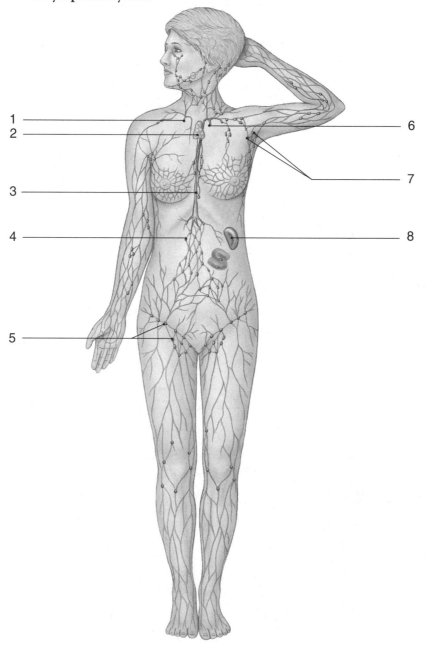

1. _____   5. _____

2. _____   6. _____

3. _____   7. _____

4. _____   8. _____

OBJECTIVE 2   Discuss the importance of lymphocytes and describe where they are found in the body.

_____ 1. The three classes of lymphocytes found in the blood are

       a. T cells, B cells, and NK cells.
       b. neutrophils, eosinophils, and basophils.
       c. WBCs, RBCs, and platelets.
       d. erythrocytes, leukocytes, and monocytes.

_____ 2. Lymphocytes that assist in the regulation and coordination of the immune response are

       a. plasma cells.
       b. helper T and suppressor T cells.
       c. B cells.
       d. NK and B cells.

_____ 3. Normal lymphocyte populations are maintained through lymphopoiesis in the

       a. bone marrow and thymus.
       b. lymph in lymphatic tissues.
       c. blood and the lymph.
       d. spleen and liver.

_____ 4. The type(s) of lymphocytes that produce antibodies are

       a. NK cells.
       b. T cells.
       c. B cells.
       d. All of the above are correct.

_____ 5. Cytotoxic T cells are the primary providers of

       a. cell-mediated immunity.
       b. immunological surveillance.
       c. the inflammatory response.
       d. phagocytic activity for defense.

_____ 6. Hemocytoblasts in the bone marrow produce lymphoid stem cells that generate

       a. B cells.
       b. NK cells.
       c. T cells.
       d. all of the above.

OBJECTIVE 3   List the body's nonspecific defenses and explain how each functions.

_____ 1. The body's nonspecific defenses that are present at birth include

       a. physical barriers and phagocytic cells.
       b. immunological surveillance and fever.
       c. interferons, complement, and inflammation.
       d. all of the above.

_____ 2. NK (natural killer) cells sensitive to the presence of abnormal cell membranes are primarily involved in

       a. defenses against specific threats.
       b. complex and time-consuming defense mechanisms.
       c. phagocytic activity for defense.
       d. immunological surveillance.

_____ 3. The protein(s) that interfere(s) with the replication of viruses is(are)

       a. complement proteins.
       b. heparin.
       c. interferon.
       d. pyrogens.

_____ 4. The nonspecific defense that breaks down cell walls, attracts phagocytes, and stimulates inflammation is

       a. the inflammatory response.
       b. the complement system.
       c. the action of interferons.
       d. immunological surveillance.

_____ 5. Circulating proteins that reset the thermostat in the hypothalamus, causing a rise in body temperature, are called

       a. pyrogens.
       b. interferons.
       c. complement proteins.
       d. lysosomes.

Labeling Exercise

Fill in the blanks (1 through 7) with the type of nonspecific defense strategy. Place your answers in the spaces provided below the figure.

FIGURE 14-2 Nonspecific Defenses

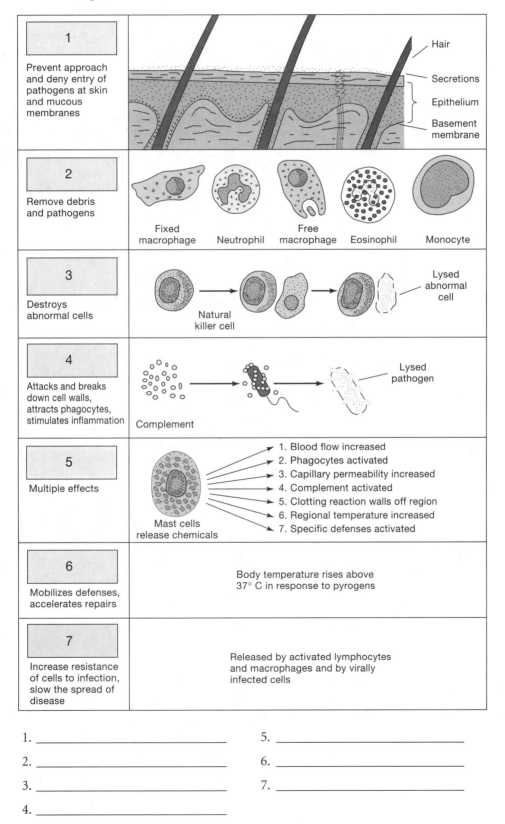

1. _____   5. _____

2. _____   6. _____

3. _____   7. _____

4. _____

OBJECTIVE 4   Define specific resistance and identify the forms and properties of immunity.

_____ 1. The four general properties of specific defenses include

        a. specificity, versatility, memory, and tolerance.

        b. innate, active, acquired, and passive immunity.

        c. accessibility, recognition, compatibility, and immunity.

        d. all of the above.

_____ 2. The two major ways the body "carries out" the immune response are

        a. phagocytosis and inflammation.

        b. immunological surveillance and fever.

        c. direct attack by T cells and circulating antibodies.

        d. physical barriers and complement.

_____ 3. A specific defense mechanism is always activated by

        a. inflammation.

        b. an antibody.

        c. fever.

        d. an antigen.

_____ 4. The first line of cellular defense against pathogens is

        a. T cells.

        b. B cells.

        c. phagocytes.

        d. NK cells.

_____ 5. Immunity resulting from natural exposure to an antigen in the environment is called

        a. passive natural immunity.

        b. active immunity.

        c. autoimmunity.

        d. innate immunity.

_____ 6. Immunity that results from the transfer of antibodies to an individual from some other source is called

        a. active artificial immunity.

        b. autoimmunity.

        c. passive immunity.

        d. active natural immunity.

_____ 7. The basic principle behind vaccination to prevent disease involves

        a. naturally acquired immunity.

        b. induced active immunity.

        c. acquired passive immunity.

        d. induced passive immunity.

OBJECTIVE 5 Distinguish between cell-mediated immunity and antibody-mediated (humoral) immunity.

_____ 1. When an antigen appears, the immune response begins with the

     a. presence of immunoglobulins in body fluids.
     b. release of endogenous pyrogens.
     c. activation of the complement system.
     d. activation of specific T cells and B cells.

_____ 2. When the immune "recognition" system malfunctions, activated B cells begin to

     a. manufacture antibodies against other cells and tissues.
     b. activate cytotoxic T cells.
     c. secrete lymphotoxins to destroy foreign antigens.
     d. recall memory T cells to initiate the proper response.

_____ 3. T cells are involved with _____ and _____ attack pathogens.

     a. cell-mediated responses; directly
     b. cell-mediated responses; indirectly
     c. humoral responses; directly
     d. humoral responses; indirectly

_____ 4. B cells are involved with _____ and create a chemical attack on _____.

     a. cell-mediated responses; antigens
     b. cell-mediated responses; pathogens
     c. humoral responses; antibodies
     d. humoral responses; antigens

_____ 5. The cells responsible for the production of circulating antibodies are

     a. NK cells.
     b. plasma cells.
     c. helper T cells.
     d. cytotoxic T cells.

OBJECTIVE 6 Discuss the different types of T cells and the role played by each in the immune response.

_____ 1. T-cell activation leads to the formation of cytotoxic T cells and memory T cells that provide

     a. humoral immunity
     b. cell-mediated immunity.
     c. phagocytosis and immunological surveillance.
     d. stimulation of inflammation and fever.

_____ 2. Destruction of target cells by the local release of cytokines, lymphotoxins, or perforin involves

     a. B cell activation.
     b. plasma cells.
     c. memory B cells.
     d. cytotoxic T cells.

_____ 3. Suppressor T cells act to

      a. suppress antigens.

      b. limit the degree of memory in memory T cells.

      c. limit antigen proliferation.

      d. depress the responses of other T cells and B cells.

_____ 4. A defense against abnormal cells and pathogens inside living cells is provided by

      a. B cells.

      b. T cells.

      c. plasma cells.

      d. antigens.

OBJECTIVE 7   Describe the structure of antibody molecules and explain how they function.

_____ 1. An active antibody is shaped like a(n)

      a. T.

      b. Y.

      c. A.

      d. B.

_____ 2. The most important antibody action(s) in the body is(are)

      a. alterations in the cell membrane to increase phagocytosis.

      b. to attract macrophages and neutrophils to the infected areas.

      c. activation of the complement systems.

      d. cell lysis and digestion of the cell membrane.

_____ 3. The specificity of an antibody is determined by the

      a. fixed segments of antigen-binding sites.

      b. size and shape of the antibody.

      c. antigenic determinants.

      d. variable segments of light and heavy chains.

_____ 4. The binding of an antigen to an antibody can result in

      a. neutralization of the antigen.

      b. agglutination or precipitation.

      c. complement activation.

      d. all of the above.

OBJECTIVE 8   Describe the primary and secondary responses to antigen exposure.

_____ 1. The antigenic determinant site is that portion of the antigen's exposed surface where

      a. the foreign "body" attacks.

      b. phagocytosis occurs.

      c. the antibody attacks.

      d. the immune surveillance system is activated.

_____   2. In order for an antigenic molecule to be a complete antigen, it must

        a. be a large molecule.
        b. be immunogenic and reactive.
        c. contain a hapten and a small organic molecule.
        d. be subject to antibody activity.

_____   3. Antibody secretion by memory B cells is the secondary response to

        a. antigen exposure.
        b. inflammation.
        c. agglutination.
        d. precipitation.

_____   4. The reason the primary response takes time to develop is that

        a. memory B cells must differentiate into plasma cells.
        b. antigen-activated B cells must differentiate into plasma cells.
        c. the release of chemical messengers must be coordinated by physical interactions.
        d. All of the above are correct.

_____   5. The antibodies produced by active plasma cells bind to the target antigen to

        a. inhibit its activity.
        b. destroy it.
        c. remove it from solution.
        d. All of the above are correct.

    6. The hormones released by synthesizing cells that make neighboring cells resistant to viral infection, thereby slowing the spread of the virus, are called _____.

    7. The ability to demonstrate an immune response upon exposure to an antigen is called

_____.

OBJECTIVE 9   Relate allergic reactions and autoimmune disorders to immune mechanisms.

_____   1. Misguided antibodies that function against normal body cells and tissues are called

        a. allergens.
        b. SCIDA.
        c. autoantibodies.
        d. cytotoxic reactions.

_____   2. Inappropriate or excessive immune responses to antigens are

        a. autoimmune diseases.
        b. allergies.
        c. immunodeficiency diseases.
        d. the result of stress.

_____ 3. When an immune response mistakenly targets normal body cells and tissues, the result is

  a. immune system failure.
  b. the development of an allergy.
  c. depression of the inflammatory response.
  d. an autoimmune disorder.

_____ 4. When the immune system fails to develop normally or the immune response is blocked in some way, the condition is called an

  a. allergy.
  b. inflammation.
  c. immunodeficiency disease.
  d. autoimmune disorder.

OBJECTIVE 10   Describe the changes in the immune system that occur with aging.

_____ 1. With advancing age the immune system becomes

  a. increasingly susceptible to viral infection.
  b. increasingly susceptible to bacterial infection.
  c. less effective at combating disease.
  d. all of the above.

_____ 2. With age, B cells become less active due to a reduced number of

  a. antibodies.
  b. cytotoxic T cells.
  c. helper T cells.
  d. plasma cells.

_____ 3. When T cells become less responsive to antigens,

  a. fewer cytotoxic T cells respond to an infection.
  b. increasing levels of circulating thymic hormones are released.
  c. an apparent enlarging of the thymus occurs.
  d. decreased susceptibility to viral infections occurs.

_____ 4. Because tumor cells are not eliminated as effectively in the elderly, the incidence of cancer reflects the fact that

  a. B cells are less responsive.
  b. immunological surveillance declines.
  c. the effectiveness of helper T cells declines.
  d. antibody levels decrease more slowly after antigen exposure.

OBJECTIVE 11   Discuss the structural and functional interactions among the lymphatic system and other body systems.

1. The lymphatic system provides IgA for secretion by epithelial glands in the

_____ system.

2. Specific defenses against infection and immune surveillance against cancer for all the body

systems is provided by the _____ system.

3. The tonsils protect against infection at entrance to the _____ tract.

4. Protection of superficial lymph nodes and the lymphatic vessels in the abdominopelvic cavity is provided by the _____ system.

5. Lymphocytes and other cells involved in the immune response are produced and stored in the _____ system.

Part II: Chapter Comprehensive Exercises

A. Word Elimination

Circle the term that does not belong in each of the following groupings.

1. thymus   lymph nodes   spleen   pineal gland   tonsils
2. B cells   plasma cells   antigens   T cells   NK cells
3. pharyngeal   salivary   adenoid   palatine   lingual
4. capsule   medulla   sinus   cortex   nephron
5. antibodies   phagocytosis   complement   fever   interferons
6. mucus   acid   blood   urine   glandular secretions
7. complement   innate   active   acquired   passive
8. specificity   versatility   memory   tolerance   compatibility
9. IgG   IgM   IgA   IgE   IgB
10. MCF   interleukins   interferons   enzymes   CSFs

B. Matching

Match the terms in Column "B" with the terms in Column "A." Use letters for answers in the spaces provided.

COLUMN A

___ 1. macrophages
___ 2. microphages
___ 3. mast cells
___ 4. acquired immunity
___ 5. specific immunity
___ 6. B cells
___ 7. passive immunity
___ 8. cytotoxic T cells
___ 9. diapedesis
___10. NK cells

COLUMN B

a. active and passive
b. humoral immunity
c. migration of phagocytes
d. transfer of antibodies
e. neutrophils and eosinophils
f. cellular immunity
g. innate or acquired
h. monocytes
i. immunological surveillance
j. nonspecific immune response

C. Concept Map I - Immune System

Using the following terms, fill in the circled numbered, blank spaces to complete the concept map. Follow the numbers that comply with the organization of the map.

Active immunization
Nonspecific immunity
Active
Transfer of antibodies
  via placenta
Passive immunization

Inflammation
Phagocytic cells
Acquired
Specific immunity
Innate

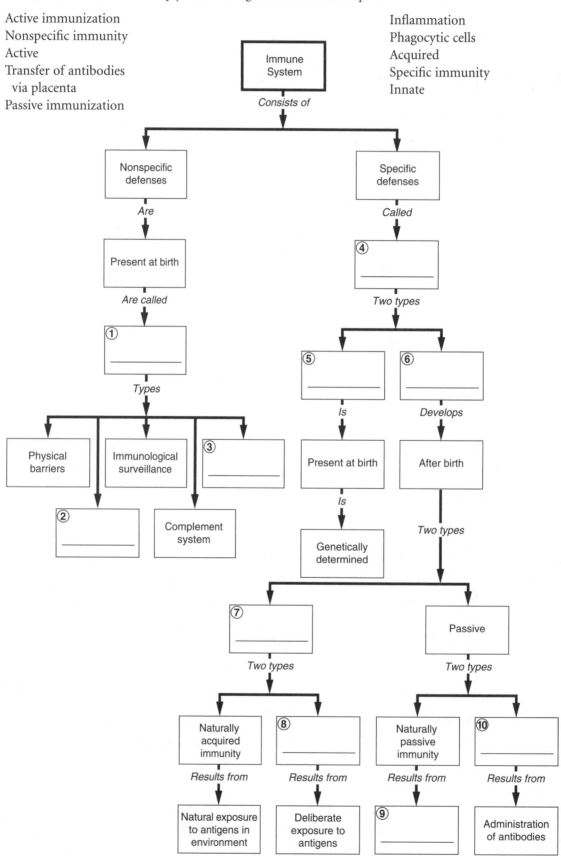

Concept Map II - The Body's Department of Defense

Using the terms below, fill in the numbered blank spaces to complete the map through the body's department of defense. Start at statement ① and proceed clockwise to statement ⑨ and ⑩. At each site you will complete the event that is taking place by identifying the type of cells or proteins participating in the specific immune response. Place your answers in the spaces provided.

Killer T cells

Viruses

B cells

Memory B cells

Antibodies

Helper T cells

Macrophages

Natural killer cells

Suppressor T cells

Memory T cells

④ _____

(the battle managers of the immune system) emit signals to B cells and killer T cells to join the attack.

⑤ _____

(produced in bones) mature into plasma cells, which in turn produce antibodies.

⑥ _____

are Y-shaped proteins designed specifically to recognize a particular viral or bacterial invader. Antibodies bind to the virus and neutralize it.

Stimulated by the release of interleukins from macrophages, helper T cells, and interferons,

③ _____

join the attack on virally infected cells. They also fight cancer cells.

⑦ _____

wage chemical warfare on virally infected cells by firing lethal proteins at them.

As the body begins to conquer the viruses,

⑧ _____

help the immune system gear down. Otherwise, it might attack the body.

② _____

quickly recognize the viruses as a foreign threat. They begin destroying viruses by engulfing them.

The race is on;

① _____

try to replicate before the immune system can gear up. Two have already taken over cells in the body.

As the viruses are being defeated, the body creates

⑨ _____   and   ⑩ _____

that circulate permanently in the bloodstream, ensuring that next time, that particular virus will be swiftly conquered.

D. Crossword Puzzle

The following crossword puzzle reviews the material in Chapter 14. To complete the puzzle, you must know the answers to the clues given, and must be able to spell the terms correctly.

ACROSS

4. Antibodies target and "attack" specific _____.
6. The type of white blood cells that can differentiate into T or B cells.
7. Inborn immunity is called _____ immunity.
8. Compounds that promote a fever.

DOWN

1. Vaccination is a type of artificially _____ immunity.
2. _____ cells produce antibodies.
3. Injecting an antigen from a weakened or dead pathogen into the body is a process called

   _____.
4. The pharyngeal tonsils are also called the _____.
5. The _____ gland converts lymphocytes to T cells.
6. After tissue fluid drains into the lymphatic vessels, it is called _____.

E. Short-Answer Questions

Briefly answer the following questions in the spaces provided.

1. What are the three primary organizational components of the lymphatic system?

2. What three major functions are performed by the lymphatic system?

3. What are the three different classes of lymphocytes found in the blood, and where does each class originate?

4. What three kinds of T cells compose 80 percent of the circulating lymphocyte population? What is each type basically responsible for?

5. What is the primary function of stimulated B cells, and what are they ultimately responsible for?

6. What three lymphatic organs are important in the lymphatic system?

7. What are the primary differences between the "recognition" mechanisms of NK (natural killer) cells and of T cells and B cells?

8. What four primary effects result from complement activation?

9. What are the four general characteristics of specific defenses?

10. What is the primary difference between active immunity and passive immunity?

The Respiratory System

Overview

The circulatory and respiratory systems interact to obtain and deliver oxygen to body cells and to remove carbon dioxide from the body. The respiratory system can be divided into upper and lower tracts. Structures in the upper respiratory tract include the nose, the nasal cavity, the paranasal sinuses, and the pharnyx.

The lower respiratory tract includes the larnyx, trachea, bronchi, bronchioles, and alveoli. The terminal bronchioles and alveoli are involved with the gaseous exchange of oxygen and carbon dioxide, whereas all the other structures of the respiratory tracts serve as passageways for incoming and outgoing air and protection of the lungs. The respiratory system also plays an important role in regulating the pH of the body fluids.

The questions and activities in this chapter reinforce the concepts of the structural organization and the primary functions of the respiratory system, control of respiration, and respiratory interactions with other systems.

Review of Chapter Objectives

1. Describe the primary functions of the respiratory system.

2. Explain how the delicate respiratory exchange surfaces are protected from pathogens, debris, and other hazards.

3. Relate respiratory functions to the structural specializations of the tissues and organs of the system.

4. Describe the physical principles governing the movement of air into the lungs and the diffusion of gases into and out of the blood.

5. Describe the actions of respiratory muscles during respiratory movements.

6. Describe how oxygen and carbon dioxide are transported in the blood.

7. Describe the major factors that influence the rate of respiration.

8. Identify the reflexes that regulate respiration.

9. Describe the changes that occur in the respiratory system at birth and with aging.

10. Discuss the interrelationships among the respiratory system and other systems.

Part I: Objective-Based Questions

OBJECTIVE 1   Describe the primary functions of the respiratory system.

_____ 1. The functions of the respiratory system include

   a. providing an area for gas exchange between air and blood.
   b. moving air to and from exchange surfaces and defending against pathogens.
   c. producing sound and providing olfactory sensations to the CNS.
   d. all of the above.

_____ 2. The breathing process is called

   a. cellular respiration.
   b. pulmonary ventilation.
   c. respiration.
   d. systemic ventilation.

_____ 3. The two primary gases involved in the respiratory process are

   a. oxygen and carbon dioxide.
   b. carbon dioxide and nitrogen.
   c. oxygen and nitrogen.
   d. All of the above are correct.

_____ 4. The movement of gases into the blood from the lungs occurs by

   a. osmosis.
   b. metabolism.
   c. net diffusion.
   d. cellular respiration.

_____ 5. The diffusion of gases between blood and interstitial fluid across the endothelial cells of capillary walls is called

   a. external respiration.
   b. internal respiration.
   c. cellular respiration.
   d. pulmonary ventilation.

_____ 6. The diffusion of gases between the blood and alveolar air across the respiratory membrane is called

   a. cellular respiration.
   b. external respiration.
   c. systemic ventilation.
   d. internal respiration.

OBJECTIVE 2   Explain how the delicate respiratory exchange surfaces are protected from pathogens, debris, and other hazards.

_____ 1. The "patrol force" of the alveolar epithelium involved with phagocytosis is composed primarily of alveolar

     a. NK cells.
     b. cytotoxic cells.
     c. macrophages.
     d. plasma cells.

_____ 2. Pulmonary surfactant is a phospholipid secretion produced by alveolar cells to

     a. increase the surface area of alveoli.
     b. reduce the cohesive force of H_2O molecules and reduce surface tension.
     c. increase the cohesive force of air molecules and raise surface tension.
     d. reduce the attractive force of O_2 molecules and increase surface tension.

_____ 3. Large airborne particles are filtered by the

     a. external olfactory meatuses.
     b. soft palate.
     c. nasal sinuses.
     d. nasal hairs in the vestibule of the nose.

_____ 4. Creating turbulence in the air to trap small particles in mucus is the function of the

     a. nasal conchae.
     b. soft palate.
     c. nasal sinuses.
     d. nasal hairs.

_____ 5. Air entering the body is filtered, warmed, and humidified by the

     a. upper respiratory tract.
     b. lower respiratory tract.
     c. lungs.
     d. alveoli.

Labeling Exercise

Identify and label the following structures in Figure 15-1. Place your answers in the spaces provided on the following page.

trachea	nasopharynx	mandible
oropharynx	tongue	epiglottis
cricoid cartilage	internal nares	hyoid bone
pharyngeal tonsil	thyroid cartilage	soft palate
auditory tube	oral cavity	palatine tonsil
external nares	vocal cord	hard palate
nasal vestibule	laryngopharynx	nasal conchae
glottis	esophagus	frontal sinus

FIGURE 15-1 The Nose, Nasal Cavity, and Pharynx

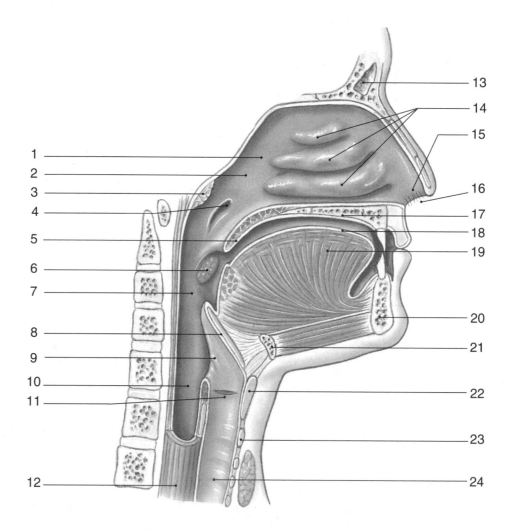

1. _____	9. _____	17. _____
2. _____	10. _____	18. _____
3. _____	11. _____	19. _____
4. _____	12. _____	20. _____
5. _____	13. _____	21 _____
6. _____	14. _____	22. _____
7. _____	15. _____	23. _____
8. _____	16. _____	24. _____

OBJECTIVE 3   Relate respiratory functions to the structural specializations of the tissues and organs of the system.

_____ 1. The respiratory system consists of structures that

  a. provide defense from pathogenic invasion.
  b. permit vocalization and production of other sounds.
  c. provide olfactory sensations to the CNS.
  d. All of the above are correct.

_____ 2. The ligaments in the larynx that are relatively inelastic and help prevent foreign objects from entering the glottis are the

  a. true vocal cords.
  b. cricoid cartilage.
  c. false vocal cords.
  d. thyroid cartilage.

_____ 3. Structures in the trachea that prevent its collapse or overexpansion as pressure changes in the respiratory system are

  a. O-shaped tracheal cartilages.
  b. C-shaped tracheal cartilages.
  c. irregular circular bones.
  d. S-shaped tracheal bones.

_____ 4. The hard palate separates the

  a. nasal cavity and the oral cavity.
  b. nasal cavity from the larynx.
  c. left and right sides of the nasal cavity.
  d. external nares from the internal nares.

_____ 5. The narrow opening through which inhaled air leaves the pharynx and enters the larynx is the

  a. epiglottis.
  b. "Adam's apple."
  c. glottis.
  d. corniculate cartilage.

_____ 6. The cartilage that makes up most of the anterior and lateral surface of the larynx is the

     a. cricoid cartilage.
     b. thyroid cartilage.
     c. cuneiform cartilage.
     d. arytenoid cartilage.

_____ 7. The diameter of the trachea is adjusted by contractions of the trachealis muscle, which is under

     a. autonomic control.
     b. the control of the CNS.
     c. vascular control.
     d. the control of the somatic nervous system.

_____ 8. The following is a list of some of the structures of the respiratory tree: (1) secondary bronchi, (2) bronchioles, (3) alveolar ducts, (4) primary bronchi, (5) respiratory bronchioles, (6) alveoli, (7) terminal bronchioles.

The order in which air passes through the structures is

     a. 4, 1, 2, 7, 5, 3, 6.
     b. 4, 1, 2, 5, 7, 3, 6.
     c. 1, 4, 2, 5, 7, 3, 6.
     d. 1, 4, 2, 7, 5, 3, 6.

_____ 9. The respiratory membrane consists primarily of

     a. ciliated pseudostratified columnar epithelium.
     b. moist cuboidal epithelium.
     c. simple squamous epithelium.
     d. ciliated squamous epithelium.

10. The openings to the nostrils are the _____.

11. The portion of the nasal cavity contained within the flexible tissues of the external nose is the_____.

12. The portion of the pharynx that receives both air and food is the _____.

13. The common passageway shared by the respiratory and digestive systems is the

_____.

14. The openings to the eustachian tube are located in the _____.

15. The vocal cords are located in the _____.

16. The airway between the larynx and the primary bronchi is the _____.

17. Secondary bronchi supply air to the _____.

18. Structures formed by the branching of the trachea within the mediastinum are

_____.

19. The actual sites of gas exchange within the lungs are the _____.

Labeling Exercise

Identify and label the following structures in Figure 15-2. Place your answers in the spaces provided below the drawing.

left lung

sphenoidal sinus

left bronchus

tracheal cartilage

tongue

cricoid cartilage

vocal cords

diaphragm

epiglottis

frontal sinus

thyroid cartilage

larynx

nasal conchae

pharynx

right lung

esophagus

hyoid

FIGURE 15-2 Components of the Respiratory System

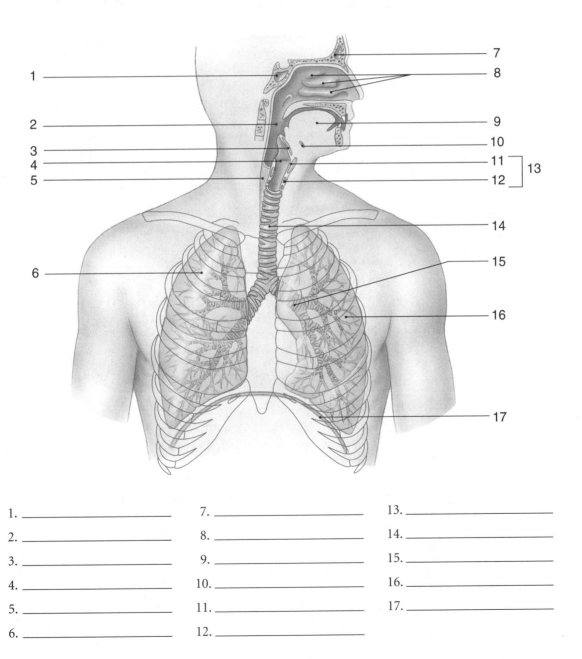

1. _____

2. _____

3. _____

4. _____

5. _____

6. _____

7. _____

8. _____

9. _____

10. _____

11. _____

12. _____

13. _____

14. _____

15. _____

16. _____

17. _____

OBJECTIVE 4 Describe the physical principles governing the movement of air into the lungs and the diffusion of gases into and out of the blood.

_____ 1. A necessary condition for normal gas exchange in the alveoli is

      a. for the alveoli to remain dry.
      b. an increase in pressure in pulmonary circulation.
      c. for fluid to move into the pulmonary capillaries.
      d. an increase in lung volume.

_____ 2. The movement of air into and out of the lungs is primarily dependent on

      a. pressure differences between the air in the atmosphere and air in the lungs.
      b. pressure differences between the air in the atmosphere and the anatomic dead space.
      c. pressure differences between the air in the atmosphere and individual cells.
      d. All of the above are correct.

_____ 3. During inspiration, an increase in the volume of the thoracic cavity is accompanied by

      a. decreasing lung volume and increasing intrapulmonary pressure.
      b. decreasing lung volume and decreasing intrapulmonary pressure.
      c. increasing lung volume and decreasing intrapulmonary pressure.
      d. increasing lung volume and increasing intrapulmonary pressure.

_____ 4. During expiration, a(n) _____ occurs.

      a. decrease in intrapulmonary pressure
      b. increase in intrapulmonary pressure
      c. increase in atmospheric pressure
      d. increase in the volume of the lungs

_____ 5. If there is a P_{O_2} of 104 mm Hg and P_{CO_2} of 40 mm Hg in the alveoli, and a P_{O_2} of 40 mm Hg and a P_{CO_2} of 45 mm Hg within the pulmonary blood, there will be a net diffusion of

      a. CO_2 into the blood from alveoli, and of O_2 from the blood into alveoli.
      b. O_2 and CO_2 into the blood from the alveoli.
      c. O_2 and CO_2 from the blood into the alveoli.
      d. O_2 into the blood from alveoli, and of CO_2 from the blood into the alveoli.

_____ 6. Each molecule of hemoglobin has the capacity to carry _____ molecules of oxygen (O_2).

      a. 6
      b. 8
      c. 4
      d. 2

_____ 7. What percentage of total oxygen (O_2) is carried within red blood cells chemically bound to hemoglobin?

    a. 5%
    b. 68%
    c. 98%
    d. 100%

_____ 8. Factors that cause a decrease in hemoglobin saturation at a given P_{O_2} are

    a. increasing P_{O_2}, decreasing CO_2, and increasing temperature.
    b. increasing temperature, decreasing pH, and increasing local P_{O_2}.
    c. decreasing DPG, increasing pH, and increasing CO_2.
    d. decreasing temperature, decreasing CO_2, decreasing P_{O_2}.

OBJECTIVE 5   Describe the actions of respiratory muscles during respiratory movements.

_____ 1. During exhalation, the diaphragm moves

    a. upward and the ribs move downward.
    b. downward and the ribs move upward.
    c. downward and the ribs move downward.
    d. upward and the ribs move upward.

_____ 2. When the diaphragm and external intercostal muscles contract, the

    a. volume of the thorax increases.
    b. volume of the thorax decreases.
    c. volume of the lungs decreases.
    d. lungs collapse.

_____ 3. The amount of air moved into or out of the lungs in a single passive respiratory cycle is the

    a. expiratory reserve volume.
    b. residual volume.
    c. tidal volume.
    d. vital capacity.

_____ 4. The amount of air exhaled with one forceful breath is the

    a. tidal volume.
    b. vital capacity.
    c. residual volume.
    d. expiratory reserve volume.

OBJECTIVE 6   Describe how oxygen and carbon dioxide are transported in the blood.

_____ 1. Most of the oxygen transported by the blood is

        a. dissolved in plasma.
        b. bound to hemoglobin.
        c. carried by white blood cells.
        d. in ionic form in the plasma.

_____ 2. Most of the carbon dioxide in the blood is transported as

        a. carbonic acid.
        b. bicarbonate ions.
        c. carbaminohemoglobin.
        d. a solute dissolved in the plasma.

_____ 3. A 10% increase in the level of carbon dioxide in the blood will

        a. decrease the rate of breathing.
        b. decrease pulmonary ventilation.
        c. increase the rate of breathing.
        d. decrease the rate of alveolar ventilation.

_____ 4. The percentage of CO_2 that binds to hemoglobin in RBCs is

        a. 7%.
        b. 23%.
        c. 70%.
        d. 93%.

_____ 5. The percentage of CO_2 converted to bicarbonate ions in RBCs is

        a. 7%.
        b. 23%.
        c. 70%.
        d. 98%.

_____ 6. An increase in CO_2 will _____ the concentration of H^+ in RBCs, which will _____ the pH of the blood.

        a. increase; decrease
        b. increase; increase
        c. decrease; decrease
        d. decrease; increase

Labeling Exercise

In the following diagram, fill in the correct percentages to complete Figure 15-3 correctly. Use the following percentages to complete the exercise, and record your answers in the spaces provided below the drawing.

70%   7%   93%   23%

FIGURE 15-3   Carbon Dioxide Transport in the Blood

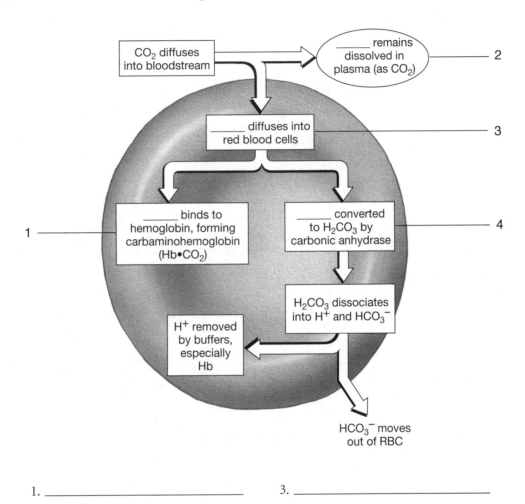

1. _____   3. _____

2. _____   4. _____

OBJECTIVE 7   Describe the major factors that influence the rate of respiration.

_____ 1. The brain's involuntary respiratory centers that regulate the respiratory muscles and control the frequency and depth of breathing are the

  a. brain stem and cerebrum.
  b. cerebrum and cerebellum.
  c. diencephalon and corpus callosum.
  d. pons and medulla oblongata.

_____ 2. The normal rate and depth of breathing are established by the

  a. inspiratory center.
  b. expiratory center.
  c. vasomotor center.
  d. dorsal respiratory group.

_____ 3. The receptors located in the carotid arteries are

  a. chemoreceptors.
  b. pressure receptors.
  c. stretch receptors.
  d. Both a and b are correct.

_____ 4. The output from baroreceptors affects the respiratory centers, causing the respiratory rate to

  a. decrease without affecting blood pressure.
  b. increase with an increase in blood pressure.
  c. decrease with a decrease in blood pressure.
  d. increase with a decrease in blood pressure.

_____ 5. Under normal conditions, the greatest effect on the respiratory centers is initiated by

  a. decreases in P_{O_2}.
  b. increases and decreases in P_{O_2} and P_{CO_2}.
  c. increases and decreases in P_{CO_2}.
  d. increases in P_{O_2}.

_____ 6. An elevated body temperature will

  a. accelerate respiration.
  b. decrease respiration.
  c. increase depth of respiration.
  d. not affect the respiratory rate.

7. The volume of air breathed in during an inhalation is controlled by stretch receptors in the

  _____.

8. The gas that establishes the rate of breathing is _____.

OBJECTIVE 8   Identify the reflexes that regulate respiration.

_____ 1. Reflexes important in regulating the forced ventilations that accompany strenuous exercise are known as the

   a. Hering-Brewer reflexes.
   b. protective reflexes.
   c. plantar reflexes.
   d. chemoreceptor reflexes.

_____ 2. Reflexes that are responses to changes in the volume of the lungs or to changes in arterial blood pressure are

   a. chemoreceptor reflexes.
   b. baroreceptor reflexes.
   c. stretch receptor reflexes.
   d. mechanoreceptor reflexes.

_____ 3. Reflexes that are a response to changes in the P_{O_2} and P_{CO_2} of the blood and cerebrospinal fluid are _____ reflexes.

   a. chemoreceptor
   b. stretch receptor
   c. mechanoreceptor
   d. baroreceptor

_____ 4. The reflex that prevents the lungs from overexpanding during forced breathing is the _____ reflex.

   a. inflation
   b. deflation
   c. chemoreceptor
   d. baroreceptor

_____ 5. The reflex that inhibits the expiratory center and stimulates the inspiratory center when the lungs are collapsing is the _____ reflex.

   a. deflation
   b. chemoreceptor
   c. inflammatory
   d. inflation

OBJECTIVE 9 Describe the changes that occur in the respiratory system at birth and with aging.

_____ 1. At birth, blood is pulled into the pulmonary circulation by

      a. the same drop in pressure that pulls air into the lungs.
      b. pulmonary surfactant.
      c. pulmonary arterial resistance.
      d. powerful contractions of the diaphragm.

_____ 2. The destruction of alveoli due to aging or by respiratory irritants is called

      a. asthma.
      b. emphysema.
      c. pneumonia.
      d. pulmonary embolism.

_____ 3. The loss of elasticity in the lungs due to aging decreases the

      a. residual volume.
      b. tidal volume.
      c. vital capacity.
      d. All of the above are correct.

_____ 4. The most probable cause of restricted movements of the chest cavity in the elderly is

      a. arthritic changes in the rib joints.
      b. excessive smoking.
      c. an increased incidence of asthma.
      d. the presence of pulmonary emboli.

OBJECTIVE 10 Discuss the interrelationships between the respiratory system and other systems.

_____ 1. All the systems of the body are affected by the respiratory system in that the respiratory system provides

      a. antigens to trigger specific defenses.
      b. bicarbonate ions to buffer pH activity in the body.
      c. increased thoracic pressure for promoting defecation.
      d. oxygen and eliminates carbon dioxide.

2. The _____ system eliminates organic wastes generated by cells of the respiratory system.

3. The _____ system releases epinephrine and norepinephrine, which stimulate respiratory activity and dilate respiratory passageways.

4. The _____ system controls the pace and depth of respiration.

5. Protection for the lungs is provided by the _____ system.

Part II: Chapter Comprehensive Exercises

A. Word Elimination

Circle the term that does not belong in each of the following groupings.

1. pharynx   larynx   alveoli   trachea   bronchi
2. frontal   mandibular   sphenoid   ethmoid   maxillary
3. glottis   epiglottis   thyroid   cricoid   arytenoid
4. apex   superior lobe   cardiac notch   inferior lobe   middle lobe
5. primary bronchi   respiratory bronchioles   alveolar ducts   alveolar sacs   alveoli
6. scalenes   pectoralis minor   internal intercostals   serratus anterior   external intercostals
7. ERV   vital capacity   IRV   residual volume P_{CO_2}
8. N_2 O_2 NH_4 H_2O CO_2
9. chemoreceptor   inflation   deflation   Hering-Brewer   mechanoreceptor
10. respiratory   surfactant   nervous   endocrine   lymphatic

B. Matching

Match the terms in Column "B" with the terms in Column "A." Write letters for answers in the spaces provided.

COLUMN A

____ 1. septal cells

____ 2. pleura

____ 3. anoxia

____ 4. Adam's apple

____ 5. alveolar macrophages

____ 6. pulmonary ventilation

____ 7. atelectasis

____ 8. upper respiratory tract

____ 9. lower respiratory tract

____ 10. hypoxia

COLUMN B

a. collapsed lung

b. thyroid cartilage

c. delivers air to lungs

d. low oxygen levels in tissues

e. breathing

f. secretion of surfactant

g. lungs

h. dust cells

i. serous membrane

j. no oxygen supply to tissues

C. Concept Map - The Respiratory System

Using the following terms, fill in the circled numbered, blank spaces to complete the concept map. Follow the numbers that comply with the organization of the map.

Lungs

Alveoli

Ciliated mucous membrane

Blood

Upper respiratory tract

Pharynx and larynx

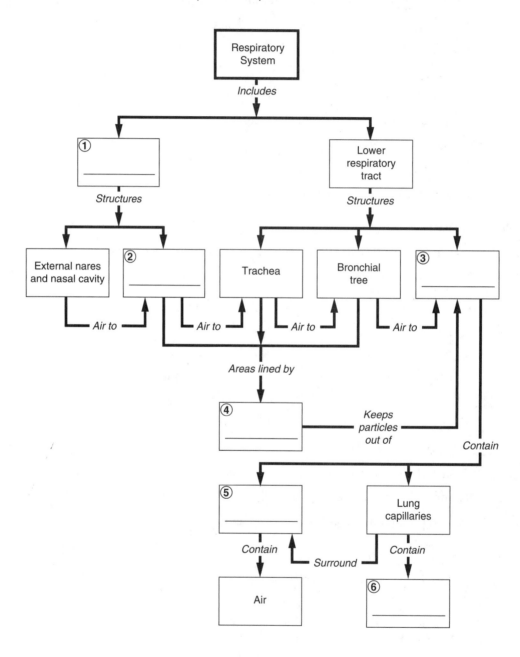

D. Crossword Puzzle

The following crossword puzzle reviews the material in Chapter 15. To complete the puzzle, you must know the answers to the clues given, and must be able to spell the terms correctly.

ACROSS

2. The amount of air we can forcibly exhale (two words).
5. The opening into the trachea.
6. These cells produce mucus to protect the lining of the respiratory tubes.
8. The tracheal tubes that enter each lung.
10. Chemoreceptors are located in the _____ arteries.
11. The amount of air we exhale passively is called the_____ volume.
12. Most of the carbon dioxide in the blood is converted to _____(two words).

DOWN

1. Low oxygen concentration in the peripheral tissues.
3. Gas exchange occurs in these.
4. About 20.8% of the atmospheric air consists of _____.
7. When the diaphragm muscle is moving upward, we are _____.
9. This volume of air in the lungs is equivalent to about 1200 ml.

E. Short-Answer Questions

Briefly answer the following questions in the spaces provided.

1. What are the five primary functions of the respiratory system?

2. How is the inhaled air warmed and humidified in the nasal cavities, and why is this conditioning of air necessary?

3. What is surfactant, and what is its function in the respiratory membrane?

4. Distinguish among external respiration, internal respiration, and cellular respiration.

5. What is vital capacity, and how is it calculated?

6. What is alveolar ventilation, and how is it calculated?

7. What are the three methods of CO_2 transport in the blood?

8. What three kinds of reflexes are involved in the regulation of respiration?

9. What is the relationship between a rise in arterial P_{CO_2} and hyperventilation?

16

The Digestive System

Overview

The average person probably knows more about indigestion than he or she knows about digestion. Perhaps you are one of many members of the "Rolaids Generation." The nutrients in food are not ready for use by cells; that is, food must be converted (digested) into chemical forms that cells can utilize for their metabolic functions. The digestive organs are responsible for ingestion of food, digestion, and elimination of undigested material from the body. Accessory digestive organs, such as the teeth, tongue, salivary glands, liver, gallbladder, and pancreas, assist in the digestive process as food moves through the digestive tract, which includes the (1) mouth; (2) pharynx; (3) esophagus; (4) stomach; and (5) the small and large intestines.

When the "processing" of food is completed by the digestive tract, the nutrients are absorbed into the bloodstream and transported to the cells and tissues of the body to be used for energy, tissue growth and repair, and the cell's metabolic activities.

The exercises in this chapter are organized to guide your study of the structure and function of the digestive tract and accessory organs. The review questions will introduce you to the endocrine and nervous systems' influences on the digestive process, and the series of steps necessary to promote absorption and eventual use of nutrients by cells for metabolic activities.

Review of Chapter Objectives

1. Identify the organs of the digestive tract and the accessory organs of digestion.

2. List the functions of the digestive system.

3. Describe the histology of each segment of the digestive tract in relation to its function.

4. Explain how ingested materials are propelled through the digestive tract.

5. Describe how food is processed in the mouth, and describe the key events of the swallowing process.

6. Describe the anatomy of the stomach, its histological features, and its roles in digestion and absorption.

7. Explain the functions of intestinal secretions, and discuss the significance of digestion in the small intestine.

8. Describe the structure and functions of the pancreas, liver, and gallbladder, and explain how their activities are regulated.

9. Describe the structure of the large intestine, its movements, and its absorptive functions.

10. Describe the digestion and absorption of carbohydrates, lipids, and proteins.

11. Describe the changes in the digestive system that occur with aging.

12. Discuss the interactions between the digestive system and other organ systems.

Part I: Objective-Based Questions

OBJECTIVE 1   Identify the organs of the digestive tract and the accessory organs of digestion.

_____ 1. Which one of the following organs is not a part of the digestive system?

    a. liver
    b. gallbladder
    c. spleen
    d. pancreas

_____ 2. Of the following groups of structures, the one that contains only accessory structures is

    a. salivary glands, pancreas, liver, and gallbladder.
    b. pharynx, esophagus, and small and large intestines.
    c. oral cavity, stomach, pancreas, and liver.
    d. tongue, teeth, stomach, and small and large intestines.

_____ 3. The digestive tube between the pharynx and the stomach is the

    a. trachea.
    b. larynx.
    c. pylorus.
    d. esophagus.

_____ 4. The correct sequence of a food particle moving through the digestive tract is

    a. oral cavity, esophagus, pharynx, stomach, small intestine, large intestine, anus, rectum.
    b. oral cavity, pharynx, esophagus, stomach, small intestine, large intestine, rectum, anus.
    c. oral cavity, esophagus, stomach, pharnyx, large intestine, small intestine, anus, rectum.
    d. pharynx, oral cavity, esophagus, stomach, small intestine, large intestine, anus, rectum.

Labeling Exercise

Identify and label the structures of the digestive tract in Figure 16-1. Place your answers in the spaces provided below the drawing after selecting from the following choices.

gallbladder

large intestine

liver

salivary glands

small intestine

esophagus

pancreas

pharynx

stomach

oral cavity/teeth/tongue

FIGURE 16-1 Components of the Digestive System

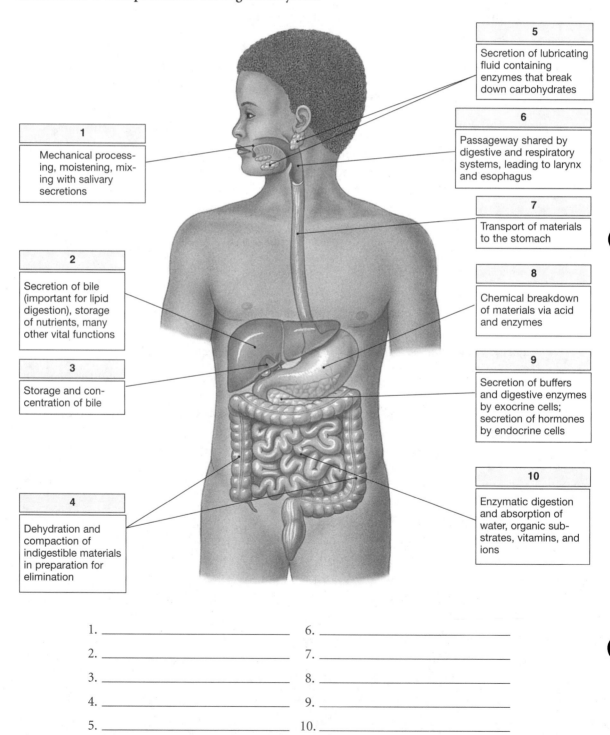

5

Secretion of lubricating fluid containing enzymes that break down carbohydrates

1

Mechanical process-ing, moistening, mix-ing with salivary secretions

6

Passageway shared by digestive and respiratory systems, leading to larynx and esophagus

7

Transport of materials to the stomach

2

Secretion of bile (important for lipid digestion), storage of nutrients, many other vital functions

8

Chemical breakdown of materials via acid and enzymes

3

Storage and con-centration of bile

9

Secretion of buffers and digestive enzymes by exocrine cells; secretion of hormones by endocrine cells

10

Enzymatic digestion and absorption of water, organic sub-strates, vitamins, and ions

4

Dehydration and compaction of indigestible materials in preparation for elimination

1. _____

2. _____

3. _____

4. _____

5. _____

6. _____

7. _____

8. _____

9. _____

10. _____

OBJECTIVE 2 List the functions of the digestive system.

_____ 1. The physical manipulation of solid foods by the tongue and teeth and the swirling and mixing motions of the digestive tract is called

      a secretion.
      b. absorption.
      c. compaction.
      d. mechanical processing.

_____ 2. The chemical breakdown of food into small organic fragments that can be absorbed by the digestive epithelium is

      a. digestion.
      b. ingestion.
      c. salivation.
      d. secretion.

3. The release of water, acids, enzymes, and buffers by the digestive tract and accessory organs

is _____.

4. The movement of small organic molecules, electrolytes, vitamins, and water across the

digestive epithelium and into the interstitium is _____.

5. The elimination of waste products from the body is _____.

OBJECTIVE 3 Describe the histology of each segment of the digestive tract in relation to its function.

_____ 1. Where mechanical stresses are most severe, such as in the oral cavity, pharynx, esophagus, and anus, the digestive tract is lined by

      a. stratified squamous epithelium.
      b. simple columnar epithelium.
      c. loose connective tissue.
      d. smooth muscle cells.

_____ 2. The cells of the gastric glands in the fundus and body of the stomach that produce the components of gastric juice are

      a. parotid cells and sublingual cells.
      b. endocrine cells and enterogastric cells.
      c. chylomicrons and lacteal cells.
      d. parietal cells and chief cells.

_____ 3. In the small intestine, fingerlike projections called _villi_ are formed by the mucosa and serve to

      a. release secretions that promote digestion.
      b. increase the area for absorption.
      c. control and coordinate contractions of the smooth muscle.
      d. All of the above are correct.

_____ 4. The layer of loose connective tissue that contains blood vessels, lymphatic vessels, and a network of nerve fibers, sensory neurons, and parasympathetic motor neurons is the

      a. circular muscular layer.
      b. submucosa.
      c. serosa.
      d. mucosal epithelium.

_____ 5. The layer of the intestinal wall that contracts and changes the shape of the intestinal lumen to move food along its length is the

      a. muscularis.
      b. mucosa.
      c. submucosa.
      d. serosa.

_____ 6. Double sheets of serous membrane composed of the parietal peritoneum and the visceral peritoneum are called the

      a. adventitia.
      b. fibrosa.
      c. serosa.
      d. mesenteries.

_____ 7. Most of the digestive tract is lined by

      a. cuboidal epithelium.
      b. stratified squamous epithelium.
      c. simple columnar epithelium.
      d. simple squamous epithelium.

_____ 8. Modifications of the mucosa of the small intestine that allow for an increase in surface area are the

      a. plicae.
      b. mucus glands.
      c. presence of striations.
      d. adventitia.

Labeling Exercise

Identify and label Figure 16-2 from the following selections. Place your answers in the spaces provided below the drawing.

plica   lumen   submucosa

mucosa   mesenteric artery and vein   mucosal gland

mesentery   muscularis externa

visceral peritoneum (serosa)

FIGURE 16-2   Histological Features of the GI Tract Wall

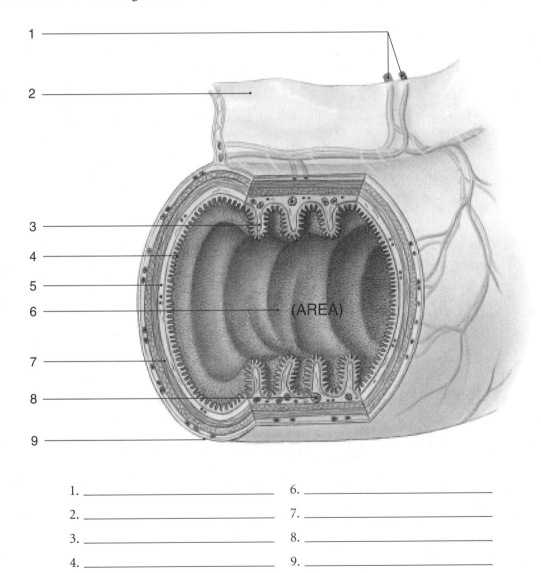

1. _____   6. _____

2. _____   7. _____

3. _____   8. _____

4. _____   9. _____

5. _____

OBJECTIVE 4 Explain how ingested materials are propelled through the digestive tract.

_____ 1. Waves of muscular contractions that propel the contents of the digestive tract from one point to another are called

      a. segmentation.
      b. peristalsis.
      c. mastications.
      d. compactions.

_____ 2. Regional movements that occur in the small intestine and function to churn and fragment the digestive materials are called

      a. segmentation.
      b. peristalsis.
      c. pendulums.
      d. mastications.

_____ 3. The backflow of materials from the stomach into the esophagus is due to the active contraction of the

      a. lower esophageal sphincter.
      b. upper esophageal sphincter.
      c. esophageal hiatus.
      d. pyloric sphincter.

_____ 4. Once a bolus of food has entered the laryngopharynx, swallowing continues involuntarily due to the

      a. swallowing reflex.
      b. size of the bolus.
      c. peristalic activity.
      d. All of the above are correct.

_____ 5. The proper sequence of swallowing involves three sequential phases consisting of the

      a. oral phase, esophageal phase, and pharyngeal phase.
      b. oral phase, pharyngeal phase, and esophageal phase.
      c. pharyngeal phase, esophageal phase, and intestinal phase.
      d. oral phase, esophageal phase, and intestinal phase.

_____ 6. Swirling, mixing, and churning motions of the digestive tract provide

      a. action of enzymes, acids, and buffers.
      b. chemical breakdown of food.
      c. mechanical processing after ingestion.
      d. peristalic activity.

_____ 7. Strong contractions of the ascending and transverse colon that move the contents of the colon toward the sigmoid colon are called

      a. defecation.
      b. pendular movements.
      c. mass peristalsis.
      d. segmentation.

OBJECTIVE 5   Describe how food is processed in the mouth, and describe the key events of the swallowing process.

_____ 1. The functions of the oral cavity include

    a. the initial digestion of lipids and carbohydrates.
    b. mechanical processing of food.
    c. lubrication and evaluation of material before swallowing.
    d. all of the above.

_____ 2. Functions of the tongue include

    a. mechanical processing of food.
    b. manipulation of food.
    c. sensory analysis of food.
    d. all of the above.

_____ 3. During swallowing, the

    a. soft palate elevates.
    b. larynx elevates.
    c. epiglottis closes.
    d. All of the above are correct.

_____ 4. Secretions from the salivary glands

    a. are mostly digestive enzymes.
    b. provide analysis before swallowing.
    c. help control bacterial populations in the mouth.
    d. all of the above are correct.

_____ 5. Food is initially ground and torn into smaller pieces by the teeth. Typically, adults have _____ incisors, _____ cuspids, _____ bicuspids, and _____ molars.

    a. 4, 2, 8, 6
    b. 8, 4, 8, 6
    c. 8, 4, 8, 12
    d. 8, 8, 4, 12

_____ 6. Salivary amylase is an enzyme, produced and released by the salivary glands, that partially digests

    a. carbohydrates.
    b. fats.
    c. proteins.
    d. all of the above.

_____ 7. The tongue is controlled by the _____ nerve.

    a. abducens
    b. facial
    c. glossopharyngeal
    d. vagus

_____ 8. When the _____ cells of the tongue are activated, they send signals to the brain via the _____ nerve to interpret the flavor of food.

        a. papillary; trigeminal
        b. gustatory; facial
        c. tastebuds; facial
        d. None of the above is correct.

_____ 9. During the swallowing process, the _____ closes off the _____.

        a. epiglottis; esophagus
        b. glottis; trachea
        c. epiglottis; trachea
        d. glottis; esophagus

10. Blade-shaped teeth that function in cutting or chopping are _____.

11. Pointed teeth that are adapted for tearing and shredding are _____.

12. Teeth with flattened crowns and prominent ridges that are adapted for grinding are the

_____.

13. The gland that empties into the upper regions of the oral cavity is the _____.

14. The structure at the posterior midregion of the soft palate is the _____.

Labeling Exercises

Identify and label the teeth in Figure 16-3. Place your answers in the spaces provided below the drawing.

FIGURE 16-3 The Secondary Teeth

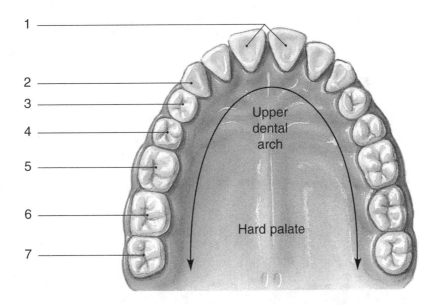

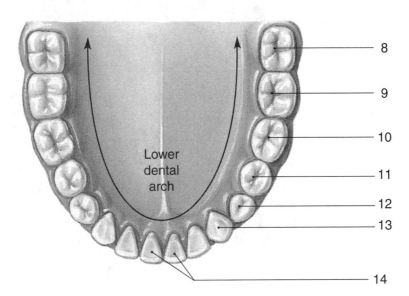

1. _____   8. _____

2. _____   9. _____

3. _____   10. _____

4. _____   11. _____

5. _____   12. _____

6. _____   13. _____

7. _____   14. _____

Labeling Exercises, continued

Identify and label the parts and areas of a typical tooth. Place your answers in the spaces provided below the drawing after selecting from the following choices.

enamel	cementum	crown
dentin	neck	root canal
blood vessels and nerves	root	alveolar bone
pulp cavity	gingival sulcus	periodontal ligament

FIGURE 16-4 Structure of a Typical Tooth

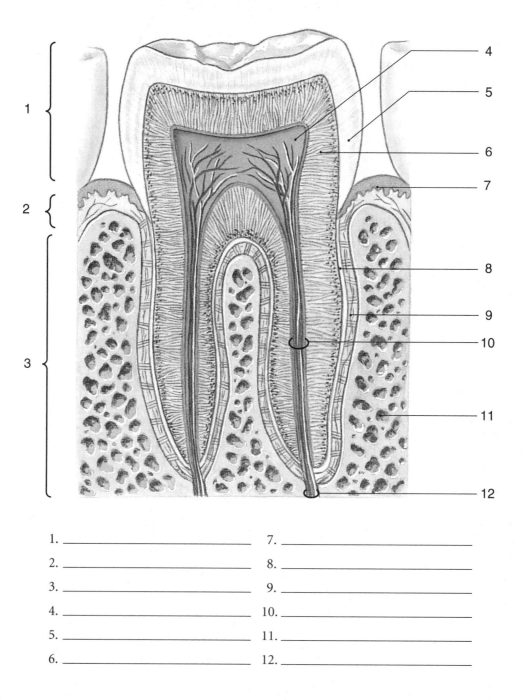

1. _____		7. _____
2. _____		8. _____
3. _____		9. _____
4. _____		10. _____
5. _____		11. _____
6. _____		12. _____

OBJECTIVE 6   Describe the anatomy of the stomach, its histological features, and its roles in digestion and absorption.

_____   1. Of the following selections, the one which is *not* a function of the stomach is

   a. storage of ingested food.
   b. denaturation of protein.
   c. digestion of carbohydrates and fats.
   d. mechanical breakdown of food.

_____   2. The greater omentum is

   a. the major portion of the stomach.
   b. attached to the stomach at the lesser curvature.
   c. important in the digestion of fats.
   d. a fatty sheet that hangs like an apron over the abdominal viscera.

_____   3. Gastric pits are

   a. ridges in the body of the stomach.
   b. pockets in the lining of the stomach that contain secretory cells.
   c. involved in absorption of liquids from the stomach.
   d. areas in the stomach where proteins are denatured.

   4. Parietal cells secrete _____.

   5. Chief cells secrete _____.

   6. The portion of the stomach that connects to the esophagus is the _____.

   7. The bulge of the greater curvature of the stomach superior to the esophageal junction is the _____.

   8. The curved, tubular portion of the J-shaped stomach is the _____.

   9. The prominent ridges in the lining of the stomach are called _____.

   10. The enzyme pepsin is involved in the digestion of _____.

Labeling Exercise

Identify and label the structures of the stomach in Figure 16-5. Select your answers from the following selections. Place your answers in the spaces provided below the drawing.

cardia   pylorus   fundus

esophagus   rugae   diaphragm

lesser curvature   greater curvature   lesser omentum

greater omentum   body

FIGURE 16-5 The Stomach

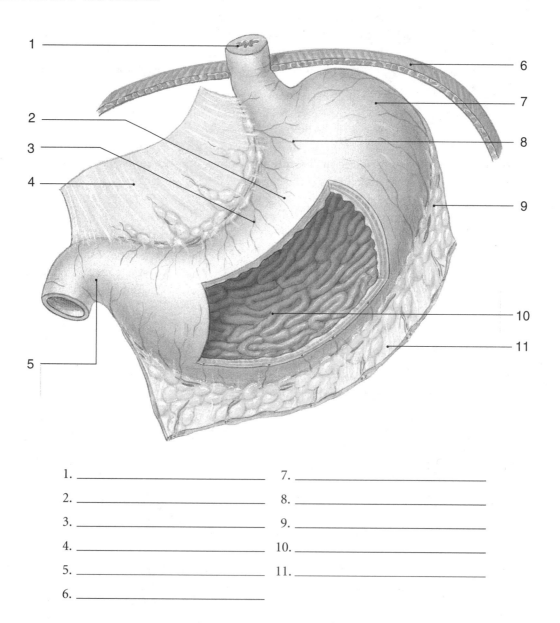

1. _____   7. _____

2. _____   8. _____

3. _____   9. _____

4. _____   10. _____

5. _____   11. _____

6. _____

OBJECTIVE 7   Explain the functions of intestinal secretions, and discuss the significance of digestion in the small intestine.

_____ 1. The three divisions of the small intestine are

    a. cephalic, gastric, and intestinal.
    b. duodenum, jejunum, and ileum.
    c. fundus, body, and pylorus.
    d. buccal, pharyngeal, and esophageal.

_____ 2. In the small intestine, immediate acceleration of glandular secretions and peristaltic activity in all intestinal segments is initiated by

    a. the gastroileal reflex.
    b. the plicae circularis.
    c. the sympathetic stimulation.
    d. the gastroenteric reflex.

_____ 3. The bulk of chemical digestion and absorption of nutrients into the bloodstream occurs in the

    a. ileum.
    b. jejunum.
    c. duodenum.
    d. cecum.

_____ 4. In order for nutrients to leave the small intestine and enter the bloodstream, the nutrients must be absorbed through the

    a. gastric pits.
    b. mucosal glands.
    c. villi.
    d. lacteals.

_____ 5. The hormone that causes the release of insulin into the bloodstream when glucose is present in the small intestine is

    a. GIP.
    b. gastrin.
    c. CCK.
    d. secretin.

_____ 6. The hormones cholecystokinin and secretin are released by the

    a. gallbladder.
    b. pancreas.
    c. small intestine.
    d. liver.

_____ 7. The intestinal hormone that stimulates the pancreas to release a watery secretion that is high in bicarbonate ions is

    a. gastrin.
    b. secretin.
    c. cholecystokinin.
    d. enterocrinin.

_____ 8. An intestinal hormone that stimulates the gallbladder to release bile is

      a. enterokinase.
      b. CCK.
      c. gastrin.
      d. secretin.

_____ 9. An intestinal hormone that stimulates the release of insulin from the pancreatic islet cells is

      a. secretin.
      b. GIP.
      c. enterokinase.
      d. enterocrinin.

_____ 10. The intestinal hormone that stimulates parietal cells and chief cells in the stomach to secrete is

      a. CCK.
      b. GIP.
      c. gastrin.
      d. enterokinase.

OBJECTIVE 8   Describe the structure and functions of the pancreas, liver, and gallbladder, and explain how their activities are regulated.

_____ 1. The hormone that causes the pancreas to release its digestive enzymes into the small intestine is

      a. cholecystokinin.
      b. secretin.
      c. gastrin.
      d. enterogastrone.

2. Bile is stored in the _____.

3. The basic functional unit of the liver is the _____.

4. The liver cells that are arranged into a series of irregular plates like the spokes of a wheel are called _____.

_____ 5. The primary function(s) of the liver include(s)

      a. metabolic regulation.
      b. hemotological regulation.
      c. synthesis and secretion of bile.
      d. all of the above.

_____ 6. The exocrine portion of the pancreas is composed of

      a. islets of Langerhans.
      b. pancreatic crypts.
      c. pancreatic acini.
      d. pancreatic lobules.

_____ 7. The pancreas produces and releases

        a. lipases.

        b. pancreatic amylase.

        c. proteases.

        d. all of the above.

_____ 8. The hormone that causes the gallbladder to release bile is

        a. cholecystokinin.

        b. secretin.

        c. gastrin.

        d. enterogastrone.

OBJECTIVE 9   Describe the structure of the large intestine, its movements, and its absorptive functional processes.

_____ 1. The three parts of the large intestine are the

        a. duodenum, jejunum, and ileum.

        b. transverse, ascending, and descending colon.

        c. cecum, colon, and rectum.

        d. sigmoid colon, rectum, and anus.

_____ 2. The major functions of the large intestine are

        a. absorption and preparation of fecal material for elimination.

        b. production of vitamins and fecal segmentation.

        c. completion of digestion and secretion of digestive secretions.

        d. metabolic and hematological regulation.

_____ 3. Movement from the transverse colon through the rest of the large intestine results from peristaltic contractions called

        a. mass movements.

        b. the defecation reflex.

        c. emulsification.

        d. the ileocecal reflex.

_____ 4. At the hepatic flexure, the colon becomes the

        a. ascending colon.

        b. transverse colon.

        c. sigmoid colon.

        d. descending colon.

_____ 5. Distension of the rectum triggers the

        a. defecation reflex.

        b. ileocecal reflex.

        c. initiation of fecal segmentation.

        d. release of hormonal secretions.

6. The external pouches of the large intestine are called _____.

7. The three longitudinal bands of muscle located beneath the serosa of the colon are the

_____.

8. The saclike structure that joins the ileum at the ileocecal valve is the _____.

9. The small, fingerlike structure attached to the "blind" end of the cecum is the

_____.

Labeling Exercise

Using the following selections, identify and label the structures of the large intestine. Place your answers in the spaces provided on the following page.

cecum	rectum	haustra
aorta	ileocecal valve	splenic flexure
transverse colon	sigmoid colon	hepatic portal vein
ascending colon	taenia coli	greater omentum
ileum	inferior vena cava	splenic vein
vermiform appendix	descending colon	

FIGURE 16-6 The Large Intestine

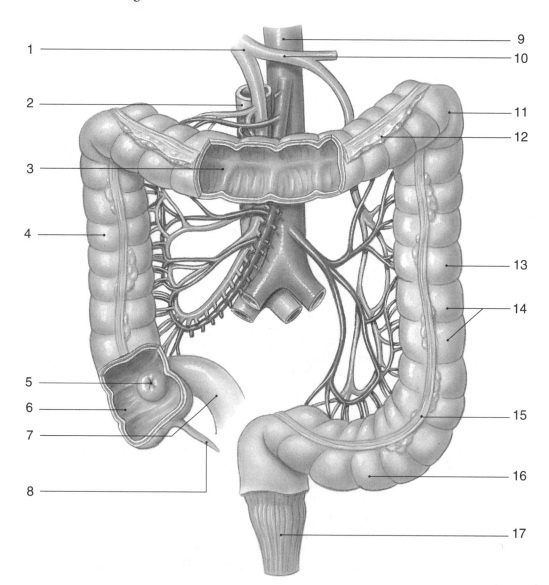

1. _____   7. _____   13. _____

2. _____   8. _____   14. _____

3. _____   9. _____   15. _____

4. _____   10. _____   16. _____

5. _____   11. _____   17. _____

6. _____   12. _____

OBJECTIVE 10   Describe the digestion and absorption of carbohydrates, lipids, and proteins.

_____ 1. Salivary amylase, which is secreted in the mouth, aids in the digestion of

    a. protein.
    b. fat.
    c. carbohydrate.
    d. all of the above.

_____ 2. An enzyme that digests proteins into polypeptides is

    a. lipase.
    b. amylase.
    c. nuclease.
    d. trypsin.

_____ 3. Enzymes involved in fat digestion are called

    a. pepsins.
    b. lipases.
    c. carboxypeptidases.
    d. amylases.

_____ 4. Hydrochloric acid in the stomach functions primarily to

    a. activate enzymes involved in protein digestion.
    b. hydrolyze peptide bonds.
    c. facilitate lipid digestion.
    d. facilitate carbohydrate digestion.

_____ 5. Digested fats are absorbed into the _____ and then enter the _____.

    a. bloodstream; lacteals
    b. lacteals; villi
    c. villi; bloodstream
    d. villi; lacteals

OBJECTIVE 11 Describe the changes in the digestive tract that occur with aging.

_____ 1. Weaker peristaltic contractions in the elderly results in more frequent

        a. diarrhea.

        b. constipation.

        c. heartburn.

        d. All of the above are correct.

_____ 2. Dietary changes that affect the entire body in the elderly result from

        a. a weakening of muscular sphincters.

        b. weaker peristaltic contractions.

        c. a decline in sense of smell and taste.

        d. decreased movement within the GI tract.

_____ 3. The types of cancer most common in the elderly who smoke are

        a. oral and pharyngeal.

        b. lung and liver.

        c. colon and stomach.

        d. skin and lymphatic.

_____ 4. Age-related changes in the digestive epithelium of the elderly may increase susceptibility to damage by abrasion, acids, or enzymes, increasing the likelihood of

        a. constipation and diarrhea.

        b. gradual loss of teeth and inflammation of the gums.

        c. erosion of tooth sockets and eventual tooth loss.

        d. peptic ulcers.

OBJECTIVE 12 Discuss the interactions among the digestive system and other systems.

1. The _____ system excretes toxins absorbed by the digestive epithelium.

2. The _____ system delivers nutrients and toxins to the liver from the digestive tract.

3. The _____ system is responsible for secreting hormones that coordinate activity along the digestive tract.

4. Hunger, satiation, and feeding behaviors are controlled by hypothalamic centers in the _____ system.

5. The _____ system provides vitamin D_3 needed for absorption of calcium and phosphorus.

Part II: Chapter Comprehensive Exercises

A. Word Elimination

Circle the term that does not belong in each of the following groupings.

1. ingestion   digestion   secretion   circulation   absorption
2. mucosa   mesentery   submucosa   muscularis externa   serosa
3. analysis   excretion   mechanical processing   lubrication   begin digestion
4. tongue   parotid   sublingual   submandibular   salivary glands
5. incisors   cuspids   dentin   bicuspids   molars
6. cardia   fundus   chyme   body   pylorus
7. gastric pits   gastric glands   parietal cells   chief cells   intrinsic factor
8. gastrin   secretin   CCK   HCl   GIP
9. trypsin   amylase   chymotrypsin   carboxypeptidase   proteolytic
10. haustra   ascending   sigmoid   transverse   descending

B. Matching

Match the terms in Column "B" with the terms in Column "A." Write letters for answers in the spaces provided.

COLUMN A	COLUMN B
____ 1. lacteal	a. secrete bile
____ 2. chylomicron	b. water-soluble vitamins
____ 3. hepatocytes	c. lipid–bile salt complexes
____ 4. Kupffer cells	d. colon pouches
____ 5. micelles	e. protein–lipid package
____ 6. B and C	f. fat-soluble vitamins
____ 7. rugae	g. lymphatic capillary
____ 8. A, D, E, K	h. secrete insulin and glucagons
____ 9. haustra	i. monocyte–macrophage phagocytes
____10. pancreatic islets	j. stomach ridges and folds

C. Concept Map I - The Digestive System

Using the following terms, fill in the circled numbered, blank spaces to complete the concept map. Follow the numbers that comply with the organization of the map.

Digestive tract movements   Hormones   Stomach

Intestinal mucosa   Amylase   Bile

Large intestine   Hydrochloric acid   Pancreas

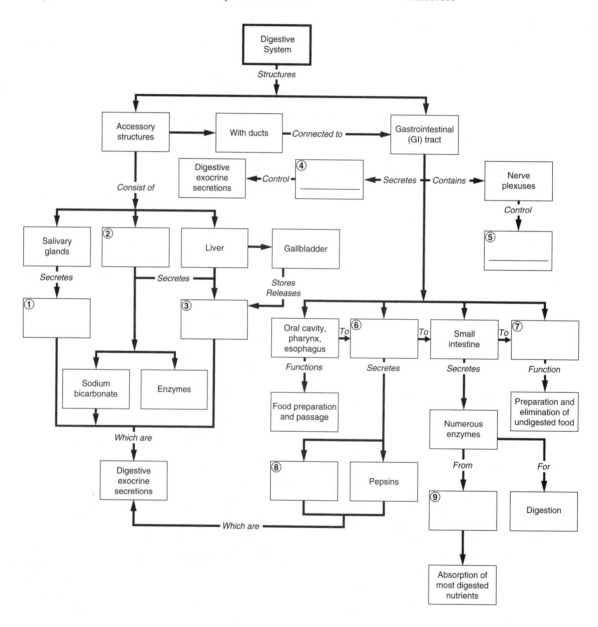

Concept Map II - Chemical Events in Digestion

Using the following terms, fill in the circled numbered, blank spaces to complete the concept map. Follow the numbers that comply with the organization of the map.

Simple sugars

Esophagus

Diglycerides, triglycerides

Monoglycerides, fatty acids in micelles

Disaccharides, trisaccharides

Lacteal

Polypeptides

Small intestine

Complex sugars and starches

Amino acids

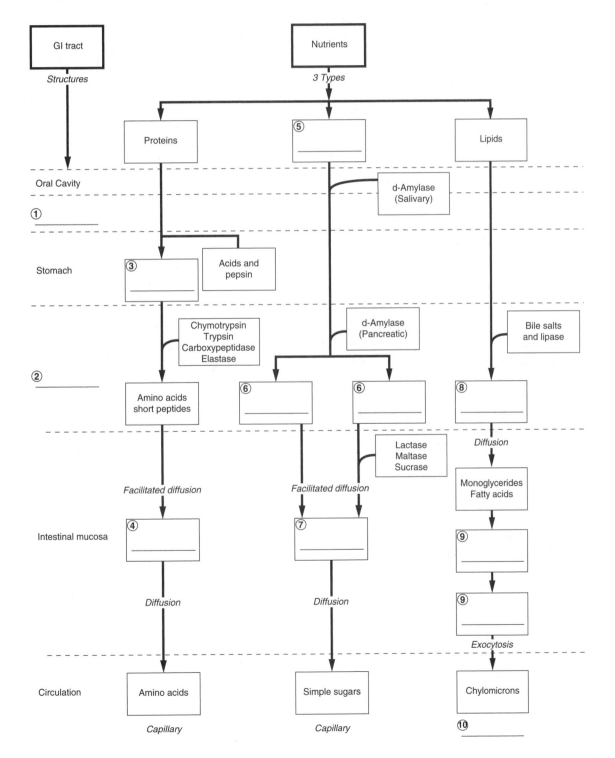

D. Crossword Puzzle

The following crossword puzzle reviews the material in Chapter 16. To complete the puzzle, you must know the answers to the clues given, and must be able to spell the terms correctly.

ACROSS

3. The process of moving nutrients from the digestive tract to the bloodstream.
4. The gland that produces salivary amylase.
5. The first portion of the small intestine.
6. Where most of the digestion in the digestive tract occurs.
8. The pancreas and gallbladder secrete their products into the _____ of the small intestine.
9. The pancreas and liver are considered to be _____ organs of the digestive system.

DOWN

1. Salivary amylase digests _____ to form glucose.
2. To reach the stomach, the esophagus passes through the esophageal _____ of the diaphragm.
7. The fleshy protrusion hanging at the back of the throat.
10. The part of the large intestine to which the appendix is attached.
11. The muscular ridges found inside the stomach.

E. Short-Answer Questions

Briefly answer the following questions in the spaces provided.

1. What six integrated steps comprise the digestive functions?

2. What three pairs of salivary glands secrete saliva into the oral cavity?

3. What four types of teeth are found in the oral cavity, and what is the function of each type?

4. What are the similarities and differences between parietal cells and chief cells in the wall of the stomach?

5. (a) What three phases are involved in the regulation of gastric function?

   (b) What regulatory mechanism(s) dominate each phase?

6. What are the three most important hormones that regulate intestinal activity?

7. What are the three principal functions of the large intestine?

8. What three basic categories describe the functions of the liver?

9. What two distinct functions are performed by the pancreas?

Nutrition and Metabolism

Overview

The knowledge of what happens to the food we eat and how the nutrients from food are utilized by the body continues to capture the interest of those who believe that "we are what we eat." Many people are more concerned with the taste of food or their "likes" than with the nutritional value of the food. Health claims about foods and food supplements have become a daily part of the news media, causing the "magic revolution" or "quick fix" for a healthy body to become believable in the minds of many people. Which claims are ridiculous, and which ones really work? A basic understanding of nutrition and knowledge of the fate of absorbed nutrients can help us answer these and other questions, so that we can make good food choices and develop food plans that provide for happy, healthy living.

All cells require energy for the processes of metabolism. Food does more than provide this energy; it also fuels tissue growth and repair and provides input for the mechanisms that regulate the body's metabolic machinery.

The exercises in this chapter provide a basic review of what you have learned in previous chapters and will be useful as you begin to understand how the integrated processes of the digestive and cardiovascular systems serve to advance the work of metabolism. They will also provide you with the basic principles of good nutrition, and what the body requires to be healthy.

Review of Chapter Objectives

1. Define metabolism, and explain why cells need to synthesize new organic structures.
2. Describe the basic steps in glycolysis, the TCA cycle, and the electron transport system.
3. Describe the pathways involved in lipid metabolism.
4. Discuss protein metabolism and the use of proteins as an energy source.
5. Discuss nucleic acid metabolism.
6. Explain what constitutes a balanced diet and why it is important.
7. Discuss the functions of vitamins, minerals, and other important nutrients.
8. Describe the significance of the caloric value of foods.
9. Define metabolic rate and discuss the factors involved in determining an individual's metabolic rate.
10. Discuss the homeostatic mechanisms that maintain a constant body temperature.
11. Describe the age-related changes in nutritional requirements.

Part I: Objective-Based Questions

OBJECTIVE 1   Define metabolism, and explain why cells need to synthesize new organic structures.

_____ 1. The term metabolism refers to

         a. the performance of essential functions.
         b. breakdown of organic molecules.
         c. the synthesis of organic molecules.
         d. all the chemical reactions that occur in the body.

_____ 2. In general, a cell with excess carbohydrates, lipids, and amino acids that needs energy will

         a. rely on lipids as an energy source.
         b. break down carbohydrates first.
         c. use amino acids as a source of energy.
         d. decrease its ability to utilize its energy resources.

_____ 3. In resting skeletal muscles, a significant portion of the metabolic demand is met through the

         a. catabolism of glucose.
         b. catabolism of fatty acids.
         c. catabolism of glycogen.
         d. anabolism of ADP to ATP.

_____ 4. The process that breaks down organic substrates, releasing energy that can be used to synthesize ATP or other high-energy compounds, is

         a. metabolism.
         b. anabolism.
         c. catabolism.
         d. oxidation.

OBJECTIVE 2   Describe the basic steps in glycolysis, the TCA cycle, and the electron transport system.

_____ 1. During glycolysis, glucose molecules are broken down into two 3-carbon molecules of

         a. pyruvic acid.
         b. acetyl-CoA.
         c. citric acid.
         d. oxaloacetic acid.

_____ 2. The mitochondrial activity responsible for ATP production is called

         a. chemiosmosis.
         b. cellular respiration.
         c. beta oxidation.
         d. deamination.

_____   3. The carbon dioxide released during cellular respiration is formed during

    a. electron transport.
    b. glycolysis.
    c. the TCA cycle.
    d. the formation of pyruvic acid.

_____   4. The mechanism for the generation of ATP that generates 95% of the ATP needed to keep cells alive is

    a. glycolysis.
    b. the electron transport system.
    c. the TCA cycle.
    d. All of the above are correct.

_____   5. During glycolysis, each molecule of glucose metabolized releases enough energy to form a net gain of _____ molecules of ATP.

    a. 2
    b. 4
    c. 36
    d. 38

_____   6. In the process of cellular respiration, each molecule of glucose metabolized releases enough energy to form _____ molecules of ATP.

    a. 2
    b. 4
    c. 36
    d. 38

OBJECTIVE 3   Describe the pathways involved in lipid metabolism.

_____   1. During lipolysis,

    a. triglycerides are converted into molecules of acetyl-CoA.
    b. lipids are converted into glucose molecules.
    c. triglycerides are broken down into glycerol and fatty acids.
    d. lipids are formed from excess carbohydrates.

_____   2. Beta oxidation

    a. occurs in the mitochondria.
    b. is the process that breaks down fatty acids into 2-carbon fragments that can be metabolized by the TCA cycle.
    c. yields large amounts of ATP, while requiring coenzymes A, NAD, and FAD.
    d. All of the above are correct.

_____   3. Lipids that can diffuse easily across cell membranes are

    a. chylomicrons.
    b. low-density lipoproteins.
    c. high-density lipoproteins.
    d. free fatty acids.

4. Lipogenesis generally begins with _____.

5. The largest metabolic reserves for the average adult are stored as _____.

6. Lipoproteins that contain triglycerides that are manufactured in the liver and transported to peripheral tissues are called _____.

7. Lipoproteins that carry mostly cholesterol and phospholipids from peripheral tissues to the liver are called _____.

OBJECTIVE 4   Discuss protein metabolism and the use of proteins as an energy source.

_____ 1. The first step in amino acid catabolism is the removal of the

      a. carboxyl group.
      b. amino group.
      c. keto acid.
      d. hydrogen from the central carbon.

_____ 2. The process of deamination prepares an amino acid for

      a. protein synthesis.
      b. generation of ketone bodies.
      c. breakdown in the TCA cycle.
      d. All of the above are correct.

_____ 3. The carbon chain remaining after deamination

      a. can be converted to pyruvic acid.
      b. can be converted to acetyl-CoA.
      c. can be converted into ketone bodies.
      d. All of the above are correct.

_____ 4. In transamination, the amino group of an amino acid is

      a. converted to ammonia.
      b. converted to urea.
      c. transferred to acetyl-CoA.
      d. transferred to another carbon chain.

_____ 5. Protein metabolism is an impractical source of quick energy because

      a. protein molecules are difficult to break apart.
      b. its by-product (ammonia) is a toxin that can damage cells.
      c. proteins are important structural and functional cell components.
      d. All of the above are correct.

OBJECTIVE 5   Discuss nucleic acid metabolism.

_____ 1. All cells synthesize RNA, but DNA synthesis occurs only in

      a. red blood cells.
      b. cells that are preparing for mitosis or meiosis.
      c. lymph and cerebrospinal fluid.
      d. the bone marrow.

_____ 2. The only parts of a nucleotide of RNA that can provide energy when broken down are the

     a. sugars and phosphates.
     b. sugars, adenine, and guanine.
     c. sugars, cytosine, and uracil.
     d. purines and pyrimidines.

_____ 3. Nucleotides from RNA

     a. are deaminated to form ammonia.
     b. can provide sugars to generate ATP.
     c. can be used to synthesize proteins.
     d. cannot be used as a source of energy for the production of ATP.

_____ 4. Even if a cell is dying of starvation, the nucleic acid it can never metabolize for energy is

     a. mRNA.
     b. DNA.
     c. tRNA.
     d. rRNA.

OBJECTIVE 6   Explain what constitutes a balanced diet and why it is important.

_____ 1. A balanced diet contains all the ingredients necessary to

     a. prevent starvation.
     b. prevent life-threatening illnesses.
     c. prevent deficiency diseases.
     d. maintain homeostasis.

_____ 2. Foods that are deficient in dietary fiber are

     a. vegetables and fruits.
     b. breads and cereals.
     c. milk and meat.
     d. rice and pastas.

_____ 3. Foods that are low in fats, calories, and proteins are

     a. vegetables and fruits.
     b. milk and cheese.
     c. meat, poultry, and fish.
     d. breads, cereals, and rice.

_____ 4. Minerals, vitamins, and water are classified as essential nutrients because

     a. they are used by the body in large quantities.
     b. the body cannot synthesize them in sufficient quantities.
     c. they are major providers of calories for the body.
     d. All of the above are correct.

_____ 5. Minerals are essential components of the diet because they

     a. determine the osmotic concentration of body fluids.
     b. play major roles in important physiological processes.
     c. are essential cofactors in a variety of enzymatic reactions.
     d. All of the above are correct.

_____ 6. Hypervitaminosis involving water-soluble vitamins is relatively uncommon because excessive amounts are

        a. stored in adipose tissue.
        b. readily excreted in the urine.
        c. stored in the bones.
        d. readily absorbed into skeletal muscle tissue.

_____ 7. The nutrients that yield approximately 4 calories per gram when metabolized are

        a. water and vitamins.
        b. carbohydrates and fats.
        c. fats and proteins.
        d. proteins and carbohydrates.

Labeling Exercise

Identify and label the five food groups that make up the Healthy You Food Pyramid. Select from the following terms and place your answers in the spaces provided below the drawing.

fruits   vegetables

grains   milk

meat and beans

FIGURE 17-1 **The Healthy You Food Pyramid** (_Source: USDA http:www.mypyramid.gov_)

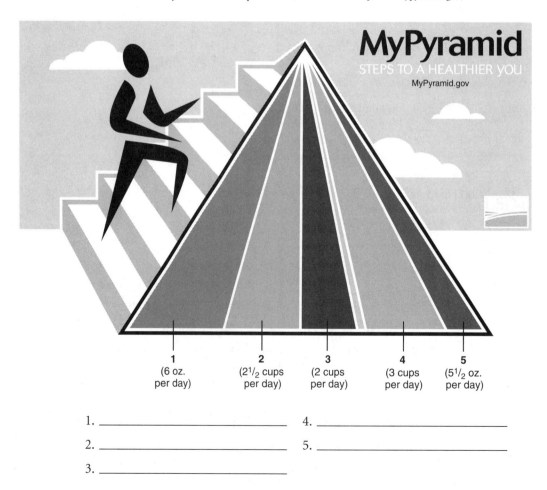

1. _____   4. _____

2. _____   5. _____

3. _____

OBJECTIVE 7   Discuss the functions of vitamins, minerals, and other important nutrients.

1. The major anion in body fluids is _____.

2. The major mineral essential for normal muscle and neuron function, and normal bone structure, is _____.

3. A mineral that is a necessary component of high-energy compounds and nucleic acids, and is a structural component of bone, is _____.

4. A mineral that is a component of hemoglobin, myoglobin, and cytochromes is

   _____.

5. A mineral that is a necessary cofactor for hemoglobin synthesis is _____.

6. The vitamin required for the synthesis of visual pigments is _____.

7. The vitamin required for proper bone growth and calcium absorption and retention is

   _____.

8. The vitamin essential for the production of several clotting factors is _____.

9. The vitamin that is a constituent of the coenzymes FAD and FMN is

   _____.

10. The vitamin that is a constituent of the coenzyme NAD is _____.

11. The vitamin that plays the role of a coenzyme in amino acid and lipid metabolism is

    _____.

12. The vitamin that is a coenzyme in amino acid and nucleic acid metabolism is

    _____.

OBJECTIVE 8   Describe the significance of the caloric value of foods.

1. The amount of energy needed to raise the temperature of 1 kilogram of water 1 degree centigrade is the _____.

_____   2. The catabolism of lipids releases approximately _____ calories per gram of energy.

       a. 4.18
       b. 4.32
       c. 9.46
       d. None of the above are correct.

_____   3. The catabolism of carbohydrates releases _____ calories per gram of energy.

       a. 4.18
       b. 4.32
       c. 9.46
       d. 12.21

_____   4. The catabolism of proteins yields approximately _____ calories per gram of energy.

       a. 4.18
       b. 4.32
       c. 9.46
       d. 2.61

OBJECTIVE 9 Define metabolic rate and discuss the factors involved in determining an individual's metabolic rate.

_____ 1. The sum of all the varied anabolic and catabolic processes occurring in the body represents an individual's

      a. bioenergetic condition.
      b. thermoregulatory status.
      c. physiological condition.
      d. metabolic rate.

_____ 2. An individual's BMR is influenced by their

      a. gender.
      b. age.
      c. body weight and genetics.
      d. all of the above.

_____ 3. An individual's metabolic state may be expressed as

      a. calories per hour.
      b. calories per day.
      c. calories per unit of body weight per day.
      d. All of the above are correct.

_____ 4. An individual's basal metabolic rate ideally represents

      a. the minimum resting energy expenditure of an awake, alert person.
      b. genetic differences among ethnic groups.
      c. the amounts of circulating hormones in the body.
      d. a measurement of the daily energy expenditures for a given individual.

OBJECTIVE 10 Discuss the homeostatic mechanisms that maintain a constant body temperature.

_____ 1. The greatest amount of daily water intake comes from

      a. consuming food.
      b. drinking fluids.
      c. metabolic processes.
      d. decreased urination.

_____ 2. The four processes involved in heat exchange with the environment are

      a. physiological, behavioral, generational, and acclimatization.
      b. radiation, conduction, convection, and evaporation.
      c. sensible, insensible, heat loss, and heat gain.
      d. thermogenesis, dynamic action, pyrexia, and thermalphasic.

_____ 3. The primary mechanisms for increasing heat loss in the body include

    a. sensible and insensible.
    b. acclimatization and pyrexia.
    c. physiological responses and behavioral modifications.
    d. vasomotor and respiratory.

4. The homeostatic process that keeps body temperature within acceptable limits regardless of environmental conditions is called _____.

5. The function of the heat gain center of the brain is to prevent _____.

Objective 11   Describe the age-related changes in nutritional requirements.

_____ 1. For each decade after age 50, caloric requirements decrease by

    a. 5%.
    b. 10%.
    c. 15%.
    d. 20%.

_____ 2. The decrease in caloric requirements with aging is associated with changes in

    a. body mass.
    b. exercise tolerance.
    c. metabolic rates.
    d. all of the above.

_____ 3. In the elderly, the supplement that may be needed to absorb calcium is

    a. vitamin C.
    b. zinc.
    c. vitamin D_3.
    d. selenium.

_____ 4. In the elderly, food is not utilized very efficiently *primarily* because

    a. their senses of taste and smell are significantly reduced.
    b. they cannot absorb food efficiently.
    c. they eat food that is unappetizing to them.
    d. they don't eat enough food.

_____ 5. In the elderly, changes in nutrition and health are related to

    a. changes in lifestyle.
    b. income.
    c. eating habits.
    d. all of the above.

Part II: Chapter Comprehensive Exercises

A. Word Elimination

Circle the term that does not belong in each of the following groupings.

1. lipids   proteins   glycolysis   carbohydrates   water

2. glycolysis   TCA   electron transport   Krebs cycle   anaerobic

3. glucose   NAD   pyruvic acid   acetyl-CoA   citric acid

4. ATP   fatty acids   glycerol   glucose   amino acids

5. linoleic acid   arachidonic   linolenic   EFA   EAA

6. leucine   lysine   tryptophan   linoleic acid   phenylalanine

7. milk   minerals   meat   vegetables   bread

8. sodium   potassium   zinc   chloride   calcium

9. vitamin A   vitamin D   vitamin C   vitamin E   vitamin K

10. thermoregulation   radiation   conduction   convection   evaporation

B. Matching

Match the terms in Column "B" with the terms in Column "A." Write letters for answers in the spaces provided.

COLUMN A	COLUMN B
____ 1. ketone bodies	a. unit of energy
____ 2. glucogenesis	b. lipid catabolism
____ 3. water-soluble vitamins	c. resting energy expenditure
____ 4. fat-soluble vitamins	d. essential fatty acid
____ 5. basal metabolic rate	e. B complex and vitamin C
____ 6. calorie	f. A, D, E, K
____ 7. linoleic acid	g. synthesis of lipids
____ 8. lipogenesis	h. glucose synthesis
____ 9. ketoacidosis	i. decrease in pH
____ 10. lipolysis	j. protein catabolism

C. Concept Map I - Healthy You Food Pyramid

Using the following terms, fill in the circled numbered, blank spaces to complete the concept map.
Follow the numbers that comply with the organization of the map.

Vitamins   Fruits   Tissue growth and repair   Proteins
Metabolic regulation   Grains   9 cal/gram   Carbohydrates

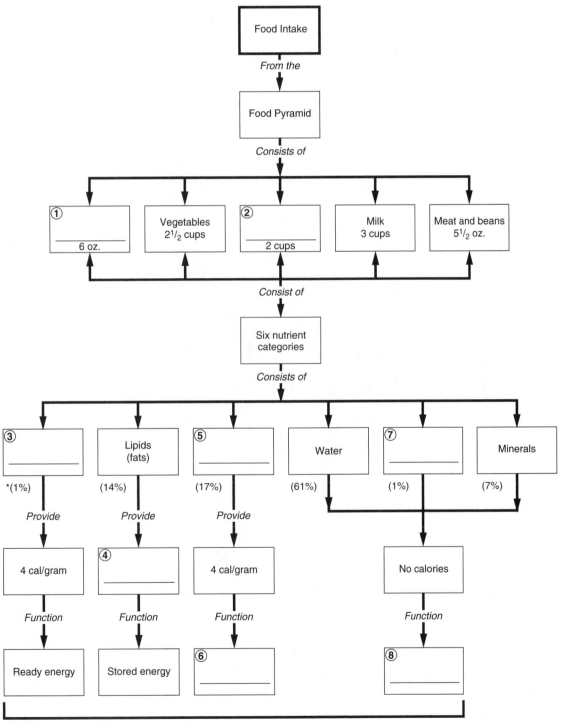

All nutrient categories are necessary —and interdependent.

*% of nutrients found in 25-year-old male weighing 65 kg (143 lbs.)

Concept Map II - Metabolism of Nutrients

Using the following terms, fill in the circled numbered, blank spaces to complete the concept map. Follow the numbers that comply with the organization of the map.

Gluconeogenesis   Amino acids   Lipogenesis
Beta oxidation   Lipolysis   Glycolysis
Electron transport   Krebs cycle

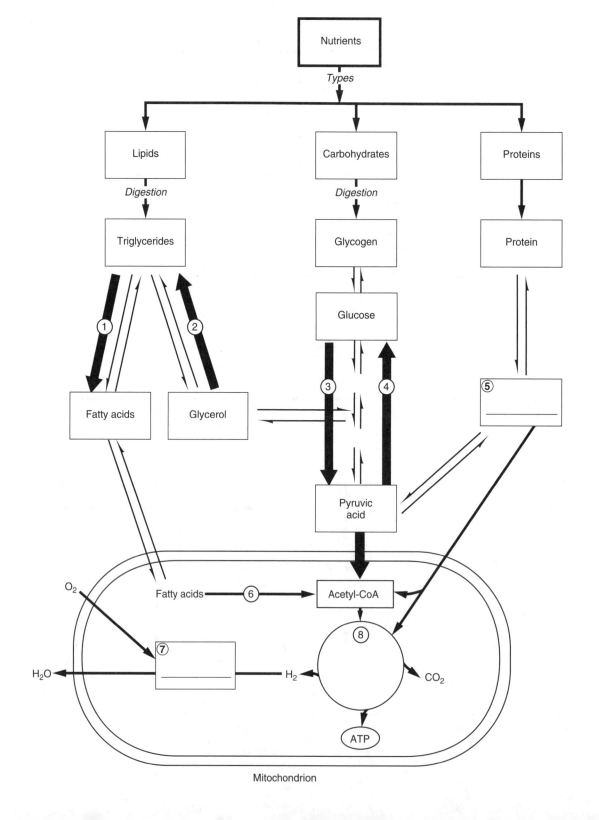

Mitochondrion

D. Crossword Puzzle

The following crossword puzzle is a review of the material in Chapter 17. To complete the puzzle, you must know the answers to the clues given, and must be able to spell the terms correctly.

ACROSS

3. A molecule required by the body that the body cannot make is considered _____.
4. Metabolic reactions that break down molecules.
5. One of the essential fatty acids (two words).
8. One of the essential amino acids.
10. A unit of measure that refers to the amount of energy in a specific type of food.
11. The digestion of fats produces fatty acids and _____.

DOWN

1. The digestion of protein produces _____ (two words).
2. The sum of all the chemical reactions in the body.
6. A food substance that has all the amino acids the body requires is known as a(n) _____ protein.
7. The digestion of carbohydrates produces _____.
9. The molecule from which mitochondria ultimately produce ATP is _____ acid.

E. Short-Answer Questions

Briefly answer the following questions in the spaces provided.

1. What factors make protein catabolism an impractical source of quick energy?

2. Why are nucleic acids not significant contributors to the total energy reserves of the cell?

3. For what four basic reasons do cells synthesize new organic components?

4. What five basic food groups and oils in the Healthy You Food Pyramid provide the basis for a balanced diet?

5. Even though minerals do not contain calories, why are they important in good nutrition?

6. (a) List the fat-soluble vitamins.

   (b) List the water-soluble vitamins.

The Urinary System

Overview

Although several organ systems are involved in the body's excretory processes, the urinary system is primarily responsible for the removal of nitrogenous wastes from the blood. The kidneys play a crucial homeostatic role by cleansing the blood of waste products and excess water by forming urine, which is then transferred to the urinary bladder and eventually excreted from the body during urination. In addition to the kidneys, the urinary system consists of the ureters, urinary bladder, and urethra, components that are responsible for transport, storage, and conduction and elimination of urine to the exterior.

Few people are aware of the many functions the kidneys perform. In addition to the preparation and excretion of urine, they (1) regulate blood pressure; (2) conserve valuable nutrients; (3) regulate blood ions; and (4) regulate blood pH. The kidneys receive more blood from the heart than any other organ. Every minute 1½ quarts of blood circulate through a complex renal pathway housed in each kidney. The blood-filtering system of the kidneys consists of millions of tubules and specialized cells that are designed to filter, reabsorb, and secrete a filtrate, ultimately leaving about 1% of the original filtrate volume as urine to be excreted.

Chapter 18 focuses on the structural and functional organization of the urinary system, the regulatory mechanisms that control urine formation and modification, and urine transport, storage, and elimination.

Review of Chapter Objectives

1. Identify the components of the urinary system and list their functions.
2. Describe the structural features of the kidneys.
3. Describe the structure of the nephron and the processes involved in urine formation.
4. Trace the path of blood flow through a kidney.
5. List and describe the factors that influence filtration pressure and the rate of filtrate formation.
6. Describe the changes that occur in the tubular fluid as it moves through the nephron and exits as urine.
7. Describe the structures and functions of the ureters, urinary bladder, and urethra.
8. Discuss the process of urination and how it is controlled.
9. Explain how the urinary system interacts with other body systems to maintain homeostasis

in body fluids.

10. Describe how water and electrolytes are distributed within the body.

11. Explain the basic concepts involved in the regulation of fluid and electrolyte regulation.

12. Explain the buffering systems that balance the pH of the intracellular and extracellular fluids.

13. Identify the most frequent threats to acid-base balance.

14. Describe the effects of aging on the urinary system.

Part I: Objective-Based Questions

OBJECTIVE 1   Identify the components of the urinary system and list their functions.

_____   1. Urine production occurs in the

    a. ureters.
    b. kidney.
    c. urethra.
    d. urinary bladder.

_____   2. Urine leaves the kidneys on its way to the urinary bladder via the

    a. urethra.
    b. nephrons.
    c. ureters.
    d. trigone.

_____   3. In addition to removing organic wastes, the urinary system

    a. regulates blood volume, blood pressure, and plasma ion concentrations.
    b. helps stabilize blood pH.
    c. conserves valuable nutrients.
    d. All of the above are correct.

_____   4. Urine exits from the body via the

    a. ureters.
    b. urinary bladder.
    c. penis.
    d. urethra.

_____   5. The initial factor that determines urine production is

    a. secretion.
    b. absorption.
    c. sympathetic activation.
    d. filtration.

_____   6. The body systems that complement and coordinate their activities with the urinary system include the

    a. nervous, endocrine, and cardiovascular systems.
    b. lymphatic, muscular, and digestive systems.
    c. digestive, cardiovascular, and respiratory systems.
    d. muscular, endocrine, and nervous systems.

Labeling Exercise

Identify and label the structures comprising the urinary system. Place your answers in the spaces provided below the drawing.

FIGURE 18-1 Components of the Urinary System

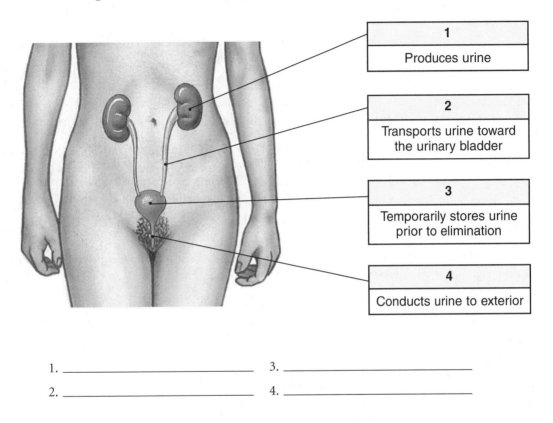

1
Produces urine

2
Transports urine toward the urinary bladder

3
Temporarily stores urine prior to elimination

4
Conducts urine to exterior

1. _____   3. _____

2. _____   4. _____

OBJECTIVE 2   Describe the structural features of the kidneys.

_____ 1. Seen in sections, the kidney is divided into

      a. renal columns and renal pelvis.
      b. an outer cortex and an inner medulla.
      c. major and minor calyces.
      d. a renal tubule and renal corpuscle.

_____ 2. The basic functional unit in the kidney is the

      a. glomerulus.
      b. loop of Henle.
      c. Bowman's capsule.
      d. nephron.

_____ 3. The three layers of connective tissue that protect and anchor the kidneys are the

      a. hilus, renal sinus, and renal corpuscle.
      b. cortex, medulla, and papillae.
      c. renal capsule, adipose capsule, and overlying peritoneum.
      d. major calyces, minor calyces, and renal pyramids.

_____ 4. Urine production begins in the renal cortex in microscopic tubular structures called

      a. the loop of Henle.
      b. renal papillae.
      c. ureters.
      d. nephrons.

_____ 5. The renal pyramids are located in the

      a. calyces.
      b. cortex.
      c. medulla.
      d. renal pelvis.

_____ 6. Once formed, urine follows which of the following sequential pathways through the kidney?

      a. renal pyramid, major calyx, minor calyx, renal pelvis, ureter
      b. renal pyramid, minor calyx, major calyx, renal pelvis, ureter
      c. renal pyramid, minor calyx, major calyx, renal pelvis, urethra
      d. renal pyramid, renal cortex, medulla, renal pelvis, ureter

Labeling Exercise

Identify and label the structures in the kidney. Place your answers in the spaces provided on the following page. Select your answers from the following choices.

ureter	cortex	renal sinus
minor calyx	renal capsule	renal column
renal pelvis	major calyx	renal pyramid

FIGURE 18-2 Sectional Anatomy of the Kidney

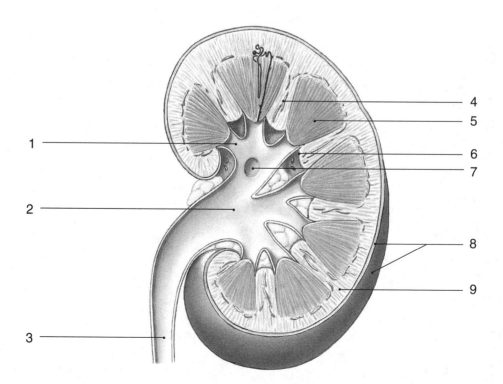

1. _____   6. _____

2. _____   7. _____

3. _____   8. _____

4. _____   9. _____

5. _____

OBJECTIVE 3   Describe the structure of the nephron and the processes involved in urine formation.

_____ 1. The "tuft" of capillaries that lies within the renal corpuscle is the

     a. glomerulus.
     b. loop of Henle.
     c. juxtaglomerular apparatus.
     d. major calyx.

_____ 2. In a nephron, the tubular passageway through which the filtrate passes includes the

     a. collecting tubule, collecting duct, and papillary duct.
     b. renal corpuscle, renal tubule, and renal pelvis.
     c. proximal convoluted tubule, loop of Henle, and distal convoluted tubule.
     d. loop of Henle and collecting and papillary ducts.

_____ 3. The primary site in the nephron where water, sodium, and potassium ion loss is regulated is the

     a. distal convoluted tubule.
     b. loop of Henle.
     c. proximal convoluted tubule.
     d. glomerulus.

_____ 4. The three processes involved in urine formation are

     a. diffusion, osmosis, and filtration.
     b. cotransport, countertransport, and facilitated diffusion.
     c. regulation, elimination, and micturition.
     d. filtration, reabsorption, and secretion.

_____ 5. The primary site for secretion of substances into the filtrate is the

     a. renal corpuscle.
     b. loop of Henle.
     c. distal convoluted tubule.
     d. proximal convoluted tubule.

_____ 6. The primary purpose of urine production is to

     a. produce urea, creatinine, and uric acid.
     b. maximize water loss to avoid dehydration.
     c. maintain homeostasis by regulating the volume and composition of the blood.
     d. reabsorb ions, organic molecules, vitamins, and water.

Labeling Exercise

Identify and label the structures comprising a nephron from the following selections. Place your answers in the spaces provided below the drawing.

proximal convoluted tubule   glomerulus   efferent arteriole

renal corpuscle   loop of Henle   collecting duct

afferent arteriole   distal convoluted tubule   papillary duct

FIGURE 18-3 Diagrammatic View of a Nephron

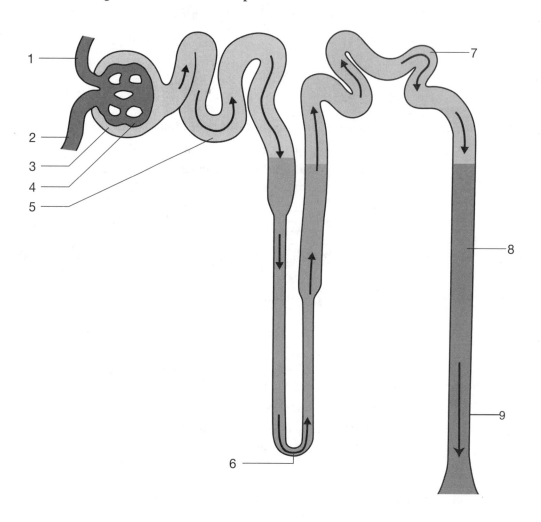

1. _____   6. _____

2. _____   7. _____

3. _____   8. _____

4. _____   9. _____

5. _____

OBJECTIVE 4   Trace the path of blood flow through a kidney.

_____ 1. Each kidney receives blood from

    a. an afferent arteriole.
    b. an arcuate artery.
    c. a renal artery.
    d. an interlobular artery.

_____ 2. The slender capillary network that accompanies the loop of Henle into the medulla is known as the

    a. macula densa.
    b. vasa recta.
    c. juxtaglomerular apparatus.
    d. papillary capillaries.

_____ 3. Blood supply to the proximal and distal convoluted tubules of the nephron is provided by the

    a. peritubular capillaries.
    b. afferent arterioles.
    c. segmental veins.
    d. interlobular veins.

_____ 4. Dilation of the afferent arteriole and glomerular capillaries and constriction of the efferent arteriole causes

    a. elevation of glomerular blood pressure to normal levels.
    b. a decrease in glomerular blood pressure.
    c. a decrease in the glomerular filtration rate.
    d. an increase in the secretion of renin and erythropoietin.

_____ 5. Blood enters the glomerulus via the

    a. renal artery.
    b. interlobar artery.
    c. efferent arteriole.
    d. afferent arteriole.

_____ 6. Blood leaves the kidney via the

    a. efferent arteriole.
    b. renal vein.
    c. interlobar vein.
    d. arcuate vein.

OBJECTIVE 5   List and describe the factors that influence filtration pressure and the rate of filtrate formation.

_____ 1. In filtration, water is forced across the filtration membrane in the renal corpuscle by

    a. osmotic pressure.
    b. hydrostatic pressure.
    c. muscle contractions.
    d. blood pressure.

_____ 2. If filtration does not occur,

      a. waste products are not excreted.
      b. pH control is jeopardized.
      c. blood volume regulation is eliminated.
      d. All of the above are correct.

_____ 3. Filtration occurs exclusively in the

      a. loop of Henle.
      b. renal corpuscle.
      c. proximal convoluted tubule.
      d. distal convoluted tubule.

_____ 4. The most selective pores in the filtration membrane are located in the

      a. podocytes.
      b. capillary endothelium.
      c. capsular space.
      d. lamina densa.

_____ 5. The first step essential to all kidney functions is

      a. secretion.
      b. reabsorption.
      c. hormonal regulation.
      d. glomerular filtration.

_____ 6. The ability to form a concentrated urine depends on the functions of the

      a. Bowman's capsule.
      b. collecting duct.
      c. loop of Henle.
      d. proximal convoluted tubule.

OBJECTIVE 6   Describe the changes that occur in the tubular fluid as it moves through the nephron and exits as urine.

_____ 1. Approximately 60–70% of the volume of the filtrate produced in the renal corpuscle is reabsorbed in the

      a. loop of Henle.
      b. proximal convoluted tubule.
      c. distal convoluted tubule.
      d. collecting duct.

_____ 2. The amount of water reabsorbed along the distal convoluted tubule and collecting duct is controlled by circulating levels of

      a. atrial natriuretic peptide.
      b. adrenalin.
      c. aldosterone.
      d. antidiuretic hormone.

_____ 3. Virtually all of the glucose, amino acids, and other organic nutrients are reabsorbed in the

      a. renal capsule.
      b. distal convoluted tubule.
      c. proximal convoluted tubule.
      d. loop of Henle.

_____ 4. Increased levels of aldosterone cause the kidneys to produce

      a. a larger volume of urine.
      b. urine with a lower specific gravity.
      c. urine with a lower concentration of sodium ions.
      d. urine with a higher concentration of potassium ions.

5. The reason water continually flows out of the tubular fluid and into the interstitial fluid by osmosis is that the

      a. descending limb of the loop of Henle is freely permeable to water.
      b. ascending limb of the loop of Henle is freely permeable to water.
      c. descending limb of the loop of Henle is impermeable to water.
      d. ascending limb of the loop of Henle is impermeable to water.

6. Over time, the highest concentration of solutes occurs near the bend in the

      a. renal capsule.
      b. proximal convoluted tubule.
      c. loop of Henle.
      d. distal convoluted tubule.

OBJECTIVE 7 Describe the structures and functions of the ureters, urinary bladder, and urethra.

_____ 1. When urine leaves the kidneys, it travels to the urinary bladder via the

      a. urethra.
      b. ureters.
      c. renal hilus.
      d. renal calyces.

_____ 2. The expanded, funnel-shaped upper end of the ureter in the kidney is the

      a. renal pelvis.
      b. urethra.
      c. renal hilus.
      d. renal calyx.

_____ 3. Contraction of the muscular bladder forces the urine out of the body through

      a. the ureter.
      b. the penis.
      c. the urethra.
      d. all of the above.

4. The muscular ring that provides involuntary control over the discharge of urine from the urinary bladder is the _____.

5. In a relaxed condition the epithelium of the urinary bladder forms a series of prominent folds called _____.

6. The hollow, muscular organ that stores urine prior to urination is the _____.

Labeling Exercise

Identify and label the following structures of the male urinary bladder. Place your answers in the spaces provided below the drawing.

detrusor muscle	urethral openings	external sphincter
prostate gland	internal sphincter	urethra
ureter	trigone	

FIGURE 18-4 The Male Urinary Bladder

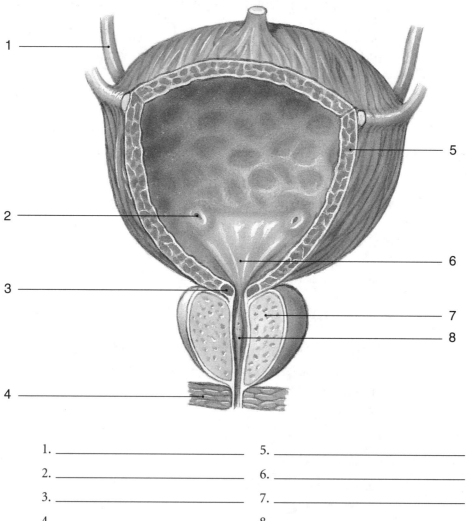

1. _____   5. _____

2. _____   6. _____

3. _____   7. _____

4. _____   8. _____

OBJECTIVE 8   Discuss the process of urination and how it is controlled.

_____ 1. The first signal that triggers urination occurs when the urinary bladder contains about
_____ ml of urine.

      a. 10
      b. 100
      c. 200
      d. 500

_____ 2. The involuntary internal sphincter opens when the urinary bladder contains about
_____ ml of urine.

      a. 100
      b. 200
      c. 500
      d. 1000

_____ 3. The external urethral sphincter consists of skeletal muscle fibers, and its contractions
are under

      a. voluntary control.
      b. involuntary control.
      c. hormonal regulation.
      d. autoregulation.

_____ 4. The muscle that compresses the urinary bladder and expels urine through the urethra
is the

      a. internal sphincter.
      b. external sphincter.
      c. rectus abdominis.
      d. detrusor.

_____ 5. During the micturition reflex,

      a. stretch receptors in the bladder are stimulated.
      b. parasympathetic stimulation initiates smooth muscle activity in the
bladder.
      c. the internal sphincter is unconsciously relaxed.
      d. the external sphincter relaxes.

OBJECTIVE 9   Explain how the urinary system interacts with other body systems to maintain
homeostasis in body fluids.

1. The system involved when water and electrolyte losses in perspiration affect plasma volume and composition is the _____ system.

2. The system involved when compounds such as acetone and water evaporate into the alveoli and are eliminated during exhalation is the _____ system.

3. The system involved when metabolic wastes are excreted in liver bile and variable amounts of water are lost in the feces is the _____ system.

OBJECTIVE 10 Describe how water and electrolytes are distributed within the body.

_____ 1. The intracellular fluid (ICF) is found in

        a. blood vessels.
        b. lymph.
        c. the cells of the body.
        d. the interstitial spaces.

_____ 2. The extracellular fluid (ECF) of the body includes

        a. blood plasma.
        b. cerebral spinal fluid.
        c. interstitial fluid.
        d. all of the above.

_____ 3. The principal cation in the ICF is

        a. sodium.
        b. potassium.
        c. calcium.
        d. chloride.

_____ 4. If the ECF solute concentration rises, water will

        a. leave the ICF.
        b. enter the ICF.
        c. move into the ICF and back out again to maintain homeostasis.
        d. leave the ECF.

_____ 5. When salt is consumed, water will

        a. enter the urinary system and raise blood pressure.
        b. leave the ECF and enter the ICF, causing a rise in blood pressure.
        c. leave the ICF and enter the ECF, causing blood pressure to rise.
        d. cause a rise in the sodium concentration, causing a rise in blood pressure.

OBJECTIVE 11 Explain the basic concepts involved in the regulation of fluid and electrolyte regulation.

_____ 1. If the ECF becomes more concentrated (hypertonic) with respect to the ICF, water will move

        a. into the cells from the ECF until equilibrium is reached.
        b. from the cells into the ECF until equilibrium is reached.
        c. back and forth between the ECF and the ICF.
        d. against its concentration gradient by active transport.

_____ 2. If the ECF becomes more dilute (hypotonic) with respect to the ICF, water will move

        a. from the ICF into the ECF, decreasing the volume of the ICF.
        b. by osmosis from the ICF into the ECF, decreasing the volume of the ECF.
        c. by carrier-mediated transport from the ECF into cells, decreasing the volume of the ICF.
        d. from the ECF into the cells, increasing the volume of the ICF.

_____ 3. Consuming a lot of salt will

    a. result in a temporary increase in blood volume.

    b. decrease thirst.

    c. cause hypotension.

    d. activate the renin-angiotensin mechanism.

_____ 4. When the level of sodium ions in the ECF decreases,

    a. osmoreceptors are stimulated.

    b. a person experiences increased thirst.

    c. more ADH is released.

    d. the level of aldosterone increases.

_____ 5. When large amounts of water are consumed, the

    a. ICF becomes hypertonic to the ICF.

    b. volume of the ECF will decrease.

    c. volume of the ICF will decrease.

    d. osmolarities of the ICF and ECF will be slightly lower.

6. The hormone that stimulates water conservation in the kidneys is _____.

7. The hormone that promotes sodium retention in the kidneys is _____.

8. Excessive potassium ions are eliminated from the body by the _____.

9. The amount of potassium secreted by the kidneys is regulated by _____.

10. Calcium reabsorption by the kidneys is promoted by the hormone _____.

OBJECTIVE 12   Explain the buffering systems that balance the pH of the intracellular and extra-cellular fluids.

_____ 1. Buffers stabilize the pH of body fluids by

    a. adding or removing bicarbonate ions from the fluid.

    b. adding or removing hydrogen ions from the fluid.

    c. adding or removing phosphate ions from the fluid.

    d. adding or removing protein from the fluid.

_____ 2. Maintaining body pH within narrow limits involves

    a. buffer systems.

    b. respiratory mechanisms.

    c. renal mechanisms.

    d. all of the above.

_____ 3. When exhaling, there is a decrease in the blood levels of

    a. carbon dioxide and oxygen.

    b. carbon dioxide and ultimately hydrogen ions.

    c. oxygen and ultimately hydrogen ions.

    d. carbon dioxide only.

_____ 4. When exhaling rapidly and excessively, blood pH

      a. drops.
      b. fluctuates.
      c. does not change.
      d. rises.

_____ 5. A rise in carbon dioxide in the blood causes blood pH to

      a. drop.
      b. fluctuate.
      c. not change.
      d. rise.

_____ 6. A rise in carbon dioxide in the blood will ultimately cause the breathing rate to

      a. decrease.
      b. fluctuate.
      c. increase.
      d. not change.

_____ 7. The part of the kidney involved in removing or adding hydrogen ions to the blood is the

      a. cortex.
      b. medulla.
      c. nephrons.
      d. renal pyramids.

_____ 8. When a person holds his or her breath, the

      a. blood CO_2 rises and blood pH drops.
      b. blood CO_2 drops and blood pH rises.
      c. blood CO_2 rises and blood pH rises.
      d. blood CO_2 drops and blood pH drops.

OBJECTIVE 13   Identify the most frequent threats to acid-base balance.

_____ 1. Hypoventilation and CO_2 buildup in tissues and blood cause

      a. an increased pH above 7.45.
      b. a decreased pH below 7.35.

_____ 2. Prolonged vomiting and associated acid loss cause

      a. a decreased pH below 7.35.
      b. an increased pH above 7.45.

_____ 3. Hyperventilation and reduction in plasma CO_2 levels cause

      a. an increased pH above 7.45.
      b. a decreased pH below 7.35.

_____ 4. Impaired H^+ excretion at the kidneys or bicarbonate loss in the urine or feces causes

      a. an increased pH above 7.45.
      b. a decreased pH below 7.35.

OBJECTIVE 14   Describe the effects of aging on the urinary system.

_____ 1. In the elderly,

     a. there is about a 40% decline in nephron function.
     b. the nephrons become less responsive to ADH.
     c. the filtration rate slows down.
     d. All of the above are correct.

_____ 2. As the aging process proceeds, the elderly may lose control of the

     a. internal urethral sphincter.
     b. external urethral sphincter.
     c. prostate gland.
     d. Both a and b are correct.

_____ 3. Urination in the elderly may occur more frequently because

     a. the nephrons are not responding to ADH.
     b. of incontinence.
     c. of the lack of ADH.
     d. of excessive ADH production and secretion.

_____ 4. Elderly men may experience difficulty with urination due to

     a. excessive secretion of ADH.
     b. an increase in the size of the glomerulus.
     c. an enlarged prostate.
     d. all of the above.

Part II: Chapter Comprehensive Exercises

A. Word Elimination

Circle the term that does not belong in each of the following groupings.

1. kidney   ureter   prostate   urinary bladder   urethra
2. cortex   nephron   medulla   pyramids   columns
3. calyces   PCT   loop of Henle   DCT   collecting duct
4. interlobar arteries   arcuate arteries   interlobular arteries   afferent arteriole   vasa recta
5. urea   creatinine   ammonia   urine   uric acid
6. sodium   potassium   glucose   chloride   bicarbonate
7. specific gravity   pH   osmolarity   color   ADH
8. adrenalin   angiotensin II   aldosterone   ADH   ANP
9. interstitial fluid   blood plasma   urine   lymph   synovial fluid
10. trigone   neck   urethral sphincter   ureter   detrusor

B. Matching

Match the terms in Column "B" with the terms in Column "A." Write letters for answers in the spaces provided.

COLUMN A

___ 1. sodium

___ 2. potassium

___ 3. decreased P_{CO_2}

___ 4. glycosuria

___ 5. urination

___ 6. aldosterone

___ 7. podocytes

___ 8. juxtaglomerular apparatus

___ 9. ascending limb of loop of Henle

___10. descending limb of loop of Henle

COLUMN B

a. glucose in the urine

b. accelerated sodium reabsorption

c. micturition

d. releases renin and erythropoietin

e. pH increases

f. reabsorbs sodium and chloride ions

g. dominant cation in ECF

h. reabsorbs water

i. filtration slits

j. dominant cation in ICF

C. Concept Map I - Urinary System

Using the following terms, fill in the circled numbered, blank spaces to complete the concept map. Follow the numbers that comply with the organization of the map.

Renal sinus   Ureters   Glomerulus
Urinary bladder   Minor calyces   Proximal convoluted tubule
Medulla   Nephrons   Collecting tubules

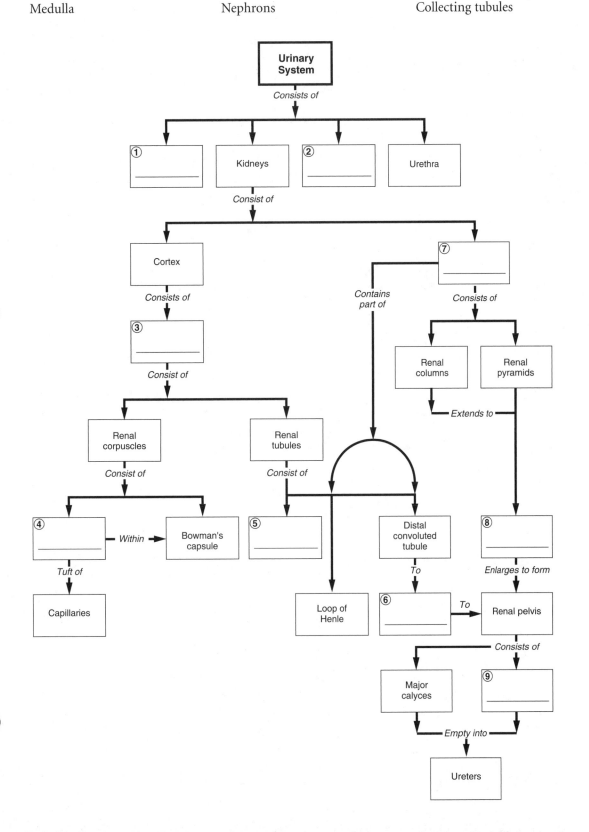

Concept Map II - Kidney Circulation

Using the following terms, fill in the circled numbered, blank spaces to complete the concept map. Follow the numbers that comply with the organization of the map.

Efferent artery   Interlobular vein   Afferent artery
Renal artery   Interlobar vein   Arcuate artery

[Kidney circulation]

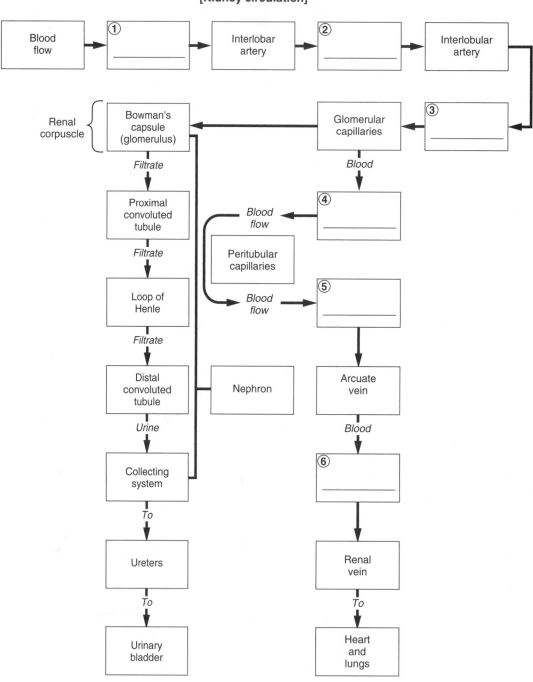

D. Crossword Puzzle

The following crossword puzzle reviews the material in Chapter 18. To complete the map, you must know the answers to the clues given, and must be able to spell the terms correctly.

ACROSS

3. The urethral sphincter that is under voluntary control.
4. An increase in carbon dioxide will increase the _____ ions in the blood.
5. Chemicals that resist changes in pH are known as _____.
9. The arteriole that takes material to the glomerulus.
10. The area where blood vessels enter and exit the kidneys.
12. When the prostate gland swells, it constricts the _____, making urination difficult.
13. The _____ ducts pass through the renal pyramid area.

DOWN

1. The capillaries inside the Bowman's capsule.
2. At about 500 ml, the ____ sphincter automatically opens.
6. This arteriole contains "cleaner" blood because it has been filtered by the glomerulus.
7. The chemical that activates angiotensin II.
8. The main functioning unit of the kidney.
11. A tube that leads from the kidneys to the urinary bladder.

E. Short-Answer Questions

Briefly answer the following questions in the spaces provided.

1. What are the essential functions of the urinary system?

2. What known functions result from sympathetic innervation of the kidneys?

3. What control mechanisms are involved with regulation of the glomerular filtration rate (GFR)?

4. What four hormones affect urine production? Describe the role of each.

5. What two major effects does ADH have on homeostatic regulation of water volume in the body?

6. How do pulmonary and renal mechanisms support the chemical buffer system?

19

The Reproductive System

Overview

The structures and functions of the reproductive system are notably different from those of any other organ system in the human body. Most organ systems show little difference between males and females. The structural differences between males and females, and the important roles these differences play in human behavior, emphasize the significance of the reproductive system. Even though major differences exist between the reproductive organs of the male and female, both are primarily involved with propagation of the species and passing genetic material from one generation to another. In addition, they produce hormones that control development of male and female sex characteristics.

The reproductive system is the only system that is not essential to the life of the individual. It is specialized to ensure survival not of the individual, but of the species. Whereas the other organ systems are functional at birth or shortly thereafter, the reproductive system does not become functional until hormonal influences are induced during puberty.

This chapter provides a series of exercises that will help you to review the principles of anatomy and physiology of the male and female reproductive tracts, hormonal influences, and changes that occur during the maturation and aging processes.

Review of Chapter Objectives

1. Describe the components of the male reproductive system.
2. Describe the process of spermatogenesis.
3. Describe the roles the male reproductive tract and accessory glands play in the maturation and transport of spermatozoa.
4. Describe the hormonal mechanisms that regulate male reproductive functions.
5. Describe the components of the female reproductive system.
6. Describe the process of oogenesis in the ovary.
7. Detail the physiological processes involved in the ovarian and menstrual cycles.
8. Discuss the physiology of sexual intercourse as it affects the reproductive systems of males and females.
9. Describe the changes in the reproductive system that occur with aging.
10. Explain how the reproductive system interacts with other organ systems.

Part I: Objective-Based Questions

OBJECTIVE 1 Describe the components of the male reproductive system.

_____ 1. The structures within the testes responsible for sperm production are the

a. seminiferous tubules.
b. interstitial cells.
c. sustentacular cells.
d. seminal vesicles.

_____ 2. The correct sequence of travel for sperm through the male's reproductive tract is

a. ductus deferens, epididymis, ejaculatory duct.
b. ejaculatory duct, ductus deferens, epididymis.
c. epididymis, ductus deferens, ejaculatory duct.
d. ejaculatory duct, epididymis, ductus deferens.

_____ 3. Seminal fluid exits the penis through the

a. ureter.
b. urethra.
c. ductus deferens.
d. ejaculatory duct.

_____ 4. A bundle of tissue that contains the ductus deferens, blood vessels, nerves, and lymphatics and serves the testes is the

a. epididymis.
b. rete testis.
c. corpora cavernosa.
d. spermatic cord.

_____ 5. Androgens are produced in

a. Sertoli cells.
b. the seminal vesicles.
c. interstitial cells.
d. sustentacular cells.

_____ 6. Sperm storage and maturation occurs in the

a. epididymis.
b. seminal vesicles.
c. interstitial cells.
d. ductus deferens.

Labeling Exercise

Identify and label the structures comprising the male reproductive tract from the following selections. Place your labels in the spaces provided below the drawing.

urinary bladder   bulbourethral gland   ductus deferens

penile urethra   urethral meatus   ureter

penis   rectum   scrotum

testis   seminal vesicle   ejaculatory duct

prostate gland   pubic symphysis   epididymis

FIGURE 19-1   Male Reproductive System

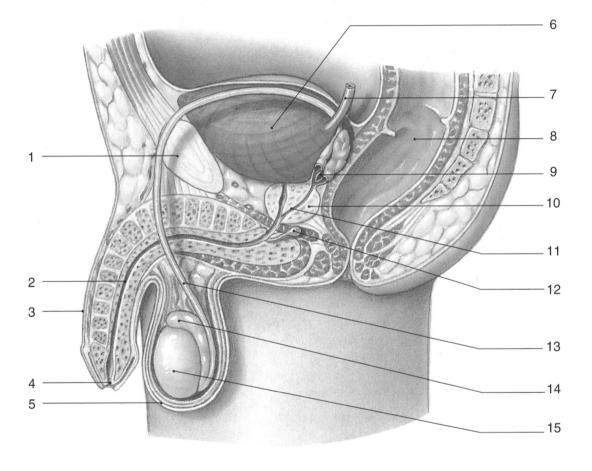

1. _____   9. _____

2. _____   10. _____

3. _____   11. _____

4. _____   12. _____

5. _____   13. _____

6. _____   14. _____

7. _____   15. _____

8. _____

OBJECTIVE 2   Describe the process of spermatogenesis.

_____ 1. Sperm production occurs in the

      a. seminal vesicles.
      b. seminiferous tubules.
      c. rete testis.
      d. epididymis.

_____ 2. The three processes involved in spermatogenesis are

      a. mitosis, meiosis, and spermiogenesis.
      b. motility, capacitation, and development.
      c. activation, capacitation, and peristaltic contractions.
      d. negative feedback, secretion of FSH, and testicular stimulation.

_____ 3. Sperm develop from "primordial cells" called

      a. spermatids.
      b. primary spermatocytes.
      c. spermatogonia.
      d. secondary spermatocytes.

_____ 4. When the process of meiosis begins, developing sperm cells become

      a. spermatids.
      b. spermatocytes.
      c. spermatozoans.
      d. sustentacular cells.

_____ 5. At the end of meiosis, the immature sperm are called

      a. spermatozoa.
      b. secondary spermatocytes.
      c. spermatogonia.
      d. spermatids.

_____ 6. The process of spermiogenesis produces

      a. spermatozoa.
      b. spermatids.
      c. secondary spermatocytes.
      d. Sertoli cells.

OBJECTIVE 3   Describe the roles the male reproductive tract and accessory glands play in the maturation and transport of spermatozoa.

_____ 1. Once sperm cells leave the testes, the route they take on their way out of the body of the male is

      a. ductus deferens → epididymis → urethra → ejaculatory duct.
      b. ejaculatory duct → epididymis → ductus deferens → urethra.
      c. epididymis → ductus deferens → ejaculatory duct → urethra.
      d. epididymis → ejaculatory duct → ductus deferens → urethra.

_____ 2. The accessory organs in the male that secrete into the ejaculatory ducts and the urethra are the

a. epididymis, seminal vesicles, and vas deferens.
b. prostate gland, inguinal canals, and raphe.
c. adrenal glands, bulbourethral glands, and seminal glands.
d. seminal vesicles, prostate gland, and bulbourethral glands.

_____ 3. Sperm move from the epididymis to the urethra via the

a. ductus deferens.
b. rete testis.
c. ejaculatory duct.
d. corpora cavernosum.

_____ 4. Seminalplasmin in the prostatic fluid is

a. a thick, sticky, alkaline mucus that helps neutralize urinary acids.
b. an antibiotic that may help prevent urinary tract infections in males.
c. a prostaglandin that stimulates smooth muscle contractions.
d. a six-carbon sugar metabolized by spermatozoa.

_____ 5. The gland that contributes about 60% to the volume of semen and produces a slightly alkaline secretion that contains fructose is the

a. prostate gland.
b. seminal vesicles.
c. bulbourethral glands.
d. Bartholin's gland.

_____ 6. The gland that surrounds the urethra at the base of the urinary bladder and produces an alkaline secretion is the

a. bulbourethral gland.
b. seminal vesicle.
c. prostate gland.
d. Bartholin's gland.

_____ 7. The small paired glands at the base of the penis that produce a lubricating secretion are the

a. bulbourethral glands.
b. Bartholin's glands.
c. seminal vesicles.
d. prostate glands.

8. The male organ of copulation is the _____.

9. The fold of skin that covers the tip of the penis is the _____.

10. The erectile tissue that surrounds the urethra is the _____.

11. The erectile tissue located on the ventral surface of the penis is the _____.

OBJECTIVE 4 Describe the hormonal mechanisms that regulate male reproductive functions.

_____ 1. The hormone that is synthesized in the hypothalamus and initiates the release of pituitary hormones is

        a. FSH (follicle-stimulating hormone).
        b. ICSH (interstitial cell-stimulating hormone).
        c. LH (luteinizing hormone).
        d. GnRH (gonadotropin-releasing hormone).

_____ 2. The hormone that promotes spermatogenesis along the seminiferous tubules is

        a. ICSH.
        b. FSH.
        c. GnRH.
        d. LH.

_____ 3. Testosterone plays a secondary role in sperm production because

        a. it causes the production of FSH.
        b. at high concentrations it stimulates GnRH to activate the release of FSH.
        c. at low concentrations it stimulates the release of FSH.
        d. it directly stimulates and initiates spermatogenesis.

_____ 4. The hormone responsible for secondary sex characteristics in the male is

        a. testosterone.
        b. FSH.
        c. LH.
        d. ICSH.

_____ 5. The pituitary hormone that stimulates the interstitial cells to secrete testosterone is

        a. FSH.
        b. LH.
        c. ACTH.
        d. ADH.

OBJECTIVE 5 Describe the components of the female reproductive system.

_____ 1. The production of female gametes and the secretion of female sex hormones is the function of the

        a. uterus.
        b. ovaries.
        c. endometrium.
        d. zona pellucida.

_____ 2. A developing embryo receives mechanical protection and nutritional support in the

        a. cervix.
        b. ovary.
        c. uterus.
        d. uterine tube.

_____   3. The mass of erectile tissue located at the anterior margin of the labia minora is the

      a. hymen.
      b. fornix.
      c. zona pellucida.
      d. clitoris.

_____   4. The muscular region extending between the uterus and the external genitalia is the

      a. mons pubis.
      b. vagina.
      c. ampullae.
      d. fornix.

_____   5. The muscular layer of the uterus is the

      a. endometrium.
      b. zona pellucida.
      c. mons pubis.
      d. myometrium.

6. The inferior portion of the uterus that projects into the vagina is the _____.

7. In the mammary glands, milk production occurs in the _____.

8. The central space bounded by the labia minora is the _____.

9. Fleshy folds that encircle and partially conceal the labia minora and vestibular structures are the _____.

10. The generally dark, pigmented skin that surrounds the mammary nipple is called the _____.

Labeling Exercise

Identify and label the structures comprising the female reproductive tract from the following selections. Place your labels in the spaces provided below the drawing.

sigmoid colon	pubic symphysis	labium minus
uterine tube	urinary bladder	ovarian follicle
urethra	ovary	clitoris
fornix	cervix	endometrium
uterus	vagina	anus
greater vestibular gland	labium majus	

FIGURE 19-2 **The Female Reproductive System**

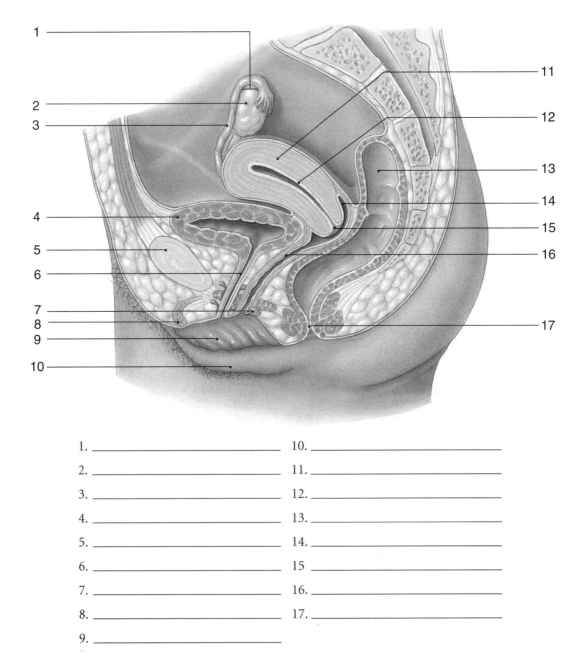

1. _____	10. _____
2. _____	11. _____
3. _____	12. _____
4. _____	13. _____
5. _____	14. _____
6. _____	15 _____
7. _____	16. _____
8. _____	17. _____
9. _____	

OBJECTIVE 6   Describe the process of oogenesis in the ovary.

_____ 1. The process of oogenesis produces three nonfunctional polar bodies and a

        a. primordial follicle.
        b. granulosa cell.
        c. functional ovum.
        d. zona pellucida.

_____ 2. Ova develop from stem cells called

        a. primary oocytes.
        b. oogonia.
        c. secondary oocytes.
        d. polar bodies.

_____ 3. The start of meiosis in the female begins between

        a. the third and seventh months of fetal development.
        b. birth and the first year of life.
        c. maturation of the female and puberty.
        d. the time of adolescence and adulthood.

_____ 4. The second meiotic division in the female is not completed until

        a. after fertilization.
        b. before fertilization.
        c. after ovulation.
        d. before ovulation.

_____ 5. The number of ova produced by the process of oogenesis is

        a. 400,000.
        b. 1.
        c. 4.
        d. 2 million.

_____ 6. The hormonal signal to complete meiosis occurs when the female

        a. completes ovulation.
        b. reaches puberty.
        c. is born.
        d. becomes an adult.

OBJECTIVE 7   Detail the physiological processes involved in the ovarian and menstrual cycles.

_____ 1. The proper sequence that describes the ovarian cycle involves the formation of

        a. primary follicles, secondary follicles, tertiary follicles, ovulation, and formation and destruction of the corpus luteum.
        b. primary follicles, secondary follicles, tertiary follicles, corpus luteum, and ovulation.
        c. corpus luteum, primary, secondary, and tertiary follicles, and ovulation.
        d. primary and tertiary follicles, secondary follicles, ovulation, and formation and destruction of the corpus luteum.

_____ 2. Under normal circumstances, in a 28-day cycle, ovulation occurs on day _____, and menses begins on day _____.

        a. 1; 4
        b. 28; 14
        c. 14; 1
        d. 6; 14

_____ 3. During the proliferative phase of the menstrual cycle,

        a. ovulation occurs.
        b. a new functional layer is formed in the uterus.
        c. secretory glands and blood vessels develop in the endometrium.
        d. the old functional layer is sloughed off.

_____ 4. During the secretory phase of the menstrual cycle,

        a. a new uterine lining is formed.
        b. the corpus luteum is formed.
        c. the old functional layer is sloughed off.
        d. glands enlarge and their rate of secretion is accelerated.

_____ 5. During the menses,

        a. the old functional layer is sloughed off.
        b. ovulation occurs.
        c. a new uterine lining is formed.
        d. the corpus luteum is formed.

_____ 6. At puberty in the male and the female,

        a. levels of FSH and LH increase.
        b. gametogenesis begins.
        c. secondary sex characteristics begin to appear.
        d. All of the above are correct.

7. The hormone that initiates oogenesis is _____.

8. The hormone that initiates ovulation is _____.

9. The principal hormone secreted by the corpus luteum is _____.

10. The hormone that causes a thickening of the endometrium to prepare the body for pregnancy is _____.

11. During pregnancy, the levels of estrogen and progesterone remain quite high to inhibit the release of _____.

OBJECTIVE 8   Discuss the physiology of sexual intercourse as it affects the reproductive systems of males and females.

_____ 1. The functional result of sexual intercourse, or coitus, is to

     a. satisfy the needs associated with arousal.
     b. introduce semen into the female reproductive tract.
     c. relieve pressure within the reproductive tract.
     d. provide viable eggs and sperm.

_____ 2. Male sexual function is coordinated by reflex pathways involving the

     a. sympathetic and parasympathetic divisions of the ANS.
     b. central nervous system.
     c. cerebrum and cerebellum.
     d. spinal cord and medulla oblongata.

_____ 3. During arousal, erotic thoughts or stimulation of sensory nerves in the genital region increase the parasympathetic outflow, causing

     a. emission.
     b. ejaculation.
     c. erection.
     d. detumescence.

_____ 4. In the female, engorgement of blood vessels at the nipples, making them sensitive to touch and pressure, is caused by

     a. parasympathetic stimulation.
     b. sympathetic stimulation.
     c. both divisions of the ANS.
     d. male manipulation.

_____ 5. In males, orgasm is an intense, pleasurable sensation associated with

     a. emission.
     b. arousal.
     c. ejaculation.
     d. detumescence.

OBJECTIVE 9   Describe the changes in the reproductive system that occur with aging.

1. In females, the time that ovulation and menstruation cease is referred to as

    _____.

2. Changes that occur in the male reproductive system over a period of time are known as the male _____.

_____ 3. Menopause is accompanied by a sharp and sustained rise in the production of
_____, while circulating concentrations of _____ decline.

  a. estrogen and progesterone; GnRH, FSH, and LH
  b. GnRH, FSH, and LH; estrogen and progesterone
  c. LH, estrogen; progesterone, GnRH, and FSH
  d. FSH, LH, and progesterone; estrogen and GnRH

_____ 4. In males between the ages of 50 and 60, circulating _____ levels begin to
decline, coupled with increases in circulating levels of _____.

  a. FSH and LH; testosterone
  b. FSH; testosterone and LH
  c. testosterone; FSH and LH
  d. LH; testosterone and FSH

OBJECTIVE 10   Explain how the reproductive system interacts with other organ systems.

1. For all other body systems, the system that provides secretion of hormones with effects on
   growth and metabolism is the _____ system.

2. The system that distributes reproductive hormones, provides nutrients and oxygen, and
   facilitates waste removal for a fetus is the _____ system.

3. The system that secretes and releases pituitary hormones that regulate sexual development
   and function is the _____ system.

4. The system that controls sexual behavior and sexual function is the _____
   system.

Part II: Chapter Comprehensive Exercises

A. Word Elimination

Circle the term that does not belong in each of the following groupings.

1. ovaries   uterine tubes   cremaster muscle   uterus   vagina
2. scrotum   epididymis   ductus deferens   ejaculatory duct   urethra
3. primary spermatocyte   secondary spermatocyte   spermatids   mitosis   sperm
4. head   neck   middle piece   tail   epididymis
5. seminal vesicles   penis   prostate gland   Cowper's glands   bulbourethral glands
6. primary oocyte   polar body   secondary oocyte   ovum   corpus luteum
7. areola   vulva   vestibule   labia minora   clitoris
8. nipple   lactiferous duct   vestibular glands   lactiferous sinus   areola
9. FSH   LH   progestin   androgens   estradiol
10. arousal   emission   coitus   ejaculation   orgasm

B. Matching

Match the terms in Column "B" with the terms in Column "A." Write letters for answers in the spaces provided.

COLUMN A

_____ 1. gametes

_____ 2. gonads

_____ 3. seminiferous tubules

_____ 4. puberty in males

_____ 5. testosterone

_____ 6. corpus luteum

_____ 7. puberty in females

_____ 8. atresia

_____ 9. human chorionic gonadotropin

_____10. oxytocin

COLUMN B

a. sperm production

b. endocrine structure

c. produces secondary sex characteristics

d. follicular degeneration

e. reproductive organs

f. indicates pregnancy

g. reproductive cells

h. milk ejection

i. menarche

j. spermatogenesis begins

C. Concept Map I - Male Reproductive Tract

Using the following terms, fill in the circled numbered, blank spaces to complete the concept map. Follow the numbers that comply with the organization of the map.

Urethra

Seminiferous tubules

Penis

Produce testosterone

FSH

Seminal vesicles

Ductus deferens

Bulbourethral glands

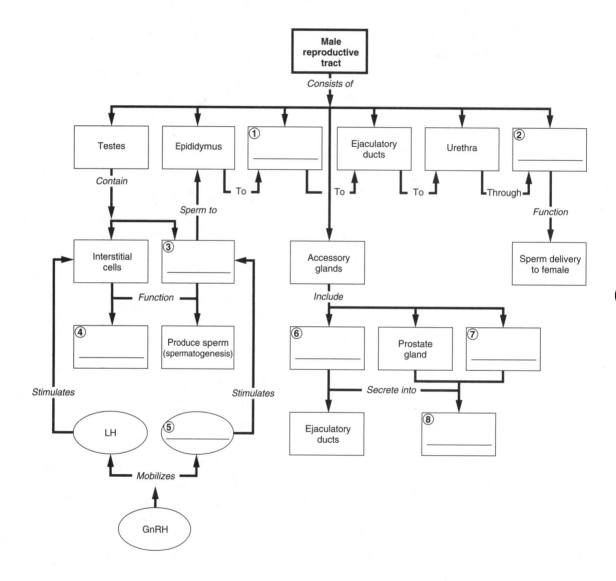

Concept Map II - Female Reproductive Tract

Using the following terms, fill in the circled numbered, blank spaces to complete the concept map.
Follow the numbers that comply with the organization of the map.

Nutrients

Follicles

Uterine tubes

Labia majora and minora

Vulva

Supports fetal development

Endometrium

Vagina

Granulosa and thecal cells

Clitoris

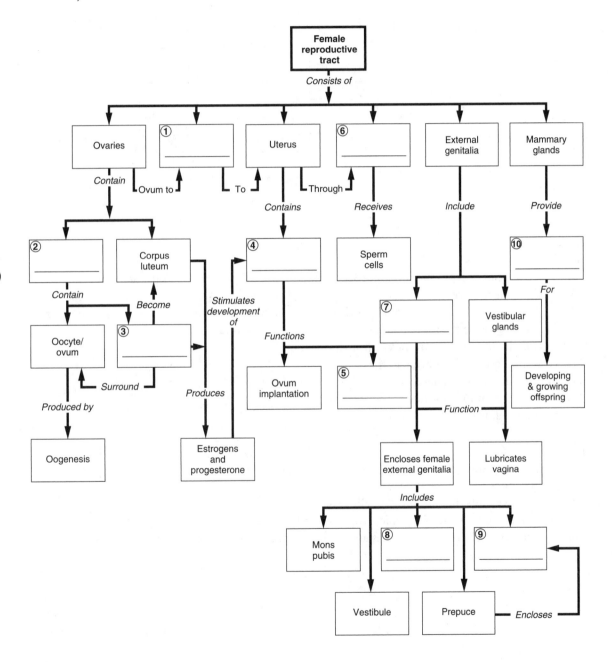

D. Crossword Puzzle

The following crossword puzzle reviews the material in Chapter 19. To complete the puzzle, you must know the answers to the clues given, and must be able to spell the terms correctly.

ACROSS

1. A type of cellular reproduction that reduces the number of chromosomes in each gamete.
5. If a zygote is not present, progesterone levels will drop, and _____ will begin.
7. _____ degrees Fahrenheit below normal body temperature is ideal for sperm production.
9. The tubules inside the testes that are responsible for sperm production.
10. Sperm cells and urine both travel through this tube.
11. Successful fertilization occurs in the _____ tube.
12. A chemical source of energy for the sperm cells that comes from the seminal vesicle.
13. The presence of this hormone indicates pregnancy.
14. A genetic name of sperm cells and egg cells.

DOWN

2. A zygote implants itself in the _____ of the uterus.
3. The hormone that causes ovulation.
4. One of the glands that produces alkaline semen.
6. Upon ovulation, the ovarian follicle ruptures and becomes a _____(two words).
8. The hormone that targets the testes and causes them to release testosterone.

E. Short-Answer Questions

Briefly answer the following questions in the spaces provided.

1. (a) What three glands secrete their products into the male reproductive tract?

   (b) What are the four primary functions of these glands?

2. What is the difference between seminal fluid and semen?

3. What is the difference between emission and ejaculation?

4. What are the five primary functions of testosterone in the male?

5. What are the three reproductive functions of the vagina?

6. What are the three phases of female sexual function, and what occurs in each phase?

7. What are the five steps in the ovarian cycle?

8. What are the three stages of the menstrual cycle?

9. What hormones are secreted by the placenta?

10. What is colostrum, and what are its major contributions to the infant?

F. Formation of Gametes – Gametogenesis

Identify the stages in each of the following processes. Place your answers in the spaces provided below each drawing.

1. Name of process: _____

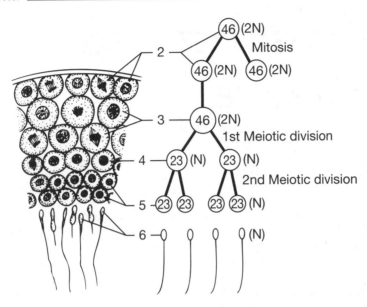

2. _____   5. _____

3. _____   6. _____

4. _____

7. Name of process: _____

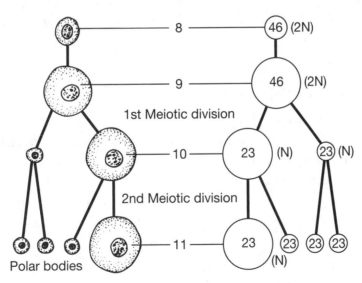

8. _____   10. _____

9. _____   11. _____

20

Development and Inheritance

Overview

The events of development, differentiation, and inheritance occur as a result of a complex and orderly sequence of changes that begin at conception and have a profound effect on an individual for a lifetime. Few topics in anatomy and physiology are as fascinating as the "miracle of life" and the events that occur during the nine months before birth. When a new life begins in the female reproductive system, new genetic combinations similar to the parents, yet different, are made and nourished until they emerge from the female tract to take up life on their own—at first highly dependent individuals but eventually growing independent as continued development and maturation occurs. What was once a single cell has developed and grown into a complex organism consisting of trillions of cells organized into tissues, organs, and organ systems—the human body, a complete living organism—carrying on all the functions of life!

Chapter 20 highlights the major events that occur during development and how our genetic inheritance profoundly affects everything about us, including our physical appearance, the way we behave, how long we live, and the likelihood of developing certain diseases. The chapter concludes with how developmental patterns can be modified for the good or ill of the individual.

Review of Chapter Objectives

1. Describe the process of fertilization.
2. List the three prenatal periods and describe the major events associated with each.
3. Describe the origins of the three primary germ layers and their participation in the formation of the extraembryonic membranes.
4. Describe the interplay between maternal organ systems and the developing embryo.
5. List and discuss the events that occur during labor and delivery.
6. Contrast the development of fraternal and identical twins.
7. Discuss the major stages of life after delivery.
8. Relate the basic principles of genetics to the inheritance of human traits.

Part I: Objective-Based Questions

OBJECTIVE 1   Describe the process of fertilization.

_____ 1. Fertilization involves the fusion of two haploid gametes, producing

        a. an egg with 23 chromosomes.
        b. a somatic cell with 23 chromosomes.
        c. a zygote that contains 46 chromosomes.
        d. a female gamete that contains 46 chromosomes.

_____ 2. Normal fertilization occurs in the

        a. lower part of the uterine tube.
        b. upper one-third of the uterine tube.
        c. upper part of the uterus.
        d. antrum of a tertiary follicle.

_____ 3. Fertilization is completed with the

        a. formation of a gamete with 23 chromosomes.
        b. formation of the male and female pronuclei.
        c. completion of the meiotic process.
        d. formation of a zygote containing 46 chromosomes.

4. Sperm cannot fertilize an egg until they have undergone an activation in the vagina

called _____.

5. The fusion of the male and female pronuclei is called _____.

6. One chromosome in each pair is contributed by the sperm and the other by the egg at

_____.

OBJECTIVE 2   List the three prenatal periods and describe the major events associated with each.

_____ 1. The period of gestation that is characterized by rapid fetal growth is the
_____ trimester.

        a. first
        b. second
        c. third

_____ 2. The period of gestation when the rudiments of all major organ systems appear is the
_____ trimester.

        a. first
        b. second
        c. third

_____ 3. The period of gestation when organs and organ systems complete most of their development and the fetus looks distinctly human is the _____ trimester.

        a. first
        b. second
        c. third

_____ 4. A blastocyst is

    a. an extraembryonic membrane that forms blood vessels.
    b. a solid ball of cells.
    c. a hollow ball of cells.
    d. a part of the placenta.

_____ 5. The inner cell mass of the blastocyst will form

    a. the placenta.
    b. the morula.
    c. the embryo.
    d. blood vessels of the placenta.

_____ 6. During implantation

    a. the syncytial trophoblast erodes a path through the uterine epithelium.
    b. inner cell mass begins to form the placenta.
    c. maternal blood vessels in the endometrium are walled off from the blastocyst.
    d. inner cell mass is temporarily deprived of nutrients.

_____ 7. During gastrulation,

    a. the blastodisc is formed.
    b. the placenta is formed.
    c. endodermal cells migrate to the ectoderm.
    d. primary germ layers are formed.

_____ 8. The chorionic villi

    a. increase the surface area for exchange between the placenta and maternal blood.
    b. form the umbilical cord.
    c. form the umbilical vein and arteries.
    d. form the major part of the placenta.

9. The process of cell division that occurs after fertilization is called _____.

10. The penetration of the endometrium by the blastocyst is referred to as

_____.

11. Identical cells produced by early cleavage are called _____.

12. The solid ball of cells formed after several rounds of cell division following fertilization is called a _____.

13. The superficial germ layer in contact with the amniotic cavity is the

_____.

14. The germ layer facing the blastocoel is known as the _____.

15. The poorly organized germ layer of migrating cells is the _____.

OBJECTIVE 3   Describe the origins of the three primary germ layers and their participation in the formation of the extraembryonic membranes.

_____ 1. Germ-layer formation results from the process of

a. embryogenesis.
b. fertilization.
c. gastrulation.
d. parturition.

_____ 2. The extraembryonic membranes that develop from the endoderm and mesoderm are the

a. amnion and chorion.
b. yolk sac and allantois.
c. allantois and chorion.
d. yolk sac and amnion.

_____ 3. The chorion develops from the

a. endoderm and mesoderm.
b. ectoderm and mesoderm.
c. trophoblast and endoderm.
d. mesoderm and trophoblast.

_____ 4. The extraembryonic membrane that contains a fluid that surrounds the developing embryo and fetus is the

a. amnion.
b. chorion.
c. allantois.
d. yolk sac.

_____ 5. The extraembryonic membrane that forms the fetal portion of the placenta is the

a. yolk sac.
b. chorion.
c. amnion.
d. allantois.

OBJECTIVE 4   Describe the interplay between maternal organ systems and the developing embryo.

_____ 1. The vital link between the maternal and embryonic systems that support the fetus during development is the

a. chorion.
b. amniotic sac.
c. placenta.
d. yolk sac.

_____ 2. The umbilical cord or umbilical stalk contains

a. the amnion, allantois, and chorion.
b. paired umbilical arteries and the amnion.
c. a single umbilical vein and the chorion.
d. the allantois, blood vessels, and yolk sac.

_____ 3. The hormone that is the basis for a pregnancy test is

      a. estrogen.
      b. progesterone.
      c. human chorionic gonadotropin (HCG).
      d. human placental lactogen (HPL).

_____ 4. The developing fetus is dependent on maternal organ systems for

      a. nourishment.
      b. respiration.
      c. waste removal.
      d. all of the above.

_____ 5. By the end of gestation, maternal blood volume has increased by almost

      a. 10 percent.
      b. 50 percent.
      c. 20 percent.
      d. 90 percent.

_____ 6. During pregnancy, maternal glomerular filtration increases by approximately 50 percent, causing the

      a. volume of urine produced to increase.
      b. volume of urine produced to decrease.
      c. volume of urine produced to be unaffected.
      d. kidneys to retain excessive amounts of fluid.

OBJECTIVE 5   List and discuss the events that occur during labor and delivery.

_____ 1. The correct sequence that describes the three stages of labor is

      a. dilation, expulsion, placental.
      b. dilation, placental, expulsion.
      c. expulsion, dilation, placental.
      d. placental, dilation, expulsion.

_____ 2. The dilation stage involves dilation of the

      a. cervix.
      b. uterus.
      c. vagina.
      d. uterine tubes.

_____ 3. When the "water breaks" the

      a. hymen is ruptured and a watery fluid is released.
      b. urinary bladder releases fluid due to excessive abdominal pressure.
      c. amniotic sac ruptures and releases amniotic fluid.
      d. chorionic villi release excessive fluid.

_____ 4. The "afterbirth" is the expelled

      a. fetal waste.
      b. maternal waste.
      c. amniotic sac.
      d. placenta.

OBJECTIVE 6   Contrast the development of fraternal and identical twins.

_____ 1. Fraternal or dizygotic twins develop when

    a. there is separation of blastomeres early in cleavage.
    b. there is splitting of the inner cell mass before gastrulation.
    c. both twins are formed from the same pair of gametes.
    d. two eggs are fertilized at the same time, forming two separate zygotes.

_____ 2. The genetic makeup and sex in identical twins is the same because

    a. the inner cell mass splits before gastrulation.
    b. the blastomeres split early in cleavage.
    c. both twins are formed from the same pair of gametes.
    d. All of the above are correct.

_____ 3. Identical twins are _____, whereas fraternal twins are _____.

    a. mitotic; meiotic
    b. monozygotic; dizygotic
    c. meiotic; mitotic
    d. dizygotic; monozygotic

Objective 7   Discuss the major stages of life after delivery.

_____ 1. The sequential stages that identify the features and functions associated with the human experience are

    a. neonatal, childhood, infancy, and maturity.
    b. neonatal, postnatal, childbirth, and adolescence.
    c. infancy, childhood, adolescence, and maturity.

_____ 2. The systems that were relatively nonfunctional during the prenatal period and that must become functional at birth are the

    a. circulatory, muscular, and skeletal.
    b. integumentary, reproductive, and nervous.
    c. endocrine, nervous, and circulatory.
    d. respiratory, digestive, and excretory.

_____ 3. Adolescence and sexual maturity begin at

    a. puberty.
    b. maturity.
    c. senescence.
    d. the neonatal period.

4. The stage associated with the end of growth in the late teens or early twenties is referred to

as _____.

5. The process of aging is referred to as _____.

OBJECTIVE 8   Relate the basic principles of genetics to the inheritance of human traits.

_____ 1. The normal chromosome complement of a typical somatic, or body, cell is

       a. 23.
       b. N or haploid number.
       c. 46.
       d. 92.

_____ 2. Gametes are different from ordinary somatic cells because

       a. they contain only half the normal number of chromosomes.
       b. they contain the full complement of chromosomes.
       c. the chromosome number doubles in gametes.
       d. gametes are diploid, or 2N.

_____ 3. During gamete formation, meiosis splits the chromosome pairs, producing

       a. diploid gametes.
       b. haploid gametes.
       c. gametes with a full chromosome complement.
       d. duplicate gametes.

_____ 4. The first meiotic division

       a. results in the separation of the duplicate chromosomes.
       b. yields four functional spermatids in the male.
       c. produces one functional ovum in the female.
       d. reduces the number of chromosomes from 46 to 23.

_____ 5. Spermatogenesis produces

       a. four functional spermatids for every primary spermatocyte undergoing
          meiosis.
       b. a functional spermatozoan with the diploid number of chromosomes.
       c. secondary spermatocytes with the 2N number of chromosomes.
       d. All of the above are correct.

_____ 6. Oogenesis produces

       a. an oogonium with the haploid number of chromosomes.
       b. one functional ovum and three nonfunctional polar bodies.
       c. a secondary oocyte with the diploid number of chromosomes.
       d. all of the above.

_____ 7. If an allele is dominant, it will be expressed in the phenotype

       a. if both alleles agree on the outcome of the phenotype.
       b. by the use of lowercase abbreviations.
       c. regardless of any conflicting instructions carried by the other allele.
       d. by the use of capitalized abbreviations.

_____ 8. If a female X chromosome of an allelic pair contains a sex-linked character for color blindness, the individual would be

      a. normal.
      b. color blind.
      c. color blind in one eye.
      d. All of the above could occur.

9. The special form of cell division leading to the production of sperm or eggs is

    _____.

10. The formation of gametes is called _____.

11. Chromosomes with genes that affect only somatic characteristics are referred to as

    _____ chromosomes.

12. If both chromosomes of a homologous pair carry the same allele of a particular gene, the

    individual is _____ for that trait.

13. When two alleles of a particular gene carry different instructions, the individual is

    _____ for that trait.

Development and Inheritance Questions

Using principles and concepts learned about development and inheritance, answer the following questions. Write your answers on a separate sheet of paper.

14. A common form of color blindness is associated with the presence of a dominant or recessive gene on the X chromosome. Normal color vision is determined by the presence of a dominant gene (C), and color blindness results from the presence of the recessive gene (c). Suppose a heterozygous normal female marries a normal male. Is it possible for any of their children to be color blind? Show the possibilities by using a Punnett square.

15. Albinism (aa) is inherited as a homozygous recessive trait. If a homozygous recessive mother and a heterozygous father decide to have children, what are the possibilities of their offspring inheriting albinism? Use a Punnett square to show the possibilities.

16. Tongue rolling is inherited as a dominant trait. For a mother and a father who are both heterozygous tongue rollers (T), show how it would be possible to produce children who do not have the ability to roll the tongue. Use a Punnett square to show the possibilities.

Part II: Chapter Comprehensive Exercises

A. Word Elimination

Circle the term that does not belong in each of the following groupings.

1. conception   birth   development   differentiation   inheritance
2. fertilization   embryology   pronucleus   spindle formation   cleavage
3. gestation   blastomere   morula   blastocyst   trophoblast
4. yolk sac   amnion   allantois   placenta   chorion
5. HCG   colostrum   prolactin   HPL   relaxin
6. childhood   infancy   fetus   maturity   adolescence
7. deafness   albinism   phenylketonuria   Tay-Sachs   Marfan's syndrome
8. curly hair   albinism   blond hair   red hair   Type O blood
9. parturition   dilation   gastrulation   expulsion   placental
10. endoderm   amnion   germ layers   ectoderm   mesoderm

B. Matching

Match the terms in Column "B" with the terms in Column "A." Write letters for answers in the spaces provided.

COLUMN A	COLUMN B
___ 1. gestation	a. visible characteristics
___ 2. neonate	b. nonreproductive cells
___ 3. phenotype	c. endocrine organ
___ 4. genotype	d. causes dilation of cervix
___ 5. somatic cell	e. prenatal development
___ 6. Peg cells	f. milk production hormone
___ 7. placenta	g. gives rise to urinary bladder
___ 8. human placental lactogen	h. newborn infant
___ 9. relaxin	i. complete capacitation process
___10. allantois	j. chromosomes and component genes

C. Concept Map I - Fertilization and Development

Using the following terms, fill in the circled numbered, blank spaces to complete the concept map. Follow the numbers that comply with the organization of the map.

Germ layer   Muscle   Endoderm   Zygote

Allantois   Relaxin   Progesterone   Yolk sac

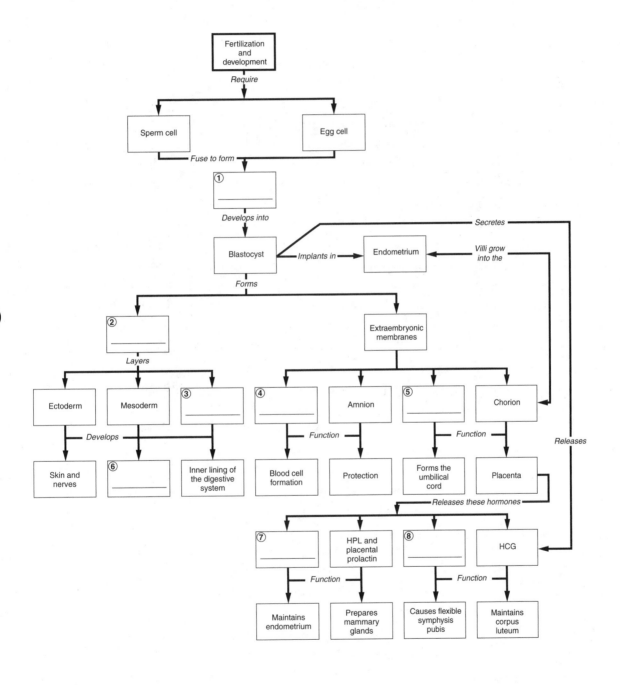

Concept Map II - Cleavage and Blastocyst Formation

Using the following terms, identify the structures or processes at the numbered locations in the illustration below concerning the female reproductive tract. Record your answers in the spaces provided below the drawing.

Early blastocyst
Morula
2-Cell stage

Fertilization
Implantation
8-Cell stage

Secondary oocyte
Zygote

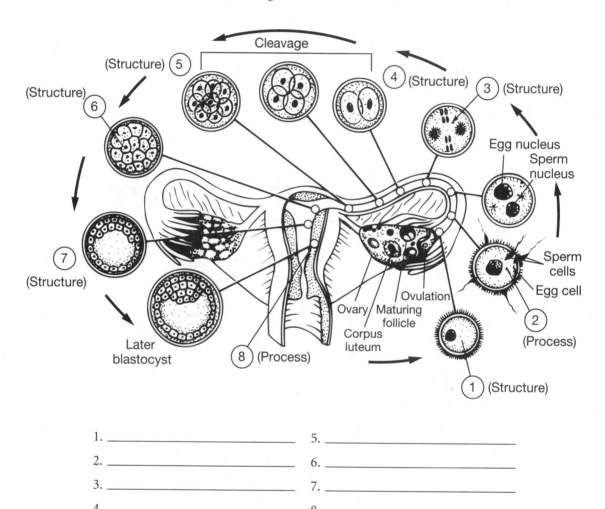

1. _____   5. _____

2. _____   6. _____

3. _____   7. _____

4. _____   8. _____

D. Crossword Puzzle

The following crossword puzzle reviews the material in Chapter 20. To complete the puzzle, you must know the answers to the clues given, and must be able to spell the terms correctly.

ACROSS

3. An induvidual that has a genetic trait that is not expressed is called a _____ of that genetic trait.
6. The expulsion of the _____ is referred to as the "afterbirth."
8. The hormone that causes milk release.
9. The gestation period is divided into _____.

DOWN

1. The membranous structure that forms the placenta.
2. The hormone that causes milk production.
4. The membranous structure that eventually becomes a part of the umbilical cord.
5. Human _____ gonadotropin hormone targets the corpus luteum.
7. A fertilized egg.

E. Short-Answer Questions

Briefly answer the following questions in the spaces provided below.

1. (a) What are the four extraembryonic membranes that are formed from the three germ layers?

   (b) From which given layer(s) does each membrane originate?

2. What are the six major compensatory adjustments necessary in the maternal systems to support the developing fetus?

3. What three major factors oppose the calming action of progesterone?

4. What three events interact to promote increased hormone production and sexual maturation at adolescence?

5. What four processes are involved with aging that influence the genetic programming of individual cells?

6. What are the three stages of labor?

Answer Key

1 An Introduction to Anatomy and Physiology

Part I: Objective-Based Questions

Objective 1

1. b
2. c
3. a
4. d

Objective 2

1. c
2. b
3. a

Objective 3

1. c
2. a
3. d
4. b

Objective 4

1. d
2. c
3. c

Labeling Exercise, Figure 1-1a

1. skeletal
2. muscular

Labeling Exercise, Figure 1-1b

1. brain
2. spinal cord
3. peripheral nerve
4. nervous
5. pineal gland
6. pituitary
7. thyroid
8. thymus
9. pancreas
10. adrenal gland
11. ovaries
12. testes
13. endocrine

Labeling Exercise, Figure 1-1c

1. heart
2. veins

3. arteries
4. capillaries
5. cardiovascular
6. thymus
7. lymph nodes
8. spleen
9. lymphatic vessels
10. lymphatic system

Labeling Exercise, Figure 1-1d

1. salivary gland
2. pharynx
3. esophagus
4. liver
5. gall bladder
6. stomach
7. large intestine
8. small intestine
9. anus
10. digestive system
11. nasal cavity
12. larynx

13. trachea
14. bronchi
15. lungs
16. respiratory

Labeling Exercise, Figure 1-1e

1. kidney
2. ureters
3. urinary bladder
4. urethra
5. excretory
6. prostate
7. urethra
8. penis
9. scrotum (testes)
10. mammary glands
11. uterine tubes
12. ovary
13. uterus
14. vagina
15. reproductive

Objective 5

1. b
2. c
3. a
4. b

Objective 6

1. a
2. b
3. c
4. d
5. b
6. nervous
7. endocrine

Objective 7

1. d
2. a
3. c
4. b
5. coronal or frontal
6. inguinal
7. gluteal
8. distal

Labeling Exercise, Figure 1-2

1. R. hypochondriac
2. R. lumbar
3. R. iliac
4. epigastric

5. umbilical
6. hypogastric
7. L. hypochondriac
8. L. lumbar
9. L. iliac

Labeling Exercise, Figure 1-3

1. orbital
2. oral
3. thorax
4. axillary
5. brachial
6. cubital
7. umbilical

8. pelvic
9. pubic
10. palmar
11. femoral
12. patellar
13. occipital
14. deltoid
15. dorsal
16. lumbar
17. gluteal
18. popliteal
19. calf

Objective 8

1. c
2. b
3. a
4. b
5. mesenteries
6. diaphragm

Labeling Exercise, Figure 1-4
1. cranial cavity
2. dorsal body cavity
3. spinal cavity
4. pleural cavity
5. pericardial cavity

6. diaphragm
7. abdominal cavity
8. abdominopelvic cavity
9. pelvic cavity
10. ventral body cavity

Part II: Chapter Comprehensive Exercises

A. Word Elimination

1. biology
2. organism
3. digestion
4. organism
5. temperature
6. supine
7. prone
8. coronal
9. caudal
10. mediastinum

B. Matching

1. g
2. j
3. a
4. h
5. c
6. b
7. i
8. e
9. d
10. f

C. Concept Map

1. cranial cavity
2. spinal cord
3. two pleural cavities
4. heart
5. abdominopelvic cavity
6. pelvic cavity

D. Crossword Puzzle

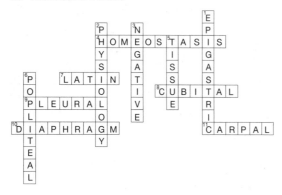

E. Short-Answer Questions

1. Any one of the following might be listed: responsiveness, adaptability, growth, reproduction, movement, absorption, respiration, excretion, digestion, circulation.

2. Subatomic particles, atoms, molecules, organelles, cell(s), tissue(s), organ(s), system(s)

3. In negative feedback a variation outside of normal limits triggers an automatic response that corrects the situation. In positive feedback the initial stimulus produces a response that exaggerates the stimulus.

4. In anatomical position, the body is erect, feet are parallel and flat on the floor, eyes are directed forward, and the arms are at the sides of the body with the palm of the hands turned forward.

5. ventral, dorsal, cranial (cephalic), caudal

6. A sagittal section separates right and left sides. A transverse or horizontal section separates superior and inferior portions of the body.

7. (a) They protect delicate organs from accidental shocks, and cushion them from thumps and bumps that occur during walking, jumping, and running.

    (b) They permit significant changes in the size and shape of visceral organs.

2 The Chemical Level of Organization

Part I: Objective-Based Questions

Objective 1

1. d
2. b
3. c
4. a
5. b
6. a

7. c
8. element
9. nucleus
10. energy
11. (Atomic structure)

12. six
13. twelve
14. four electrons
15. chemically active
16. C

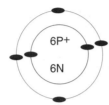

Objective 2

1. c
2. a
3. d
4. c

5. a
6. b
7. b
8. covalent bonds

9. ionic bond

Labeling Exercise, Figure 2-1
1. ionic
2. covalent

Objective 3

1. d
2. c

3. b
4. d

5. b

Objective 4

1. a
2. d

3. b
4. catabolism

5. equilibrium

Objective 5

1. a
2. c

3. b
4. d

5. b

Objective 6

1. b
2. d

3. organic
4. inorganic

Objective 7

1. c
2. b

3. b
4. c

5. solution
6. electrolytes

Objective 8

1. c
2. b
3. a
4. d

5. c
6. b
7. neutral

Labeling Exercise, Figure 2-2
1. acidic
2. neutral
3. alkaline

Objective 9

1. d
2. b

3. c
4. d

5. b
6. d

Objective 10

1. c
2. a
3. c
4. b
5. d
6. d
7. b
8. c
9. d
10. a
11. b
12. b
13. c
14. d
15. peptide bond
16. deoxyribose
17. uracil

Labeling Exercise, Figure 2-3

1. deoxyribose
2. adenine
3. thymine
4. guanine
5. phosphate
6. cytosine
7. hydrogen bond

Labeling Exercise, Table 2-1

Table 2–1	Classification of Various Organic Molecules				
Organic molecules	Carbohydrate	Lipid	Protein	Nucleic acid	High-energy compound
Amino acid			X		
ATP					X
Cholesterol		X			
Cytosine				X	
Disaccharide	X				
DNA				X	
Fatty acid		X			
Glucose	X				
Glycerol		X			
Glycogen	X				
Guanine				X	
Monosaccharide	X				
Nucleotide				X	
Phospholipid		X			
Polysaccharide	X				
RNA				X	
Starch	X				

Part II: Chapter Comprehensive Exercises

A. Word Elimination

1. isotope
2. compound
3. buffer
4. glucose
5. carbonic acid
6. glycogen
7. glycogen
8. uracil
9. carbon dioxide
10. monosaccharide

B. Matching

1. f
2. l
3. h
4. j
5. d
6. a
7. b
8. k
9. e
10. c
11. g
12. i

C. Concept Map

1. lipids
2. nucleic acids
3. dissacharides
4. fatty acids
5. amino acids
6. DNA

D. Crossword Puzzle

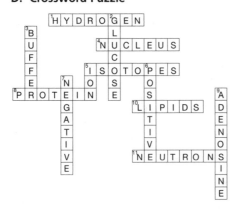

E. Short-Answer Questions

1.

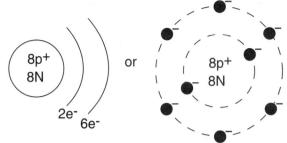

2. Their outer energy levels contain the maximum number of electrons so they will not react with one another nor combine with atoms of other elements.

3. The oxygen atom has a much stronger attraction for the shared electrons than do the hydrogen atoms, so the electrons spend most of the time in the vicinity of the oxygen nucleus. Because the oxygen atom has two extra electrons part of the time, it develops a slight negative charge. The hydrogens develop a slight positive charge because their electrons are away part of the time.

4. (a) freezing point 0 degrees C; boiling point 100 degrees C, (b) capacity to absorb and distribute heat, (c) heat absorbed during evaporation, (d) solvent properties

5. (a) carbohydrates, ex. glucose; (b) lipids, ex. steroids; (c) proteins, ex. enzymes; (d) nucleic acid, ex. DNA

6. In a saturated fatty acid, each carbon atom in the hydrocarbon tail has four single covalent bonds. If some of the carbon-to-carbon bonds are double covalent bonds, the fatty acid is unsaturated.

7. (a) Adenine nucleotide; (b) thymine nucleotide; (c) cytosine nucleotide; (d) guanine nucleotide

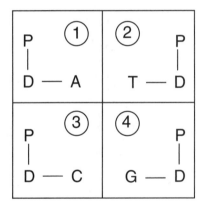

8. adenine, ribose, and phosphates

3 Cell Structure and Function

Part I: Objective-Based Questions

Objective 1

1. b
2. d
3. a
4. homeostasis

Objective 2

1. c
2. d
3. d
4. a
5. phospholipid bilayer
6. cell membrane

Labeling Exercise, Figure 3-1

1. heads
2. phospholipid bilayer
3. protein with channels
4. carbohydrate chain
5. tails
6. cholesterol
7. proteins
8. cytoskeleton
9. cell membrane

Objective 3

1. a
2. c
3. b
4. d
5. b
6. d
7. b
8. c
9. filtration
10. phagocytosis
11. isotonic

Labeling Exercise, Figure 3-2

1. hypertonic
2. hypotonic
3. isotonic

Objective 4

1. a
2. c
3. b
4. d
5. b
6. c
7. cytosol
8. microtubules

Labeling Exercise, Figure 3-3

1. cilia
2. secretory vesicles
3. centrioles
4. Golgi apparatus
5. mitochondrion
6. rough E.R.
7. nuclear envelope
8. nuclear pores
9. fixed ribosomes
10. microvilli
11. cytosol
12. lysosome
13. cytoskeleton
14. cell membrane
15. smooth E.R.
16. free ribosomes
17. nucleolus
18. chromatin

Objective 5

1. c
2. b
3. d
4. c
5. a

Objective 6

1. a
2. c
3. a
4. d
5. a
6. d
7. a
8. amino acids

Labeling Exercise, Figure 3-4

1. tRNA
2. translation
3. ribosomes
4. mRNA
5. transcription
6. DNA
7. nuclear pore

Objective 7

1. c
2. d
3. a
4. b
5. b

Labeling Exercise, Figure 3-5

1. nucleus
2. nucleolus

3. interphase
4. centrioles
5. spindle fibers
6. chromatin
7. early prophase
8. centromere
9. chromosome
10. late prophase
11. metaphase plate
12. metaphase
13. daughter chromosomes
14. anaphase
15. cytokinesis
16. daughter cell
17. telophase

Objective 8

1. c
2. a
3. b
4. d

Part II: Chapter Comprehensive Exercises

A. Word Elimination

1. organelle
2. lysomes
3. glycocalyx
4. distance
5. saturation
6. diffusion
7. ribosomes
8. mitochondria
9. DNA
10. interphase

B. Matching

1. b
2. i
3. c
4. a
5. j
6. e
7. d
8. g
9. f
10. h

C. Concept Map

1. proteins
2. cytosol
3. membranous
4. nucleus
5. centrioles

D. Crossword Puzzle

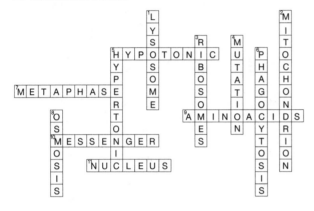

E. Short-Answer Questions

1. (a) Circulatory—RBC; (b) muscular—muscle cell; (c) reproductive—sperm cell; (d) skeletal—bone cell; (e) nervous—neuron. (Other systems and cells could be listed for this answer.)
2. (a) Physical isolation; (b) regulation of exchange with the environment; (c) sensitivity; (d) structural support
3. Cytosol—high concentration of K^+; extracellular fluid (ECF)—high concentration of Na^+
   Cytosol—higher concentration of dissolved proteins
   Cytosol—smaller quantities of carbohydrates and lipids
4. Cytoskeleton—centrioles, ribosomes, mitochondria, nucleus, nucleolus, ER, Golgi apparatus, lysosomes
5. Centrioles—move DNA during cell division
   Cilia—move fluids or solids across cell surfaces
   Flagella—move cell through fluids
6. (a) Lipid solubility; (b) channel size; (c) electrical interactions

4 The Tissue Level of Organization

Part I: Objective-Based Questions

Objective 1

1. d
2. b
3. c

Objective 2

1. c
2. d
3. b
4. c
5. simple squamous
6. pseudostratified columnar epithelium

Objective 3

1. b
2. c
3. d
4. a
3. c
4. e
5. a
6. f
7. h
8. l
9. i
10. j
11. g
12. k

Labeling Exercise, Figure 4-1
1. b
2. d

Objective 4

1. c
2. a
3. a
4. d
5. c
6. b
7. d
8. c
9. b
10. a
11. connective
12. collagen
13. areolar
14. reticular

Labeling Exercise, Figure 4-2
1. adipose tissue
2. loose connective tissue
3. collagen fibers
4. central canal
5. canaliculi
6. matrix
7. bone tissue
8. hyaline cartilage
9. dense connective tissue

Objective 5

1. a
2. c
3. b
4. c
5. a
6. d
7. lamina propria
8. synovial

Labeling Exercise, Figure 4-3
1. cutaneous
2. mucous
3. serous
4. synovial

Objective 6

1. d
2. a
3. b
4. d
5. d
6. contraction
7. skeletal

Labeling Exercise, Figure 4-4
1. muscle fiber (cell)
2. striations
3. skeletal muscle tissue
4. nucleus
5. smooth muscle cell
6. smooth muscle tissue
7. nucleus
8. intercalated disc
9. striations
10. cardiac muscle tissue

Objective 7

1. b
2. d
3. b
4. a
5. b

Labeling Exercise, Figure 4-5
1. dendrite
2. nucleus
3. soma
4. axon

Objective 8

1. c
2. a
3. d
4. b

Objective 9

1. c
2. d
3. d

Part II: Chapter Comprehensive Exercises

A. Word Elimination

1. adipose
2. storage
3. microvilli
4. flagella
5. connective
6. covering
7. matrix
8. lymph
9. visceral
10. neuroglia

B. Matching

1. i
2. f
3. a
4. j
5. b
6. d
7. c
8. l
9. k
10. h
11. g
12. e

C. Concept Map

1. connective
2. columnar
3. skeletal
4. neuron
5. loose
6. adipose
7. ligament
8. cartilage
9. blood

D. Crossword Puzzle

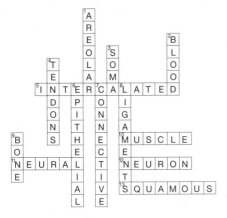

E. Short-Answer Questions

1. Epithelial, connective, muscle, and neural tissue

2. Provides physical protection, controls permeability, provides sensations, and provides specialized secretion.

3. Microvilli are abundant on epithelial surfaces where absorption and secretion take place. A cell with microvilli has at least 20 times the surface area of a cell without them. A typical ciliated cell contains about 250 cilia that beat in coordinated fashion. Materials are moved over the epithelial surface by the synchronized beating of cilia.

4. Merocrine secretion—the product is released through exocytosis.

   Apocrine secretion—loss of cytoplasm as well as the secretory product.

   Holocrine secretion—product is released, cell is destroyed.

   Merocrine and apocrine secretions leave the cell intact and able to continue secreting; holocrine secretion does not.

5. Serous glands—watery solution containing enzymes.

   Mucous glands—viscous mucous.

   Mixed glands—serous and mucous secretions.

6. Specialized cells, extracellular protein fibers, and ground substance.

7. Connective tissue proper, fluid connective tissues, supporting connective tissues.

8. Collagen, reticular, and elastic fibers.

9. Mucous membranes, serous membranes, cutaneous membranes, and synovial membranes.

10. Skeletal, cardiac, smooth.

11. Neurons—transmit nerve impulses from one region of the body to another.

    Neuroglia—provide support framework for neural tissue.

5 The Integumentary System

Part I: Objective-Based Questions

Objective 1

1. c
2. a
3. d
4. b
5. d

Objective 2

1. d
2. a
3. a
4. d
5. stratum corneum
6. stratum lucidum

Labeling Exercise, Figure 5-1

1. epidermis
2. dermis
3. hypodermis
4. hair shaft
5. sebaceous gland
6. arrector pili muscle
7. hair follicle
8. touch pressure receptor
9. nerve fiber
10. sweat gland
11. blood vessel
12. fat (adipose) tissue

Objective 3

1. c
2. d
3. a
4. b
5. c
6. vitamin D$_3$
7. melanin

Objective 4

1. d
2. c
3. a
4. b
5. d

Objective 5

1. d
2. d
3. d
4. DNA
5. ultraviolet light

Objective 6

1. c
2. d
3. c
4. a
5. b
6. b
7. nails
8. follicle
9. eyelashes
10. goose bumps

Labeling Exercise, Figure 5-2

1. free edge
2. hyponychium (underneath)
3. nail bed (underneath)
4. lateral nail groove
5. lunula (moon)
6. eponychium (cuticle)
7. nail root
8. eponychium
9. lunula
10. nail body
11. hyponychium
12. phalanx (bone of fingertip)

Objective 7

1. d
2. c
3. d
4. b
5. c
6. a

Objective 8

1. a
2. d
3. b
4. c
5. d

Objective 9

1. d
2. a
3. c
4. b
5. melanocyte
6. glandular

Part II: Chapter Comprehensive Exercises

A. Word Elimination

1. cutaneous
2. dermis
3. secretion
4. melanocytes
5. stabilize
6. apocrine
7. sebaceous
8. arrector pili
9. increased immunity
10. epidermis

B. Matching

1. e	3. g	5. a	7. j	9. i
2. h	4. c	6. b	8. f	10. d

C. Concept Map

1. dermis
2. deep reticular layer
3. loose connective tissue
4. elastic and collagen fibers
5. hair
6. sweat glands (suderiferous)

D. Crossword Puzzle

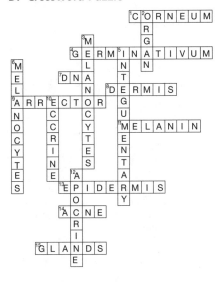

E. Short-Answer Questions

1. Palms of hand; soles of feet. These areas are covered by 30 or more layers of cornified cells. The epidermis in these locations may be six times thicker than the epidermis covering the general body surface.

2. Bacteria break down the organic secretions of the apocrine glands.

3. Stratum corneum, stratum granulosum, stratum spinosum, stratum germinativum, papillary layer, reticular layer.

4. Long-term damage can result from chronic exposure to sunlight, and an individual attempting to acquire a deep tan places severe stress on the skin. Alterations in underlying connective tissue lead to premature wrinkling, and skin cancer can result from chromosomal damage or breakage.

5. Hairs are dead, keratinized structures, and no amount of oiling or shampooing with added ingredients will influence either the exposed hair or the follicles buried in the dermis.

6. "Whiteheads" contain accumulated, stagnant secretions. "Blackheads" contain more solid material that has been invaded by bacteria.

6 The Skeletal System

Part I: Objective-Based Questions

Objective 1

1. d
2. b
3. a
4. c

Objective 2

1. a
2. d
3. c
4. b
5. osteon (Haversian system)
6. epiphysis

Labeling Exercise, Figure 6-1
1. proximal epiphysis
2. diaphysis
3. distal epiphysis

4. spongy bone
5. articular cartilage
6. compact bone
7. marrow cavity
8. endosteum
9. periosteum
10. blood vessels

Labeling Exercise, Figure 6-2
1. lamellae
2. central canal

3. endosteum
4. osteons
5. artery
6. vein
7. periosteum
8. perforating canal
9. compact bone
10. trabeculae

Objective 3

1. a
2. b
3. c
4. c
5. a

6. a
7. b

Labeling Exercise, Figure 6-3
1. disintegrating chondrocytes
2. enlarging chondrocytes

3. epiphysis
4. diaphysis
5. marrow cavity
6. blood vessels
7. epiphyseal plate

Objective 4

1. c
2. b
3. d
4. a

5. a
6. a
7. d
8. c

9. b
10. d

Objective 5

1. b
2. c
3. a
4. d
5. c
6. a
7. c
8. muscles
9. extremities
10. clavicle

Labeling Exercise, Figure 6-4
1. parietal bone
2. frontal bone

3. clavicle
4. scapula
5. humerus
6. vertebrae
7. os coxae
8. femur
9. patella
10. talus
11. metatarsals
12. temporal bone
13. maxilla
14. mandible
15. sternum

16. rib
17. radius
18. sacrum
19. ulna
20. carpals
21. metacarpals
22. phalanges
23. tibia
24. fibula
25. tarsals
26. phalanges

Objective 6

1. b
2. a
3. b
4. d
5. c
6. d
7. c
8. d
9. b

Labeling Exercise, Figure 6-5
1. frontal bone
2. sphenoid bone
3. lacrimal bone
4. ethmoid bone

5. nasal bone
6. zygomatic bone
7. maxilla
8. mandible
9. parietal bone
10. temporal bone
11. occipital bone
12. zygomatic arch
13. mastoid process
14. styloid process

Labeling Exercise, Figure 6-6
1. parietal bone
2. frontal bone
3. sphenoid bone

4. temporal bone
5. zygomatic bone
6. maxilla
7. nasal bone
8. ethmoid bone
9. lacrimal bone
10. nasal concha
11. vomer
12. mandible

Labeling Exercise, Figure 6-7
1. zygomatic bone
2. zygomatic arch
3. vomer
4. styloid process

5. mastoid process
6. occipital bone
7. maxillary bone
8. palatine bone
9. sphenoid bone
10. temporal bone
11. occipital condyle
12. foramen magnum

Labeling Exercise, Figure 6-8
1. coronal suture
2. frontal bone
3. sphenoidal fontanel
4. maxillary bone
5. mandible

6. squamosal suture
7. mastoid fontanel
8. occipital bone
9. lambdoidal suture
10. frontal fontanel
11. coronal suture
12. sagittal suture
13. parietal bone
14. occipital fontanel

Objective 7

1. b
2. c
3. c
4. b
5. c
6. a
7. b
8. c
9. a
10. c
11. coccyx
12. atlas (C_1)

Objective 8

1. a
2. c
3. b
4. a
5. d
6. b
7. d
8. a
9. c
10. b
11. c
12. d
13. a
14. d
15. b
16. c
17. clavicle
18. coxae
19. styloid
20. malleolus

Objective 9

1. c
2. b
3. d
4. b
5. b
6. d
7. d
8. suture
9. synarthrosis

Objective 10

1. a
2. c
3. d
4. a
5. d
6. b
7. c
8. c
9. d
10. a

Labeling Exercise, Figure 6-17
1. extension

Objective 11

1. d
2. c
3. a
4. d
5. b

---

13. cervical

Labeling Exercise, Figure 6-9
1. cervical
2. thoracic
3. lumbar
4. sacral
5. coccygeal

Labeling Exercise, Figure 6-10
1. lamina
2. pedicle
3. spinous process
4. transverse process

21. acetabulum
22. knee
23. childbirth
24. clavicle
25. fibula

Labeling Exercise, Figure 6-12
1. superior border
2. spine
3. medial border
4. coracoid process
5. acromion process
6. glenoid cavity
7. body
8. lateral border

Labeling Exercise, Figure 6-13
1. ilium
2. sacrum
3. pubis
4. symphysis pubis
5. ischium (inferior ramus)

10. symphysis
11. synovial
12. hip
13. knee
14. elbow

Labeling Exercise, Figure 6-16
1. extensor muscle
2. bursa
3. femur

2. flexion
3. hyperextension
4. flexion
5. extension
6. flexion
7. extension
8. hyperextension
9. abduction
10. adduction
11. supination
12. pronation
13. head rotation

6. d

Labeling Exercise, Figure 6-19
1. gliding joint
2. hinge joint
3. pivot joint

---

5. vertebral foramen
6. vertebral body

Labeling Exercise, Figure 6-11
1. sternum
2. manubrium
3. body of sternum
4. xiphoid process
5. floating ribs
6. true ribs
7. false ribs
8. costal cartilage

6. iliac crest
7. coccyx
8. acetabulum
9. obturator foramen

Labeling Exercise, Figure 6-14
1. ulna
2. radius
3. carpals
4. metacarpals
5. phalanges

Labeling Exercise, Figure 6-15
1. tarsals
2. navicular bone
3. cuneiform bone
4. metatarsals
5. phalanges
6. tibia
7. talus
8. calcaneus

4. tendon
5. patella
6. fat pad
7. joint capsule
8. meniscus
9. joint cavity
10. intracapsular ligament
11. patellar ligament
12. tibia

14. limb rotation

Labeling Exercise, Figure 6-18
1. inversion
2. eversion
3. dorsiflexion
4. plantar flexion
5. opposition
6. retraction
7. protraction
8. elevation
9. depression

4. ellipsoidal joint
5. saddle joint
6. ball-and-socket joint

Objective 12

1. d
2. d
3. b
4. d

Part II: Chapter Comprehensive Exercises

A. Word Elimination

1. secretion
2. vitamin D_3
3. ostopenia
4. pelvis
5. hyoid bone
6. occipital
7. mastoid
8. scoliosis
9. olecranon
10. pronation

B. Matching

1. d
2. g
3. a
4. i
5. c
6. h
7. e
8. b
9. f
10. l
11. k
12. j

C. Concept Maps

Concept Map I - Skeletal System

1. vertebral column
2. cranium (8 bones)
3. ribs
4. pectoral girdle
5. upper limbs
6. coxal bone
7. lower limbs

Concept Map II - Joints

1. no movement
2. sutures
3. cartilaginous
4. amphiarthrosis
5. fibrous
6. symphysis
7. synovial
8. monoaxial
9. wrist

D. Crossword Puzzle

E. Short-Answer Questions

1. The functions of the skeletal systems are support, storage, blood cell production, protection, and leverage.

2. In compact bone, the basic functional unit is the *osteon* within a *Haversian system*. The lamella (bony matrix) fills in spaces between the osteons. Spongy bone has no osteons; the lamella forms bony plates called *trabeculae*.

3. *Calcification* refers to the deposition of calcium salts within a tissue; *ossification* refers specifically to the formation of bone.

4. The thoracic and sacral curves are called primary curves because they begin to appear late in fetal development. They accommodate the thoracic and abdominopelvic viscera.

   The lumbar and cervical curves are called secondary curves because they do not appear until several months after birth. They help position the body weight over the legs.

5. *Kyphosis*: normal thoracic curvature becomes exaggerated, producing "roundback" appearance.

   Lordosis: exaggerated lumbar curvature produces "swayback" appearance.

   Scoliosis: abnormal lateral curvature.

6. *Intramembranous* ossification begins when osteoblasts differentiate within a connective tissue; *endochondral* ossification begins with the formation of a cartilaginous model.

7. Pectoral girdle: scapula, clavicle
   Pelvic girdle: ilium, ischium, pubis
8. A tendon attaches muscle to bone; ligaments attach bones to bones.
9. (a) Bursae are small, synovial fluid-filled pockets in connective tissue that form where a tendon or ligament rubs against other tissues. Their function is to reduce friction and act as shock absorbers.
   (b) Menisci are articular discs that (1) subdivide a synovial cavity, (2) channel the flow of synovial fluid, and (3) allow variations in the shape of the articular surfaces.
10. Synovial fluid provides lubrication, acts as a shock absorber, and nourishes the chondrocytes.
11. The knee joint and elbow joint are both hinge joints.
12. The shoulder joint and hip joint are both ball-and-socket joints.
13. Intervertebral discs are not found between the first and second cervical vertebrae (atlas and axis), the sacrum, and the coccyx. C_1 the atlas, sits on top of C_2, the axis; the den of the axis provides for rotation of the first cervical vertebra, which supports the head. An intervertebral disc would prohibit rotation. The sacrum and the coccyx are fused bones.
14. (a) inversion
    (b) opposition
    (c) plantar flexion
    (d) protraction
    (e) depression
    (f) elevation

7 The Muscular System

Part I: Objective-Based Questions

Objective 1
1. b
2. d
3. c
4. a

Objective 2
1. b
2. a
3. d
4. d
5. c
6. a

Labeling Exercise, Figure 7-1
1. tendon
2. skeletal muscle
3. epimysium
4. blood vessels and nerves
5. perimysium
6. muscle fascicle
7. endomysium
8. muscle fiber

Objective 3
1. a
2. b
3. d
4. a
5. b

Labeling Exercise, Figure 7-2
1. actin
2. A band
3. I band
4. M line
5. myosin
6. Z line

Objective 4
1. d
2. a
3. c
4. b
5. c

Labeling Exercise, Figure 7-3
1. resting sarcomere
2. active site exposure
3. cross-bridge attachment
4. pivoting of myosin head
5. cross-bridge detachment
6. myosin reactivation

Objective 5
1. c
2. a
3. c
4. a
5. muscle tone
6. incomplete

Objective 6
1. d
2. c
3. a
4. c
5. a
6. b

Objective 7
1. b
2. d
3. b
4. b
5. b
6. d
7. a
8. c

Objective 8
1. c
2. d
3. d

Objective 9
1. d
2. d
3. b
4. b
5. a
6. c
7. d
8. a
9. b
10. c
11. c
12. a
13. d
14. b
15. c
16. c
17. a
18. b
19. d
20. b

Labeling Exercise, Figure 7-4
1. temporalis
2. orbicularis oculi
3. zygomaticus
4. orbicularis oris
5. pectoralis major
6. deltoid
7. biceps brachii
8. rectus abdominis
9. external oblique
10. adductor muscles
11. gracilis
12. sartorius
13. tibialis anterior
14. frontalis
15. masseter
16. sternocleidomastoid
17. external oblique
18. tensor fascia lata
19. rectus femoris
20. vastus lateralis
21. vastus medialis
22. peroneus longus

Labeling Exercise, Figure 7-5
1. gluteus maximus
2. semimembranosus
3. biceps femoris
4. semitendinosus
5. gastrocnemius
6. occipitalis
7. trapezius
8. deltoid
9. triceps brachii
10. latissimus dorsi
11. external oblique
12. gluteus medius
13. soleus

Objective 10

1. d   3. b
2. a   4. c

Objective 11

1. skeletal   3. lymphatic   5. nervous
2. cardiovascular   4. endocrine

Part II: Chapter Comprehensive Exercises

A. Word Elimination

1. support   3. contraction   5. DNA   7. jogging   9. sartorius
2. sarcomere   4. myogram   6. myoglobin   8. anaerobic   10. heart

B. Matching

1. e   3. a   5. b   7. f   9. h
2. g   4. c   6. d   8. j   10. i

C. Concept Maps

Concept Map I - Muscle Tissue

1. heart   4. involuntary   7. multinucleated
2. striated   5. nonstriated
3. smooth   6. bones

Concept Map II - Muscle Structure

1. muscle bundles (fascicles)   4. actin   7. H zone
2. myofibrils   5. Z lines
3. sarcomeres   6. thick filaments

D. Crossword Puzzle

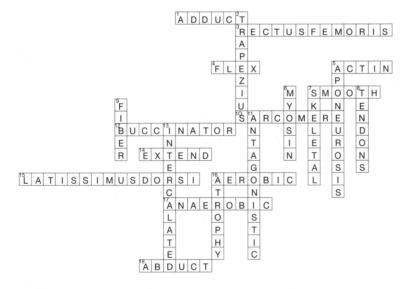

E. Short-Answer Questions

1. (a) produce skeletal movement
   (b) maintain posture and body position
   (c) support soft tissues
   (d) guard entrances and exits
   (e) maintain body temperature

2. (a) an outer *epimysium*, (b) a central *perimysium*, and (c) an inner *endomysium*

3. When fatigue occurs and the oxygen supply to the muscles is depleted, aerobic respiration ceases, owing to the decreasing oxygen supply. Anaerobic glycolysis supplies the needed energy for a short period of time. The amount of oxygen needed to restore normal pre-exertion conditions is the oxygen debt.

4. *Isometric* contraction: tension rises to maximum but the length of the muscle remains constant.

   Isotonic contraction: tension in the muscle builds until it exceeds the amount of resistance and the muscle shortens. As the muscle shortens, the tension in the muscle remains constant at a value that just exceeds the applied resistance.

5. Biceps femoris, semimembranosus, and semitendinosus

6. Rectus femoris, vastus intermedius, vastus lateralis, and vastus medialis

7. Fast fiber muscles produce powerful contractions, which use ATP in massive amounts. Prolonged activity is primarily supported by anaerobic glycolysis, and fast fibers fatigue rapidly. Slow fibers are specialized to enable them to continue contracting for extended periods. The specializations include an extensive network of capillaries so supplies of O_2 are available, and the presence of myoglobin, which binds O_2 molecules and results in the buildup of O_2 reserves. These factors improve mitochondrial performance.

8. The origin remains stationary while the insertion moves.

9. (a) muscles of the head and neck

   (b) muscles of the spine

   (c) oblique and rectus muscles

   (d) muscles of the pelvic floor

10. (a) muscles of the shoulders and arms

    (b) muscles of the pelvic girdle and legs

8 The Nervous System

Part I: Objective-Based Questions

Objective 1

1. a
2. c
3. d
4. c
5. a
6. a

Objective 2

1. b
2. c
3. d
4. b
5. c
6. a
7. d
8. b
9. a
10. c

Labeling Exercise, Figure 8-1

1. dendrite
2. soma
3. nucleus
4. axon hillock
5. axon
6. neurilemma
7. axon terminals/synaptic knobs
8. multipolar

Labeling Exercise, Figure 8-2

1. neuron
2. astrocyte
3. myelinated axon
4. oligodendrocyte
5. microglial cell
6. capillary

Objective 3

1. b
2. c
3. a
4. b
5. d
6. d
7. b

Objective 4

1. a
2. c
3. b
4. a
5. b
6. d

Objective 5

1. c
2. a
3. a
4. c
5. b
6. b

Objective 6

1. d
2. c
3. c
4. b
5. a
6. d

Labeling Exercise, Figure 8-3

1. posterior median sulcus
2. white matter
3. pia mater
4. central canal
5. anterior horn
6. anterior median fissure
7. spinal nerve
8. dorsal root
9. ventral root
10. dura mater
11. posterior horn
12. subarachnoid space
13. gray commissure

Objective 7

1. d
2. b
3. a
4. b
5. d
6. b
7. a
8. d
9. c
10. b

4. occipital lobe
5. cerebellum
6. medulla oblongata
7. postcentral gyrus
8. precentral gyrus
9. frontal lobe
10. lateral fissure
11. temporal lobe
12. pons

Labeling Exercise, Figure 8-4

1. central sulcus
2. parietal lobe
3. parieto-occipital fissure

Labeling Exercise, Figure 8-5

1. choroid plexus
2. cerebral hemispheres
3. corpus callosum
4. pineal gland
5. cerebral peduncle
6. cerebral aqueduct
7. fourth ventricle
8. cerebellum
9. thalamus
10. fornix
11. third ventricle
12. corpora quadrigemina
13. optic chiasma
14. pituitary gland
15. mammilary gland
16. pons
17. medulla oblongata

Objective 8

1. b
2. c
3. b
4. a
5. c
6. a
7. a

8. c
9. d
10. b

Labeling Exercise, Figure 8-6
1. precentral gyrus
2. premotor cortex
3. frontal lobe

4. temporal lobe
5. central sulcus
6. postcentral gyrus
7. parietal lobe
8. occipital lobe

Objective 9

1. c
2. b
3. d
4. olfactory
5. optic
6. oculomotor
7. opthalmic
8. VII

9. vagus
10. tongue

Labeling Exercise, Figure 8-7
1. olfactory N I
2. oculomotor N III
3. trigeminal N V
4. vestibulocochlear N VIII
5. glossopharyngeal N IX

6. hypoglossal N XII
7. optic N II
8. trochlear N IV
9. abducens N VI
10. facial N VII
11. vagus N X
12. accessory N XI

Objective 10

1. b
2. a

3. d
4. c

Objective 11

1. a
2. d
3. d
4. b
5. c

Labeling Exercise, Figure 8-8
1. white matter
2. gray matter
3. interneuron
4. sensory neuron

5. stimulus
6. receptor
7. motor neuron
8. effector
9. synapse

Objective 12

1 c
2. b
3. b
4. a
5. d
6. b

7. c
8. d
9. a

Labeling Exercise, Figure 8-9
1. lateral corticospinal

2. anterior corticospinal
3. posterior spinocerebellar
4. lateral spinothalamic
5. anterior spinocerebellar
6. anterior spinothalamic

Objective 13

1. b
2. d
3. d
4. c
5. b

6. c
7. b
8. c
9. c
10. b

11. d
12. a
13. a
14. fight; flight
15. rest; repose

Objective 14

1. b

2. c

3. d

Objective 15

1. reproductive
2. skeletal

3. endocrine
4. digestive

5. cardiovascular

Part II: Chapter Comprehensive Exercises

A. Word Elimination

1. CNS
2. muscle

3. neuroglia
4. neuron

5. conduction
6. adrenergic

7. N IV
8. CNS

9. gyrus
10. meninges

B. Matching

1. f
2. h

3. b
4. g

5. c
6. e

7. a
8. j

9. d
10. i

C. Concept Maps

Concept Map I - Nervous System Overview

1. central nervous system (CNS)
2. arachnoid matter
3. gray mater
4. columns
5. ascending and descending tracts
6. afferent division
7. cell bodies
8. motor neurons

Concept Map II - Major Regions of the Brain

1. diencephalon
2. hypothalamus
3. corpora quadrigemina
4. 2 cerebellar hemispheres
5. pons
6. medulla oblongata

Concept Map III - Autonomic Nervous System

1. sympathetic
2. motor neurons
3. smooth muscle
4. first-order neurons
5. ganglia outside CNS
6. postganglionic

Concept Map IV - Sympathetic Division of ANS

1. thoracolumbar
2. spinal segments T_1–L_2
3. second-order neurons (postganglionic)
4. sympathetic chain of ganglia (paired)
5. visceral effectors
6. adrenal medulla (paired)
7. general circulation

Concept Map V - Parasympathetic Divisions of ANS

1. craniosacral
2. brain stem
3. ciliary ganglion
4. N VII
5. nasal, tear, salivary glands
6. otic ganglia
7. N X
8. segments S_2–S_4
9. intramural ganglia
10. lower abdominopelvic cavity

D. Crossword Puzzle I

Crossword Puzzle II

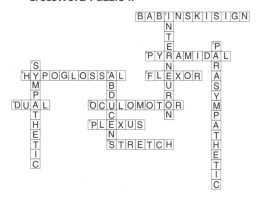

E. Short-Answer Questions

1. (a) providing sensation of the internal and external environments
   (b) integrating sensory information
   (c) coordinating voluntary and involuntary activities
2. CNS consists of the brain and the spinal cord.
   PNS consists of the somatic nervous system and the autonomic nervous system.
3. astrocytes, oligodendrocytes, microglia, and ependymal cells

4. *Neurons* are responsible for information transfer and processing in the nervous sytem.
   Neuroglia are specialized cells that provide support throughout the nervous system.

5. (a) cerebrum; (b) diencephalon; (c) mesencephalon; (d) cerebellum; (e) pons; (f) medulla oblongata

6. (a) The cerebellum oversees the postural muscles of the body, making rapid adjustments to maintain balance and equilibrium. (b) The cerebellum programs and times voluntary and involuntary movements.

7. (a) preganglionic (first-order) neurons located between segments T_1 and L_2 of the spinal cord
   (b) ganglionic (second-order) neurons located in ganglia near the vertebral column (sympathetic chain ganglia, collateral ganglia)
   (c) specialized second-order neurons in the interior of the adrenal gland

8. (a) preganglionic neurons in the brain stem and in sacral segments of the spinal cord
   (b) ganglionic neurons in peripheral ganglia located within or adjacent to the target organs

9. The sympathetic division stimulates tissue metabolism, increases alertness, and generally prepares the body to deal with emergencies.

10. The parasympathetic division conserves energy and promotes sedentary activities, such as digestion.

11. (a) a reduction in brain size and weight; (b) a decrease in blood flow to the brain; (c) changes in synaptic organization of the brain; (d) intracellular and extracellular changes in CNS neurons

9 The General and Special Senses

Part I: Objective-Based Questions

Objective 1

1. c
2. a
3. a
4. b

Objective 2

1. c
2. c
3. a
4. d
5. b
6. c
7. d

Objective 3

1. a
2. c
3. b
4. d
5. d

Labeling Exercise, Figure 9-1

1. olfactory tract
2. cribriform plate
3. olfactory bulb
4. afferent nerve fiber
5. basal cell
6. olfactory gland
7. bipolar neuron
8. cilia
9. mucus layer

Objective 4

1. d
2. a
3. c
4. b

Labeling Exercise, Figure 9-2

1. bitter taste
2. sour taste
3. salty taste
4. sweet taste
5. taste buds
6. stratified squamous epithelium
7. transitional cell
8. gustatory cell
9. cranial nerve fibers
10. taste hairs

Objective 5

1. c
2. c
3. a
4. c
5. c
6. a
7. d
8. a
9. sclera
10. pupil
11. rods
12. cones
13. occipital

Labeling Exercise, Figure 9-3

1. ciliary body
2. suspensory ligament
3. iris
4. aqueous humor
5. lens
6. cornea
7. vitreous humor
8. optic disc
9. optic nerve
10. fovea centralis
11. sclera
12. choroid coat
13. retina

Labeling Exercise, Figure 9-4

1. superior oblique
2. superior rectus
3. lateral rectus
4. inferior rectus
5. inferior oblique

Objective 6

1. c
2. b
3. a
4. c
5. b
6. d
7. iris
8. myopia
9. macula lutea
10. accommodation

Labeling Exercise, Figure 9-5

1. pigment layer of retina
2. rod
3. cone
4. amacrine cell
5. horizontal cell
6. bipolar cells
7. ganglion cells

Objective 7

1. b
2. c
3. d

Objective 8

1. b
2. c
3. b
4. d
5. d
6. c

Objective 9

1. a
2. d
3. b
4. c
5. b
6. c
7. c

Labeling Exercise, Figure 9-6

1. outer ear
2. middle ear
3. inner ear
4. pinna
5. malleus
6. incus
7. stapes
8. vestibular complex
9. temporal bone
10. cochlea
11. vestibulocochlear nerve
12. bony labyrinth
13. auditory tube
14. tympanum
15. external auditory canal

Objective 10

1. c	3. d	5. c	7. b
2. b	4. a	6. a	8. d

Part II: Chapter Comprehensive Exercises

A. Word Elimination

1. touch	3. stereoreceptors	5. choroid	7. tympanum	9. auditory tube
2. balance	4. cornea	6. propriopia	8. otolith	10. cerumen

B. Matching

1. f	3. a	5. c	7. i	9. d
2. h	4. j	6. b	8. e	10. g

C. Concept Maps

Concept Map I - Special Senses

1. olfaction	4. ears	7. balance and hearing
2. audition	5. smell	8. retina
3. tongue	6. taste buds	9. rods and cones

Concept Map II - General Senses

1. pain	5. tactile	9. Pacinian corpuscles
2. pressure	6. muscles spindles	10. aortic sinus
3. proprioception	7. baroreceptors	11. dendritic processes
4. thermoreceptors	8. Merkel's dics	

D. Crossword Puzzle

E. Short-Answer Questions

1. Sensations of temperature, pain, touch, pressure, vibration, and proprioception.
2. Smell (olfaction), taste (gustation), balance (equilibrium), hearing (audition), and vision (sight).
3. (a) Nociceptors—variety of stimuli usually associated with tissue damage.
   (b) Thermoreceptors—changes in temperature.
   (c) Mechanoreceptors—stimulated or inhibited by physical distortion, contact, or pressure on their cell membranes.
   (d) Chemoreceptors—respond to presence of specific molecules.
4. Baroreceptors monitor changes in pressure. Proprioceptors monitor the position of joints, the tension in tendons and ligaments, and the state of muscular contraction.
5. Sensations leaving the olfactory bulb travel along the olfactory tract (N I) to reach the olfactory cortex, the hypothalamus, and portions of the limbic system.
6. Sweet, salty, sour, bitter.
7. Receptors in the saccule and utricle provide sensations of gravity and linear acceleration.
8. (a) Provides mechanical support and physical protection.
   (b) Serves as an attachment site for the extrinsic eye muscles.
   (c) Assists in the focusing process.

9. (a) Provides a route for blood vessels and lymphatics to the eye.
    (b) Secretes and reabsorbs aqueous humor.
    (c) Controls the shape of the lens (important in the focusing process).
10. The pigment layer (a) absorbs light after it passes through the retina and (b) biochemically interacts with the photoreceptor layer of the retina.

    The retina contains (a) photoreceptors that respond to light; (b) supporting cells and neurons that perform preliminary processing and integration of visual information; and (c) blood vessels supplying tissues lining the vitreous chamber.
11. During accommodation the lens becomes rounder to focus the image of a nearby object on the retina.

10 The Endocrine System

Part I: Objective - Based Questions

Objective 1
1. d
2. c
3. b
4. c

Objective 2
1. d
2. b
3. c
4. a

Objective 3
1. d
2. b
3. d
4. d
5. a
6. c

Objective 4
1. b
2. a
3. c
4. d
5. b
6. d

Objective 5
1. posterior pituitary
2. oxytocin
3. ACTH
4. FSH
5. MSH
6. calcitonin
7. iodine
8. parathyroid
9. thyroid
10. E epinephrine and NE norepinephrine
11. aldosterone
12. kidneys
13. heart
14. pancreas (beta cells)
15. glucagon
16. testes
17. estrogen
18. pineal

Labeling Exercise, Figure 10-1
1. hypothalamus
2. pituitary
3. thyroid
4. thymus
5. adrenals
6. ovary
7. pineal
8. parathyroids
9. atria (heart)
10. pancreas
11. testis

Labeling Exercise, Figure 10-2
1. a
2. h
3. e
4. c
5. f
6. g
7. d
8. b
9. l
10. m
11. k
12. I
13. j
14. n
15. q
16. o
17. p

Objective 6
1. d
2. a
3. b
4. b

Objective 7
1. d
2. b
3. b

Objective 8
1. a
2. c
3. a
4. b
5. c

Objective 9
1. b
2. c
3. a
4. d

Objective 10
1. nervous
2. cardiovascular
3. digestive
4. urinary
5. muscular

Part II: Chapter Comprehensive Exercises

A. Word Elimination

1. prostate
2. keratin
3. PTH
4. elastin
5. aldosterone
6. hemoglobin
7. calcitonin
8. testes
9. melatonin
10. permissive

B. Matching

1. e
2. h
3. a
4. j
5. b
6. g
7. c
8. f
9. d
10. i

C. Concept Maps

Concept Map I - Endocrine Glands

1. hormones
2. epinephrine
3. peptide hormones
4. testosterone
5. pituitary
6. parathyroids
7. pineal
8. heart
9. male/female gonads
10. bloodstream

Concept Map II - Endocrine System Functions

1. cellular communication
2. homeostasis
3. target cells
4. contraction
5. ion channel opening
6. hormones

D. Crossword Puzzle

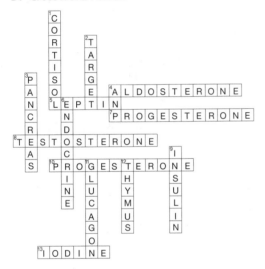

E. Short-Answer Questions

1. The hypothalamus (a) contains autonomic centers that exert direct neural control over the endocrine cells of the adrenal medulla. Sympathetic activation causes the adrenal medulla to release hormones into the bloodstream; (b) acts as an endocrine organ to release hormones into the circulation at the posterior pituitary; and (c) secretes regulatory hormones that control activities of endocrine cells in the pituitary glands.

2. (a) Control by releasing hormones; (b) control by inhibiting hormones; (c) regulation by releasing and inhibiting hormones.

3. Thyroid hormones elevate oxygen consumption and rate of energy consumption in peripheral tissues, causing an increase in the metabolic rate. As a result, more heat is generated, replacing the heat lost to the environment.

4. Erythropoietin stimulates the production of red blood cells by the bone marrow. The increase in the number of RBCs elevates blood volume, causing an increase in blood pressure.

5. The secretion of melatonin by the pineal gland is lowest during daylight hours and highest during the darkness of night. The cyclic nature of this activity parallels daily changes in physiological processes that follow a regular pattern.

6. (a) The two hormones may have opposing, or antagonistic, effects; (b) the two hormones may have an additive, or synergistic, effect; (c) one hormone can have a permissive effect on another. In such cases the first hormone is needed for the second to produce its effect; (d) the hormones may have integrative effects, i.e., the hormones may produce different but complementary results in specific tissues and organs.

11 The Cardiovascular System: Blood

Part I: Objective-Based Questions

Objective 1

1. b
2. a
3. d
4. c
5. d

Objective 2

1. d
2. c
3. d
4. c
5. a

Objective 3

1. b
2. c
3. b
4. d
5. erythropoiesis
6. leukopoiesis
7. thrombopoiesis

Objective 4

1. a
2. d
3. d
4. c
5. a
6. d
7. d
8. c

Objective 5

1. b
2. d
3. c
4. a
5. c
6. a
7. d

Labeling Exercise, Figure 11-1
1. B antigen
2. A antigen

Labeling Exercise, Figure 11-2
1. compatible
2. incompatible
3. incompatible
4. compatible
5. incompatible
6. compatible
7. incompatible
8. compatible
9. compatible
10. compatible
11. compatible
12. compatible
13. incompatible
14. incompatible
15. incompatible
16. compatible

Objective 6

1. c
2. d
3. a
4. a
5. d
6. b
7. a
8. c
9. b
10. a

Labeling Exercise, Figure 11-3
1. neutrophil
2. basophil
3. monocyte
4. eosinophil
5. lymphocyte

Objective 7

1. b
2. d
3. c
4. b
5. d
6. a
7. c
8. b
9. d
10. b

Part II: Chapter Comprehensive Exercises

A. Word Elimination

1. analysis
2. lymph
3. serum
4. vitamin D
5. urinalysis
6. Rh factor
7. platelets
8. RBC
9. platelet
10. transferrin

B. Matching

1. e
2. h
3. a
4. j
5. c
6. b
7. d
8. f
9. g
10. i

C. Concept Maps

Concept Map I - Blood

1. plasma
2. solutes
3. albumins
4. oxygen
5. leukocytes
6. neutrophils
7. monocytes

Concept Map II - Blood Clotting

1. vascular spasm
2. platelet phase
3. plug
4. blood clot
5. clot retraction
6. clot dissolution
7. plasminogen
8. plasmin

D. Crossword Puzzle

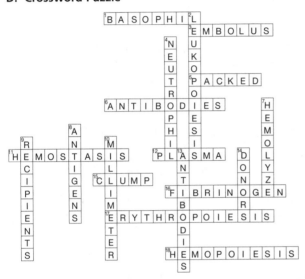

E. Short-Answer Questions

1. Blood (a) "transports" dissolved gases; (b) "regulates" the pH and electrolyte composition of interstitial fluid; (c) "restricts" fluid losses through damaged vessels; (d) "defends" the body against toxins and pathogens; and (e) helps "regulate" body temperature by absorbing and redistributing heat.

2. (a) albumins, (b) globulins, and (c) fibrinogen.

3. Granular leukocytes: neutrophils, eosinophils, basophils
   Agranular leukocytes: monocytes, lymphocytes

4. (a) transport of chemicals important to the clotting process
   (b) formation of a plug in the walls of damaged blood vessels
   (c) active contraction after clot formation has occurred

5. (a) vascular phase: spasm in damaged smooth muscle
   (b) platelet phase: platelet aggregation and adhesion
   (c) coagulation phase: activation of clotting system and clot formation
   (d) clot retraction: contraction of blood clot
   (e) clot destruction: enzymatic destruction of clot

6. embolus: a drifting blood clot
   thrombus: a blood clot that sticks to the wall of an intact blood vessel

12 The Cardiovascular System: The Heart

Part I: Objective-Based Questions

Objective 1

1. d
2. c
3. a
4. a
5. b
6. d
7. a

8. b
9. d
10. atria
11. fibrous skeleton
12. intercalated discs

Labeling Exercise, Figure 12-1
1. right side
2. coronary vessels
3. aortic arch
4. pulmonary trunk
5. base
6. left side
7. apex

Objective 2

1. a
2. c
3. b
4. c

Labeling Exercise, Figure 12-2
1. individual muscle cells
2. endocardium
3. epicardium
4. pericardial cavity
5. parietal pericardium
6. myocardium

Objective 3

1. a
2. c
3. b
4. d
5. c
6. a
7. b
8. c
9. d
10. c
11. a
12. b
13. c
14. a

Labeling Exercise, Figure 12-3
1. right pulmonary arteries
2. superior vena cava
3. fossa ovalis
4. opening of coronary sinus
5. right atrium
6. triscuspid valve
7. inferior vena cava
8. right ventricle
9. aorta
10. aortic arch
11. pulmonary trunk
12. pulmonary semilunar valve
13. left pulmonary arteries
14. left pulmonary veins
15. interatrial septum
16. aortic semilunar valve
17. biscuspid valve
18. chordae tendineae
19. papillary muscles
20. left ventricle
21. interventricular septum

Labeling Exercise, Figure 12-4
1. tricuspid valve (O)
2. bicuspid AV valve (O)
3. aortic semilunar valve (C)
4. pulmonary semilunar valve (C)
5. tricuspid (right AV) valve (C)
6. bicuspid valve (C)
7. aortic semilunar valve (O)
8. pulmonary semilunar valve (O)

Objective 4

1. c
2. d

3. c
4. a

Objective 5

1. b
2. d
3. c
4. a
5. d

Labeling Exercise, Figure 12-5
1. SA node
2. AV node
3. AV bundle
4. bundle branches
5. Purkinje fibers

Objective 6

1. c
2. c

3. d
4. b

5. a

Objective 7

1. b
2. a
3. b

4. b
5. c

Part II: Chapter Comprehensive Exercises

A. Word Elimination

1. L. pulmonary artery
2. semilunar
3. chordae tendineae
4. anastomoses
5. systole
6. tachycardia
7. auricles
8. AV valve
9. multinucleated
10. aortic arch

B. Matching

1. i
2. f
3. g
4. j
5. h
6. d
7. c
8. a
9. b
10. e

C. Concept Maps

Concept Map I - The Heart

1. two atria
2. blood from atria
3. endocardium
4. epicardium
5. pacemaker cells
6. two semilunar
7. aortic
8. deoxygenated blood
9. tricuspid
10. oxygenated blood

Concept Map II - Path of Blood Flow through the Heart

1. superior vena cava
2. right atrium
3. tricuspid valve
4. right ventricle
5. pulmonary semilunar valve
6. pulmonary arteries
7. pulmonary veins
8. left atrium
9. bicuspid valve
10. left ventricle
11. aortic semilunar valve
12. L. common carotid artery
13. aorta
14. systemic arteries
15. systemic veins
16. inferior vena cava

D. Crossword Puzzle

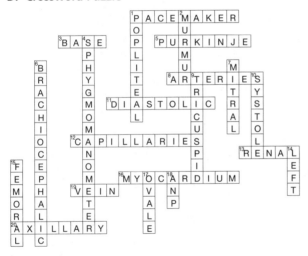

E. Short-Answer Questions

1. CO = SV × HR

   CO = 75 ml × 80 beats/min = 6000 ml/min

   6000 ml = 6.0 l/min

2. Anastomoses are interconnections of the left and right coronary arteries, causing the blood supply to the cardiac muscle to remain relatively constant regardless of pressure fluctuations in the R. and L. coronary arteries.

3. ↓ (decreasing) CO, ↓ SV, ↓ length of systole, ↓ ventricular filling

4. CO = SV × HR

   Therefore, $\dfrac{CO}{HR} = \dfrac{SV \times \cancel{HR}}{\cancel{HR}}$

   Therefore, $SV = \dfrac{CO}{HR}$

   $SV = \dfrac{5 \text{ l/min}}{100 \text{ bpm}} = 0.05 \text{ l/beat}$

5. The visceral pericardium, or epicardium, covers the outer surface of the heart. The parietal pericardium lines the inner surface of the pericardial sac that surrounds the heart.

6. (a) epicardium; (b) myocardium; (c) endocardium

7. Cardiac muscle fibers are connected by gap junctions at intercalated discs, which allow ions and small molecules to move from one cell to another. This creates a direct electrical connection between the two muscle fibers, and an action potential can travel across an intercalated disk, moving quickly from one cardiac muscle fiber to another. Because the cardiac muscle fibers are mechanically, chemically, and electrically connected to one another, the entire tissue resembles a single, enormous muscle fiber. For this reason cardiac muscle has been called a functional syncytium.

8. SA node → AV node → bundle of His → bundle branches → Purkinje cells → contractile cells of ventricular myocardium

9. bradycardia: heart rate slow than normal

   tachycardia: faster-than-normal heart rate

10. (a) Ion concentrations in extracellular fluid:

    (*Note:* EC = extracellular)

    decreasing EC K^+ → decreasing HR

    increasing EC Ca^{2+} → increasing excitability and prolonged contraction

    (b) Changes in body temperature:

    decreasing temp. → decreasing HR and decreasing strength of contraction

    increasing temp. → increasing HR and increasing strength of contraction

    (c) Autonomic activity:

    parasympathetic stimulation → releases ACh → decreasing heart rate

    sympathetic stimulation → releases norepinephrine → increasing heart rate

13 The Cardiovascular System: Blood Vessels and Circulation

Part I: Objective-Based Questions

Objective 1

1. a
2. d
3. b
4. c

5. d
6. a

Labeling Exercise, Figure 13-1
1. artery

2. arteriole
3. capillaries
4. venules
5. vein

Objective 2

1. c
2. d

3. d
4. c

5. c

Objective 3

1. b
2. a

3. b
4. a

5. hydrostatic pressure
6. osmotic pressure

Objective 4

1. d
2. b

3. b
4. d

5. d
6. b

Objective 5

1. b
2. a

3. c
4. d

5. b

Objective 6

1. b
2. a

3. d
4. c

5. d
6. a

Objective 7

1. c
2. c

3. c
4. d

5. c

Objective 8

1. circle of Willis
2. pulmonary veins
3. pulmonary arteries
4. internal jugular
5. axillary
6. brachial
7. radial, ulnar
8. basilar
9. diaphragm
10. common iliac
11. femoral, deep femoral
12. superior vena cava
13. brain
14. brachial
15. brachiocephalic
16. superior vena cava
17. femoral
18. inferior vena cava
19. hepatic portal
20. inferior vena cava

Labeling Exercise, Figure 13-2
1. R. common carotid
2. vertebral
3. R. subclavian
4. brachiocephalic

5. ascending aorta
6. celiac
7. brachial
8. radial
9. ulnar
10. palmar arches
11. external iliac
12. popliteal
13. posterior tibial
14. anterior tibial
15. peroneal
16. plantar arch
17. L. common carotid
18. aortic arch
19. L. subclavian
20. axillary
21. descending aorta
22. renal
23. superior mesenteric
24. gonadal
25. inferior mesenteric
26. common iliac
27. internal iliac
28. deep femoral
29. femoral

30. dorsalis pedis

Labeling Exercise, Figure 13-3
1. external jugular
2. vertebral
3. subclavian
4. axillary
5. cephalic
6. brachial
7. basilic
8. hepatic
9. median cubital
10. cephalic
11. median antebrachial
12. ulnar
13. palmar venous arches
14. digital vein
15. great saphenous
16. popliteal
17. small saphenous
18. peroneal
19. dorsal venous arch
20. plantar venous arch
21. internal jugular
22. brachiocephalic
23. superior vena cava

Objective 8 (continued)

24. intercostals
25. inferior vena cava
26. renal
27. gonadal
28. lumbar
29. common iliac
30. external iliac
31. internal iliac
32. deep femoral
33. femoral
34. posterior tibial
35. anterior tibial

Labeling Exercise, Figure 13-4
1. anterior cerebral
2. internal carotid
3. middle cerebral

Objective 9
1. b
2. d
3. d
4. b

Objective 10
1. lymphatic
2. nervous
3. urinary
4. reproductive
5. skeletal

4. basilar
5. vertebral
6. anterior communicating
7. anterior cerebral
8. posterior communicating
9. posterior cerebral
10. circle of Willis

Labeling Exercise, Figure 13-5
1. inferior vena cava
2. hepatic veins
3. liver
4. cystic vein
5. hepatic portal vein
6. superior mesenteric vein
7. colic veins
8. ascending colon
9. aorta
10. esophagus
11. stomach
12. L. gastric vein
13. gastroepiploic veins
14. spleen
15. splenic vein
16. pancreas
17. L. colic vein
18. inferior mesenteric vein
19. descending colon
20. sigmoid branches
21. small intestine
22. superior rectal vein

Part II: Chapter Comprehensive Exercises

A. Word Elimination
1. valves
2. tunica lumen
3. compression
4. baroreceptors
5. ACh
6. increased pH
7. pulmonary vein
8. carotid artery
9. phrenic
10. increased hematocrit

B. Matching
1. h
2. b
3. g
4. j
5. a
6. i
7. e
8. f
9. c
10. d

C. Concept Maps

Concept Map I - The Cardiovascular System
1. pulmonary veins
2. arteries and arterioles
3. veins and venules
4. pulmonary arteries
5. systemic circuit

Concept Map II - Major Branches of the Aorta
1. ascending aorta
2. brachiocephalic artery
3. L. subclavian artery
4. thoracic aorta
5. celiac trunk
6. superior mesenteric artery
7. R. gonadal artery
8. L. common iliac artery

Concept Map III - Major Veins
1. superior vena cava
2. azygous vein
3. L. hepatic veins
4. R. suprarenal vein
5. L. renal vein
6. L. common iliac vein

D. Crossword Puzzle

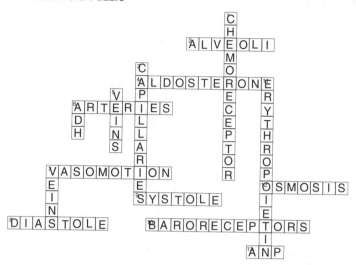

E. Short-Answer Questions

1. heart → arteries → arterioles → capillaries (gas exchange area) → venules → veins → heart

2. In the pulmonary circuit, oxygen stores are replenished, carbon dioxide is excreted, and the "reoxygenated" blood is returned to the heart for distribution in the systemic circuit.

   The systemic circuit supplies the capillary beds in all parts of the body with oxygenated blood and returns deoxygenated blood to the heart of the pulmonary circuit for removal of carbon dioxide.

3. (a) vascular resistance, viscosity, turbulence

   (b) Only vascular resistance can be adjusted by the nervous and endocrine systems.

4. $F = \dfrac{BP}{PR}$.

   Flow is directly proportional to blood pressure, and inversely proportional to peripheral resistance. Put another way, (1) an increase in blood pressure results in increased flow, while a decrease in blood pressure results in decreased flow, and (2) an increase in peripheral resistance results in decreased flow, while a decrease in peripheral resistance results in increased flow.

5. $\dfrac{120 \text{ mm Hg}}{80 \text{ mm Hg}}$ is a "normal" blood pressure reading.

   The top number, 120 mm Hg, is the systolic pressure, i.e., the peak blood pressure measured during ventricular systole.

   The bottom number, 80 mm Hg, is the diastolic pressure, i.e., the minimum blood pressure at the end of ventricular diastole.

6. Cardiac output, blood volume, and peripheral resistance.

7. Aortic baroreceptors, carotid sinus baroreceptors, and atrial baroreceptors.

8. Epinephrine and norepinephrine, ADH, angiotensin II, erythropoietin, and atrial natriuretic peptide.

9. Arteries lose their elasticity, the amount of smooth muscle they contain decreases, and they become stiff and relatively inflexible.

14 The Lymphatic System and Immunity

Part I: Objective-Based Questions

Objective 1
1. d
2. c
3. d
4. d
5. b

6. thoracic duct
7. lymph nodes

Labeling Exercise, Figure 14-1
1. R. lymphatic duct
2. thymus
3. thoracic duct
4. lumbar lymph nodes
5. inguinal lymph nodes
6. L. lymphatic duct
7. axillary lymph nodes
8. spleen

Objective 2
1. a
2. b

3. a
4. c

5. a
6. d

Objective 3
1. d
2. d
3. c
4. b
5. a

Labeling Exercise, Figure 14-2
1. physical barriers
2. phagocytes
3. immunological surveillance
4. complement system
5. inflammatory response
6. fever
7. interferons

Objective 4
1. a
2. c
3. d

4. c
5. b
6. c

7. b

Objective 5
1. d
2. a

3. a
4. d

5. b

Objective 6
1. b
2. d

3. d
4. b

Objective 7
1. b
2. c

3. d
4. d

Objective 8
1. c
2. b
3. a

4. b
5. d
6. interferons

7. immunological competence

Objective 9
1. c
2. b

3. d
4. c

Objective 10
1. d
2. c

3. a
4. b

Objective 11
1. reproductive
2. lymphatic

3. respiratory
4. muscular

5. skeletal

Part II: Chapter Comprehensive Exercises

A. Word Elimination
1. pineal gland
2. antigens
3. salivary
4. nephron
5. antibodies
6. blood
7. complement
8. compatibility
9. IgB
10. enzymes

B. Matching

1. h	3. j	5. g	7. d	9. c
2. e	4. a	6. b	8. f	10. i

C. Concept Maps

Concept Map I - Immune System

1. nonspecific immunity
2. phagocytic cells
3. inflammation
4. specific immunity
5. innate
6. acquired
7. active
8. active immunization
9. transfer of antibodies via placenta
10. passive immunization

Concept Map II - The Body's Department of Defense

1. viruses
2. macrophages
3. natural killer cells
4. helper T cells
5. B cells
6. antibodies
7. killer T cells
8. suppressor T cells
9. memory T cells
10. memory B cells

D. Crossword Puzzle

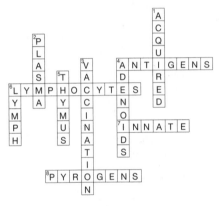

E. Short-Answer Questions

1. (a) lymphatic vessels; (b) lymph; (c) lymphatic organs
2. (a) production, maintenance, and distribution of lymphocytes
   (b) maintenance of normal blood volume
   (c) elimination of local variations in the composition of the interstitial fluid
3. (a) T cells (thymus); (b) B cells (bone marrow); (c) NK or natural killer cells (bone marrow)
4. (a) cytotoxic T cells—cell-mediated immunity
   (b) helper T cells—release lymphokines that coordinate specific and nonspecific defenses
   (c) suppressor T cells—depress responses of other T cells and B cells
5. Stimulated B cells differentiate into plasma cells that are responsible for the production and secretion of antibodies. B cells are said to be responsible for humoral immunity.
6. (a) lymph nodes; (b) thymus; (c) spleen
7. NK (natural killer) cells are sensitive to the presence of abnormal cell membranes and respond immediately. When the NK cell makes contact with an abnormal cell, it releases secretory vesicles that contain proteins called perforins. The perforins create a network of pores in the target cell membrane, allowing free passage of intracellular materials necessary for homeostasis, thus causing the cell to disintegrate.

   T cells and B cells provide defenses against specific threats, and their activation requires a relatively complex and time-consuming sequence of events.
8. (a) destruction of target cell membranes
   (b) stimulation of inflammation
   (c) attraction of phagocytes
   (d) enhancement of phagocytosis
9. (a) specificity
   (b) versatility
   (c) memory
   (d) tolerance
10. Active immunity appears following exposure to an antigen, as a consequence of the immune response.
    Passive immunity is produced by transfer of antibodies from another source.

15 The Respiratory System

Part I: Objective-Based Questions

Objective 1
1. d
2. b
3. a
4. c
5. b
6. b

Objective 2
1. c
2. b
3. d
4. a
5. a

Labeling Exercise, Figure 15-1
1. internal nares
2. nasopharynx
3. pharyngeal tonsil
4. auditory tube
5. soft palate
6. palatine tonsil
7. oropharynx
8. epiglottis
9. glottis
10. laryngopharynx
11. vocal cord
12. esophagus
13. frontal sinus
14. nasal conchae
15. nasal vestibule
16. external nares
17. hard palate
18. oral cavity
19. tongue
20. mandible
21. hyoid bone
22. thyroid cartilage
23. cricoid cartilage
24. trachea

Objective 3
1. d
2. c
3. b
4. a
5. c
6. b
7. a
8. a
9. c
10. external nares
11. vestibule
12. oropharynx
13. pharynx
14. nasopharynx
15. larynx
16. trachea
17. lobes of the lungs
18. primary bronchi
19. alveoli

Labeling Exercise, Figure 15-2
1. sphenoidal sinus
2. pharynx
3. epiglottis
4. vocal cords
5. esophagus
6. right lung
7. frontal sinus
8. nasal conchae
9. tongue
10. hyoid
11. thyroid cartilage
12. cricoid cartilage
13. larynx
14. tracheal cartilage
15. left bronchus
16. left lung
17. diaphragm

Objective 4
1. a
2. a
3. c
4. b
5. d
6. c
7. c
8. b

Objective 5
1. a
2. a
3. c
4. b

Objective 6
1. b
2. b
3. c
4. b
5. c
6. a

Labeling Exercise, Figure 15-3
1. 23%
2. 7%
3. 93%
4. 70%

Objective 7
1. d
2. a
3. d
4. d
5. c
6. a
7. lungs
8. CO_2

Objective 8
1. a
2. d
3. a
4. a
5. a

Objective 9
1. a
2. b
3. c
4. a

Objective 10

1. d
2. urinary
3. endocrine
4. nervous
5. skeletal

Part II: Chapter Comprehensive Exercises

A. Word Elimination

1. alveoli
2. mandibular
3. glottis
4. middle lobe
5. primary bronchi
6. internal intercostals
7. P_{CO_2}
8. NH_4
9. chemoreceptor
10. surfactant

B. Matching

1. f
2. i
3. j
4. b
5. h
6. e
7. a
8. c
9. g
10. d

C. Concept Map - The Respiratory System

1. upper respiratory tract
2. pharynx and larynx
3. lungs
4. ciliated mucous membrane
5. alveoli
6. blood

D. Crossword Puzzle

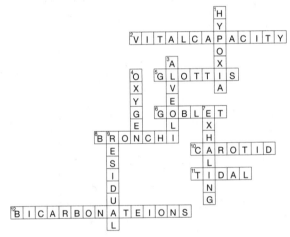

E. Short-Answer Questions

1. (a) Providing a site for gas exchange between air and blood.
   (b) Moving air to and from the exchange surfaces of the lungs.
   (c) Protecting the respiratory surfaces from dehydration, temperature changes, and airborne pathogens.
   (d) Producing sounds that permit speech, singing, and nonverbal communication.
   (e) Providing olfactory sensations to the central nervous system for the sense of smell.

2. The air is warmed to within 1 degree of body temperature before it enters the pharynx. This results from the warmth of rapidly flowing blood in an extensive vasculature of the nasal mucosa. For humidifying the air, the nasal mucosa is supplied with small mucus glands that secrete a mucoid fluid inside the nose. The warm and humid air prevents drying of the pharynx, trachea, and lungs, and facilitates the flow of air through the respiratory passageways without affecting environmental changes.

3. Surfactant cells scattered among the simple squamous epithelial cells of the respiratory membranes produce an oily secretion containing a mixture of phospholipids that coat the alveolar epithelium and keep the alveoli from collapsing like bursted bubbles.

4. External respiration includes the diffusion of gases between the alveoli and the circulating blood.
   Internal respiration is the exchange of dissolved gases between the blood and the interstitial fluids in peripheral tissues.
   Cellular respiration is the absorption and utilization of oxygen by living cells via biochemical pathways that generate carbon dioxide.

5. The vital capacity is the maximum amount of air that can be moved into and out of the respiratory system in a single respiratory cycle.
   Vital capacity = inspiratory reserve + expiratory reserve + tidal volume.

6. Alveolar ventilation, or V_e, is the amount of air reaching the alveoli each minute. It is calculated by subtracting the anatomic dead space, V_d, from the tidal volume (V_t) using the formula
   $$V_e = F_x (V_t - V_d)$$

7. (a) CO_2 may be dissolved in the plasma (7 percent).
   (b) CO_2 may be bound to hemoglobin in RBCs (23 percent).
   (c) CO_2 may be converted to a molecule of carbonic acid (70 percent).
8. (a) mechanoreceptor reflexes
   (b) chemoreceptor reflexes
   (c) protective reflexes
9. A rise in arterial P_{CO_2} immediately elevates cerebrospinal fluid CO2 levels and stimulates the chemoreceptor neurons of the medulla. These receptors stimulate the respiratory center, causing an increase in the rate and depth of respiration, or hyperventilation.

16 The Digestive System

Part I: Objective-Based Questions

Objective 1
1. c
2. a
3. d
4. b

Labeling Exercise, Figure 16-1
1. oral cavity/teeth/tongue
2. liver
3. gallbladder
4. large intestine
5. salivary glands
6. pharynx
7. esophagus
8. stomach
9. pancreas
10. small intestine

Objective 2
1. d
2. a
3. secretion
4. absorption
5. excretion

Objective 3
1. a
2. d
3. b
4. b
5. a
6. d
7. c
8. a

Labeling Exercise, Figure 16-2
1. mesenteric artery and vein
2. mesentery
3. plica
4. mucosa
5. submucosa
6. lumen
7. muscularis externa
8. mucosal gland
9. visceral peritoneum (serosa)

Objective 4
1. b
2. a
3. a
4. a
5. b
6. c
7. c

Objective 5
1. d
2. d
3. d
4. c
5. c
6. a
7. c
8. b
9. c
10. incisors
11. cuspids
12. molars
13. parotid
14. uvula

Labeling Exercise, Figure 16-3
1. central incisors
2. cuspid
3. 1st premolar
4. 2nd premolar
5. 1st molar
6. 2nd molar
7. 3rd molar
8. 3rd molar
9. 2nd molar
10. 1st molar
11. 2nd premolar
12. 1st premolar
13. cuspid
14. central incisors

Labeling Exercise, Figure 16-4
1. crown
2. neck
3. root
4. pulp cavity
5. enamel
6. dentin
7. gingival sulcus
8. cementum
9. periodontal ligament
10. root canal
11. alveolar bone
12. blood vessels and nerves

Objective 6
1. c
2. d
3. b
4. HCl
5. pepsinogen
6. cardia
7. fundus
8. pylorus
9. rugae
10. proteins

Labeling Exercise, Figure 16-5
1. esophagus
2. body
3. lesser curvature
4. lesser omentum
5. pylorus
6. diaphragm
7. fundus
8. cardia
9. greater curvature
10. rugae
11. greater omentum

Objective 7
1. b
2. d
3. b
4. c
5. a
6. c
7. b
8. b
9. b
10. c

Objective 8

1. a
2. gallbladder
3. lobule
4. hepatocytes
5. d
6. c
7. d
8. a

Objective 9

1. c
2. a
3. a
4. b
5. a
6. haustrae
7. taeniae coli
8. cecum
9. appendix

Labeling Exercise, Figure 16-6

1. hepatic portal vein
2. inferior vena cava
3. transverse colon
4. ascending colon
5. ileocecal valve
6. cecum
7. ileum
8. vermiform appendix
9. aorta
10. splenic vein
11. splenic flexure
12. greater omentum
13. descending colon
14. haustra
15. taeniae coli
16. sigmoid colon
17. rectum

Objective 10

1. c
2. d
3. b
4. a
5. d

Objective 11

1. b
2. c
3. a
4. d

Objective 12

1. urinary
2. cardiovascular
3. endocrine
4. nervous
5. integumentary

Part II: Chapter Comprehensive Exercises

A. Word Elimination

1. circulation
2. mesentery
3. excretion
4. tongue
5. dentin
6. chyme
7. intrinsic factor
8. HCl
9. amylase
10. haustra

B. Matching

1. g
2. e
3. a
4. i
5. c
6. b
7. j
8. f
9. d
10. h

C. Concept Maps

Concept Map I - Digestive System

1. amylase
2. pancreas
3. bile
4. hormones
5. digestive tract movements
6. stomach
7. large intestine
8. hydrochloric acid
9. intestinal mucosa

Concept Map II - Chemical Events in Digestion

1. esophagus
2. small intestine
3. polypeptides
4. amino acids
5. complex sugars and starches
6. disaccharides, trisaccharides
7. simple sugars
8. monoglycerides, fatty acids in micelles
9. diglycerides, triglycerides
10. lacteal

D. Crossword Puzzle

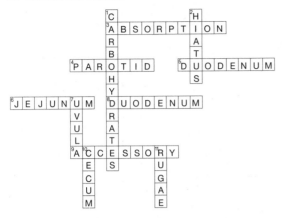

E. Short-Answer Questions

1. (a) ingestion
   (b) mechanical processing
   (c) digestion
   (d) secretion
   (e) absorption
   (f) excretion (defecation)

2. (a) parotid glands
   (b) sublingual glands
   (c) submandibular glands

3. (a) incisors—clipping or cutting
   (b) cuspids (canines)—tearing or slashing
   (c) bicuspids (premolars)—crushing, mashing, and grinding
   (d) molars—crushing, mashing, and grinding

4. Parietal cells and chief cells are types of secretory cells found in the wall of the stomach. Parietal cells secrete intrinsic factors and hydrochloric acid. Chief cells secrete an inactive proenzyme, pepsinogen.

5. (a) cephalic, gastric, intestinal
   (b) CNS regulation; release of gastrin into circulation; enterogastric reflexes, and secretion of cholecystokinin (CCK) and secretin

6. Secretin, cholecystokinin, and glucose-dependent insulinotropic peptide (GIP)

7. (a) resorption of water and compaction of feces
   (b) the absorption of important vitamins liberated by bacterial action
   (c) the storing of fecal material prior to defecation

8. (a) metabolic regulation
   (b) hematological regulation
   (c) bile production

9. (a) Endocrine function—pancreatic islets secrete insulin and glucagon into the bloodstream.
   (b) Exocrine function—secrete a mixture of water, ions, and digestive enzymes into the small intestine.

17 Nutrition and Metabolism

Part I: Objective-Based Questions

Objective 1

1. d
2. b
3. c
4. c

Objective 2

1. a
2. b
3. c
4. b
5. a
6. c

Objective 3

1. c
2. d
3. d
4. acetyl-CoA
5. triglycerides
6. LDLs—low-density lipoproteins
7. HDLs—high-density lipoproteins

Objective 4

1. b
2. c
3. d
4. d
5. d

Objective 5

1. b
2. c
3. b
4. b

Objective 6

1. d
2. c
3. a
4. b
5. c
6. b
7. d

Labeling Exercise, Figure 17-1
1. grains
2. vegetables
3. fruits
4. milk
5. meat and beans

Objective 7

1. chloride ion
2. calcium
3. phosphorus
4. iron
5. copper
6. vitamin A
7. vitamin D
8. vitamin K
9. riboflavin
10. niacin
11. vitamin B_6
12. folacin

Objective 8

1. calorie
2. c
3. a
4. b

Objective 9

1. d
2. d
3. d
4. a

Objective 10

1. a
2. b
3. c
4. thermoregulation
5. hypothermia

Objective 11

1. b
2. d
3. c
4. b
5. d

Part II: Chapter Comprehensive Exercises

A. Word Elimination

1. glycolysis
2. anaerobic
3. NAD
4. ATP
5. EAA
6. linoleic acid
7. minerals
8. zinc
9. vitamin C
10. thermoregulation

B. Matching

1. j
2. h
3. e
4. f
5. c
6. a
7. d
8. g
9. i
10. b

C. Concept Maps

Concept Map I - Healthy You Food Pyramid

1. grains
2. fruits
3. carbohydrates
4. 9 cal/gram
5. proteins
6. tissue growth and repair
7. vitamins
8. metabolic regulation

Concept Map II - Metabolism of Nutrients

1. lipolysis
2. lipogenesis
3. glycolysis
4. gluconeogenesis
5. amino acids
6. beta oxidation
7. electron transport
8. Krebs cycle

D. Crossword Puzzle

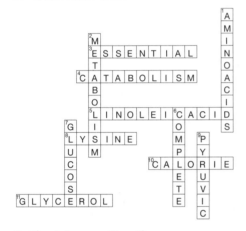

E. Short-Answer Questions

1. (a) proteins are difficult to break apart; (b) their energy yield is less than that of lipids; (c) the by-product, ammonia, is a toxin that can damage cells; (d) proteins form the most important structural and functional components of any cell; extensive protein catabolism threatens homeostasis at the cellular and system levels.

2. When nucleic acids are broken down, only the sugar and pyrimidine bases (cytosine, thymine, uracil) provide energy. Purine bases (adenine, guanine) cannot be catabolized; instead, they are deaminated (the amine is removed) and excreted as uric acid, a nitrogenous waste.

3. (a) to perform structural maintenance and repairs; (b) to support growth; (c) to produce secretions; and (d) to build nutrient reserves.

4. (a) milk; (b) meat and beans; (c) vegetables; (d) fruits; (e) grains

5. Minerals (i.e., inorganic ions) are important because they (a) determine the osmolarities of fluids; (b) play major roles in important physiological processes; and (c) are essential cofactors in a variety of enzymes.

6. (a) A, D, E, K; (b) B complex and vitamin C (ascorbic acid)

18 The Urinary System

Part I: Objective-Based Questions

Objective 1

1. b
2. c
3. a
4. d

5. d
6. c

Labeling Exercise, Figure 18-1
1. kidneys
2. ureters
3. urinary bladder
4. urethra

Objective 2

1. b
2. d
3. c
4. d
5. c
6. b

Labeling Exercise, Figure 18-2
1. minor calyx
2. renal pelvis
3. ureter
4. renal column
5. renal pyramid
6. renal sinus
7. major calyx
8. renal capsule
9. cortex

Objective 3

1. a
2. c
3. c
4. d
5. c
6. c

Labeling Exercise, Figure 18-3
1. efferent arteriole
2. afferent arteriole
3. renal corpuscle
4. glomerulus
5. proximal convoluted tubule
6. loop of Henle
7. distal convoluted tubule
8. collecting duct
9. papillary duct

Objective 4

1. c
2. b

3. a
4. a

5. d
6. b

Objective 5

1. d
2. d

3. b
4. a

5. d
6. c

Objective 6

1. b
2. d

3. c
4. b

5. a
6. c

Objective 7

1. b
2. a
3. c
4. internal sphincter
5. rugae

6. urinary bladder
Labeling Exercise, Figure 18-4
1. ureter
2. urethral openings
3. internal sphincter
4. external sphincter
5. detrusor muscle
6. trigone
7. prostate gland
8. urethra

Objective 8

1. c
2. c

3. a
4. d

5. b

Objective 9

1. integumentary

2. respiratory

3. digestive

Objective 10

1. c
2. d

3. b
4. a

5. c

Objective 11

1. b
2. d
3. a
4. d

5. b
6. ADH
7. aldosterone
8. kidneys

9. aldosterone
10. calcitriol

Objective 12

1. b	4. d	7. c
2. d	5. a	8. a
3. b	6. c	

Objective 13

1. b	3. a
2. a	4. b

Objective 14

1. d	3. a
2. b	4. c

Part II: Chapter Comprehensive Exercises

A. Word Elimination

1. prostate	3. calyces	5. urine	7. ADH	9. urine
2. nephron	4. vasa recta	6. glucose	8. adrenalin	10. ureter

B. Matching

1. g	3. e	5. c	7. i	9. f
2. j	4. a	6. b	8. d	10. h

C. Concept Maps

Concept Map I - Urinary System

1. ureters	4. glomerulus	7. medulla
2. urinary bladder	5. proximal convoluted tubule	8. renal sinus
3. nephrons	6. collecting tubules	9. minor calyces

Concept Map II - Kidney Circulation

1. renal artery	3. afferent artery	5. interlobular vein
2. arcuate artery	4. efferent artery	6. interlobar vein

D. Crossword Puzzle

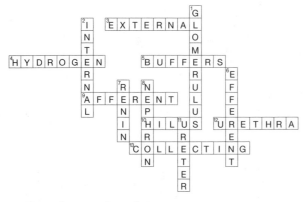

E. Short-Answer Questions

1. (a) regulates plasma concentrations of ions; (b) regulates blood volume and blood pressure; (c) contributes to stabilization of blood pH; (d) conserves valuable nutrients; (e) eliminates organic wastes

2. (a) powerful vasoconstriction of the afferent arteriole, thereby decreasing glomerular filtration rate and slowing the production of filtrate; (b) stimulation of renin release; (c) direct stimulation of water and sodium ion reabsorption

3. (a) autoregulation; (b) hormonal regulation; (c) autonomic regulation

4. (a) ADH—decreased urine volume; (b) renin—causes angiotensin II production; stimulates aldosterone production; (c) aldosterone—causes increased sodium ion reabsorption; causes decreased urine concentration and volume; (d) atrial natriuretic peptide (ANP)—inhibits ADH production; results in increased urine production.

5. (a) stimulates water conservation at the kidney, reducing urinary water losses; (b) Stimulates the thirst center to promote the drinking of fluids. The combination of decreased water loss and increased water intake gradually restores normal plasma osmolarity.

6. (a) secrete and/or absorb hydrogen ions; (b) control excretion of acids and bases; (c) generate additional buffers when necessary

19 The Reproductive System

Part I: Objective-Based Questions

Objective 1

1. a
2. c
3. b
4. d
5. c
6. a

Labeling Exercise, Figure 19-1
1. pubic symphysis
2. penile urethra
3. penis
4. urethral meatus
5. scrotum
6. urinary bladder
7. ureter
8. rectum
9. seminal vesicle
10. prostate gland
11. ejaculatory duct
12. bulbourethral gland
13. ductus deferens
14. epididymis
15. testis

Objective 2

1. b
2. a
3. c
4. b
5. d
6. a

Objective 3

1. c
2. d
3. a
4. b
5. b
6. c
7. a
8. penis
9. prepuce
10. corpus spongiosum
11. corpus cavernosa

Objective 4

1. d
2. b
3. c
4. a
5. b

Objective 5

1. b
2. c
3. d
4. b
5. d
6. cervix
7. lobules
8. vestibule
9. labia majora
10. areola

Labeling Exercise, Figure 19-2
1. ovarian follicle
2. ovary
3. uterine tube
4. urinary bladder
5. pubic symphysis
6. urethra
7. greater vestibular gland
8. clitoris
9. labium minus
10. labium majus
11. uterus
12. endometrium
13. sigmoid colon
14. fornix
15. cervix
16. vagina
17. anus

Objective 6

1. c
2. b
3. a
4. a
5. b
6. b

Objective 7

1. a
2. c
3. b
4. d
5. a
6. d
7. FSH
8. LH
9. progesterone
10. progesterone
11. FSH

Objective 8

1. b
2. a
3. c
4. a
5. c

Objective 9

1. menopause
2. climacteric
3. b
4. c

Objective 10

1. reproductive
2. cardiovascular
3. endocrine
4. nervous

Part II: Chapter Comprehensive Exercises

A. Word Elimination

1. cremaster muscle   3. mitosis   5. penis   7. areola   9. androgens
2. scrotum   4. epididymis   6. corpus luteum 8. vestibular glands 10. coitus

B. Matching

1. g   3. a   5. c   7. i   9. f
2. e   4. j   6. b   8. d   10. h

C. Concept Maps

Concept Map I - Male Reproductive Tract

1. ductus deferens   4. produce testosterone   7. bulbourethral glands
2. penis   5. FSH   8. urethra
3. seminiferous tubules   6. seminal vesicles

Concept Map II - Female Reproductive Tract

1. uterine tubes   5. supports fetal development   9. clitoris
2. follicles   6. vagina   10. nutrients
3. granulosa and thecal cells   7. vulva
4. endometrium   8. labia majora and minora

D. Crossword Puzzle

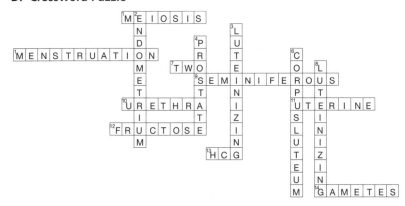

E. Short-Answer Questions

1. (a) seminal vesicles, prostate gland, bulbourethral glands
   (b) activate the sperm; provide nutrients for sperm motility; provide sperm motility; produce buffers to counteract acid conditions

2. Seminal fluid is the fluid component of semen. Semen consists of seminal fluid, sperm, and enzymes.

3. *Emission* involves peristaltic contractions of the ampulla, pushing fluid and spermatozoa into the prostatic urethra. Contractions of the seminal vesicles and prostate gland move the seminal mixture into the membranous and penile walls of the prostate gland.

   Ejaculation occurs as powerful, rhythmic contractions of the ischiocavernosus and bulbocavernosus muscles that push semen toward the external urethral orifice.

4. (a) promotes the functional maturation of spermatozoa
   (b) maintains accessory organs of male reproductive tract
   (c) responsible for male secondary sexual characteristics
   (d) stimulates sexual behaviors and sexual drive
   (e) stimulates metabolic operations, specifically protein synthesis, and muscle growth

5. (a) serves as a passageway for the elimination of menstrual fluids
   (b) receives penis during coitus; holds sperm prior to passage into uterus
   (c) in childbirth forms the lower portion of the birth canal

6. (a) arousal—parasympathetic activation leads to an engorgement of the erectile tissues of the clitoris and increased secretion of the greater vestibular glands.
   (b) Coitus—rhythmic contact with the clitoris and vaginal walls provides stimulation that eventually leads to orgasm.
   (c) Orgasm—accompanied by peristaltic contractions of the uterine and vaginal walls and rhythmic contractions of the bulbocavernosus and ischiocavernosus muscles, giving rise to pleasurable sensations.

7. Step 1: formation of primary follicles

   Step 2: formation of secondary follicles

   Step 3: formation of a tertiary follicle

   Step 4: ovulation

   Step 5: formation and degeneration of the corpus luteum

8. (a) menses

   (b) proliferative phase

   (c) secretory phase

9. (a) human chorionic gonadotropin (HCG)

   (b) relaxin

   (c) human placental lactogen (HPL)

   (d) estrogens and progestins

10. By the end of the sixth month of pregnancy the mammary glands are fully developed, and the glands begin to produce colostrum. This contains relatively more proteins and far less fat than milk, and it will be provided to the infant during the first two or three days of life. Many of the proteins are immunoglobulins that may help the infant ward off infections until its own immune system becomes fully functional.

F. Formation of Gametes: Gametogenesis

1. spermatogenesis
2. spermatogonia
3. primary spermatocytes
4. secondary spermatocytes
5. spermatids
6. sperm
7. oogenesis
8. oogonia
9. primary oocyte
10. secondary oocyte
11. ovum

20 Development and Inheritance

Part I: Objective-Based Questions

Objective 1

1. c	3. d	5. amphimixis
2. b	4. capacitation	6. fertilization

Objective 2

1. c	6. a	11. blastomeres
2. a	7. d	12. morula
3. b	8. a	13. ectoderm
4. c	9. cleavage	14. endoderm
5. c	10. implantation	15. mesoderm

Objective 3

1. c	3. d	5. b
2. b	4. a	

Objective 4

1. c	3. c	5. b
2. d	4. d	6. a

Objective 5

1. a	3. c
2. a	4. d

Objective 6

1. d	2. c	3. b

Objective 7

1. c	3. a	5. senescence
2. d	4. maturity	

Objective 8

1. c	6. b	11. autosomal
2. a	7. c	12. homozygous
3. b	8. a	13. heterozygous
4. d	9. meiosis	
5. a	10. gametogenesis	

Development and Inheritance Questions

14. Color blindness is an X-linked trait. The Punnett square shows that sons produced by a normal father and a heterozygous mother will have a 50 percent chance of being color blind, while the daughters will all have normal color vision.

Maternal alleles

Paternal alleles	X^C	X^c
X^C	$X^C X^C$	$X^C X^c$
Y	$X^C Y$	$X^c Y$ (color blind)

Objective 8 (continued)

15. The Punnett square reveals that 50 percent of their offspring have the possibility of inheriting albinism.

Maternal alleles

		a	a
Paternal alleles	A	Aa	Aa
	a	aa (albino)	aa (albino)

16. The Punnett square reveals that there is a 25 percent chance of having children who are not tongue rollers and a 75 percent chance of having children with the ability to roll the tongue.

Maternal alleles

		T	t
Paternal alleles	T	TT (yes)	Tt (yes)
	t	Tt (yes)	tt (no)

Part II: Chapter Comprehensive Exercises

A. Word Elimination

1. inheritance
2. embryology
3. gestation
4. placenta
5. colostrum
6. fetus
7. Marfan's syndrome
8. curly hair
9. gastrulation
10. amnion

B. Matching

1. e
2. h
3. a
4. j
5. b
6. i
7. c
8. f
9. d
10. g

C. Concept Maps

Concept Map I - Fertilization and Development

1. zygote
2. germ layer
3. endoderm
4. muscle
5. yolk sac
6. allantois
7. progesterone
8. relaxin

Concept Map II - Cleavage and Blastocyst Formation

1. secondary oocyte
2. fertilization
3. zygote
4. 2-cell stage
5. 8-cell stage
6. morula
7. early blastocyst
8. implantation

D. Crossword Puzzle

E. Short-Answer Questions

1. (a)   (b)
   - yolk sac   • endoderm and mesoderm
   - amnion   • ectoderm and mesoderm
   - allantois   • endoderm and mesoderm
   - chorion   • mesoderm and trophoblast

2. (a) respiratory rate goes up and tidal volume increases; (b) the maternal blood volume increases; (c) maternal requirements for nutrients increase; (d) glomerular filtration rate increases; (e) uterus increases in size; (f) mammary glands increase in size, and secretory activity begins

3. (a) rising estrogen levels; (b) rising oxytocin levels; (c) prostaglandin production

4. (a) hypothalamus—increases production of GnRH; (b) increasing circulatory levels of FSH and LH (ICSH) by the anterior pituitary; (c) FSH and LH initiate gametogenesis and the production of male or female sex hormones that stimulate the appearance of secondary sexual characteristics and behaviors

5. (a) dilation stage; (b) expulsion stage; (c) placental stage

6. infancy, childhood, adolescence, maturity, senescence